THE LIBRARY
ST. MARY'S COLLEGE OF MARYLAND
ST. MARY'S CITY, MARYLAND 86

T3-BOG-958

SUBSTANCE, FORM AND PSYCHE:
AN ARISTOTELEAN METAPHYSICS

Substance, form and psyche: an Aristotelean metaphysics

Montgomery Furth

Professor of Philosophy,
University of California, Los Angeles

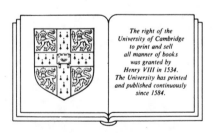

The right of the
University of Cambridge
to print and sell
all manner of books
was granted by
Henry VIII in 1534.
The University has printed
and published continuously
since 1584.

CAMBRIDGE UNIVERSITY PRESS

CAMBRIDGE

NEW YORK   NEW ROCHELLE

MELBOURNE   SYDNEY

Published by the Press Syndicate of the University of Cambridge
The Pitt Building, Trumpington Street, Cambridge CB2 1RP
32 East 57th Street, New York, NY 10022, USA
10 Stamford Road, Oakleigh, Melbourne 3166, Australia

© Cambridge University Press 1988

First published 1988

Printed in Great Britain at the University Press, Cambridge

British Library cataloguing in publication data

Furth, Montgomery
Substance, form and psyche: an Aristotelean metaphysics.
1. Aristotle
I. Title
185   B485

Library of Congress cataloguing in publication data

Furth, Montgomery.
Substance, form, and psyche.
Bibliography: P.
1. Aristotle – Contributions in metaphysics.
2. Metaphysics. I. Title.
B491.M4F87   1987   110'.92'4   87-23872

ISBN 0 521 34143 4

SE

To Charlotte

CONTENTS

Contents

Contents

Contents

PREFACE

This book began when I resolved to take a sabbatical leave in 1971–2. My proposed research consisted of three limited projects, as I thought: one on Aristotle's biology and metaphysics, one on Leibniz's monadology, and one on Frege's philosophy of language. Because I had written previously on the second and third of these topics, I decided (with a logic that seemed persuasive at the time but now escapes me) to work first on the Aristotle.

That was in the summer of 1971. I am writing these final words in the summer of 1986. Leibniz and Frege are still in my file drawer.

There have to be many reasons why a project should prove so intractable, besides the incapacities of its author, and there is little ground to expect the author to be aware of all of them. The main reason that I myself know about is the size and complexity of the subject, which I adequately realized only gradually. I have felt like a builder who contracted to construct a modest country church from a plan supplied by the vestry, but who finds that as each phase of the construction is supposedly completed, the plan has mysteriously become that of a larger and more elaborate building, and eventually that of a huge and pretentious cathedral – one which he would never have agreed to build at the start, but which he must now try to finish in view of the efforts already invested. (That is a personal and subjective simile; a different constructional image better suited to the subject-matter is pursued in §0.)

Another factor has certainly been the very high degree of internal connectedness in the subject-matter. This is what has defeated my many attempts at piecemeal publication, because it has seemed there is hardly any part that can stand properly independent of the rest, and so it seemed that until the whole was finished, even the parts that existed were really not finished either.[1]

These features of size and complexity have combined to produce a consequence I have found quite striking: for some years I have known that the theory described in this book is larger and more complex than my mind is able to contain simultaneously, even though all the description in

1 In terms of interim publications, only the article Furth (1978) ("Transtemporal Stability in Aristotelean Substances") was somehow cobbled up, from §§1, 4, 9, 13, 15, 18, 19, for an invited symposium paper for the American Philosophical Association's Eastern Division meeting in Washington, D.C., December 1978. Here I should also like to acknowledge with gratitude the support of the National Science Foundation in the first year of the project (1971–72, #GS-30655).

this book is of my own composition. Returning briefly to the cathedral of two paragraphs back, I have sometimes imagined myself as the builder now hoisting into place a piece of vaulting here, now polishing a gargoyle there, now stepping back to regard the overall structure but ignoring the details – but unable to visualize the overall design *and* all its details at once. Of course, the problem with the theory (and here we take leave of the cathedral, for good) is not the *details*, but the *multidimensionality* – keeping every distinction and dimension going simultaneously is simply too much, at least for me. (Occasionally I have wondered idly whether Aristotle was mentally able to do this, i.e. keep every distinction and dimension going simultaneously. Whether he was or not, we shall find that he either could not or did not try to do so in his text as we have it. For one example, some cases of this that have made much hermeneutic trouble are discussed in §22.)

A third kind of recalcitrance, as the project grew, resided in its sheer weight; the labor of revisions and further enlargements rapidly approached my limit of strength; it became very difficult to make the thing march. It is a safe conjecture that had the manuscript not been moved from the physical basis of typing and paper to that of electronic text processing, in the fall of 1982, it would not have been completed.

Having been composed over so long a period, the work is irregularly stratified, with newer parts next to much older ones, some of the latter no longer the way I would write them today. (Some of the most recent material is in §§5, 15(iii)(iv), 16, 23; some of the oldest in §§7, 14, 15(i)(ii), 18, 24.) Also, were I to start over now, I would rearrange the presentation, mostly in the direction of simplicity. And I am acutely aware that many matters could be taken very much deeper than they are here, especially in Part V.

With all these doubts and misgivings, however, for better or worse, this work *is* basically the work I had in mind to produce. There is a paradox here (it is the paradox of the *Meno*). How could I have known fifteen years ago that *this* was what I wanted to do? If I knew that, why did it take fifteen years? How can I know now that *this* was what I wanted to do then? (Of course, it is well known how the *Meno* answers this question. It's not the right answer, needless to say. Whatever the fifteen-year odyssey has been, it certainly has not had anything to do with recollection. But this is also where the author's lack of cognizance comes in.)

Whom is it intended for, and what advice can I give the reader, or uncertain reader-candidate, how to tackle it? The book should be of interest to anyone knowledgeable about ancient Greek philosophy and science, and such a person can read it straight through or in any other way that may seem suitable. But I also hope that it will find a place with a more general philosophical audience, persons simply interested in general metaphysics, and perhaps among some classicists, and historians of science other than antiquity specialists, and possibly even some specimens of that near-extinct order, the general reader. And many members of these types, especially if lulled by the relatively accessible discourse on method (§0), may have trouble at first with Part I (§§1–5), which is a quite dense and technical discussion of the metaphysics of Aristotle's *Categories*. Starting with §6, the treatment broadens out again and becomes more available to non-experts. I suggest that the reader who finds Part I rough going and feels he or she isn't getting enough out of it to warrant the effort, should skip to §6 and go on, and perhaps return to §§1–5 after assimilating the rest of the book. There are many backward references in §§6–25, which can point a reader who proceeds in this way to the important differences to look for between the smaller and larger theories.

My indebtedness to friends and colleagues is so extensive that a complete acknowledgement of it would run on interminably; short of that, I must confine myself to major debts – some going so far back that the generous creditors may have forgotten that they were helpful to me. However, I have not forgotten. At various stages the work in progress was read and criticized by David Blank, Myles Burnyeat, Alan Code, Allan Gotthelf, Nicholas White, and an anonymous referee for the Cambridge University Press; very helpful suggestions came from this, which I have done my limited best to incorporate or otherwise respond to here.

Beyond this, in innumerable invited lectures, symposia, seminars, and discussions, I have had valuable feedback from many sources, among them: Marilyn Adams, Rogers Albritton, David Balme, Jonathan Bennett, Tyler Burge, William Charlton, Marc Cohen, John Cooper, Russell Dancy, James Dybikowski, Michael Frede, Mary Louise Gill, Marjorie Grene, Sally Haslanger, David Hills, Jaakko Hintikka, Rosalind Hursthouse, David Kaplan, David Keyt, Aryeh Kosman, Joan Kung, James Lennox, Frank Lewis, Mohan Matthen, Gary Matthews, John McDowell, Ernan McMullin, Julius Moravcsik, Alexander Mourelatos, Martha Nussbaum, Joseph Owens, Jeffry Pelletier, Sandra Peterson, Anthony Preus, William Prior, Gerasimos Santas, Daniel Shartin, Gregory Vlastos, and Jennifer Whiting.

I have greatly benefited from the opportunity to teach this material at several venues besides UCLA, in seminars at Harvard, the University of British Columbia, the University of Texas at Austin, and the University of California at Irvine.

With all this distinguished help, I should like to have produced a better book; but at this point I am glad to settle for a book.

Montgomery Furth   *Los Angeles, June 1986*

§0. Preliminary: a short discourse on method

My aim in what follows is to explain and to motivate a theory of essence, existence and individuation that I think is to be found in the later and more advanced of the extant writings of Aristotle. The view to be explored has several features that are noteworthy from a scientific as well as a philosophical standpoint: it centers especially, though not exclusively, on a concept of what an *individual material object* is – a concept that has both intrinsic interest and (if some suggestions I shall advance as to its provenance and motivation are accepted) a historical significance that has not always been accurately appreciated.

The subject has of course had a great many discussants over the millennia, and so inevitably there is overlap at most points here with what others have had to say. Yet anyone familiar with the richness, elusiveness and originality of Aristotle's thought in this area will readily agree that present understanding of it remains imperfect and that new points and perspectives regarding it are still to be gained; the topic is limitless. Such novelties of content as I shall recommend will emerge in their due order. But there are also some unconventional and very likely exceptionable aspects to my method in this study which should be identified at once.

One is a variation on the usual approach to a historical philosopher – that of working from his text to his meaning. For my interpretive practice here is in places frankly reconstructive in character, synthetic rather than analytic; where it seems needed, or even merely helpful, I do not stick at approaching the text by convergence, rather than by trying to extract doctrine from it in the conventional way. This interpretive practice is in fact guided by an interpretive ideal: to recreate in imagination the world the philosopher saw, the problems it presented to him, and the conceptual instrumentalities with which he sought to reduce what was problematic to intelligibility and order – and to do this so completely and so vividly that in the light of this understanding arrived at in our own terms, it becomes possible to "*deduce* the text", to validate a reaction that goes: "But someone who assumed *that*, or looked at the world in *that* way, or noticed and was impressed by very general facts of *that* sort, would quite naturally say things like *this*" – where *this* is some characteristic verbal behavior with well-established standing in the philosopher's text, which has discouraged, if not outright baffled, standardly cautious essays at picking out a plausible meaning directly *ex ipsissimis verbis*. There are of

I

course obvious hazards and potentials for irresponsibility in an approach that makes such a use of philosophical imagination. On the other side, the possible access of philosophical understanding, of a conceptual scheme that there is every reason to expect to be markedly different from what we are used to, may be greater than timider approaches can ever likely furnish. And the fact that the proof of an interpretive hypothesis is still firmly lodged in the success with which the textual phenomena can in practice be "saved" thereby is, if not a guarantee against errors and excess, still at least a public check against their propagation and acceptance. Even if it is indeed our dangerous purpose not merely to disinter, but to resurrect, there remain intersubjective criteria whose application is to be welcomed, not discouraged, for helping verify the identity of the resurrectee who speaks anew.

Thus much for the ideal. Returning to the real world and the problem of interpreting Aristotle, there are several complicating factors that, paradoxically, both motivate us in the direction of the ideal and militate against its attainment. For the problem is this: the view of his that I wish to explore is not something that is stated by him compact, entire and consistent. Rather, first, the various outcroppings of the view that do occur in his text as received, are surrounded and separated by sizeable stretches of other material that is either older, or representative of other standpoints, or concerned with other topics, or otherwise off our reservation. When to this is added the pervasive general difficulty of his written record – overpacked, sometimes concise to the point of being cryptic, sometimes patently confused, sometimes palpably inconsistent – it becomes quite obvious that we must be selective in what we can expect to explain, rather than trying to reconcile it all into a total consensus; there is no possible way to make it all fit. Moreover, second, a related vexation arises from the fact that the views in question not only are ones which Aristotle arrived at in stages, and perhaps never fully disentangled from their superseded antecedents in earlier thought of his, but beyond this they are in a number of important directions not completely worked out: there are concepts and issues that can be seen on his own principles to be critically significant and requiring detailed analysis and discussion, which in the extant corpus are simply not squarely addressed, and where the relevant points of theory must be pieced together from scattered remarks, or inferred from patterns of practice, or supplied by "deduction" from interpretive hypothesis (on the principle that filling gaps in this way is permissible if points so supplied are not in conflict with explicit statements in the canon).

For an analogy to the problem and the procedure, imagine us set the task of restoring a shattered ancient colossal statue. We have to hand by way of materials a number of fragments of various sizes, many of them readily recognizable as to what they are and where they should go (a portion of right forearm, a portion of left pectoral, etc.), and from which also a sense of the majestic scale of the completed entirety can be inferred. Still, all is not straightforward. There is reason to believe that the final grand design was never actually finished. Many parts that obviously are needed to go with those we have are missing (whether lost or never fabricated now undeterminable). There is some duplication of parts, indicating that our remnants stem from more than one stage of construction, and implying furthermore that even the *hapax tunkhainonta* (one-time occurrers) require critical scrutiny and should by no means be automatically assigned to the final version. Finally, there also survives from the same master's hand another sculpture, quite perfect within its strict limitations: a comparatively miniature figure that may possibly have been some sort of study model for the monumental one (though the relationship is itself a much-disputed topic); in any case it offers several clues of incalculable value to the intended design of the larger work, which however cannot be simply copied from it because it is also demonstrably simplified in important ways, and not merely reduced in scale.

It is our task as restorers of such an object to find the most straightforward, historically plausible, and (within these parameters) aesthetically best statue that relevantly utilizes as many of the fragments as possible. Of course, solving such an equation for so many values simultaneously is not amenable to an effective procedure (in the logicians' sense), but it is not just witchcraft either, and when an attempt has been made, it is open to all who are qualified to judge such matters to assess the justness of the product's proportions and its verisimilitude as a specimen of its producer and period of production. However, it is important in fairness to the beholder and the assessment process that we restorers not try to efface the joins between the marble of the original fragments and the plaster that fills out the remainder of the reconstruction: by some means at once unobtrusive – not distracting from the perception of the whole – and still noticeable, the distinction must remain visibly available between what we have been given and what we have done with it. One way would be by lightly tinting the plaster. On that understanding, the attempt at a reconstruction meeting the conditions described is not merely allowable but loudly called for, since while much may be uncertain about what the ancient sculptor had in mind to produce, it most assuredly was not a pile of fragments.

It is plain enough how this analogy is to be cashed. To hand is an extensive body of written material scattered through Aristotle's works on logic, on method, on nature, on First Philosophy, and on other matters too, that concerns itself with an interrelated cluster of topics called Substance (*ousia*), being an Individual or a "This" (*tode ti*), that which is "the Same and One in Number" (*tauton kai hen arithmōi*), "What Something Is" (*ti estin, touth' hoper estin*), Species, Genus and Differentia (*eidos, genos, diaphora*), Essence (*ti ēn einai*), Form and Matter, Actuality and Potentiality – to name a few, for a start. The task of an interpreter of this material is to find the most straightforward, historically plausible, and (within these parameters) philosophically and scientifically most comprehensible set of assumptions, motivations and questions that will generate, help explain, or merely assist us in seeing the point of so much as writing down, as much of it as possible. In making the reconstruction, some passages and even whole chapters fit in so naturally that they can be utilized just about as they are in the course of its primary exposition. In other places, the materials that we have do not address adequately, or at all, some matter that can be seen to be of great importance for the whole, and we find ourselves thrown back on our own resources to piece together from whatever indications there are, how the scheme *ought* to handle the matter; these parts must be openly indicated, along lines of the tinting of the plaster. When the main features of the reconstruction are in place, some other fragments can be understood as first approximations, or intermediate developmental stages, or adaptations to another application, or the like, of the overall metaphysical structure arrived at. Inevitably, some parts will not fit at all; or I cannot see a place for them but others, cleverer and more learned practitioners of restorer's art, will be able to do so. Finally, what corresponds to the simplified miniature or well-crafted study model of the statue analogy is the metaphysical theory of the *Categories*, which deals with the same universe of substances as does the larger theory, but does so with a cut-down and simplified conceptual apparatus (using only about the first half of the notions enumerated at the beginning of this paragraph). The full theory is much more complex, yet so carefully contrived is the *Categories* theory that it can serve as, even if it was not intended as, an introduction to the whole.

I have alluded once or twice above to "earlier" and "later", and to "developmental stages". As will emerge in more detail, I do find signs of progression and evolution in the theory of substance between different parts of the corpus, and it is only natural to think of more "advanced" parts as being more "final", and it is but a short step from there to "later" and such. However, I should state here that my overriding concern is the content of the "advanced" theory and its relationships of content to some of the other versions that surface here and there, and I presume to make no contribution here to the body of learning known as *Entwicklungsgeschichte*, the history of his development. If some unknown diagnostic instrument of the future – e.g. an Infallible Stylometer – were to demonstrate that a view I call "advanced" belonged to Aristotle's young middle age and that something I call "intermediate" was in fact a later production of his Lyceum period, then I should stand corrected, then presumably in all consistency I ought to be privately disappointed in what was from my own standpoint a falling-off on his part, but I need not regard it as contradicting any important historical thesis propounded by this work. On the other hand, it seems unnatural and unnecessary to systematically detoxify the exposition by relentlessly expunging all temporal language; so the temporal references remain, where they do, indicating what is to me plausible surmise that also simplifies the telling of the story.

There is a second major matter of method in this study requiring mention here as not altogether standard, having to do with my use of the biological writings. It springs from a hypothesis, stated more fully in §9 where it first comes into operation, that Aristotle's metaphysical inquiries about essence, substance, individual, and so on were (or came to be) motivated in an extremely concrete and specific way by his theoretical preoccupations in biology. It is of course well known that these biological researches of his were of unexampled depth and extent; but my belief – and one of the interpretive hypotheses in this work – goes farther: it is my view that Aristotle asked himself a series of very profound questions about the animal kingdom, to which the metaphysics of substance was part of a response, so that the latter was to a sizeable extent motivated, and thus should be read, as a deep theoretical foundation, a "methodology" in Tarski's sense, for the biological sciences – much as the work of Frege and his successors was to stand to the "deductive sciences" two millennia later. (Indeed Aristotle's questions were *so* good, if I am right, that we have only in the light of rather recent developments returned – the rest of us, that is – to a position from which to appreciate them; and it may well be that ultimately, the best way to understand and appreciate his questions fully is to know even more than is known at present about the *right* answers to them.) The idea of a biological provenance for his "more strictly philosophical work" (in D'Arcy Thompson's phrase) is not of itself new and has indeed been pursued in the present century by several distinguished interpreters; it is pursued here on a more specific basis and

5

from a more systematic and theoretically-oriented standpoint than in other treatments to date.

A third, no doubt less important methodological aspect of this study has to do with style. Some readers may not be annoyed by the changes from the language of sober history of science to that of present-day analytical philosophy, from that to a more literary and evocative mode, and occasionally from that to something less anything else than poetical. Others will certainly find it irritating. I can sympathize, and have to say only that it was not planned that way, and eventually was allowed only because after prolonged struggle I became convinced that unless written in the unforeseen way it was insisting upon being written, it would not be written at all. To paraphrase from Frege's apologia for strange-seeming, "fremdartige", innovations in his *Grundgesetze* that he knew would repel many a reader whom he wanted to keep: I have not arrived at them haphazardly or out of a craving for novelty, but driven as it developed by the nature of the enterprise.

One more point about method must be candidly avowed: during most of the composition of this, I have worked largely independent of the burgeoning secondary literature concerned with these matters, not because I thought it misleading or unhelpful, but out of a sense (the imperative strength of which I found surprising) that my prolonged pondering of the issues and convergent vector with respect to the text must be allowed to proceed to its conclusions without outside influence of that kind. Subsequent to the main lines of the study's being laid down, I have tried to do something to correct this, and some dissents from other interpreters have been recorded, as well as all the points where I find I have been anticipated. But it has to be understood that such appearance as may result of attentiveness to the corpus of scholarship in this area is superficial and misleading. In fact, not the least of the faults of this – I hope, actually, one of the greatest ones – is that it does not intersect enough with other secondary literature, by which it has been either anticipated or antecedently refuted. I have been most assiduous, however, in trying to record my debt wherever I have been influenced. I recognize that it has been a peculiar way to proceed.

Finally, the purview of this work is strictly limited to the portion of the Aristotelean universe that lies near the surface of the Earth, i.e., on its land, in its waters, and in its skies, all beneath the orbit or "sphere" of the Moon. It ignores, almost completely, all astronomical and theological matters, the outer "spheres", and the Movers. There can be no good methodological defense for these omissions, nor even a truly good excuse.

6

My weak excuse is that there is already much more than I can handle at the sublunary level. But although Aristotle sometimes says that it is *one* motivation for studying the sublunary, material and (therefore) perishable substances that it may help us to "get clearer about" substances that are eternal and divine, I am certain beyond the slightest question that he thinks the sublunary substances worthy of the fullest interest and attention in their own right – as he quotes from the anecdote about Heraclitus in his opening lecture in the course on animal anatomy and physiology, "even here there are gods".

I. CROSS- AND INTRA-CATEGORIAL PREDICATION IN THE CATEGORIES[1]

§1. Categories: preliminary rationale

It was suggested in §0 that the metaphysical theory of the *Categories* could be seen as a miniature or cut-down study model relative to the theory of the *Metaphysics*; but although the *Categories* is indeed limited in apparatus, that is not to say that there is anything modest about its scope, which is nothing less than to offer a logical/semantical analysis or 'philosophical grammar' for the entirety of *predicative being* – that is, for every state of affairs in the world that ordinary language (the immediate object-language of the theory is of course Greek of the mid fourth century, but we may for our purposes pass rather freely between that medium and our own) casts into the form

$$X \text{ is } Y$$

for any subject X, and any predicate Y. The purported analysis regards this immense field of situations as falling into eight distinguishable types, exemplified by the following instances (the selection here is arbitrary, but the arrangement deliberate), so that it claims to analyze the *being* of

(1) Socrates' *being* man' or animal, and of
(2) Socrates' *being* brave or grammatical, or Coriscus' *being* ghastly pale or precisely 52.39 kilograms in weight, and of
(3) Socrates' *being* virtuous or knowledgeable, or Coriscus' *being* somehow-colored or a bantamweight, and of
(4) (a) man's *being* (a) mammal, (an) animal, and of
(5) (a) man's, (an) animal's, *being* brave, grammatical, ghastly pale, precisely 52.39 kilograms in weight, and of
(6) (a) man's, (an) animal's, *being* virtuous, knowledgeable, somehow-colored, a bantamweight, and of

---

1 This Part was circulated in a very early draft among a number of friends and has benefited from their criticism: John Cooper, Gareth B. Matthews, Julius Moravcsik, Alexander Mourelatos, Sandra Peterson, Richard Sorabji, Nicholas White.

(7) bravery's *being* (a) virtue, grammar's *being* (a) knowledge, ghastly pallor's *being* (a) color, and of

(8) (a) knowledge's *being* (a) state, (a) chill's *being* (a) condition, (a) color's *being* (a) quality.

Indeed, the enormous reach of the theory extends even beyond such 'beings' as these, to encompass '*X beings Y*' that happen in colloquial expression not to contain any "is" or "being" in their surface grammar – e.g., such as

Socrates' running, winning, cutting, having-shoes-on (which sort with types (2) and (3)),

(a) man's running, sitting, getting-burnt, wearing-armor (which sort with types (5) and (6)).[2]

The 'regimentation' that differentiates these eight varieties of *Sachverhalt* arises from a small number of distinctions that seem to us quite simple, but nonetheless prove to involve some interpretive subtleties. To begin, the colloquial forms of expression

X is Y,   X Y's ("Socrates runs", e.g.),

are first thrown for analysis into a standard or canonical notation, technicalese:

Y is-predicated of X,

and then either of two significantly different underlying structures are seen as indifferently expressed (and therefore their difference effaced, or even concealed) by the analysandum: roughly, one in which the entity designated by "Y" *inheres in* the subject X (this is not exact),[3] the other in which Y is *said-of* the subject X.

It needs to be understood from the outset that in the *Cats.*, *predicated-of a subject* and *said-of a subject* are not the same, despite some minor carelessness in the exposition that can misguide an unwary reader into conflating

2 There is *one* type of 'being' that in principle cannot be brought within the reach, vast as it is, of the *Cats.* theory, and which I mention here for the record: that of a statue's *being* wooden, or that a sphere *is* of-bronze. The entire dimension of the relation between a material substance and the matter of which it is composed, is shut off from view in the *Cats.* treatment. It will begin to open in §6, and will be fairly completely analyzed by §21. For 'being wooden', in particular, see §20(ii), §23(i).

3 The complication here is that the entity designated by "Y" in actual fact *is* (= , is identical with) X. "Y" is something like "brave", which names Socrates (that is, if Socrates *is* brave); whereas what inheres in Socrates is named by "bravery". The *Cats. does not* say that either bravery or "bravery" is *predicated-of* Socrates – one may think there is no deep reason why it could not, but it does not; and if it did, this would run against the important doctrine about 'predicability of the definition'. Further details are in §§2 and 3. For an alternative reconstruction of the matter, see Frank A. Lewis (1982).

them. *X is-predicated-of Y* is simply the converse of *Y is X*, regardless of the category of X and Y or the underlying structure that is unrevealed by either of these two forms. Rewriting the ordinary-language "is" form in the canonical "predicated-of" form makes no analytical advance; and that no more than this is involved is attested by numerous litanies of the form, "X is predicated-of Y, for Y is X" – e.g. $1^b 14$–15, $2^a 24$–6, 31–2; cf. $3^a 27$–8 (slightly more complicated, since definition and the said-of connection are here implicated also). *X is-said-of Y*, on the other hand, is a heavily theory-laden technical configuration requiring close and exact study, some of which it will get in §3 and §4 below. The carelessnesses that can lead to confusing the two, all take the form of the author's stating in terms of *predicated-of*, points that actually hold only for the special case of predicated-of that is *said-of*; the context (particularly the illustrative example) usually shows clearly that this *is* the case that is meant. (For example, $1^b 10$–12, $2^b 16$–17, $3^b 4$–5; cf. $2^a 21$–6, $2^a 36$–$b1$.)[4]

Before getting into the first of this pair of analysantia – namely, *inherence* – it is useful to mark more sharply what sort of thing the analysis is meant to be an analysis of. I have phrased the last few paragraphs in terms of analysis of *Sachverhalte*, situations, states of affairs, rather than of statements or propositions or assertions or sentence-types, and I think that it is most basic, in-principle fidelity to the *Cats.* to keep the discussion in the material rather than the formal mode of speech.[5] However, it has to be recognized that in that work the observance of our settled distinction between use and mention is anything but scrupulous.[6] It is true that in ch. 2 "things that are said" or *legomena* are differentiated from "things that are" or *onta*, and some apparent floutings of the distinction to be encountered shortly will turn out under scrutiny to be explainable (such as "said-of" for a relationship between "things that are", $1^a 20$ ff., and the seeming carelessness as to whether it is white or the name "white" that is predicat-

---

4 I believe that this observation, together with the analysis to follow, goes some way to resolve the difficulties of R. M. Dancy (1975b), at 349–60.

5 Though this terminology (originally, I believe, from Carnap's *Logical Syntax*) is needed to make the point, it is not very happy given the heavy technical usage to be made in this work of "formal" and "material" in their direct, hylomorphic connection. The reader must be relied upon to disambiguate as needed.

6 I am quite sure that this was a main spring of the vigorous though largely inconclusive debate, extending in recent times at least over a century and a half (Trendelenburg (1833), (1846); Bonitz (1853); Apelt (1891), for a start – leaving aside ancient controversy), over whether the *Categories* is basically a work of "logic" or of "metaphysics". For more recent reviews, see Owens (1960) (reprinted in Owens (1981)), and de Rijk (1952), pp. 1–5, 73. Rijk notes (pp. 4–5) that the chronic effacement in the *Cats.* of use-mention concerns has suggested an "intentional" interpretation of the linguistic entities in question. Cf. Ross, *AM* lxxxii–xc.

ed-of a subject, $2^a31–34$).[7] But other difficulties about use and mention will not go away – for example, the notorious, tortured paragraph 3^b10 ff. ("every substance seems to signify a certain 'this'");[8] and it might even be that in the interest of forward progress in interpreting the *Cats.*, the best policy regarding the use-mention issue is to forget it.[9] In any case, I understand Aristotle's interest in analyzing X *is* Y and X Y's (and, accordingly, Y *predicated-of* X) to be an interest in laying bare and articulating the structure(s) of realities obtaining in the world, both their constituent entities (*onta*) and the relationships that link up the constituent entities into the various classes of states of affairs (according to the *Cats.*, eight classes). It is much more that than it is an interest in language, and terminology like "philosophical grammar" needs to be employed on that understanding.

This 'concern with realities' can be enlarged upon briefly by stating intuitively what the relationship is between the world that the *Categories* looks at, and the world of the biological and metaphysical treatises, which will occupy us later. The relationship, as I see it, is this: *they are the same world*; however, the *Categories* sees this world in much less depth and detail than do the latter works. Anticipating the terms we are eventually to elaborate at length, the *Categories* surveys, takes in, the entire sublunary universe that the latter works encompass, but it *notices* only a fraction of it: namely, the individual substances, their species and genera, and their individual and general accidents – in the enumeration of the next paragraph, items 4, 1, 2 and 3. That is, the total universe under study also contains a great deal more, both between and beneath (so to speak) the scattered items that the eyes of the *Categories* are constructed to perceive; all this the *Categories* simply ignores. We shall look further at the rest of the universe beginning with §6, and shall express the difference in the terms of "wider and deeper"; but the difference is that of the same universe, more widely and deeply taken in. That said, let us examine the *Categories*' world, the world as seen less fully.

All the entities, or "things that are", the *Categories* teaches, may be divided into four parts. First, some are *said-of* a subject, but are not *in* any subject: these are the *substantial kinds* or "secondary substances", substan-

---

7 For these two, see §3, p. 23 and §2, p. 19 and note 10 respectively.
8 For this one, see §4, pp. 30–1.
9 This advice is partly prompted by J. L. Ackrill's (1963) notes to his otherwise admirable Clarendon translation of the *Cats.* and *de Int.*, which I follow here wherever possible, i.e. usually. In at least one instance, fixating on use-mention problems diverted attention from an important technical point; see §2, note 10.

tial species such as Man[10] or Horse, substantial genera such as Animal. For example, Man is said-of a subject, the individual man (*anthrōpos kath' hupokeimenou legetai tou tinos anthrōpou*), but is not in any subject.[11]

Second, some are *in* a subject but are not *said-of* any subject: these are the *nonsubstantial individuals*, such as the individual item of grammatical knowledge (*hē tis grammatikē*) and the individual shade of light color (*to ti leukon*). For example, the individual item of grammar is *in* a subject, namely, the psyche or psyches of some individual man or men, but is not said-of any subject.

Third, some are both *in* a subject and *said-of* a subject: these are the *nonsubstantial kinds*, such as Knowledge, and Color. For example, Knowledge is said of a subject, the individual item of grammatical knowledge, and also is in a subject, i.e. in some individual man's (men's) psyche(s) that the individual item of grammar is in.[12]

Fourth, some are neither *in* any subject nor *said-of* any subject: these are the *substantial individuals* or "primary substances", such as Socrates, the individual man, and Boukephalos, the individual horse.[13]

These, then, are 'the things that are'; in terms of them and relations between them all that in ordinary language is said predicatively to *be* is to be reductively analyzed. A further, organizing condition on the notion of *kind* is the following: first, it is evidently intended that the substantial individuals fall within the successively wider substantial kinds (species, genera) that are said-of them, in such a way that the kinds form a hierarchy extending finally to a *widest substantial kind*, which the *Cats.* calls: Substance. But also evidently intended – though hardly worked out past the barest beginnings – is a set of analogous conditions on the non-substances: for example, the individual shade of light color falls within successively wider nonsubstantial kinds (Light Color, Color) that are said-of it, in a sequence extending finally to a widest kind which the *Cats.*

---

10 "Man" as used in this work translates *anthrōpos*, human being, and (like English "Horse") does not connote gender.

11 "Said-of" in English, connoting *saying*, looks like a peculiar name for a relationship between "things that are". For a suggestion as to how *legetai kata* might look less incongruous, and even felicitous, in ancient Greek, see §3, p. 23.

12 As will be seen (§2, §5), there is an issue over whether *to ti leukon* (in the second division of the tetrachotomy) can or cannot inhere in many subjects. According to me, Aristotle holds that it can. But regardless of one's view about this, it is beyond any question that Color (third division of the tetrachotomy) *must* be capable of inhering in the many subjects that are colored$_a$ with the many individual colors$_n$, on *either* construal of individual colors$_n$. Therefore whatever one's view of the latter, it cannot be generally true of inherence that for all x, y and z, if x inheres in y and x inheres in z, then y = z. Cf. Frede (1978), and §2 below.

13 At 2^{a}14 the primary substances are referred to as "in" the kinds that are the secondary substances; but this is not the "in" of "in a subject". See §4, §8.

calls: Quality; the particular lengths (e.g. two-cubits, three-cubits) likewise have wider kinds said-of them extending finally to: Quantity; and so generally for all the nonsubstances, resulting in a group of *widest nonsubstantial kinds*, by the *Cats.* account totalling nine. These of course, together with the widest substantial kind, are the famous Categories of tradition; according to *Cats.* 4 (1^b25-7), each and every one of the "things that are" is to be found in one (and, the language here implies, only one, though exceptions are contemplated at 11^a37-8) of them.

My main concern in this work being the concept of substance, I shall largely dispense with questions like what differentiates the various nonsubstantial categories from one another, the rationale (if there be one) for comprehending into a single category the monstrous motley horde yclept Quality, the justification (which seems to me quite hopeless) for a category, co-ordinate with the others, of Time, and other such. It will be seen that numerous particular points will emerge along the way in the course of the general discussion of Inherence. But enough has even now been ·fixed to allow statement of three general truths about the relationship between the tetrachotomy of "things that are" and the total categorial scheme. None of them is explicitly stated in the work, but all of them are in practice observed with great fidelity, and their controlling place in the theory will become more evident in what follows (were one to essay the project, conceivably worthwhile, of axiomatizing the theory, they would be plausible candidates for axioms):

(i) *said-of* is always intra-categorial, and conversely,
(ii) *inherence* is always cross-categorial, and conversely,
(iii) substances and only substances can be subjects of inherence.

Brief note on the rendering of OUSIA. With misgivings that in the last analysis have proved superable, I have followed long English-speaking tradition in translating Aristotle's technical coinage *ousia* as "substance". But any who do not already know, should be made aware that this rendering is both etymologically and historically suspect, and should take care to let the word acquire its associations strictly from its use in the Aristotelean context. *Ousia* in Greek is a noun formed from the present participle of the verb meaning "to be". The corresponding noun in Latin is that from which English derives "entity". One distinguished interpreter has not only thoroughly argued the case for "entity" as rendering for *ousia*, but actually consistently employed it.[14] If we do this, we must be prepared to

---

14 Joseph Owens, *Doctrine of Being* (hereafter *DOB*), ch. 4 for the argument.

speak not only of "an entity" but of "the entity *of* something", at which point we are not much better off (so far as English goes) than in having to do the same with "substance", though we may with reason feel etymologically purer. Another possibility for *ousia* is "reality"; and no doubt we can swallow "a reality" (as in "an individual ox is a reality"). However, in normal English "the reality *of* something" means its existence, which is not what Aristotle means by its *ousia*; another problem is that there is no adjective related to the noun "reality" as "substantial" is related to "substance" (it could not be "real", it would have to be something like "realitative"), and since we cannot possibly get on without such an adjective (and no force on earth could make me use "realitative"), it seems better to use an English noun that forms such an adjective naturally than to use "reality" for the noun and "substantial" for the adjective.[15] If I could invent it without two millennia of background, I would render *ousia* as "entity", but it is a small choice, and "substance" is deeply entrenched. With this explanation, henceforth *ousia*, in all its complexity, is "substance".

15 This is not an imaginary predicament; see Barnes (1975), e.g. p. 169.

§2. Inherence

If *Socrates is X*, i.e. if *X is predicated-of Socrates*, by way of something's being *in* him, the applicable sense of "in" is supposed to be elucidated by the following explanation:

By '*in* a subject', I mean that which (i) subsisting in something, not as a *part*, (ii) cannot exist separately from what it is in.

This is then applied to the examples of the second class of the tetrachotomy:

– For example, the particular item of knowledge of letters[1] is *in* a subject, viz. the psyche, but it is not *said-of* any subject; and the particular shade of light color is *in*

1 I take *grammatikē* in its literal meaning of knowledge of letters, *grammata*, although the shift in its colloquial sense to the Hellenistic "grammar" no doubt was well under way (the sense clearly felt at e.g. *Meta.* 1003^{b}20; ambiguous: e.g. *Postpraed.* 14^{b}1–2). *hē tis grammatikē* is then a specific parcel of literacy, a point to be drilled into the boys by the master on Day *n* of Reading 1–A. (Also consonant with what is known by "grammatical art" according to *Sophist* 253a.)

a subject, viz. the body (for every color is in a body), but it is not *said-of* any subject. (1ᵃ23–9)

That is not the most enlightening explanation ever given, but in fact in conjunction with what comes later a good deal can be extracted from it. What is meant, I believe, is as follows (on the understanding that many matters in this area are disputed and that consensus upon any interpretation as definitive is highly unlikely). To begin, we should put aside a misinterpretation still seemingly widespread, that by *to ti leukon* is meant a particular occurrence of pallor on Socrates' surface and no other, Socrates' very own proprietary white, and coordinately that by "cannot exist separately from what it is in" is meant that Socrates' demise (or even his retirement to sunny Southern California) would entail the permanent destruction of that particular white that had been just his.[2] This reading seems to me thoroughly implausible on a variety of grounds, many of which were convincingly argued by G. E. L. Owen in his paper on the matter of 1965;[3] deferring further details for §5 below, I will proceed on the basis that *leukon* covers all light colors (as *melan* covers all dark ones),[4] and *to ti leukon* means some particular fully determinate shade of light color (*chalk white*, let us say); likewise, we may add, *grammatikē* is knowledge of letters, and *hē tis grammatikē* is a particular item of such knowledge – say, that the voiced palatal consonant that we all inarticulately know as [g] is written: Γ, Gamma, or that the name on this shard is that of the politician who has bought my vote (or, if the shard is an actual *ostrakon*, of his enemy). Such a color, and such a fragment of literacy, can exist *in* many subjects,[5] and the point of the "cannot exist separately" clause is to fix upon a *manner* of 'being': these are *onta* that can exist in no other fashion than by inhering in things other than themselves; they cannot exist on their own, like primary substances – but no imputation is made of

---

2 Recall from note 12 of §1 that it is quite out of the question that *everything* that inheres, inheres in only a single subject. The next outcropping of the issue is in §5.

3 Owen (1965b). But it should be noted that my overall view of the *Cats.* doctrine is different on a couple of significant points, particularly: (a) the said-of/predicated-of distinction seems not to have been part of his picture in that paper (cf. his p. 97), and (b) he did not there attach the importance that I do here to *paronymy* (cf. his p. 99 top, also Owen (1957), p. 175). The most powerful defense published since Owen's of the general tendency to be advocated here on this matter is that of Frede (1978); it argues, among much else, that 1ᵃ24–5 requires a *sort* of primary substance (i.e., a species or genus) for the individual nonsubstance to inhere in: colors must inhere in *body*, knowledges must inhere in *psyche* (*ibid.*, pp. 27–28). It also has what I think may be the definitive diagnosis of the intuitive fallacy on which the "proper to their bearers" interpretation rests (*ibid.*, pp. 30–31). See §4, note 1, and §5.

4 Platnauer (1921).

5 Note that the use of "knowledge" as correlative of "knowable" in *Cats.* 7 7ᵇ23–5 certainly does not suggest that points of knowledge cannot be shared; such things are "the same for all", *de Int.* 16ᵃ6.

exclusive proprietorship or of the vast horizontal multiplication of particular entities that that would entail. The 'particularity' of such an item rather is explicitly stated to reside in its *specificity*: in its not being *sayable-of* anything, which means, of anything less general than it.[6]

That last is slightly premature, but will be set in context before we are done (see §3). Now, the next point about "in a subject" cannot be extracted directly from the passage (1^a23–9) just quoted, but has to be seen in the use to which the notion is put. It will be recalled that we were dealing with situations of the form *X is predicated-of Socrates*, where *X* is unchanged from its predicative form in the original, colloquial *Socrates is X*. And the idea is this: if, in *X predicated-of Y*, *X* and *Y* are not of the same category (thus here, if *Y* is and *X* is not in the category of substance – cf. (ii) and (iii) at the end of §1 above), then the statement is not yet in fully analyzed form and does not fully show forth the nature of the 'being' in question; it always reduces to a more fundamental form in which a 'particular item' is said to exist *in* a subject, in the enormously broad present sense of "in".[7] Examples of such items, beyond those just given (a color, some knowledge) are a particular specific virtue (e.g. bravery, 1^a15) or a particular position or posture (6^b11), or – now to make some up – a definite degree or stage of exophthalmia ("ophthalmia = a particular disease" at *Top.* iv 3, 123^b35–6; cf. §5 below), or total baldness, or just *this* snubness of nose. (Of course, it sounds odd to say that such things are "in" someone, though possibly no more odd than to say that he "partakes of" them. In Greek it is about equally odd; but except for remarking (1^a24, 3^a31–2) that by "in" is not meant "in as a part", which anyway at this point we presumably can see for ourselves, the author is strikingly unperturbed over its interpretation. A lesson to take may be that we can reach what is interesting about this more quickly if we do not strain at the jargon.)

These items that inhere, being individuals, have names that are nominal in form, like "bravery" or "the particular pallor"; and it is from being-inhered-in by these items that the individual substances get *their* names, like "brave" or "pale", by way of a transformation that Aristotle calls *paronymy*: $brave_a$ is predicated-of Socrates (i.e. Socrates *is* $brave_a$) paronymously, from the $bravery_n$ that's *in* him, and $grammatical_a$ from the

6 *Cat.* 2, 1^b6–7; my phrasing is owed to Owen (1965b), p. 98 (which, however, has "predicable of"). Note also *Cat.* 7, 6^b11–12, "lying and standing and sitting are *particular positions* (*theseis tines*)"; no need is suggested to identify the *poseurs* in order to obtain the identity of the positions. See the previous note; the entire matter is worked over in §5 below.

7 Anticipating forthcoming refinements, strictly speaking the *situation* invariably contains a nonsubstantial 'particular item' inhering in a substantial subject; the *statement* may be less explicit (as "Socrates is of-some-color", "Socrates is somehow-qualified"), and remain accessible to analysis. See the last paragraph of §3 below.

grammar$_n$ that's in his mind. We are *knowledgeable$_a$* (*epistēmones*) through our having (*tōi ekhein*) some particular items of knowledge (*tōn kath' hekasta epistēmōn tina*, 11ᵃ33–4, cf. 15ᵇ17–21) – "having" being here the converse of "in". Honey is sweet$_a$ by having taken on sweetness$_n$ (*tōi glukutēta dedekhthai*, 9ᵃ33). A man becomes now pale$_a$ and now dark$_a$ (4ᵃ18) by "receiving" paleness$_n$ and darkness$_n$ (4ᵇ14). And so on. "Paronymy" is itself defined even more telegraphically than "in", but is also to be understood as a relationship between things not linguistic expressions: paronymous things (grammatical and brave ones, for example, like grammatical and brave Socrates) "get their name [i.e. grammatical$_a$ and brave$_a$] from something, with a change of ending or inflection [from grammar$_n$ and bravery$_n$]" (1ᵃ12–15).

The details can wait. For now, the critical thing is that where *X predicated-of Socrates* is cross-categorial, where the adjectival *X* ascribes to him quality, or quantity, or character, or position (still disregarding details such as what to make of the category of Time and various other such items), the adjectival 'being' expressed as X_a is thought of as derived, by way of the paronymy transformation,[8] from a deeper nominal form X_n *naming* an *individual quality*, quantity or whatever it may be, and the whole statement accordingly breaks up into a relational assertion that two particular individuals stand to one another in the relation of one attaching to or 'inhering in' the other.

It is that which is named by the deeper, nominal form, and not the adjectival one, that receives a *definition*: we ask, What is bravery$_n$?, for example, not, What is brave$_a$?, and the definitory response (typically, "Such-and-such a virtue"), is not, Aristotle correctly remarks, predicable

---

8 W.D. Ross claims (*AM* i 256) that the *Metaphysics* concept of a *pros hen kai mian phusin legomenon* (*Meta. Γ* 2, 1003ᵃ33) is essentially that of a paronym with respect to its eponymous inherent. This is only superficially right; it is true that *pros hen* meaning meets the definitional conditions for paronymy, but they radically underdescribe it: for the paronymy-transformation $X_n \rightarrow X_a$ yields only a *single* adjectival meaning, there is no sign of the *family* of related adjectival applications that radiate from the kernel of a focal term like "health(y)"; in the latter case the situation is perhaps something like:

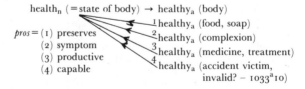

The approach here is in agreement with that of Owens in *DOB²*, p. 111, n. 20. He also cites *Topics* i 15 106ᵇ29–107ᵃ2.

For my own version of how the *pros hen* concept fits into the total apocalypse, see §23(i).

of the original subject (Socrates is not such-and-such a virtue), nor, we might add, is it predicative in nature at all.[9] (At this point we pass by, but will not now try to grasp, a handle on the Unity of Definition problem which raises some highly instructive difficulties later in connection with the metaphysics of substances; we shall get back to this in §23 below.) However, in this connection occurs something very interesting. Consider the specimen statement, *That animal is pale* (I am shifting the grammatical subject to *animal* temporarily as a word – *zōion* – that is neuter in Greek, unlike "man" or "Socrates"). This goes into technicalese as *pale predicated-of that animal*, where *pale* is: *leukon*, the adjective agreeing with *zōion*. This comes by paronymy from: *leukon*, the nominal that names the color, and the whole sentence is: *leukon* (in fact, some determinate shade of light color, e.g. *ghastly pallor*) *inheres in that animal*. But the adjectival and nominal forms look just alike! True; we may call this a case of 'degenerate paronymy', but it is anything but trivial. It is the case Aristotle has in mind in *Cat.* 5, 2^a27–4, 3^a15–17: most cases, he says, are like bravery, where neither the name (bravery) nor the definition (such-and-such a virtue) is predicated of the subject, only the paronymous offspring (brave$_a$); but in some cases, like *leukon* (with neuter name of subject), "nothing prevents the name of what inheres in the subject from being predicated" (= the name and the predicate look just alike), but nonetheless the underlying *Sachverhalt* is still the same and "it is still impossible for the definition to be predicated" (ibid.).[10] A remarkable little point, it seems, which he evidently saw quite clearly and distinctly: that

$$leukon \neq leukon$$

in the sense just explained,[11] one deriving paronymously from the other.

9 I have in mind here Frege's use of "predicative nature" to evoke (in his terminology) the special character of *concept* as opposed to *object*; cf. *Kleine Schriften*, p. 171 (= "Ueber Begriff und Gegenstand", p. 197). The reader to whom the allusion is unfamiliar need not pursue it.

10 Ackrill (1963) notes: "At 2^a31–4 Aristotle is careless. He says that white is in a subject and is predicated of a subject; he should have said that white is in a subject and its name is predicated of the subject" (p. 75). This misses a mark, not so much by reimporting the use-mention issue, there generally overworked (cf. §1, note 9), as by overlooking the authentic insight in the idea of degenerate paronymy. Nor is this "homonymy or something like it" (1^a12 n., p. 72), except as the technical triviality that if the color and the man are both white, and the definition of the color can be predicated of the white color but not of the white man, then these whites are 'homonyms' by 1^a1–6. But this only obscures the important relationship. Similar considerations apply to Dancy (1975b), at 358–359. Owens (*DOB²*, p. 111, n. 21), cites a 'problem' raised by Zabarella, in the supposition that on the "change-of-ending" condition of paronymy, a female grammarian (*grammatikē*) couldn't get her name from grammar (*grammatikē* – no change of ending in Greek!). But the degeneracy analysis is also applicable here.

11 But of course this is no "little point" in its ramifications; the significance of the predicability-of-the-definition aspect is critical, as we shall see (§4, §5). And although the

Of course, if required for some reason, *leukotēs*, pallor, was ready at hand, and indeed surfaces explicitly at e.g. 9^a34, 9^b9, 10^a30.[12]

In general, then, the predication that a particular something, like Socrates, is thus-and-so particularly qualified, as e.g. ghastly pale$_a$, is to be understood as a particular quality's inhering in him; this is the true form of the fact, and is not confined to the *category* of so-called quality, but runs through the nonsubstantial categories generally (cf. 11^a15, the particular positions or relatives at 6^b11, etc.), to encompass all those 'beings', a particular something being a particular something, that fall within the second of the eight classes enumerated at the beginning of §1. The only even apparent exceptions are the cases in which a nominal form, naming the inhering particular something, does not happen to exist in current ordinary speech (10^a32 ff.); these should not pose any special problem in principle, nor does the author seem to think that they do (he evinces no timidity about "inventing names" as the occasion may call for, 7^a5–22, $^b11$–12, 10^a32 ff.).[13]

There are, needless to say, a great many problems associated with these 'particular *enonta*' or inherents; following the illustrious lead of Aristotle himself, I wish to evade all of them to the maximum extent possible. Clearly inherence is a catch-all, an omnium-gatherum generated above all by the motive of obtaining maximum contrast ("The Category of Everything Else"), between all its many and various and by-the-*Cats.*-ill-distinguished instances on the one hand, and intracategorial predication, especially in the category of substance, on the other – to which we should now proceed. Thus (i) there is the puzzling question raised by the *Cats.* account, how is it that *color*, for example, is supposed (as it apparently is) to split up its reference into *the particular colors*, through *white* etc. into *chalk*

language of "essence" (*hoper, ti ēn einai, anthrōpōi einai*, etc.) is hardly at all deployed in the *Cats.* (though, obliquely, at 3^b36, 6^a19; cf. too 1^a5, 11) – cf. §3, note 4 –, the point of *Cat.* 2^a27–34 meshes precisely with that of *Meta.* Gamma 4, 1007^a32–3: "*leukon* attaches to (*sumbebēken*)" the man, because he's *leukos*, but he's not *hoper leukon* (just what is (=) white, i.e. the color^n)" (nor *hoper chrōma* either, *Top.* iii 1, 116^a27 (cf. §5)). And an unbroken line leads from this direct to the Things Identical With Their Essences problem in *Meta.* Zeta 6; for the link see 1031^b22–8, on this §23(iii) below.

12 The contrast (*leukotēs* versus *leukon*, etc.) itself goes back to, and perhaps originates in, the *Theaetetus* (145de, 156e, 159cde, 182ab, 186b; it seems that the notion of *poiotēs* does originate at 182a). As John Cooper has reminded me, all that is strictly licensed by the official explanation of paronymy at 1^a12 ff. is a derivation like *leukotēs*→*leukon* with an *explicit* "change of ending or inflection" (cf. pp. 18f. above); thus Aristotle's clear recognition of the degenerate possibility here at 2^a27–34, 3^a15–17 should have caused him either to revise the earlier explanation to accommodate it, or else (rather less plausibly) to try to argue that *leukon* (i.e., *leukon*$_n$) and *leukon* (i.e. *leukon*$_a$) are despite surface appearances somehow or other really distinct in "ending or inflection". 13 Noted by Dancy (1975b), 369.

white$_n$, *ghastly pale*$_n$ and the other particular shades of light, dark, etc., color – is it that Aristotle conceives this as if on a par with the way *man* splits up into the individual men, a syllepsis that would come rather unnaturally to us?[14] Some further light can in fact be shed on this, and we shall find ourselves having to return to it in §5. But (ii) I hope to evade entirely the vexatious difficulties in the 'particular points of knowledge', which presents especially severe problems of individuation, as latter-day treatments of the semantics of knowledge and belief have once again made apparent. Yet again, (iii) I want to shelve for the present the difficulties surrounding *differentia*, and what category to put it in (for the differentiae of a substance, the correct answer of course has to be: substance, but it is sometimes hard to motivate concrete suggestions in particular cases, and there are some confusing texts in the corpus pointing in various other peculiar directions); this one, we shall find, is not soluble with *Cats*. machinery and requires assistance from the theories of the biological works and the *Metaphysics*.[15] Then there is (iv) the type of problem that comes up repeatedly in trying to apply the *Cats*. theory to the real world: however beautiful a theory of "predicative being" it may or may not be, it is a thoroughly wretched theory of color, of knowledge, of virtue, of grammar, and of most everything else in nonsubstance. These and many other questions and difficulties I resolutely pass by, in order to go back to *X predicated of Y* and to ask after the other underlying structure, claimed to differ so profoundly from 'this inhering in that': namely, 'this said-of that, being said-of a subject'.

14 On this cf. Frede (1978), pp. 22–23. A different idea of "counting" in connection with nonsubstantial individuals is suggested by Jones (1972), pp. 114 ff., and queried by Annas (1974).

15 See §13(ii), §23–4; the nearest the *Cats*. comes to hinting at lore in this area is 3ᵃ21ff., 3ᵃ33 ff. *Meta*. Delta 14 *init*. reports a use of "quality" (*poion*) to mean substantial differentia, but this cannot possibly be taken as meaning the *category* of quality (as Ross *AM* xci and perhaps (?) Pellegrin (1982), p. 79n.); cf. Kirwan (1971) *ad loc*. (pp. 162–3). Cf. also Anscombe (1961), pp. 13, 33.

§3. Said-of a subject: the general case

It is a difficulty in the exposition of the *Categories* that the *said-of* structure is nowhere laid out in its own right – that is, though it seems clear from the tetrachotomy of ch. 2 that the structure is supposed to occur not exclusively in the category of substance but elsewhere as well,[1] almost everything else that is said about it is in ch. 5, on substance. As a consequence, it is hard to see clearly which properties ascribed to *said-of* in the case of substance also carry over to the other categories (as some certainly do), and which are peculiar to it (as some certainly are). The only way to proceed, then, is to extract whatever we can from the indications of ch. 5, bearing the difficulties in mind.

Perhaps the first lesson of ch. 5 in order of significance is one that it is at first sight surprising not to have had stated in the tetrachotomy of ch. 2: just as the things that inhere "cannot exist separately from what they are in", but have *inhering* in substances, and ultimately in substantial individuals, as their unique mode of being, so too the things that are said-of also cannot exist separately from substances, and ultimately from substantial individuals.[2] Thus it turns out in ch. 5 to be a central principle of the theory that the substantial individuals are absolutely basic and ultimate, not only overlying no deeper subject in either of the two possible ways (1^b3-4), but themselves underlying all the other 'things that are': "*all* of the other things are either said-of the primary substances as subjects or else in them as subjects" (2^a34), so that "if the primary substances did not exist it would be impossible for *any* of the other things to exist" (2^b5). This fact about the substantial individuals is indeed explicitly cited as what especially qualifies them for the title of 'substance' ($2^b15-17, 2^b37-3^a1$), a point to which we shall more than once have to return (§§4, 6, 8, 17, 19): it is *why* as substances they are 'primary' (in the *Categories*).

In fact, at second sight the silence of ch. 2 on this point is not so surprising, because the dependence of the substantial kinds upon the primary substances is different from and more involved than that of the nonsubstantial kinds in certain ways, and ch. 2 is not ready for the complications (nor yet are we; but see §4). But for immediate present purposes, the point is that as regards dependence on the substantial individuals, both all that inheres and all that is said-of are in the last analysis thus dependent.

Then how are they different?

---

1 Some confirmation of this comes from the important chapter *Topics* i 9, for whatever that may be worth in interpreting the *Cats.*: there, protases both of *what it is* (= genus) and of *definition* (= species) are to be found throughout all the categories, not substance alone. For a full discussion see Frede (1981), pp. 9f.
2 Cf. Dancy (1975b), 344.

(1) 2^a19–34. The first indication is perhaps the most significant:

It is clear from what has been said[3] that of the things that are *said-of* a subject, both the name *and the definition* necessarily are predicated of the subject. (2^a19–21)

This already makes a sharp contrast with inherence, for which, as we have seen, it is firmly claimed that the definition of what inheres can *never* be predicated of the subject (2^a30–4, 3^a16–17, cf. §2 above). The example that is then taken as illustrative, not too luminously (2^a21–7), is a substance (viz. a man), but a generalizable moral is near at hand. It lies in the fact that unlike the English locutions "said-of" and "definition", which are wholly unrelated to one another (and partly for this reason, "said-of" in English rings oddly for a relationship that is supposed to hold between *onta*, things that are), the Greek verb *legesthai* (*kata*) is connected in etymology and meaning with *logos* – the *Cats.* word for *definition* – and thus to the Greek reader could perhaps connote a sort of material-mode *defining*, marking-out-the-nature-of. Thus the entire context *ho anthrōpos kath' hupokeimenou tou tinos anthrōpou legetai* (e.g., 3^a11) could be understood along the lines, Man (the species) *defines* the individual man as subject. To develop the intuition a bit further, the thought would be that that which is *said-of* a subject is part – or, in the limiting case, all – of the *nature* of that subject, something that must hold of it necessarily and permanently, all of this being familiarly connoted by the Greek associations of "definition".[4] As phrased here, there is evidently nothing in this thought that would confine its application to substance alone; indeed, as we shall see when we encounter some complications in §4 about the interpretation of "substance" in the *Cats.*, its application to substances is if anything the more controversial of the two. Certainly the example used for the third division of the tetrachotomy in ch. 2, Knowledge (*epistēmē*) said-of grammar

---

3 "From what has been said" apparently must refer to 1^b10 ff., which hardly makes "clear" anything of the sort here being inferred, and beyond that is a plain misstatement as it stands (cf. p. 11 above).

4 I do not know why the *Categories* does not use the expression *ti ēn einai*, usually Englished as "essence". It means, standardly in all of Aristotle, *that which is articulated by a definition* of anything – that is, in our terminology, by the *definiens*. Since in any good definition, the meanings of definiendum and definiens are identical, it follows at once that any kind, substantial or otherwise, is identical with its own essence – this is for us a rather trivial theorem of our identity theory, but for Aristotle was a major metaphysical crux requiring laborious (and not always altogether followable) argumentation to get the right answers in this connection (for further references and details, see §23(iii) on *Meta.* Zeta 6). In any case, it would somewhat lessen the use-mention horrors of 2^a19–34 if the passage were phrased in terms of predicability of the essence, i.e. the 'objective correlate' of the definiens, which is obviously what is meant, and the word "definition" could be left out of it.

(*grammatikē*), seems conformable to such an interpretation; but to spell it out I prefer to change the example (for one reason, the problems about individuating "knowledges", mentioned at the end of §2, are just too difficult): 'Such-and-such a virtue' *defines* bravery, a particular virtue, as subject. (There is more to be said about the individuation of virtues, too, however. See §5.)

(2) *3ª7–21*. The indications of the last paragraph as to the intended contrast between said-of and inherence are mainly drawn from 2ª19–34; a related line is pursued in 3ª7–21, which is to the effect that "no substance is *in* a subject." This is simply asserted *ex vi termini* for primary substances = substantial individuals, and then argued for secondary substances = substantial kinds to be "obvious at once", on grounds similar to the last paragraph: that in the case of Man and the individual man, the definition of the former is predicated-of the latter (he could and should have said said-of, in the "material-mode" sense) and by this the inherence relation is ruled out. (As he proceeds to point out, the same argument can be made for differentia, which tells in favor of the suggested answer to question (iii) at the end of §2.) If we ask what parallel to this argument could be made for nonsubstantial kinds, the answer is that in one sense there is no analogy, since inherence is only in substances (thus such a claim as "it is obvious at once that Color is not *in* the particular white" is immediately verified by the fact that *nothing* is *in* the particular white); but in another sense, the *reason* why Man or Animal are not *in* the individual man (and plenty of things *are in* the individual man), namely the predicability of him of the *definitions* of Animal and Man, also applies to Color and the particular white, and to nonsubstantial said-of relatees generally.

(3) *3ª33–ᵇ9*. The contrast between inherence and all of said-of is put in a third and final way, also stemming from the predicability-of-definition criterion: according to ch. 1, things are *synonymous* when they share a name and the definition answering to the name is predicable of both, *paronymous* when "one gets its name from the other with a change of ending" – in this way, whereas Socrates is called *brave* paronymously, from *bravery*, Socrates is called *man* synonymously, from *man* (3ª33–ᵇ9). (There is *no* such thing as a paronymy of *man* from *humanity* or *anthrōpotēs*, or anything like it.) Once again, nothing is said explicitly here about nonsubstantial said-of, but on the basis of the rest of the view there is no evident reason why the particular knowledge-of-grammar should not be regarded as called that (*knowledge*) synonymously, from the *knowledge* that's said-of it.

Thus all of the features of the said-of structure that flow from the predicability of the definition in that case, seem to apply to the nonsubstantial categories at least as validly as to the substantial.

In the light, then, of these gleanings from *Cat.* 5, let us see what we can infer about the contrast that is intended between the two configurations as considered so far.

First, as to inherence. The only case of inherence that we were yet in a position to deal with in §2 (that corresponding to the second type of 'being' in the list, a particular something's 'being' particularly-qualified$_a$, quantified$_a$, or the like) turned out to be a special relationship between two particular entities, a particular substance and a particular nonsubstance (a particular quality$_n$, quantity$_n$, or whatever) which the substance 'has' (11^a33–4) or 'receives' (4^b14–16, 9^a33) (cf. p. 18 above). The nonsubstance is dependent on substance(s) in the sense that it cannot exist except by inhering in a substance, whether (a) in many at one time or (b) in different ones at different times or (c) in one at one time and not at another (these of course are not exclusive); but if and when it does not inhere in *any* substance, then it does not exist at all (2_a34–5) – let us call this the *"no-toehold situation"*. Except for this, however, the particular substance and nonsubstance can be seen to enjoy a certain *in*dependence, in two ways. First, the nonsubstance is at least conceptually and in many instances actually detachable from any particular substance in which it may reside at a given juncture; it can disappear from *that* substance without being totally annihilated, if only it retain a toehold in some other, and within that limit, it has all the range of freedom indicated in alternatives (a)(b)(c) above. Second, the substance is conceptually and in many intances actually detachable from any particular nonsubstance that may reside in it at a given juncture,[5] and indeed as we shall see (§4 (ii) below), its ability to endure intact as "the same and numerically one" while contrary inherents shuffle through it, is to be saluted as its most distinctive feature. And the particular substance is of course independent in the sense in which "all the other things" are dependent, the sense of existing in such a manner as to have need of no other thing in order to exist. In short, in any given inherence of particular in particular, we have *an attachment between two distinct entities, each of which is capable of surviving their detachment* save only when the result is the "no-toehold" condition which spells annihilation for the nonsubstance.

5 It is as well to keep the picture rather general at this point and not try to focus too sharply. (For a single example, it might be doubted that an individual man is even conceptually, let alone actually, detachable from the inherent in the category of Relation that is whose daughter she is.) (Here recall §1, n. 10, p. 13 above).

For the relata of the said-of configuration, things look quite different from this. Let us take the nonsubstances first (for they are the easier, also we have not yet looked at the substances as such), and use Quality for purposes of illustration. It seems that what is envisaged is like this: we noted already that at one end of the scale are (1) the particular qualities$_n$, *ghastly pallor*$_n$ and *chalk white*$_n$, etc., all of which have (2) *light color*$_n$ (i.e., *leukon*$_n$) said-of them; then there are (e.g.) (1) *ducal maroon*$_n$ and *coal black*$_n$, etc., all of which have (2) *dark color*$_n$ (i.e., *melan*$_n$) said-of them; then (e.g.) there is (3) *color*$_n$, said-of all of the foregoing; farther along there is perhaps (4) *affection*$_n$, which picks up not only everything so far mentioned but other more-particular qualities$_n$ like (2?) *hotness*$_n$; farther out we get to (9?) state$_n$, (12?) condition$_n$, and finally terminate at (20?) *quality*$_n$. (It will be recognized that the specifics are mostly my invention, eked out with a few borrowings from *Cats*. ch. 8) Now it seems, from the indications about said-of that we have extracted from *Cats*. chs. 2 and 5, that each said-of predication, and therefore the entire branching structure of Quality just outlined, must hold "necessarily and permanently" (p. 23 above); we do *not* have here the detachability of the relata from these relationships, that appeared to hold for the relation of particular subject to particular inherent-in-that-subject. In fact, from the indications it looks very much as if the entire arboreal complex must be entirely unchanging in every way, save one: just as before, for so long as a particular quality$_n$ goes "no-toehold", for that long it altogether ceases to be, so here, the more-general qualities$_n$ will go "no-toehold" and disappear for so long as this may happen to all of the more-particular qualities$_n$ they are said-of; and this is the interpretive expansion (for those *onta* we have dealt with so far) of precisely how it is that "if the primary substances did not exist it would be impossible for any of the other things to exist" (2^b5–6).

If this is the interpretation intended, then, it seems that according to the *Categories*, where X is *said-of* Y, this situation is *not* an attachment between entities that can become unattached, but rather one which is *entirely unalterable except for the possibility that Y may cease to exist* (a possibility that will occur, for those *onta* we have dealt with so far, by Y's going "no-toehold").[6]

6 Mention has already been made above of the *Theaetetus*, esp. 182a, in connection with the concept *poiotēs* (§2, note 12, p. 20 above); it seems highly plausible that the character of the structure as described, including its unalterability, derives in some fairly direct way from that of the domain of Forms as envisaged in later Platonic writings (the *Sophist*, for example). The relationship seems especially apt just in connection with the argument against "Total Instability" at *Tht*. 181c–183b, in which *poiotēs* emerges; cf. also John McDowell's discussion in the Clarendon Plato version, pp. 180–4. Also *Timaeus* 49–52.

Another way of putting what I believe is extensionally the same contrast, is to say that X *inhering in* Y is a relation between Y and something X that Y *has* (we have seen above that the *Cats.* sometimes so phrases it), whereas X *said-of* Y is a relation between Y and something X that Y *is*, in some stronger and more theory-laden sense of "is" than the ordinary-language word of the eight analysanda-types (we shall see Aristotle struggling to clarify the desiderated sense of "is" in some very instructively difficult chapters of *Meta.* Zeta: cf. §23(iii)) – several note-worthy recent interpretations make use of this turn; but it will be desirable, if possible, not to leave it at this for primitive terminology.[7]

In §4, we shall return to deal with some interpretive complications about this view in connection with *said-of* in the category of substance, which is the topic we should proceed to next.

Before proceeding, however, let us quickly catch up on the types of 'being' that the scheme as so far developed is able to encompass. Most straightforwardly, the nonsubstantial *said-of*'s analyze the 'beings' of types (7) and (8) in the enumeration of §1, "Grammar is (a) knowledge", "(a) color is (a) quality" (e.g.), the first (7) seen as nonsubstantial kind said-of nonsubstantial particular, the second (8) as wider (indeed widest) kind said-of narrower. But another, spectacular consequence of bringing in the kinds that are said-of the nonsubstantial atoms is the inherence of those kinds in the substances in which the nonsubstantial atoms inhere; for from the standpoint of the analysis of the 'beings', this effects a truly enormous expansion of the *domain* (in the sense of the logic of functions) of the paronymy-transformation – the fact that if a particular like *ghastly pallor*$_n$ inheres in Socrates, then so does everything said-of it, from *light color*$_n$ to *color*$_n$ all the way out to *quality*$_n$, is what explains the fact that if Socrates is ghastly pale,$_a$, then he is also light-colored$_a$ and colored$_a$ . . . and qualified$_a$, the exceedingly large class of 'beings' represented in §1 as type (3).[8]

---

7 Anscombe (1961), p. 27; Owen (1965a), pp. 137–8; Code (1985a), p. 411.

8 Both points *contra* Rijk (1952), *op. cit.*, p. 72: "From the point of view of the theory of predication, . . . it would serve no useful purpose to distinguish within the secondary [= nonsubstantial] categories the individual accidents from their genres [sic] and species."

§4. Said-of a subject: the case of substance

One would expect that what is supposed to be understood for *said-of* in general, should also carry over into the special case of it that is within the category of substance; and we shall find this expectation largely borne out in the end, though not without some intervening complications. However, in addition to this, the "special case of substance" is *very* special.

The substantial individuals or "primary substances" are special as the ultimate subjects (*hupokeimena*), ultimate in the sense that nothing underlies or is subject for (*hupokeitai*) them, so that metaphysically they lie at the floor of the world, and everything else ("*all* the other things", 2^a34) can only *be* by being in them or said-of them. As already noted, this ultimacy is said to earn them the title of substance "most of all", "preeminently" (*malista*, 2^b17; cf. p.22 above).

The substantial kinds or "secondary substances" are also special, in several ways. For one thing, and importantly, they too get to be subjects of inherence: for what inheres in a substantial individual also inheres in the substantial kinds said-of it (this is obviously intended, though the point is made in the looser and technically less precise language of "predicated" and "stands to", 3^a1–6)[1] – and with this, another two of the eight predication-types of §1 come within the scope of the analysis: (5), (a) man's *being* grammatical, (6), (a) man's *being* virtuous. (But here there is a little gap in what is made explicit about this case in the *Cats*. It surely is intended, but is never quite nailed down, that if a nonsubstantial kind inheres in a substantial individual, it *must* do so in virtue of some nonsubstantial individual's doing so which that kind is said-of; thus if, e.g., "Color inheres in Body", not only must Color inhere in some individual body (which is long ago provided for, as most lately noted in the last paragraph), but some individual color must inhere in that individual body.[2] At least, this seems so reasonable that the absence of explicit provision for the general case can be taken as most likely an oversight.)

This sharing with the primary substances in the role of subjecthood for the inherents is part of what makes the substantial kinds *substantial*, in

---

1 "Importantly": for *form* as subject-of in the *Meta.*, cf. §8, §19(iv). Frede (1978), op. cit., pp. 26–7, makes use of this fact in an ingenious argument against the "unit-nonsubstance" misinterpretation (cf. §2, n. 3, p. 16 above).

2 Recall that the nature of these individual nonsubstances is still scheduled for further discussion in §5.

accordance with the *Cats.* view that the more of a *subject* something is, the more of a *substance* it is; and so it is not surprising that in these stakes it turns out that the species is "*more* substance" than the genus, since it is subject for more than the genus is, namely for the genus itself, which is said-of the species but not conversely (2^b17–22).

However, at this point there enters a somewhat different criterion for (secondary) substance:

> It is reasonable that, after the primary substances, only their species and genera should be called ('secondary') substances; for they alone, of things that are predicated, *reveal, make clear* (*dēloi*) the primary substance. (2_b29–31)

This is because "if someone is to render of [e.g.] the individual man what he is, he'll do so appropriately (*oikeiōs*) if he renders the species or the genus", whereas if he renders "any of the other things, he'll have done so inappropriately (*allotriōs*), – e.g., if he renders white$_a$ or runs$_a$ or anything like that" ($^b31$–6). Here it is not fully clear what the force is of "appropriately"; and in fact it is my suspicion that the author is moving at this point with the greatest possible caution, for reasons that will be explained shortly (pp. 32–33, 37–39). However, to complete the point, it turns out that on this criterion, too, species is "more substance" than is genus: this is because

> it is 'nearer' to the primary substance. For if someone is to render of the primary substance what it is, he'll render it better-known and more fitting (*gnōrimōteron kai oikeioteron*) if he renders the species than the genus; e.g., he would render the individual man better known rendering *man* than *animal*, – for the former is more distinctive (*idion mallon*) of the individual man, the latter is more common (*koinoteron*), – and he'll render the individual tree better-known rendering *tree* than *plant*. (2^b8–14)

This is one of those places, mentioned at the start of §3 above, where it is hard to tell how much of the point being made is peculiar to substance and how much holds categories-wide. That is, could it be contended *pari passu* with the foregoing that *light color*$_n$ (*leukon*$_n$) is "more quality" than (say) *color*$_n$ (*chrōma*$_n$), because it is 'nearer' the particular color, (say) *chalk white*$_n$? Because in rendering of the particular color what it is, one will render it better known by declaring it a light color$_n$ than merely a color$_n$? Because the latter is more common, the former more distinctive? And so on? There seems to be no way of deciding this; what is clear is that for the case of substance this is one of the most delicate *topoi* there is, as we shall appreciate when we return to it at the end of §4. Meanwhile, we first must deal with another *topos* which is (or seems to be) more peculiar to substance, as well as in some ways just plain peculiar.

(i) Presentiment of synchronic individuation

There is a fact about the examples of substance that occur in the *Cats.*
which is both noteworthy in itself and, I think, of considerable signficance
in its implications: to put it first anachronistically, in the formal-versus-
material-mode of speech to whose niceties Aristotle is so oblivious, it is
that the predicates naming the substantial kinds are *individuative* predicates, in the sense of terms marking off objects severally by way of a
criterion of individuation that is part of their meaning: terms of the type
today sometimes called "count terms", as opposed to "mass-terms" like
blood and "adjectival terms" like *blue*.[3] Thus they pick out individuals as
wholes, and accordingly accept numerical modifiers and form plurals:
the property remarked by Frege in those "concepts that isolate what falls
under them in a definite manner", the only type of concept to which a
finite *number* can belong (*Grundlagen*, p. 66); and connected is the fact that,
because such terms *F* are true of each member of their divided or
distinguished reference as discrete *wholes*, the result of splitting an *F* in two
will generally not be two *F*'s. (This characterization is only heuristic and
approximate, not to be regarded as hard-and-fast or criterial; we shall
frequently revisit the business of individuativeness before we are done,
and it will be considerably refined as we proceed (cf. esp. §8, §13(i), §15(i),
§23 (iv)).

As stated, in the formal mode of speech, the above is of course straightforward enough: the substantial predicate "man", we say, is an
individuative term, that is, 'divides its reference', multiply-denotes the
discrete individual men. Now it has already been sufficiently pointed out
(here and elsewhere) that the author of the *Cats.* is not finely attuned to
the distinction between mention and use of expressions – but all the
allowance in the world for that fact would not excuse the following
passage, if the above were all it were struggling to find expression for:

Every substance seems to signify a certain 'this' (*tode ti*). As for the primary
substances, it's true and quite beyond dispute that each of them signifies a certain
'this'; for the thing revealed is in-dividual (*atomon*) and numerically one (*hen
arithmōi*). But as for the secondary substances, though it appears from the form of

---

3 The term "sortal" has sometimes been used for the type of predicate here called
"individuative", but in such a way as to incorporate some suggestion of an *essence* condition,
beyond that of individuativeness; this has the effect of conflating two strands that, as will be seen,
I will need to distinguish in order to make a point about their delicate relationship in Aristotle's
theory, and so I prefer the more restricted word. My usage is modeled on that of W. V. Quine's
classic "Speaking of Objects", see *Ontological Relativity* (Columbia, 1969), p. 8. Cf. "divided
reference", *Word and Object*, pp. 90–5.

the name – when one says *man*, or *animal* – that it likewise signifies a certain 'this', this isn't really true; rather it signifies a certain *qualification* (*poion ti*). – for the subject (of the species or the genus) is not 'one' in the *way* that the primary substance is (one), but man and animal are said-of many things. – But then, it doesn't signify a certain qualification just like that (*haplōs*), in the way that *pale* (= pallor$_n$) does; for pale signifies *nothing but* a qualification, whereas the species and the genus mark off the qualification-of-a-*substance*; they signify *substance*-of-a-certain-qualification. (3^{b}10–21)

Here, it is true, the mention-use confusion embodied in the application of the semantical concepts "signify" and "reveal" and "mark off" is well-nigh total; but even that is not the main problem of expression in this passage. In what sense is it that the passage is trying to say that Man, the species, as well as the individual man, is "a certain 'this'", and why is this so difficult for it to do? The only possible interpretive strategy for this statement, compressed as it is to the point of strangulation, is to venture a hypothesis as to the broader view that it is a compression of, and then to try to see why the present expression of it is so constricted. In that spirit, as considerations that may with some plausibility be surmised to figure in Aristotle's thought that there is something 'thislike' about the substantial species, I hazard the following:

(1) *Man* (meaning the species), though it is not *atomon* in the technical *Cats.* sense of *individual*, since there are things that it is said-of, nonetheless *IS atomon* in the sense of *indivisible*, for *it is a fully differentiated and not further differentiable species*: a "lowest" or *infima* species (as it was later to be miscalled; for this use of "atomic" in connection with species, in the *Organon* and elsewhere, see Bonitz, *Index* 120^{a}58–b4, and §8, §23(iv) below; for "miscalled", §13 where eidos is really *above* genos, not below, in the two-stage domain).

(2) In some way that is related to (1), *Man* (the species) also *divides what it is said-of, its 'reference' in the material-mode sense, into individuals, into 'thisses' in the sense that is "true and beyond dispute"* (3^{b}11) – in this case, the discrete individual men.

It will transpire as developments proceed, that this pair of theses, and particularly the idea that there is some causal dependency of the second on the first, are deeply insinuated in Aristotle's metaphysics of substance (§8, §13(v), §15, §23). Evidently, the *Cats.* has reason to be extremely circumspect in this area, and its statement is cautious and relatively inexplicit, and consequently incomplete; shortly we shall consider some possible reasons for this. With the above as background, let us re-read and paraphrase the passage:

There is an obvious sense in which Coriscus, an individual man, is a "this', both atomic and numerically one, a unitary package: let us accept this for the moment as "true and quite beyond dispute". Now, the passage struggles on, let us try to see how something similar is true of the species (I leave the genus out of it for the time being). As a first shot, someone might think a species was *itself* a 'this' (e.g. a Platonist, albeit not very sophisticated in this Platonism, might so think), but that of course could not be right just as it stands; for that would not adequately reflect the multiplicative nature of the species, the fact that it is duplicated over and over again in a multiplicity of specimens (obviously that is not the technical *Cats.* sense of "in"), the "many things" that it is said-of. The passage phrases this fact, not very happily, by bringing in the word "qualification" or "such" (*poion*), which at once has to be modified so as to distinguish the predicability of *man* from that of *pale*, resulting in the strange contortions of the final sentence, *peri OUSIAN to poion, poion tina OUSIAN.*

What is going on here? Certainly the "this-hood" of the species does not spring forth from the paraphrase much if any more clearly than it does from the original; and the idea of thesis (1) is not articulated at all. What does come out is a muffled form of (2): *Man* is a kind *that comes in the form of ("qualified") 'thisses'*, a kind whose nature is to constitute the sorts of entity called primary substances ("of-a-certain-qualification"), each of which *is* 'one' and a 'this' in the fashion that is "true and beyond dispute".

As much as gets expressed, then, of the "this-hood" of species, is that the species is, not an individual, but *a kind of individual*, in the sense of a kind in which individuals come. (That phrasing is a slight variant on the phrasing of *Cats.* 2^{a}14–16, "the species in which the things primarily called substances are, are called secondary substances, as also are the genera of these species". But note that here the seas of language run dizzily high indeed: both

a species is a kind of individual

in English, and its translation into Greek (*eidos esti atomon ē tode ti*), are ambiguous as between *two* readings, one of which – the second – is the not-very-sophisticated-Platonic reading which the passage is at pains to rule out:

– a species is a kind.
– a species is an individual (of a peculiar kind).)

The idea is expressed in 3^{b}10–21 with great obscurity and with a terseness unusual even for Aristotle. Why? The reason for the obscurity is that the idea cannot possibly be explained properly in the absence of the distinction of form *versus* matter, which is being kept entirely out of the picture in the *Cats.* (deliberately, in my view, see below, end of §4). And the reason for the terseness is that at this point the discussion is verging on an area that the author of the work is doing everything he can to stay away from: the surpassingly complex interrelationship between substantial individuals and substantial *eidos* (thus far translated "species", appropriately for the *Cats.*); and I believe it may be a sign of this avoidance that thesis (1) is not made explicit. Both of these points will be elaborated upon in what follows (§4, pp. 37–39, §8, to begin).

This fact about substance, the fact that at any given moment the existence of substance consists in the existence of a population of discrete, well-distinguished unitary 'thisses' or *tade tina*, each of them "in-dividual (*atomon*) and numerically one (*hen arithmōi*, $3^{b}12$)", I will call the fact of substance's "*synchronic individuation*". We shall see that it gets somewhat more thoroughly exposed in the works to be treated later than it does here. The *Cats.* does not say whether this fact of synchronic individuativeness, though characteristic of substance, is exclusive to it, or whether something similar should be thought to hold for nonsubstance also; it may be recalled that this question was raised at the end of §2, only to be pushed aside; and such further light as I am able to shed on the contrast between the substantial and nonsubstantial individuals, which will be taken off the table in §5, will not much clarify this particular issue.

As against this, there is another aspect to the substantial individuals as to which the *Cats.* is clear and emphatic that it is "distinctive" and indeed unique to them, which is our next concern.

(ii) Presentiment of diachronic individuation, and a deviant but nonetheless unexcluded possibility

The longest sustained argument in all the *Cats.* is that ending the chapter on Substance ($4^{a}10-^{b}19$), to the effect that the "most distinctive" characteristic of the substantial individuals is their capability of existing as continuants "numerically one and the same" across time while undergoing change or "receiving contraries".[4] And indeed the bulk of that argument is an effort to prove that this mark is not merely "distinctive" of substantial individuals (in a modern sense of "distinctive"), but absolutely unique to them: *only* the substances can change (= alter, $4^{a}31$) while remaining numerically one and the same, "nothing like this is to be seen

---

4 Recall that *x receiving y* in this context is the same as *y inhering in x*; cf.$4^{b}14-16$, and §2, p. 18.

in any other case" (4^a21). The reason for this is not that the concept of something "individual and numerically one" lacks application outside substance, which as we know is not true (cf. 1^b6–7, §2, pp. 17–18), but is rather that individual nonsubstances are totally and entirely unchangeable: no such thing, it is insisted, "is changed *at all, by anything. . . . .Nothing comes-to-be 'in' them*" (4^b10–13), which also is no surprise, since we already have found reason to surmise that anything said-of a nonsubstance must hold of it necessarily and permanently (cf. §3, p. 23 above), and that nothing can inhere in a nonsubstance at all (cf. §1, p. 14).[5]

Substances alone, then, can persist identical through change (= succession) of inherents: let us call this fact about them their transtemporal or *"diachronic individuation"*.[6] However, at this point we encounter the question what limits, if any, are set by the *Cats.* upon the sorts of changes a substance can persist identical through; and the somewhat astonishing fact eventuates that *no limits whatever are made explicit.* The type of case that is not explicitly provided for runs so counter to the clearly intended interpretation of the work as to seem slightly shocking – in fact, it testifies to the intuitive beauty and power of the over-all intended design that the possibility left open by the words of the work does not seem to have been noticed or, if noticed, pondered for its possible significance. In any event, what is surprising is this: *neither here in 4^a10–$^b19$ nor anywhere else in the work is it explicitly excluded that a single substantial individual can belong to one substantial kind at one time and to another at another while remaining throughout numerically one and the same, nor for that matter is it provided that a substantial individual has to belong to a substantial kind at all.* In the former case the question, What is it? could elicit different answers concerning the same individual at the two times; in the latter case it could elicit presumably no better answer than "an individual substance"; at any rate no basis is actually articulated for any objection to either. In other words, the text of the *Categories* is compatible with a deviant interpretation under which some or all of the

5 This is perhaps the best place to mention the difficult problem of how the *Categories* theory should handle *adverbial* predications, such as Socrates' running *slowly* (how it "should", because clearly it does not). I will only point to two sub-problems. First, as will be discussed at more length in §5, there is uncertainty in many cases where the final nonsubstantial particularity lies; perhaps running$_n$ should be seen as divided into particular running$_n$, some fast and some slow (as color$_n$ is into particular colors$_n$, some light and some dark), and the problem generally handled in that way. Or perhaps that will not work. Second, a possible alternative would be to introduce into the theory a new, third relationship, of the adverbial 'being' to the nonsubstance (this relationship *cannot* be inherence or 4^a10–$^b19$ must be dropped). Cf. F.A. Lewis (1982), p. 10.

6 Dancy (1978), calls this idiosyncrasy an "alleged peculiarity of substances" and is critical of authors who find it criterial (377–8).

substantial individuals may be "bare particulars" capable of retaining their numerical identities through arbitrary migrations between substantial kinds or out of the kinds altogether; it determines the property of *being of a kind* with respect to the temporal termini of a substantial individual no more narrowly than does the common/legal concept of *nationality* with respect to human beings, whereby one and the same human being can (with some legal but no metaphysical difficulty) change her nationality or, like Philip Nolan, come to lack one entirely.

I am by no means implying that we are left clueless in this area; to the contrary, there is much to influence our understanding when the evidence is sifted carefully. Something might be made of 4^a5–7 ("a man isn't *more man* now than before"). More generally, we have found reason to believe that at least for the nonsubstance, the configuration *x said-of y* is an attachment that cannot be broken or altered in any way, save for the sole possibility that *y* may cease to exist (p. 26). Reasoning along the lines there advanced, it could plausibly be suggested that we are supposed to understand the possibility of substantial individuals' changing kinds as excluded by Aristotle's provisions that (a) if something *F* is said-of a subject then the *definition* of *F* is said-of that subject also, so that if *F* is a substantial species, then the definition of *F* is said-of *the individual F* (since the species is), and (b) surely a definition must hold permanently of what it applies to at all, *ergo* he can't mean that a thing that is now *F* (for this sort of *F*) could become not-*F*. To which I would respond: an excellent suggestion, very likely correct; I am not suggesting that there is any doubt about what we are supposed to understand. It is perhaps less than conclusive as it stands, in that the *Cats.* is introducing a technical concept of "definition" that has the novelty, among others, of countenancing talk of definitions applying to individual things (as opposed to kinds) at all;[7] it is not automatic from the sheer use of the word how it is supposed to interact with "substance" and "numerically one and the same" (two further novelties in the technical sense they bear in this work).

But in any case, not to prolong debate over whether or not the exclusion of substantial individuals' changing kinds is successfully *insinuated* by the *Cats.*, the point is that making the exclusion definite and explicit beyond question is not *difficult*: it is done clearly enough at *Topics*

---

7 By "novelty" I do not mean that definitions of kinds applying to members of those kinds is previously unheard of; Myles Burnyeat points out to me that the *Euthyphro* paradigm looks like a case of this. But the methodological explicitness with which it is incorporated into theory is new. And the relations between kind, definition and individual continue to give trouble well into Zeta; see §23(iii). The argument sketched in (a) and (b) could be more clearly phrased in terms of *essence* (cf. §3, n. 4).

125^b37-9,[8] and we shall see how it could have been done without any undue travail in the received *argot* of the *Cats*. ("*4^b19 ff." below); so the question becomes, if that is what is meant (as no doubt it is), then why does the *Cats*. not just come out with it?

One possibility is simple oversight, like the little gap we noticed earlier about Color and the individual color (p. 28); and this of course cannot be summarily ruled out. Yet, the precision and control that are generally manifest in the crafting of the work, and the obvious importance of the case, suggest the prima facie advisability in this instance of looking farther than that. And one need not look too far for the outline of an interesting explanation to begin to emerge. Once again, as with synchronic individuation, our author is being *exceedingly* careful.

For the *Categories* is a carefully limited work – arguably, an introductory one – which seems determined to contain the discussion at a metaphysical level that is, though in some ways sophisticated, still simple, and especially to block any descent from its own curtailed universe into the much deeper as well as wider universe of the *Metaphysics*. There are also signs of a notable concern not to get involved in "causes" – to analyze the varieties of predicative 'being' by setting out some ontological phenomena about individuals, kinds, inherences, survival of changes, and the like, without delving – here – into the underlying structure of the nature of things from which these phenomena eventuate. And a critical factor in maintaining that simplicity is the designation of the substantial individuals as ultimate subjects, at the "floor of the world", such that the nonsubstances must inhere in them and the substantial kinds be said-of them in order to exist, whereas they themselves are not thus existentially dependent on anything further, but are wholly self-sufficient: the dependencies all terminate in them, and with them "everything" comes to an end ("*all* the other things", "*none* of the other things"). Now, what happens to this agreeable simplicity if we (or he) should try to incorporate into the statement of the theory an explicit condition that would block the nonstandard model that it admits as it is actually written? Suppose *Cats.* 5 be continued another thirty lines or so past its present end, by an essentializing paragraph, e.g., as follows:

4^b17 (. . . It is, therefore, distinctive of substance that what is numerically one and the same is able to receive contraries. [Delete: This brings to an end our discussion of substance.])

---

8 "It's impossible for the same thing to remain, if it be entirely transferred out of its species, just as neither could the same animal at one time be, and at another time not be, a man". Also *Meta.* Zeta 15 1040^a29-33.

4^{b}19 ff.: However, it is impossible even among substances that what is numeri-cally one and the same should at one time have one thing said-of it and at another time not that, but something else, or that nothing should be said-of it at all. For as for things that are *in* a subject, it is of course obvious and true that this is impossible, for the individual shade of light color, numerically one and the same, cannot be at one time (a) Color, and at another time (a) Knowledge,[9] nor can it be neither-(a)-Color-nor-anything-else, but what's said-of it holds of it necessar-ily and always. But even for substances, something analogous is true. Of course, if a primary substance were to have one thing said-of it at one time and something different at another, this would not be a case of "what is numerically one and the same receiving *contraries*", since we have already said that "one substance – including secondary substance – is not contrary to another". [Cf. 3^{b}24–7.] But in any case, it is impossible. For when we said that the species and genera of substances – the secondary substance –, and only they, "reveal the primary substance", on the ground that "if someone is to render of the individual man what he is, he'll do so appropriately (*oikeiōs*) if he gives the species or the genus" [Cf. 2^{b}29–33, and p. 29 above], we didn't mean *just* "appropriately" (*oikeiōs monon*). Rather, what's said-of (*legetai kata*) the individual primary substance states *just what that individual is*, and is definition (*logos*) of just what that individual is, so that, e.g., the individual man could not continue to be, numerically one and the same, unless Man were to continue to be said-of him. For what's said-of him, too, holds of him necessarily and always.[10] And the same holds in the other cases. Nor can there be a primary substance of which no genus or species is said, for it would be without definition (*alogos*). This brings to an end our discussion of substance.

I take it that the foregoing is not something the author of the *Categories* was incapable of writing down, and it is my belief that when he wrote the work he subscribed to the view it articulates (thus that it *is* the intended interpretation), yet he did not definitively settle the matter by making it explicit, instead skirting it with insinuations. Why not, then?

"Paragraph *4^{b}19 ff.*", though it obviously echoes a basic line in *Metaphysics* Z and elsewhere, nonetheless if introduced into the *Categories* would considerably agitate the glassy-smooth surface that the author is at such pains to maintain upon its waters. For it injects a large complication: now, in addition to the agreeably simple *existential* dependency of "all the other things" – all the nonsubstances and the substantial kinds – on the substantial individuals, we are being told that there is also a reverse dependency that the substantial individuals have upon the substantial

9 I take this to be not question-begging, but to be interpreted, "what *starts* as an individual shade of light color", etc. –ed. (= M.F.)

10 "Always", i.e., as long as he lasts, not (necessarily) "eternally". The implications of "necessarily" are another, long story; cf. §25.

kinds – an *essential* dependency, in virtue of which (generalizing "$*4^b19$ ff.") "the individual F cannot continue to be, numerically one and the same, while F (its species) ceases to be said-of it". Abruptly we are facing species (or *eidos*) in a role wholly different from and more powerful than anything the *Cats.* is prepared to deal with: not a (mere) class, or even kind, but something constitutive or even causal, *required* for the continuity of the substantial individuals across time, "numerically one and the same while sustaining alteration". The newly explicit dependency of the substantial individuals on their kinds must immediately begin to erode their ultimacy as subjects, *eo ipso* they must cease to be *methodologically* "atomic" and opaque, as they are in the *Cats.* (that is, prior to "$*4^b19$ ff."), new questions must arise regarding their *analysis* in terms of this new concept of constitutive *eidos*, and the transformation of the *Categories* universe of *eidos* and individual with the individuals at its "floor" into the *Metaphysics* universe of *eidos* and matter, with the individuals *constructed*, "out of" the latter "by" the former, is irrecoverably under way.[11] (It is very interesting that the mere attempt to state an essentializing condition on the *Cats.* theory in normal *Cats.* terminology, as is done in the second half of "$*4^b19$ ff.", has the immediate effect of turning the discussion into the language of *Metaphysics* Zeta 4 – which I regard as representing an intermediate stage in that total transformation. The reader is encouraged to experiment with the task to see if this consequence can be avoided, as I think it cannot.)

My suggestion is that the omission of an explicit essentializing condition in the *Categories* is no oversight, but that the author, seeing plainly the edge of the abyss and knowing it could not possibly be plumbed within the scope of the work in hand, deliberately, silently drew back. He hoped, perhaps, that no one would notice, and hardly anyone did. It was no doubt for the same reason, i.e., because it would attract unwanted attention in the same quarter, that while he was at it he also did not bother to say that a primary substance should normally have some nonsubstantial inherents, even quite a few of them; in the text the possibility that some might not have any is nowhere excluded either.[12]

11 See §8 on the "opaqueness" in the *Categories* of substantial coming-to-be, ceasing-to-be, and plurality. – The whole question of the relationship between *eidos* in the *Categories* and *eidos* in the *Metaphysics* is one of the most interesting and deeply vexed in all Aristotle. I will argue that the *eidē* of these two works are the same entity or being, but that the associated theory of them in the *Metaphysics* is vastly richer and more complex, in ways that will be elaborated in some detail. See below §6, note 2, p. 50.

12 My belief in the Aristotelean authorship of the *Categories* is indeed based chiefly on the unlikelihood that there should have been a second person having so deep and exact a comprehension of Aristotelean metaphysics as to be able to write an introductory text to it that everywhere comes precisely to the edge of what can be rounded off in a plausible way without

That is a suggestion, and controversial. On the other hand, something definite and in which we can have some confidence is this: the *Categories* postulates at the theoretical level the existence of four determinately distinct types of beings or things-that-are, and proposes to analyze the entirety of common-parlance 'X being Y' in terms of relationships among these four. Although there are existential dependencies between the other three and the substantial individuals, the four are not *reducible*: they all, in their own right, *are*. If we take care to go no farther, that much carries through from *Categories* to *Metaphysics*.[13]

Let us return briefly to our starting-point in §1. We have now before us the comprehensive analysis of 'predicative being' that was there promised, having treated each segment of the octochotomy of possible configurations of 'things that are'.[14] In the hope that it may be of some help in assimilating the analysis in the right spirit, I offer on Aristotle's behalf a little fable or myth, in which an important part of that spirit seems to me to be nicely embodied. The fable follows. The story will have to be retold in a less fabulous form before we are done, but its appositeness here in the present form will nonetheless be recognized.

In the beginning, humankind spoke Philosophical Grammar. Language did not contain the word "is" (*esti*), and instead represented the things that are (*ta onta*) properly and in themselves; where what was meant was that a particular nonsubstance inhered in a particular substance, that is the way it was expressed, and where the relationship was said-of, it was so put. Naturally language at that point also did not have the paronymous forms, like "brave$_a$" from "bravery$_n$", there being no need for them. Language and reality were in paradisial conformity.

toppling off into the depths of the *Metaphysics* – and that we should know nothing else whatsoever about him. From the same qualities I infer it to be a mature rather than a juvenile production. However, it is also compatible with the materials that the work is early, or alternatively that the author is simply avoiding *topics* that he knows to be peril-filled, rather than withholding doctrines already worked out. I do not mean (and have no need) to require that Aristotle is holding back a written-down Zeta–Eta. A good recent discussion of the authenticity of the *Cats.* is that of Driscoll (1981), note 4.

13 *Contra* Dancy (1975b), 371. The *Cats.–Meta.* relationship recurs again in §8.
14 Here is a checklist of the octochotomy and where the cases are treated:

(1) (SK/SI) §4,
(2) (NSI/SI) §2 (see pp. 17–18),
(3) (NSK/SI) §3 (see p. 27),
(4) (SK/SK) §4,
(5) (NSI/SK) and (6) (NSK/SK) §4 (see p. 28),
(7) (NSK/NSI) and (8) (NSK/NSK) §3 (see p. 27).

(2), (3), (5) and (6) are inherences; (1), (4), (7) and (8) are said-of.

Then came the Fall, not in this story from a craving to know that which it is not given to humankind to know, but rather from a simpler failing: laziness. We tired of these many and cumbersome forms of expression, and thought to lighten our lot by using a single one for all: first perhaps it was "predicated-of", later some ingenious sluggard invented the inver-. sion of subject and predicate and the tiny little all-purpose "is". Paronymy entered the scene to confuse matters yet more.

Yet all was not lost: for redemption was at any point possible in the retrievability of the Philosophical Grammar, by calling the hideous *patois* into which humankind had blundered or lapsed, an *abbreviation* for everyday purposes of the Philosophical Truth, a "convention" allowable to mortals in the spirit of Wittgenstein's Say what you like, as long as it doesn't prevent you from seeing what the facts are, and long before, of Empedocles' similar injunction, allowing even the philosopher to employ the slipshod idioms of ordinary speech:

This is custom, and I myself assent to it.[15]

But then, of a sudden arose a dreadful jeopardy, in the thought of the greatest philosopher humankind would or ever could produce: this was Plato, who was so bewitched by the everyday vernacular that he dreamed of establishing a *science* that would study something univocally called 'predicative being', as if there really was *one* thing that was called by that name, a *single* reality that answered to the name of "is". (*The Wizard of Iz??*) Such a move would of course be the most grievous of all possible mistakes, for it would enshrine the error of the univocity of 'predicative being' at the level of *theory*, as opposed to mere "convention": and thus it would close off the avenue of at-least in-principle accessibility to the Philosophical Truth.

Fortunately for us all, the error was seen and exposed by the acutest of the great pseudoscientist's followers, who argued cogently and convincingly that because the concept of so-called 'being' in contexts of the form *X Is Y* really answered to different configurations depending on the respective *categories* of X and Y, the master's vision of a single Science of Being (and for that matter, of the Good) was a mirage; and thus it was that in time's nick, Philosophical Grammar, the paradisial idiom so nearly lost, was regained.[16] The Redeemer, a lad of becoming modesty, asked as reward only our "warm thanks" (*SE, fin.*).

15 *Philosophical Investigations*, §79; *Peri Phuseōs*, DK 9.4.
16 The story I am here caricaturing derives from the pioneering paper, Owen (1957), *init.*, which will figure in the nonfabulous retelling of the tale; cf. §23(i).

§5. Substantial and nonsubstantial particulars

In §2, an interpretive question was raised concerning the 'particular nonsubstance' of the *Cats.*, the particular white, grammar and so on, there being a view with some currency to the effect that their 'particularity' consists in uniqueness of each to the particular substance it inheres in, so that the particular whiteness of Callias and that of Coriscus would be distinct whitenesses, even though both these substantial individuals were, as we would ordinarily put it, of precisely the same color. This question was then dropped for the nonce, and the subsequent discussion has been on the alternative basis that is by now thoroughly enough shaken out. But with the *Categories* concept of substantial particular now more firmly in hand, it is worthwhile to return to the topic; for we are now in a position to refine the points of similarity and difference between the substantial and nonsubstantial cases.

The literature on this matter is vast and contentious,[1] and as observed in §2, the issue is not likely to be settled, soon or ever, to the satisfaction of all. Yet there remain a few points that even now have not yet received adequate attention.

We have had a look in §4 at the relationship between substantial species and individuals. The substantial species has a way of splitting up into the individual 'thisses', *tade tina*, which are the specimens of the species and are 'called synonymously after' it; this "way of splitting up" remains fairly obscure in *Cat.* 5, but we followed Aristotle's game though somewhat desperate struggles to explicate the idea in 3^{b}10–23. Bracketing those difficulties, let us be reminded of the relatively uncontroversial intuition that the substantial species is "a kind in which the substantial individuals come" (§4, p. 32).

Looking now at the nonsubstantial individuals or particulars, I will first state what seems to me the main point of contrast that we are now

---

1 Here is a *fractional* sampling: very roughly, on one side, Anscombe (1961), pp. 7–8; Ackrill (1963), pp. 74–6; Matthews and Cohen (1968); Allen (1969); Jones (1972); Annas (1974); Hartman (1976), ch. 1; Heinaman (1981); very roughly, on the other side, Owen (1965b); Frede (1978). Cherniss (1944), *ACPA* 348 n. 255, maintains that the particular/general distinction for nonsubstances is not observed outside the *Cats*, but he has in mind the "proprietary" interpretation of "particular" (which I claim is not observed in the *Cats*. either). Jones (1972), p. 107, for reasons unknown to me, also asserts that nonsubstantial individuals are mentioned only in the *Cats*. In the interpretation advocated here, the distinction is found pervading the Organon and even farther afield; see below. Note Heinaman (1981), p. 299, on the legitimacy of the *Topics* as a comparison source for *Cats*. philosophical usages.

properly placed to appreciate, and then rehearse some of the relevant evidence that indicates in its favor.

The contrast is this. In the case of substance, let the whole definition of the species *man* be, *animal that travels on two feet*; then the most particular possible said-of configuration is that in which the species, so defined, is said-of ('defines', §3 above), i.e. determines the nature of, every individual man – of which there are many. Whereas in the case of nonsubstance, it is *the individual nonsubstance* that itself gets the specific definition – let the definition of $bravery_n$ be, *virtue that's knowledge of what's to fear and what's to dare*: now, $bravery_n$ as a particular virtue cannot be said-of anything, so the most particular possible said-of configuration is that in which $virtue_n$ is said-of $bravery_n$ – *but this is not species to specimen, but genus to species*.

The individual nonsubstance is a species!? In one way that makes a kind of sense, for we knew already that nonsubstantial individuals had each one its own definition, which accords with each being a species, whereas the substantial individuals do not. But it is still a strange sort of species; for it is also an atomic particular, which means that it is not said-of anything (1^b6–9); i.e., it does not "split up into individual thisses", which would have to be multiple individual $braveries_n$ – but we were already down to the ultimate individual along *that* axis; instead, it has to pluralize along the other configuration, which is exactly what it does: into the multiple individual $braves_a$ 'called paronymously after' it, i.e. the *substances* that are $brave_a$, the substances in which the atomic nonsubstantial particular $bravery_n$ has a "toehold" (§3). But the plurality has to be of substances, not of braveries. Of $virtues_n$ there can be a plurality, but this is the plurality of species in a genus, an intuition going all the way back to the *Meno* (73–4), and the Sting-ray of the Agora trying to make poor befuddled Meno comprehend how it is that that Justice is not Virtue, but *a certain* Virtue.[2]

Here a personal concession/confession is necessary: because I am not a Board-certified aretologist or chromatologist, etc., I cannot claim authority on exactly where the final specificity in each line of nonsubstantial said-of's actually comes. Perhaps there are *tines andreiai*, particular braveries, such as bravery about wild animals, or heights, or illness, or battle; or perhaps not, because some analytical flaw can be elenched out of such a supposition, and there is only atomic *bravery* – I do not know. But however

---

2 In the terms of *Metaphysics* Zeta 6, the individual *non*substances are identical with their essences; the individual substances are not identical with theirs. (But the statement makes an imperfect contrast, because of an (*important*) ambiguity in "their". See §23(iii).)

this may be, the final said-of, which *ex hypothesi* terminates in the *atomon*, must still here in non-substance be genus of atomic species, and not species of atomic specimen.[3]

The idea of a species that is also an atomic particular is one that is severely hedged by remarks of Aristotle's elsewhere (such as *Meta.* Zeta 4), and may seem to some an outright impossibility in Aristotelean terms; so we must hasten to call up some Aristotelean testimony, not rendered totally disreputable by coming largely from the *Topics*.

> *Top.* iv 3 123^{b}35: the particular disease (*hē tis nosos*), e.g. *fever*, *ophthalmia*, being a species of disease . . .

> *Top.* vi 6 144^{a}7: jeering$_n$ is a particular *hubris*, so that jeering$_n$ is [not differentia but] species . . .

> *Top.* vi 9 147^{a}23–27: Again, in the case of relatives, look to see whether for 'that in relation to which' (*pros ho*) he's rendered the genus, he's rendered the species 'in relation to a particular that' (*pros ekeino ti*). E.g., if *conception* (G) is *relative to the conceivable*, then *the particular conception* (S) is *relative to the particular conceivable*, and if *multiple* (G) is *relative to the fraction*, then *the particular multiple* (S) is *relative to the particular fraction*. For if it's not rendered like this, it's clear that it's gone wrong.

These cases show that the idiom

$$S = \text{a particular } G,$$

for nonsubstantial species S and genus G, has at least some currency in the *Organon*;[4] without explicit mention of species and genus, there are far

---

3 Dancy (1978), 380 n. 20, suggests that a similar uncertainty may afflict *Cat.* 15 15^{b}17–21: "Ar. . . . might, in [ch.] 15, only be thinking of *definite* heights (see 15^{b}20–21)". For more on the connection between specificity and individuality in the case of substance, see §15.

4 *Top.* iv 6 127^{a}21–6 might be thought difficult from the viewpoint being elaborated here, and perhaps it is:

"Look to see whether the things that share in the genus rendered (*ta metekhonta tou apodothentos genous*), fail to be different in species, e.g. *ta leuka*; for these do not differ from one another in species, but of every genus the species are different; therefore *to leukon* can't be the genus of anything";

here I must regard *ta leuka* as *ta leuka*$_a$, and *to leukon*$_n$ as entirely particular, i.e. as *to ti leukon*$_n$. Then is it a problem that "sharing" (*metekhein*) is defined in the *Topics* as admitting the definition of what is shared in (iv 1, 121^{a}11–12), and "that which belongs by sharing" (*to kata methexin huparkhon*) is assigned to the essence of that to which it belongs (v 4, 133^{a}1–3), so that "sharing" more cases than can be cited here, but in the interest of diminishing the plausibility of the proprietary interpretation (if two substances, then necessarily two particular whites) I will cite a few. Observe in each instance that no need is stated to know the identity of the proprietor in order to know *which* particular so-and-so is meant: leafing through *Top.* iv, we encounter:

124^a12, justice = a particular knowledge;

124^a20, decomposition = a particular destruction;

124^b4, blindness = a particular insensibility, sight = a particular sensibility;

126^a12, if *philia* is in the appetitive [psyche] it can't be *boulēsis tis*, for all *boulēsis* is in the calculating [psyche];

128^a37, music (i.e. *mousikē*) is a particular knowledge, walking is a particular movement. Etc.

Ranging a bit farther afield:

GA ii 6 745^a5, "for all animals there's a particular limit to their size", the theoretical context makes plain (we shall see in §15(i) below) that this "particular limit" is *species-specific*, we are not being handed the bromide that every individual animal has a size of his or her very own.

Meta. Zeta 12 1038^a15, "clovenfootedness is a particular footedness", surely not an allusion to a footedness exclusive to *Napoleon* (the pig).

Meta. Eta 3 1043^b34, horismos = arithmos tis ("definition a sort of number")

Meta. Theta 8 1050^b1, eudaimonia = zōē poia tis ("well-being a particular sort of life")

Meta. Iota 3 1054^b32, enantiōsis = diaphora tis ("contrariety a particular sort of difference")

Meta. Iota 4 1055^b3, 7. sterēsis = antiphasis tis ("lack a particular sort of contradiction")

DA iii 9 433^a25, epithumia = orexis tis ("wanting is a particular sort of desire")

PA ii 5 651^b11, phthora = oligaimia tis ("decay is a particular sort of blood-deficiency").

Etc.

must be exclusively intracategorial, which is not, on the above interpretation, the relationship of *ta leuka*$_a$ and *to leukon*$_n$? I think not. It does not follow that *ta leuka* must therefore be individual colors$_n$; for observe that according to the iv 6 passage, *to leukon* has turned out *not* to be genus and *not* to be "shared in" by *ta leuka* – it has been "rendered genus" *unsuccessfully*, so that "share in" means "are alleged (by the renderer) to share in". Thus construed, perhaps the passage is not "an embarrassment for the new interpretation" (Heinaman (1981), p. 302). But the points are not easy ones.

There is another bit of technical *argot* that has a use, especially in the *Organon* but elsewhere also, that is to just the same effect as

$$S = \text{a particular G}$$

for (arbitrary, substantial or not) species S and genus G: it is

$$S \text{ is } hoper \text{ G.}$$

This has to be translated, not very transparently, "S is just what is (a) G" (and "S is *hoper* G *ti*" as "S is just what is some G – or a particular G"); the idea it expresses is, "S is one *form* of G", "S is one of the things being G comes to".[5] For some cases that convey the flavor:

> *APr.* i 39 49^{b}6: . . . there is no difference between
> saying "the conceivable is not genus of the
> opinable" and "the opinable is not *hoper* conceivable
> *ti*" (for the meaning is identical) . . .

The purport of the foregoing I take to be:

$$X \text{ is genus of } Y \leftrightarrow Y \text{ is } hoper \text{ X } ti.$$

> *Top.* iii 1 116^{a}23–28: Next, *to hoper tode ti* [is more
> worthy of choice] than what's not in the genus, e.g.
> justice$_n$ [more worthy of choice] than the just$_a$
> [thing]; for the former is in the genus [a] Good$_n$,
> the latter is not, and the one is *hoper* Good$_n$, the
> other not. For nothing is *hoper to genos* which doesn't
> fall within the genus; e.g. the pale$_a$ man isn't *hoper*
> Color$_n$. And likewise in the other cases.

(In passing, note the use of *tode ti* in the above to refer to genus.) The following ties the threads together succinctly:

> *Top.* iv 6 128^{a}33–37: . . . if [you want to establish
> constructively that] knowledge is *hoper* belief, [look
> and see] whether the knower, *qua* he knows,
> believes; for [in that case] it's clear that knowledge
> would be [=] a particular belief.

To sum up, the foregoing makes a case for

$$S = \text{a particular G} \leftrightarrow S \text{ is } hoper \text{ G } (ti),$$

---

5 For some reason *X is hoper Y* is persistently mis-rendered as "X is just what *Y* is", which gets the idea backwards. The right reading is stated by Barnes, *APo.* 83^{a}1 n. (p. 168), following Bonitz, *Index* 533^{b}19–534^{a}23 s.v. *hosper*. Slightly different: Charlton, *Physics i–ii*, p. 60.

where S is a nonsubstantial particular and is regularly called a species; only a minute fraction of the evidence has been cited.[6]

While on the subject of equivalent terminologies for relationships between more or less particular entities of the same category, we can mention two further ones, of which one will occupy us later on, and the other is little heard of outside the *Topics*. As for the latter, to render a protasis of the form "X is *hoper* Y" is sometimes called, "to place X within Y", and various sorts of possible dialectical blunders are described in these terms ("see if he's placed the genus inside the species", i.e. proposed that G = *hoper* S; "see if he's placed the differentia inside the genus", i.e. proposed that D = *hoper* G, etc., cf. *Top.* 122ᵇ18, ᵇ25, ᵇ37, 123ᵃ1). As for the other idiom, "X is *hoper* Y" also coincides with *one* of the several senses of that most dreadfully overworked Aristotelean phrase, "Y belongs to X *kath' hauto*", *per se* or "in respect of itself", the sense in which "Y belongs to X in what it (= X) is", equivalent to the *Cats.* meaning of "Y is said-of X". The phrase is canonically introduced in *APo.* i 4, *Meta.* Delta 18, and we shall be seeing it again (§23(ii)).

We shall find ourselves having a return to Pallors$_n$, *Hoper*, *Kath' hauto* & Company when we investigate the *Metaphysics* version of these matters, and shall find that some important signals have been changed: especially on the question whether the extension (once again in our material-mode sense) of something like pallor$_n$ – which as we have seen, would have to be the totality of the substances that are pale$_a$ – ought to be called a species or not. (There the consensus is, Not.)

This survey of that which is *atomic* among substance and nonsubstance, respectively, in the *Categories* leads to one further interesting consequence which can be stated even now, but will be found to have profound ramifications in the larger setting to come. We can now see that even at the *Cats.* level, *there are, besides the individual substances, two additional types of ultimate and irreducibly 'atomic' 'beings'*. That is, there are (1) the individual nonsubstances, which are fully particular in their category, and which pluralize only along the inherence dimension. And there are also (2) the fully determinate specific forms, which *do* indeed pluralize by being said-of the individual substances as specimens, but which *do not* stand to them as genus (less determinate) to species (more determinate); they are not further divided by differentiae, and they too are therefore, in that sense, atomic. Already we may recognize a potentially dangerous simple-

6 For the readiest access to more, cf. the voluminous references in Bonitz, *loc. cit.* Typical: snow is not *hoper* white, *ergo* white is not the genus of snow, *Top.* iv 1 120ᵇ23–4.

mindedness in the commonplace characterization of a 'universal' as 'that which belongs to a multitude of things' (all the way from *de Int.* 7 17^{a}39 to, so famously, Zeta 13 1038^{b}11). For (1) the individual white does that (i.e., 'belongs to a multitude'), by inhering, yet it is also an atomic particular, and explicitly so described, as we have seen. And (2) the species (i.e., the *eidos*) Man also does that, but it is atomic as well; it can pluralize, but it does so, as the *Cats.* says, not by inhering, but by – the best we could say it – *defining* (§3), i.e. by imposing the same specific nature, both singular and unitary, upon its specimens, each of which (specifically speaking, so to speak) is an identical duplicate of any other. Only a substantial *eidos* can do this; it is unique to substance.[7] Put another way, the substantial specific nature does not break up, in the way that the generic nature breaks up into species.[8]

And so there is a powerful sense in which, even in the *Cats.*, *both* the individual white *and* the species Man *should not* be called 'universal' (a word the *Cats.* of course does not use). They both meet the 'belong to many' criterion, but that criterion does not cut to the depth even of the *Cats.* theory; in a way at least as important, they are not 'universal', because they are fully unitary and determinate and specific, and thus, in their way, atomic.

In the case of the specific form Man (and all the other animate specific forms), this determinacy and unitariness represents both one of the most fundamental and to-be-saved phenomena of the Aristotelean natural universe, and one of the deepest problems of Aristotelean metaphysics; we shall see much of both as we proceed (§9, §15(i), §23).

It is evident that we are now at (if not well beyond) the limits of what the *Categories* can tell us about these matters. So recalling now the broken stones and the finely crafted miniature sculpture of §0: we have now learned as much about substance metaphysics as the miniature study model of it that is the *Categories* can teach us on its own, and it is time to begin trying to put together the main job.

7 This is the ultimate reason why I think Aristotle does not, as some think he does, regard the whiteness$_n$ of Socrates, Coriscus, etc., as distinct individual whites$_n$, which (note 2 above) would stand to anything X above them as things that X was said-of.

8 Though as we shall see, "breaking up into" certainly is not the best way to try to visualize the genus-species relation. And there are always the *terata* to keep in mind (cf. §13(iv) *fin.*, §15(ii), §23(iv)).

II. SUBSTANCE IN THE METAPHYSICS: A FIRST APPROXIMATION

§6. Two criteria for the substantial

Proceeding from the "philosophical grammar" (as it was once or twice styled in the foregoing) of the *Categories*, to the full theory of substance that is attempted in the *Metaphysics*,[1] is like travelling from the complex surface of a solid into its multiply-complex interior. In fact, the problem of complexity is one that can very easily get out of hand with this theory, for the object or "solid" in question is highly multidimensional; and this makes for difficulties of both organization and tactics, to which very likely no solution is ideal. Also, the full picture requires of us moderns some rather considerable mind-bending if we are to take it all in. The best course, it seems, is to proceed in stages, by degrees; for while bending one's mind is highly salutary for the philosophical soul, I would not wish to break any minds, or blow them. It has been indicated in §0 that particular emphasis is going to be placed on Aristotle's biological writings as a source of concrete metaphysical intuitions, and we shall move in that direction shortly. But it will both help us in focusing on the right issues, and also work in the spirit of proceeding-by-degrees, first to indicate roughly and provisionally some main features of the *Metaphysics* concept of the sort of thing a substance is, and from the outset to separate some questions that it is very important to separate. The first of these tasks is for the present section; the second is undertaken in §7.

It was also let fall in §0 that my interpretive approach would be, in places, "reconstructive", "approaching the text by convergence". This first approximation to the *Metaphysics* substance idea is the first such place; as a preliminary sketch of this idea is outlined in §6, and as

1 The reference is consciously imprecise; it will be seen that I have in mind centrally books Zeta, Eta and Theta of that particular compilation that has come down to us as "the *Metaphysics*", but I do not hesitate to invoke portions of doctrine from other parts of it, or from other works, particularly *Physics* and *Coming-to-be and Ceasing-to-be*, where their adaptability (or, sometimes, unadaptability) to the reconstructive project at hand (§0) needs remarking. And I shall take the biological treatises as continuous with the foregoing as regards the "full theory of substance", as in §9 and III–V generally.

questions are separated in §7, we shall find ourselves tacking more independently of the text than hitherto. The reconvergence begins in earnest with the look at the biology in Part III.

(i) Synchronic individuation

So far as substance is concerned, the theories of the *Categories* and of the *Metaphysics* are simultaneously very like, and very unlike. They are like, among other things, in treating of two particular sorts of entity, substantial individuals on one hand, and substantial *eidē* and *genē* on the other. They are unlike in the theoretical treatment of these.[2] By far the most important difference between the theories, a difference from which many and varied consequences flow, is the entire absence in the *Categories*, and the conspicuous presence in the *Metaphysics*, of the idea of matter,[3] and the corollary, that the individual substances are no longer, as in the *Cats.*, simple, methodologically "atomic" and opaque, but are "composites" (*syntheta*), constituted or formed by form out of matter. This is a complicated business of which a good deal will be heard as we proceed;[4] the main thing to be stipulated now is that the introduction of matter into the picture and the "composite" reading of the substantial individuals have as an immediate consequence a de-coupling of the concepts, which coincide in the *Cats.*, of ultimate *substance* (in the *Cats.*, the substantial individuals) and ultimate *hupokeimenon* or *subject* (in the *Cats.* the substantial individuals, but in the *Meta.* the ultimate matter, whatever that may turn out to be). (For the identification in the *Cats.*, recall §3, p. 22, §4, p. 28; for the decoupling, see next §8, p. 61.)

2 My view that it is the same thing, the same 'being', that is called *eidos* in the *Cats.* and in the *Meta.* theories, is superficially at odds with that of Driscoll (1981). Driscoll argues that the *Meta.* correspondent to the *Cats. eidos* is what the *Meta.* calls "the composite of form and matter taken universally", at Zeta 10 1035^{b}27–30, Zeta 11 1037^{a}6–7 (*op.cit.*, p. 146). My problem with this identification is that the latter looks to me like the material totality of the species, the total collectivity of (say) Tibetan Yaks, either synchronically or (better) diachronically taken – which is some sort of "universal" *subject*, whereas the *Categories eidos* is of course a thing-predicated. But there seems to be good agreement between my view and Driscoll's as to the nature of all the entities in the two theories; the only difference is over whether (a) *eidos* in the *Cats.* is the same as *eidos* in the *Meta.*, but with a different, and richer, associated theoretical apparatus (mainly coming from the *Meta.* importation of matter), which in my view, or whether (b) *eidos* in the *Cats.* is the same as something else in the *Meta.*, which is Driscoll's view. It is a problem of transtheoretical identification, between two theories over which our outlooks do not otherwise seem to differ much.

3 Not, of course, a novel observation. It is true that *Cat.* 8^{a}9–10 mentions "fire and water and suchlike, out of which the animal is constituted"; but it is the only such mention and is without theoretical significance.

4 For most immediately impending developments, cf. §12(ii) on "Complexity of Matter", §13(ii) and (iv) on the reconstruction of Differentia and Genus, §15(i) for metaphysical morals of the embryology, §20(i) on *Meta.* Zeta 3.

With that in mind, I wish to proceed for the present on the basis that substance in the *Metaphysics* setting still retains the feature that was called in §4 "*synchronic individuation*": the material-mode version of "divided reference" in the substantial *eidos* that consists in the substantial specimens' being integral *units* or *tade tina*, "thisses", each "atomic and numerically one", as the *Cats.* puts it. As a result, I am going to take it that despite some tentative suggestions to the contrary that are to be found in the text, the natures or properties that are candidates for substantial status but are *not* individuative in their character are *not* according to the *Meta.* theory of substance to be classed as substances. This particularly applies to the material elements, the "simple" or "natural bodies", such as earth, water, air and so on,[5] which certainly do not "divide their reference" in the sense with which we are here concerned. (And the *Meta.* knows that they do not: "water, for instance, is *much*, but not *many*" – Iota 6 1056^{b}16.) The point will begin to be better grounded when we have a look into the foundations of "unity" in the actual corporeal composites, i.e. living things, in §13 and §15; later, the metaphysical aspects will be explored through *Meta.* Zeta 3 and 16 (§17 *init.*, §20, §23) and eventually to the Unity of Form question (§24). For the present, to get started, let it be stipulated that material natures, like *water*, though stable through changes in a way and thus meeting an analogue to the other criterion for substance in the sense we are trying to characterize, still fail to meet the criterion of *synchronic individuativeness*: "none of them's a *one*, but they're like a *heap*, until they're worked up and some kind of unity is made out of them" (Zeta 16, 1040^{b}8–10). And accordingly, are not composite substances, although they are that which composite substances are out of, and in the terms of §§20 ff. they could be termed sub-substances. I shall argue (§§8–9, for a start) that in the context of matter as Aristotle conceives it, the occurrence of synchronically unified material individuals is a phenomenon calling for explanation, and (§15, for a start) that according to him, the explanation lies in the nature of fully specific form.

Of course, while a property's or a nature's meeting this individuativeness criterion is necessary for its being substantial in our desiderated sense, this obviously cannot be sufficient – though the reasons *why* it should be the case that, of the candidate natures that *prima facie* may seem to pass the individuative test, most nonetheless fail to qualify as substances, are reasons which the *Cats.* furnishes no slightest inkling of.

These reasons are of two different sorts. The first sort is best put in terms of the general question itself: *What things are substances?* (Alternatively put,

5 For substantial claims on their behalf in the *Meta.*, see Delta 8 1017^{b}10, Zeta 2 1028^{b}10, Eta 1 1042^{a}8, etc.

Which characters of things are substantial kinds?) Is the Sun a substance? The Moon? Animals? Plants? Artefacts, like houses, hatchets, statues? The "Heaven" (*ouranos*)? Any immaterial thing? Et cetera. – This, the question of which things are and which are not substances, I call the "Population Problem": it requires independent discussion, which it will begin to receive in §7 and which will not be finally and definitively concluded until §21. (So far as material substances are concerned, my own *answer* will be: animals and plants and very little else. As for immaterial things, my answer is: I don't know.) Aristotle's answers will be dealt with in their proper places: cf. Part III *passim*, Part V §18, §19(iii), §21. But my analysis of the problem is such that the widest latitude of opinion is possible on the topic of what things are substances, all entirely compatible with the account I think Aristotle means to give of what a substance *is*. That, then, is the first type of case in which a sort of thing that seems to meet in individuativeness condition can fail to be substantial – it is the type where, for example, *houses* or *hatchets* are (or can be) ruled out as substances by concerns of the kind I will call "Population concerns".

A second type of case, equally unadvertised in the *Categories*, we shall later see should ultimately be viewed as a variety of the Population type, but because it is a topic specifically addressed and indeed somewhat agonized over in the *Metaphysics*, it may be noted separately here. Reverting momentarily to the formal mode of speech,[6] it arises in connection with terms that are grammatically individuative but which there is a case for regarding as denoting not a substantial thing as such but some actual or possible stage of a substantial thing: terms like "scholar", "coward", "tadpole", "octogenarian"; Aristotle adduces such examples as *to badizon, the walker* or *thing that walks*, and *to kathēmenon, the sitter* (*Meta.* Zeta 1, 1028ᵃ24). Also in this category, and coming up frequently, are (again formal mode) certain phrases consisting of a modifier attached to some admitted substantial term, like "pale man" (*Meta.* Zeta 4, Delta 6, 7, 9, etc.); such nominalizations do divide their reference, but do not, as wholes, 'signify substance'. Why? Why are *the walker* and *the pale man* not substances?

(ii) Diachronic individuation

This brings us to the second condition on substantial properties or natures in the *Meta.* setting: that of being the constitutive nature or "essence" of

---

6 Cf. the cautionary reminder of §1, note 5.

the individuals that have them, the condition that we saw in §4 to be insinuated by some features of the *Cats.* account, but never quite made completely explicit. But to avoid prejudging the relationship between real Aristotelean essentialism and the many varieties that have circulated under that and other titles since his day, I will temporarily adopt a neologistic and, in intention at least, maximally neutral way of isolating the phenomenon for study: I will say of a particular thing that it "migrates" when, in ordinary pre-theoretic terms, it ceases to have a property it formerly had, or comes to have a property it formerly lacked, *while remaining throughout the change numerically one and the same object*. We may then note that Aristotelean substantial properties or kinds are to be seen as endowed with a striking characteristic of resistance to migration, in the sense that where F is part or all of the substance of something, it is impossible that an object be at one time F and at another time not F, while remaining numerically one and the same object; in general, for F in substance, an object's ceasing to be F is its ceasing to exist, ceasing to be (the thing it is) at all. Thus this condition can be seen as a descendant of the *Cats.* idea that substances are things (even, the only things) that persist through time as "numerically one and the same while receiving contraries"; but it is stronger: it adds that the substantial form of a substantial individual is something it can neither change nor lose without ceasing to exist.[7] – It is important that the terminology of "migration-resistance" of itself does not, and is not meant to, tell us anything about the *structure* of substance or the *analysis* of what-it-is-to-be-F for such an F; its purpose is to allow thought about, and discussion of, the persistence and nonpersistence of numerically one and the same individual through changes of various sorts, without calling up in sophisticated present-day philosophical minds any of the semantic-cum-metaphysical *mechanisms* that have been devised since Aristotle's day to deal with such questions, in order to try to get at his own mechanism, the first. Which, as it will prove, is different from any now in circulation in some fundamental ways. This condition may be called, as in §4, that of transtemporal or *"diachronic individuativeness"*.

This second condition on substance is the one that operates to exclude as substances the coward and the octogenarian, as well as the pale man; yet that is not exactly what it does, and what it does do, it does not do by itself. That is not exactly what it does, because *nothing but* a substance can be an octogenarian, or a pale man; so it cannot be right just as it stands to

---

7 Dancy (1978), pp. 377–9, seems to see the *Cats.* and *Meta.* versions of this not as weaker versus stronger, but as in conflict. I try to show how they fit together; see Part V.

say that the criterion operates to "exclude them as substances". And what it does do, it does not do by itself, but in tandem with specific solutions for particular cases of the Population Problem. At this point, before we can profitably try to get deeper into the nature of substance, it is necessary that we clarify the dimensions of Population, for otherwise we shall find progress everywhere impeded by entanglement with that.

To sum up: these two conditions add up to a first approximation, no more than rough and superficial, of Aristotelean substantial kinds or species (i.e., *eidē*), in this sense: Aristotle's reflections on the problem "What *is* substance?" can be seen as efforts to bring to light *what underlying metaphysical framework or structure in the nature of things could plausibly be thought to eventuate in the two phenomena, those of (i) individuality or "this"-hood, and of (ii) a certain type of natural persistence as the same F through change, that the conditions identify.*[8]

8 The centrality of these conditions is emphasized by Hartman (1977), chs. 1–2. But I do not, as he does, think that Aristotle *identifies* an individual substance with its essence or form. Cf. §20(iii).

§7. The Population Problem

There are two related but distinct problems revolved by Aristotle on substance: (1) What things are substances?; (2) What is the substance *of* such a thing? – or, in his vernacular, what *makes* it a substance, or *why* is it one (the "cause")?

Now the first of these questions – the Population Problem – certainly is of great importance, but it is also important not to become excessively consumed with it, nor to allow it to distract us from the second. To say this is not to recommend the offhand attitude reportedly once taken by Wittgenstein, that the question what things are substances is "a merely *empirical* matter";[1] it is more serious than that; but in the final analysis perhaps it is right to say that it is not a philosophical question, or at least, it very often is not – the "science of being" does not tell us which things are the substances, or whether anything is; or, as has long ago been noted, the Population Problem cannot be solved by metaphysics. The final resolu-

1 See Malcolm's *Memoir*, p. 86, also Russell's second lecture on Logical Atomism (*Logic and Knowledge*, p. 199). In fairness to Wittgenstein, his remark to Malcolm about this was perhaps more retrospective self-caricature than a serious avowal. Russell in contrast evidently speaks for himself, at the time.

tion of the matter will not be reached until §21, when the second question has been more fully dealt with (in the spirit that it is premature to try to count things when one does not yet know what they are); but several points have to be established now, so that we do not stumble over them from the very start. It will be suggested below that the most plausible Aristotelean material substances are the living beings – as he remarks, such things as plants and animals "are substances if anything is";[2] whereas such specimens as bronze spheres, thresholds, houses, hatchets, statuary and so forth, introduced here and there for various illustrative purposes, tend to deflate and collapse under any pressure. Later we shall in fact see good grounds for regarding artefacts in general as at best borderline substances if at all (§16(i), §19(iii)). But in any case, even for someone sharing Wittgenstein's old view, there is still a legitimate point in separating the question of the *nature* of substance from that of Population; possibly at a minimum we might agree to take the query, "Are *F*'s substances?" simply to mean, in relevant part, "is there no such possibility as an object's being at one time *F* and at another time other-than-*F*, while remaining throughout one and the same object?", and then let everyone consult her own intuitions in particular cases. According to me, *tadpole* and *teenager* would not qualify as substantial kinds by this criterion; but others' intuitions could go different ways about this, while we meanwhile got on with the metaphysically more pressing inquiry, into the Nature question. (In fact it is to be hoped that forthcoming clarity on Nature will bring about, *de facto*, better alignment of intuitions about Population; but it will prove all the same that the resolution of the Nature question remains logically compatible with views about Population that would strike most of us as highly eccentric. Even in the corpus itself: in *CTBPA* i 4 319^{b}25–31, for a single example, there are contemplated, as if they were alternative possible renderings of the same event, (1) an unmusical man's becoming musical, (2) an unmusical man's ceasing to be and a (new) musical man's coming to be.)

It is in a similar vein, I think, that we are wisely admonished in *Meta.* Iota to keep distinct the questions what sorts of things are said to be *one* (*poia hen legetai*), and what it is to be one, what's the 'account' of it (*ti esti to heni einai kai tis autou logos*, Iota 1, 1052^{b}1–3). An exactly analogous relationship holds, though I do not believe Aristotle ever remarks this, between "What is truth?" and "What things are true?", i.e. "What are the truths?".[3]

---

2 *Meta.* Zeta 7, 1032^{a}19; Zeta 8, 1034^{a}4 (tr. Ross)
3 I cannot find a basis for Richard Rorty's claim in Rorty (1973) (p. 399) that questions of these two types are not distinguishable by Aristotle.

"Separating the questions" of Nature and Population also helps us to see the underlying reason why it is that metaphysics cannot solve the Population Problem: it is because the condition here called "migration-resistance" does not itself include any *criterion* for the identity or distinctness of the temporarily separated individuals – or stages thereof – involved, and that is why there is space for varying intuitions that can duly be made to collide. Consider the following bizarre eventuality: Socrates, before our very eyes, commences to sprout fur and fangs; additional and even more amazing changes ensue, and thirty gripping minutes later there is a wolf just where Socrates was.[4] Is the same individual, then, still there? It is very important to understand that the "science of being" does not answer this question for us, it only teaches us how to formulate it correctly. (1) IF *man* and *wolf* are (distinct) substantial kinds, *THEN* they include migration-barriers such that one and the same object cannot be earlier a man and later a wolf; Socrates accordingly has perished, and a new individual has now come into existence which, on pain of both philosophical and practical confusion, it is highly advisable to give a new name. *IF*, on the other hand, it is thought on one ground or another (see (2) below) that Socrates has not perished, but has become and now is a wolf, *THEN* it must be concluded that *man* and *wolf* are not (distinct) substantial kinds, but instead the applicable migration-barriers lie elsewhere from where we no doubt formerly thought; it is after all possible for one and the same object to migrate from one of these alleged species into the other, and therefore the alleged species are not really so. (If this sort of thing happened all the time, *and* we did indeed wish to regard the individuals involved as identical continuants through these changes, rather than as being generated and destroyed in hitherto-unheard-of ways, then it is doubtful whether this whole scheme of "substance" would have any application whatever. At this point we pass by, but will not now try to grasp, a handle on the Law of Non-Contradiction connection in *Meta.* Gamma.)[5]

---

4 Let us grant that it *is* a wolf, although generated in a manner most uncommon for wolves (Transylvanian, rather than traditional), enough so to provoke legitimate doubt that anything *so* produced *could be* such – compare the puzzle whether anything constructed out of basic materials in a laboratory *could be* a human being. I do not mean to prejudge such scruples, either way, by the Gedankenexperiment in progress in the text.

5 See Furth (1986); also the unintended interpretation of diachronic individuation in the *Cats.* (§4 above). Another possible explanation of the strange appearances described in the text would be that *man* and *wolf* are substantial as we formerly thought, but that Socrates belongs to neither, instead being a specimen of a third species known traditionally though not very accurately as *wolf-man*. This saves the phenomena as described, but requires modification of the hypothesis that what faced us at the end of the transformation was a *wolf* (cf. previous footnote).

(2) We also can see in this case how it is that Aristotelean metaphysics will not adjudicate for us among the various *criteria* of identity that may be assigned different weights and priorities, resulting in different judgments about Population (in this case, two individuals or one). As it was formulated, Socrates and the wolf (the wolf that replaced him, that is, or the wolf he became, respectively), were spatiotemporally contiguous. Philosopher A will find this circumstance especially compelling, being impressed by the fluidity and smoothness of the half-hour transition, and vote for "same individual"; whereas Philosopher B above all needs to know whether the wolf recalls Socrates' childhood and youth as his own, a criterion that for B overrides all others to the extent that it would rule even had the wolf *not* been spatiotemporally contiguous with (the *earlier*, in this case) Socrates – as it certainly does, e.g., with astronauts "beamed" up and down between planetary surfaces and the Starship Enterprise. (Later we shall find further discrepancies between "same individual" and "spatiotemporally continuous" that militate against the latter's being held generally criterial for the former: §21(ii), "Continuity of Form".) Philosopher C, a fanatical believer in the substantial specieshood of *man* and *wolf*, must hold that Socrates has ceased to be, and a new wolf come to be, whatever the spatiotemporal connection between them and even regardless of any ostensible memory-relationships, common traits of character, or anything else. I do not suggest that there is no reason to prefer one of these sample positions to the others, or some yet-unstated position to them all, only that no particular answer will be dictated by the "science of being". In §21, the "watchword" will be sounded that real cases are best decided not by metaphysics, but by the close and accurate study of nature.

Having introduced a fantastic and implausible example, I had better explain in a justificatory way the spirit in which it is meant to be taken. For it seems that much time and ingenuity are expended, and much of that wasted, by philosophers in debating outlandish hypothetical changes: changes from being of-wood to being of-steel, brain transplants, the ship of Theseus, Jekyll/Hyde transformations, spatiotemporal discontinuities, strange divisions-in-two, et cetera; whereas the whole point of separating the Population Problem from the question of the nature of substance is to prevent the discussion of the latter from being contaminated and confused, as it frequently is, by irresolvable collisions of competing criteria. It may surely be questioned whether Aristotle's substance theory can usefully be asked to deal with fantastic cases which it was not designed to treat and which its author did not consider in his wildest imaginings (to the extent that his wildest imaginings have come down to us). My excuse for resorting to them, to the quite limited extent that I shall do so, is that there are several important methodological morals, concerning the apportionment of weights in Population decisions between metaphysical and nonmetaphysical factors, that can be more sharply and quickly pointed using specially-crafted fantastic cases than in any other way. But beyond this limited purpose, the "watchword" in the pursuit of Population and the use of fantastic cases is, and will remain, restraint.

That, it is hoped, will hold the Population Problem until we are ready to take a more definitive position on it, in the light of intervening developments (§18, §21(i) ff.).

§8. Constitutive predicates and basic individuals

In this section I wish to delineate, provisionally but still as accurately as possible at this stage, both the relationship between the *Categories* and the *Metaphysics* theory of substance, and some of the large differences that divide the orientation common to them both from our own.

Let us begin with the latter task. The universe of the *Categories* is built upon *the individual F's and G's*; it is a world whose ultimate constituents are those well-distinguished countable individual and indivisible units (*atoma*), retaining their individual identities through time as they "sustain contraries" and all else that may "happen to" them (*sumbebēken autois*): the individual man, the individual ox, and all the denumerable rest. Now delving into the metaphysical interior (§6, *init.*), we see that the characteristics just evoked are understood in the *Metaphysics* setting as springing from two coordinate properties of the substantial forms or kinds: the synchronic property of individuativeness, and the diachronic property of anti-migration. We have found traces of both these properties in the *Categories*, but in both cases treated in a strangely tentative and incomplete way, amid numerous signs that the author is walking a precipice (§4, pp. 30–33, 34–38).

To make the requisite comparisons, it is necessary to calibrate some rather fundamental historical bearings. For the *Categories* universe may have a certain deceptive appearance of familiarity to us moderns, yet that appearance masks an underlying difference whose identification is central to the understanding of the *Metaphysics* theory. The modern cast of mind that lends itself to the deception can be described in several ways; I will try to do so first in a narrower and more technical way, and then in larger (and hence, alas, inevitably also cloudier) terms.

The first characterization is this: we post-Fregean analytical philosophers, born and raised in the analytical setting of twentieth-century quantification theory, are accustomed to thinking of the domain, or universe, of a language as already consisting of individuals, well-demarcated and so on – the domain is customarily a *class*, so that its elements are assumed as – so to speak 'given' as – 'well-distinguished' at the outset;[1] and then we think of each predicate constant of the language as picking out a subset of that totality. The universe being already organized into individuals, it is also natural to conceive every predicate as picking out a class of objects in the same fashion – to take a single classical example: Carnap, introducing the idea of a "degree-one predicator" in *Meaning and Necessity*, unhesitatingly varied his examples between "Human", "Biped", "Blue", "Hot", "Hard", and "20 Feet High"; the assumption is that our *objects* are 'given', and our predicates distribute properties over them.

From such a standpoint, it is easy to think of the *Categories* as stating a view that is much like the foregoing but is merely complicated by the distinction between the substantial and nonsubstantial "predicated-of", with (formal mode of speech, temporarily) the substantial predicates functioning as count-terms (synchronically speaking) and essence-indicators (diachronically speaking, and going by the intended interpretation) with respect to a universe of objects already assumed countable, marked off as numerically distinct – a complication that could easily be assimilated by the theory of *Meaning and Necessity* or any like it. And there is hardly anything in the *Categories* to tell a post-Fregean analytical philosopher that it is wrong to think of the *Categories* in this way – except for the signs of precipice-walking, and anyone who can read those must already know this. But wrong it is, and not just by gross anachronism, but – as the *Metaphysics* shows – it also basically misrepresents the historical situation and the nature of the problem Aristotle was confronting.

It is central to the interpretation to be pursued here that the existence of material

---

1 The idea goes all the way back to Cantor's baptism of *class* in 1895: "The collection, *S*, into a totality, of definite, well-distinguished objects of our intuition or our thought – called the *elements* of *S*" (*Gesammelte Abhandlungen*, p. 282); cf. Frege's similar remark cited above (§4, p. 30). I am aware that there are major differences of outlook dividing Frege, Cantor and Carnap on many of these matters, and even larger differences between them and others of the past hundred years. Here I am trying to limn a difference greater than any of these, within a reasonable compass.

individuals is for Aristotle a "given" only in the sense of a datum requiring explanation, a phenomenon that calls for saving, and that the concept of a material individual is thoroughly problematic, in a state of active development in the theory, and not something that can be regarded as assumed as part of the primitive basis of that theory. In this perspective, the "atomicity", in the sense of both primitive ness and methodological opacity (cf. §4, p. 38), enjoyed by the substantial individuals in the *Categories*, is quite unrepresentative of the problematic status of the concept of material individual in the *Metaphysics*, where it is the subject of a difficult and painstaking analysis. And not to prejudge that analysis, which is after all our main topic here, I will suggest that Aristotle's problem in the *Metaphysics* is not that of fitting a theory of various sorts of things-predicated around a primitive notion of "atomic" individual that is just assumed, but is rather *to delineate a kind of thing-predicated that somehow, in some way, marks something out as an individual in the first place.* His approach to this problem is along these lines: we have no antecedently-given array of objects to be the subjects of things-predicated; instead, we have two types of things-predicated: first, the ones that *constitute* individuals as individuals (these are the specific substantial kinds), and second, the ones that *characterize* individuals presupposed to be constituted as such (the ones that comprise what "happens to" or "afflicts" them – these are the ones of the nonsubstantial categories), and no logically or metaphysically prior individuation of objects (prior to individuation by a constitutive – substantial – thing-predicated, that is) is imagined or, according to the approach he proposes, imaginable.[2]

That is the more technical characterization of a generic contrast between our outlook and Aristotle's. To put it more broadly and less clearly, it is my belief, and an active hypothesis of this work, that our Western-philosophical concept of a material individual, as explicitly and consciously opposed to that of a (quantity of a) material stuff, is largely an original formulation – I am tempted to say, a deliberate invention – of Aristotle's, and that according to his way of thinking, the distinctive way to the concept is *via* the substantial kind – the intuition being that for him there is no other way to them, Aristotelean individuals come *only* in, and *via*, kinds (thus the individual *tree*, the individual *man*) – and that this is

---

2 For the requisite consequent reorganization of the notion of the *domain* of a language, from what we today are used to (sketched above, p. 59) to something more along the *Meta.* line, see §19. This way of setting things up of course can make no claim for novelty; the Aristotelean essence/accident distinction is probably the hardiest perennial of all Western philosophy. The leading specimen of the last generation is perhaps Strawson's division of 'sortal and characterizing universals' (*Individuals*, 168).

true to such an extent that for him, the two aspects of the notion of substance that we stated separately in §6, namely, individuativeness and essence, are merged together in a way that they are not for us.

That is not yet clear enough, and it will be helpful in clarifying it to enlarge a little on the relationship between the *Categories* and the *Metaphysics* view of what sort of substance is *"primary"*, and why.

In the *Cats.*, where *being a substance* is *being a subject*, and the *more* 'subject' something is, the *more* 'substantial' it is (2^b15–17, 2^b37–3^a1: cf. §3, p. 22, §4, p. 28), it is natural that on this criterion the 'most prior' and thus 'first' or '*primary*' type of substance will be that which is '*most* subject' – namely, in the *Cats.*, the individual such-and-such, the *atomic substance*.

In *Metaphysics* Zeta, *being a substance* is straightway decoupled from *being a subject* (Zeta 3, cf. §20(i)), and is associated instead with *whatever it is that MAKES the individual such-and-such to be 'what it is and a this'*. On this criterion, the 'most prior' and thus 'first' or '*primary*' type of substance will be that which is *most* responsible for this kind of 'making', 'the substance *of*' the individual such-and-such. Various candidates for this office are examined and criticized in Zeta, until the one best meeting the changed criterion eventually wins out, namely substantial form and actualization (Zeta 17 ff.). The individual such-and-such is now no longer 'atomic', but instead is a composite thing (*suntheton* or *sunolon*), composited (*sunistamenon* or *sunestēkotos*) out of matter by form. Instead of the individual such-and-such, the *form* comes to be called 'atomic' – and sometimes even a 'this'.

This is the point at which the individuativeness and the essence conditions are found, as I think, to be merged together in Aristotle's thought about substance. There is a serious interpretive crux here that has baffled interpreters as thoroughly as anything in all of Aristotle: the occasions when terms like *tode ti* ("this") and *atomon* ("un-divided", "individual") are applied to the 'most definite *eidos*', which is 'the substance *of*' its individuals, rather than the individuals themselves. The crux of "the *form* as separate and a 'this'" consists in the fact that expressions like "*substance means a 'this'*" apparently were for him multistable, like an optically reversing figure: oscillating between

> *Man* splits up into thisses, *atoma tade tina*

and

> *Man* is itself a most definite and specific and not further specifiable or differentiable species, is itself *atomon kai tode*,

and *khōriston*, and *eskhaton*, and *oikeion*, i.e. undivided, and 'this', and separate, and final, and proprietary.[3]

As said above, this is a deep and complicated problem whose untangling will require some careful treatment, but already visible is a wide difference between his ways of mind and ours on this point. We are used to an abstract or attenuated concept of individual which can float free of any particular count-concept with respect to which the individual is individuated; whereas for Aristotle the notion of *individual* is so tightly linked to that of *kind of individual* that the terminologies for the two notions can sometimes coalesce in a way that we are likely to find extremely confusing.

Another way of approaching the point is to briefly anticipate our later reading of *Meta.* Zeta 3, by saying that in this substance-theory, there is no more basic or "purer" individual than an individual as marked off by a substance-property. This appears in Zeta 3, when a Gedanken-experiment is made of trying to crack open, break down, a substantial *tode ti* and to find in it, as a kind of bare substantial particular, something that *just* meets the technical specifications for a "subject" (*hupokeimenon*) and nothing further, something that is *just* "that of which the other things are said, but itself is never said of any other thing" (1028^{b}36–7). But the result of the attempt is, significantly, *not* a "purer individual", but a "subject" of a wholly different kind, viz., matter – the whole notion of a discriminable *individual* or *particular* "subject" of things-predicated begins to fall apart. (It will be seen that I attach great significance to *Meta.* Zeta 3: it presages the doctrine that "'being a subject' or 'underlying' is *twofold*", *dikhōs hupokeitai*", at the root of the later theory; cf. §19.)

Here is a different perspective on the difference between *Categories*-metaphysics and the larger theory. In both, it is obviously contemplated

---

3 A few representative samples: *Meta.* Delta 8 1017^{b}25, where *form* is alluded to as *tode ti* and *khōriston*; likewise, e.g., Eta 1 1042^{a}29, Theta 7 1049^{a}35. *Eskhaton*, *PA* i 4 644^{a}24; *oikeion*, *DA* ii 3 414^{b}27. On the other hand *Socrates is tode ti* at Zeta 8 1033^{b}24. Some cases of virtually flawless ambiguity between the two alternatives: Zeta 3 1029^{a}27–9; Zeta 4 1030^{a}4; Zeta 7 1032^{a}15, 18–19. The problem seems under slightly better control at Eta 3 1043^{a}29 ff., "sometimes it's hard to tell ('escapes notice') whether" a name like *man* means the complex substance (*tēn sunthetēn ousian*) or the actuality or form (Ar.'s example is "house", but on artefacts see §7 above); the identical contrast is made in Zeta 15 *init.*, 1039^{b}20 ff. At *Meta.* Zeta 17 1041^{b}11 ff., form is responsible for the syllable's not only being whatever syllable it is, but being "one" as opposed to a heap. And *DA.* ii 1 412^{a}8, "form, *in virtue of which* (Socrates) is called *tode ti*" (for both these last, cf. §23(iv)). *Top.* vi 6 144^{b}1–3, "Each *animal* is *either* a species *or* an individual" (??). Joseph Owens addressing this issue justly remarks, "One is standing before the feature of Aristotelian thought that has exasperated certain commentators" (*Doctrine of Being*, 1st ed., p. 242; 2d ed., p. 390).

that the substantial individuals come-to-be and pass-away. But in the *Categories*, there is nothing that substantial coming-to-be or passing-away *is*. An individual man *is not*, then she *is*, and then she *is not*; but it is a consequence of what I have called the "methodological opacity" of the substantial individuals in the *Cats.* that such an occurrence is an unanalyzable brute fact, which does not *consist in anything*. The contrast with the larger theory is dramatic: in the larger theory, when a substantial individual comes-to-be, *what happens* is that a matter is informed by a form into the composite, which is what has come-to-be; and when a substantial individual ceases-to-be, *what happens* is that the individual disintegrates into its component matter, as the matter loses the form. In the *Categories*, there is no such *story*. By exactly the same token, the plurality of many substantial individuals of the same specific form is in the *Categories* another brute fact that has no *rationale*; in the larger theory it is explicable, in terms of that form's being re-applied, repeatedly, in a material medium. We shall visit this aspect again in §19(ii).

Or finally, the point about substantial individuals and their kinds can be approached in the terms of a dusty nineteenth-century dispute. When in one connection or another, Aristotle trots out his list of Categories, he sometimes signalizes the category of substance as *ti* (i.e., *what*) or *ti estin* (*what it is*), and sometimes as *tode ti* – and a few times, interestingly from our viewpoint, as both.[4] Accordingly contention broke out as to which of the two was "more fundamental" and which "secondary" or derivative. Bonitz thought that the more basic idea was *tode ti*.[5] Otto Apelt, on the other hand, assiduously combed the corpus, fished out sixty-odd occurrences of lists of various lengths, and found that *ti estin* heavily predominated; on the basis of this "Uebergewicht" he concluded that the basic idea must be *ti estin*.[6] We can infer from the foregoing that of the two, Apelt's *conclusion* was the more nearly right – the individuals in this theory are constituted by or through "what"-properties –, though for the wrong reason, since the predominance of *ti estin* in the lists can be explained by the fact that the concept of categories, and the use of "what" for substance at their head, considerably pre-dated the preoccupation with the metaphysics of substantial individuals that pervades Aristotle's later work – and indeed that concept was employed by Aristotle and others far earlier,

---

4 E.g., *Meta.* 1028ᵃ11, 1032ᵃ14–15. The variant *ousia kai tode*, *Meta.* 1030ᵃ19, *DA* 402ᵃ24, *CTBPA* 317ᵇ9. 5 Bonitz (1853).
  6 Apelt (1891).

within a wholly Platonic setting in the Academy (as the *Topics* makes plain).[7]

Let us then review where we stand: for in some ways the present view has carried through relatively intact from the *Categories*, but in others it is fundamentally transformed. (1) Here, as in the *Cats.*, we have a theory of *basic individuals*: the individual men, horses, trees. (2) Here, as in the *Cats.*, these individuals are 'said' or 'called to be what they are', not by way of any 'inherence' or 'coincidence' (*sumbebēkos*) of anything, *in* or *to* them; Socrates' manner of being man is no more than before parallel with his way of being pale or short. However, the concept of a constitutive thing-predicated opens up an analytic route as to the inner structure of these substantial individuals that is closed, even invisible, in the *Cats.*; and it is the shift of 'primacy' in substance, *from* the individual so-and-so *to* what causes the individual so-and-so to be 'what it is and a this', with all its internal ambiguity as to the location of the 'this', that is the key to the opening.

Suppose we ask ourselves: what is a substantial thing-predicated predicated *of*? In the *Cats.* the answer is extremely straightforward: the deep structure is the *said-of* structure, and the scheme, constantly repeated, is, *Man said-of the individual man*, of the atomic unit (*kata tou atomou*).[8] What then of here, in the *Metaphysics*? Much more complicated, and there is much uncertainty and a lot of wavering along the way (cf. §23(iii) on the struggles of Zeta 4 and 6); but the line that eventually crystallizes is quite clear on some points. (a) The true subject or *hupokeimenon* of "Socrates is (a) man" is *not* Socrates, the individual man:

---

7 At least according to Apelt's list, the category of substance is never called *tode* or *tode ti* in the *Topics* or indeed anywhere in the *Organon*, and is so called only in *Physics* iii, *CTB/PA* i, *de An.* i, *Meta. ZH*, once in *Meta.* N and once in the *Rhetoric.* – Something partially resembling the co-ordinacy of constitutive and individuative components in the meanings of the substantial predicates which I am advocating here was suggested long ago by one of the Oxford translators, Smith (1921): *tode ti* meant, according to him,

"'anything which is both a this and a somewhat', the two expressions being co-ordinate. *x* is *tode ti*, if it is both (a) singular and so signifiable by 'this', and (b) possessed of a universal nature, the name of which is an answer to the question *ti estin* in the category of *ousia*; in other words *x* is a *prōtē ousia*".

This is solid good sense as far as it goes; but it goes not far enough to encompass the full extent of the ambivalence. W. D. Ross rejoined (*AM* i 247 f., Beta 4 1001^{b}32 n.), "generally speaking it is singularity and not the possession of a universal nature that Ar. seems to have in mind when he uses the phrase"; in support of this view he then cited *Cat.* 5 3^{b}12 ff., a passage that we have already found to be a good specimen of precisely Aristotle's (not usually very successful) struggles to articulate the co-ordinacy (§4, pp. 30–33). More recently, a similar outlook is recommended in Georgiadis (1973).

8 *Cat.* 1^{a}21–2, 2^{a}21–2, 34–5, ^{b}3–5, 15–17, 22–6, 2^{b}37–3^{a}1, 3^{a}11, 13, 23–4, 37–9 (another *a fortiori* occurrence of *katēgoreisthai*, where *legesthai* would have been legitimate and strictly more correct, cf. §1, pp. 10–11).

"this much is plain, it's *not* being asked 'why he who's a man is a man'"

(Zeta 17, 1041^{a}21–22)

or, as we could rephrase it, the question is not "Why does *man* attach to (or get said-of) *him*?". (b) The true subject of "Socrates is (a) man" also is not some more basic, logically prior individual or particular object ("pure" or "bare" Socrates, not essentially a man) whose combination with or participation in, or getting said-of by, *Man* is what makes up human Socrates and therewith the truth of the proposition. Rather, the anti-migration condition on the substantial kind Man entails that the generation and destruction of human Socrates *is identical with* the generation and destruction of Socrates the individual (what's "numerically one and the same"), there is in this theory no "more basic" individual continuant. Such is the import of the concept of Man as constitutive rather than characterizing, and such is the moral of the cautionary tale that we just now were (anticipatorily) reading out of *Meta.* Zeta 3.[9]

In that case, how *is* Socrates the substance constructed? What *is* the true logico-philosophical form of this evidently idiosyncratic fact, Socrates'-being-man? It *is* a fact, so something *is* predicated of something, *ti kata tinos* (Zeta 17, 1041^{a}23), but what of what?

---

9 The assumption here should be made audible, that I am here assuming an answer to a special case of the Population Problem, namely that Man *is* a substantial kind (and thus that the episode which we might be inclined to describe as the transformation of Socrates into a wolf or vice versa *is* necessarily the generation of a new individual and not the alteration of a continuant). As for the viability of any such assumption, with respect to Man or any other putative kind, that is still in abeyance (§7, §18, §21).

III. THE ZOOLOGICAL UNIVERSE

§9. Methodological reorientation

We have noted (§4) that in the *Categories*, the substantial individuals are (as it was put) "methodologically opaque", so prodigiously "atomic" as to display no internal structure.[1] And we saw (also in §4) that the treatment of both the synchronic and the diachronic unity or "oneness" of substantial individuals is unusually terse and obscure: synchronically, the explanation of the "this"-hood of substance quickly gets into deep trouble (pp. 30–33). And diachronically, the requirement that a substantial individual have a permanent essential nature which it cannot "migrate" out of while remaining the same and numerically one, is at most insinuated there by some not very luminous outgivings about "definition", rather than made unmistakably explicit (pp. 34–38). Subsequent to that, some few main features of substantial individuals according to the *Metaphysics* concept have been sketched out, in a rather schematic way; but we have not yet tried to see very deeply into their internal structure, to conceptualize with any vividness what "substantial being" comes to. To get further, we must try to do this.

However, the best way to do this is not, I believe, to try to wring an intuitive understanding directly out of Aristotle's own positive outgivings on the topic, particularly those coming down to us as the *peri tēs ousias*, "On Substance", i.e., *Metaphysics ZHΘI*. That is an abstruse and imperspicuous work, as is well-known in itself and well-attested-to by the notably uneven successes of the interpretive tradition, and this tends to discourage such a frontal approach; but besides, for an *intuitive* understanding there is a better way in, one that can for now circumvent some of the perplexities of the metaphysical writings, and that may later enable us, as it were, to come up beneath them under our own power.

It consists in following up the consequences of the hypothesis, first, that the actual Aristotelean substances are pre-eminently the biological objects, living things – which means in practice the higher animals,

[1] §4, p. 38 and note 11, §6, p. 50, §8, p. 60.

metazoans, the ones he could see. (Higher plants, metaphytans, are not excluded – to the contrary, much of what will be said here applies to them as well – but they do not seem to have been the focus of nearly the intense concern that the animals drew. Of course he had no inkling of microbial forms of any sort.) Thus, let us take seriously and in earnest the tender concerning Population, that "plants and animals are substances *malista*, most of all" (Zeta 8, cf. §§7–8 above), and look to his biological studies for both the common "principles" and the distinguishing "differences" most characteristic of substances, as they are to be found in the real world: the manner of their construction, how they come into existence, their modes of self-sustenance, how they relate to the remainder of the world surrounding them, what is specifically meant by a substance's decline and eventual ceasing-to-be, *et cetera*.

Second, in studying the nature of these "beings" and endeavouring to analyze the "causes" that are at work in bringing them about and endowing them with their immensely absorbing and unique characteristics, we are embarking (in Aristotle's tracks) on a highly ambitious enterprise of biological *theory*, in which a number of deep and difficult problems must be faced and resolved: theoretical problems, we shall see, that are not at all primitive, or naive, or superannuated, but that are in large part still unresolved today, and go to the very nature of life itself.

Third, these problems, and the theoretical framework that Aristotle devised to deal with them, raise in turn very important general issues of a foundational character; – in fact, it is my belief that Aristotle the biologist asked himself a series of very profound questions about the animal kingdom, and at this point enters my thought, as was mentioned in §0, that the metaphysics of substance was to a great extent motivated (and that hence "The Metaphysics Of Substance" should to a great extent be approached) as a deep theoretical foundation, a "methodology" in Tarski's sense, for the biological sciences, much as the work of Frege and his successors was to stand to the "deductive sciences" two millennia later.

The present work does not masquerade as a free-standing original dissertation on Aristotelean biology; nor can all the biological problems he contended with be discussed here, nor his attempted resolutions be definitively evaluated. But if this general perspective is at all sound, it suggests that only by grasping at least the basics of this complicated subject can we hope to acquire a good intuitive view of what he was up to. Or more positively, perhaps by tracing his ideas as to the manner in which the complex biological objects are constructed and what they are like, we may not only lay a firm grasp on the strands that form some of the snares of ontology, but even see to some of their unravelling.

So let us now use our imagination. We now must truly try to put our feet in Aristotle's tracks. Let us go all the way back to first principles, and consider from scratch.

(i) We are endeavoring to understand the fundamental character of the natural world at a time when its *micro structure* was quite unknown. The (perhaps better, *an*) atomic theory of matter has been stated, with luminous clarity and precision by Democritus, yet seems quite impossible to accept. Why? – all the way back to first principles: it asks us to found everything on unobservables, which is contrary to sound scientific practice; it requires the existence of a *void* – an endless source of paradox and absurdity; and it asserts the *law of inertia*, which is patently falsified by experience. Thus we are moved to accept instead an Empedoclean concept of matter, whose "elements" are stuffs, bulks, fluids, gases ("Earth", "Air"), and where "combination" of elements therefore is likened to the squeezing-together of pigments by a painter (Empedocles, fr. 23 Diels).[2] Thus the logic of our matter, if such a phrase be permitted, is inescapably a *mass* logic; and there is the related, most radical consequence that "combination" is not structural but chemical in nature – the elements can mingle and merge, but of itself, on its own (*kath' hautēn*), the nature of this basic matter is not to build up *into* complex structures and superstructures in the way that can be made at least intuitively plausible on, for one example, an atomic basis.

This nonstructural character of the basic matter is very significant. I believe it goes to the fundamental reason why Aristotle makes such ado about Form in connection with organic substances.

Put the other way, the material elements are such that, the deeper we go into the infrastructure of the world, the more homogeneous and "uniform" (technically, *homoiomeres* – see §11 below) its character becomes, and the less structure it manifests – there is in this matter-theory nothing corresponding to the notion of an atomic and molecular architecture; rather at that level discreteness gives way to continuity, and organization of components to commingling, blending, alloying of ingredients in a mixture.[3]

2 It will be seen that here and below (especially §12), I do not hesitate to take an Aristotelean view of Empedocles, and do not trouble much whether this view does justice to the historical personage of that name. In the final analysis I think the injustice is not altogether and impossibly gross, but I acknowledge that such an analysis is not provided here.

3 For Aristotle's awareness of this distinction in principle, *sunthesis* versus *krasis* or *mixis*, see §12.

(ii) In the light of this, the occurrence in the megascopic world of these endlessly repeated, specifically identical, highly organized, sharply demarcated, integral structures or systems (*sustēmata*, he calls them or *sustaseis*) – the biological objects which are the substantial individuals, each one a unitary individual entity or "this", each one exemplifying over its temporal span a sharply defined complete specific nature or substantial kind – stands out as a remarkable fact of nature which invites explanation. "Invites", not "defies" – how *do* such entities come to take shape, out of the Empedoclean swirl of mixing and unmixing, clumping and unclumping?[4]

This phenomenon, "(ii)", will be enlarged upon shortly; but even going no further than this, there is already a real question here, not less real in contemporary than in ancient terms, and it seems that Aristotle saw it very clearly: how is it, what principles must be at work to make it the case, that in the environmental circumstances that terrestrially prevail, the world of bio-organic substances takes this form of numerous species of independent, integral *units* – the individual men, dogs, chambered nautili, catfish, grasshoppers, whales? That "how is it?" answers to Aristotle's "why?": why this, rather than say, a general bio-organic swamp, or some other organic distribution built on a completely different principle from that of the *constantly repeated individual?* This stupendous superquestion of course resolves into a great many subquestions, to which even today only the dimmest beginnings of answers are apparent: and *we* know that even these beginnings of the answers that are currently unfolding are possible only through the resurrection of the atomic theory, and then (among much else) the beginning comprehension of the molecular bond, the successful analysis of the proteins, the decipherment of nucleic acid, and the interweaving of all these factors with what is known of evolution. Of all this Aristotle of course knew nothing whatever; most of it was unknown to anyone before yesterday afternoon. But he did know, and constantly reiterates, that much more must be involved in the construction of these intricate specifically identical units than the Empedoclean clumping and commingling of material stuffs. On the basis of this (perfectly correct) insight, he evolves a theory of the (onto)logical

---

4 I do not suggest by any means that a similar question cannot or should not be asked about the occurrence of such entities as higher animals on the basis of an atomic as opposed to an Empedoclean matter theory; obviously the reverse is true, as indicated below. The point is rather that whereas in dealing with such objects on an atomic view of matter, the need for a concept like Aristotelean *form* – as opposed to the possibility of completely reductionistic explanations in terms of micro-states of elementary matter – is at least debatable, on an Empedoclean view of matter it is in principle inescapable. As Aristotle indeed argues, often and at length, against Empedocles himself; cf. §12 below.

working-up of materials into a unity, through a succession of progressively more complex stages ("parts", as his language makes him call them), from the mass-logic level of the original materials to the count-logic level of the completed individual. This occurs through the progressive advent of *form*, and to Aristotle's mind would be totally unintelligible without it.

As can be seen from these remarks but should be made explicit, my hypothesis is that the philosophical concept of substantial form should basically be seen as an *invention*: as a conceptual instrumentality deliberately fashioned in the course of seeking a theoretical understanding of the agencies (or "causes") responsible for the simultaneous unity and complexity of biological objects, in the setting of an Empedoclean physics and chemistry (if we may call it that) of itself nowhere nearly powerful enough to accomplish such a task.[5] This does not imply that it is devoid of contemporary value – the question of its possible applicability today, at least in part, to biological questions of the kind that interested Aristotle, is a separate one. The important thing is the task it was devised to do at the time it was devised – a *task* that is still with us.

It will now be useful[6] to look more closely at some of the biological *phainomena* that Aristotle was endeavoring to deal with, since my claim is that he was deeply impressed by a number of extremely basic and pervasive "facts of nature"[7] concerning the biosphere which should strike observers today as equally notable. They are all of course totally obvious (at least once formulated), yet, ridiculously banal as such points as the following appear when one troubles to state them, a first perception of them and of their potentially profound implications was a feat of no mean biological intuition: they are indeed banal, but they are also global. Although hard to formulate without using some words that have been pre-empted at one time or another for some philosophical or scientific purpose, I take them to be thoroughly untechnical in principle.

5 The line I am here suggesting is thus in contrast to Rorty's view in Rorty (1973), in that I take Aristotle to be *introducing* a concept in a theoretically self-conscious way rather than defending a common-sense concept in everyday use against "reductionist attack" from materialists and Platonists (p. 395). In terms of the (dubious, to me) distinction of revisionary versus descriptive metaphysics, my Aristotle is much more revisionary than is usually assumed. If his "metaphysical arguments" sometimes strike *us* as "attempts to defend something like a common-sense view of the world" (Hartman (1977), p. 51, and many others), I would say that (*a*) that does not mean they played that role for Aristotle, (*b*) we should not underestimate the extent to which our common sense has been shaped by Aristotelean influence. It is a risky thesis that holds, "Ordinary thought is spontaneously 'ousiological'" (Pellegrin (1982), p. 68).

6 Most of the rest of §9 and §§10–13 were pre-distributed, read and discussed at the Princeton Classical Philosophy Colloquium in December 1976. I am indebted to the audience, and particularly to my co-symposiasts, David Balme and Marjorie Grene, and my commentator, Martha Nussbaum, for their comments.   7 This is a phrase of art; see §21 (iii) below.

Fact 1. Biological objects are individuals or "thisses"; as observed above, for some reason the animal kingdom (i.e., mainly the metazoans, as was said) comes in the form of countable, repeated specifically identical unitary parcels, *tade tina*, each one a *tode ti*: the individual *F*s, *G*s, and so on.[8] Simultaneously,

Fact 2. Each one of these biological individuals is permanently endowed with a highly definite specific nature, a characteristic specific constitution, which it shares with other individuals (the ones we say are *homogenē*, of its kind, co-specific) and which incorporates a very large number of features and aspects of its make-up, among these: (a) an overall physical structure of the living thing as a whole, and underlying this, very typically fashioned subassemblies, substructures and subcomponents, extending down to quite minute details of its construction – its minute as well as gross anatomy and physiology – and to a considerable extent even including the kinds of basic materials that compose its various parts; all of this apparently specifically determined. And founded on this structure, (b) also incorporated in its specific character is a characteristic life-style, a total pattern of functioning typical for its species – including, e.g., a manner of growth and development, manner of nutrition at different stages of development, mode of reproduction, mode of homemaking, mode of relationship to co-specific individuals, to potential enemies, to the general animal population, to the total circumambient environment. For discussion of these thousands of features of structure and function that specifically typify any biological object, Aristotle takes over and adapts to the purpose an old technical term from the Academy, calling them the object's *differentiae (diaphorai)*;[9] in any concrete case their comprehensive description would fill volumes. Indeed, it is notable and deserving of separate mention, that:

Fact 3. These biological individuals are by a wide margin and without exception the most complex and highly organized objects to be found on the Earth; in particular, they display to a marked degree a hierarchical structure of *levels* of organization, in which what is a "whole" at one level is a "part" at the next, and in which the part-whole relationship itself assumes a variety

8 It should be remembered that this is not the *only* meaning of *tode ti* in Aristotle, cf. e.g. §4 above (on the second half of *Cat.* 3ᵦ10–21), §8, §15(i), §17(iii), §23.

9 In actual usage these are usually called differentiae of the species rather than of the individual; however, a species being after all simply a kind of individual (= a kind in which they come, cf. §4, p. 32 and §8, pp. 60–61), in effect they are really differentiae of every individual of the species. On that understanding, the terminologies are equivalent. The development of the "logical" idea of differentia discussed in the Organon into the biological idea introduced here, is treated in §13(ii) below. See also notes 11 and 12 below.

of forms beyond that of ingredience in a mixture, or aggregation into a bulk or a "heap". In complexity of behavior, too: these objects are strikingly more elaborate in what they *do* than are non-living objects such as stones and lakes, even than are rivers and fires (which so impressed Heraclitus). In particular, they are constantly and at all levels engaged in natural processes and routines that are *future-oriented*, i.e., ones that are aimed at natural *telē*, "completions" (this is not unique to them, but is very highly characteristic). Such future-directed processes and activities need not involve conscious planning and explicit purposes, which is only one variety found in higher forms,[10] although that case can sometimes be used (with great care) as an illustrative model for the non-conscious natural processes that aim at a *telos*. (It is noteworthy that although the dimension of transtemporal persistence through change was identified as "most distinctive" of substances in the *Categories*, the aspect of future-directedness, of the utmost import for organic substances, is there entirely absent. We shall enlarge on this in §16.)

Fact 4. Yet, all these complexities granted, nonetheless *the intricate constitutive nature that typifies such things is very highly species-specific, to the extent that a detailed examination of relatively few specimens is sufficient to smooth out the variation attributable to environmental influence* and ascertain the basic character, and basic behavior-types, of all, past, present and future, species members.[11] A fact of some significance: it suggests (particularly in view of the fact about complexity) that the causal agencies at work must be extremely stable and regular, so much so that the underlying mechanisms involved must be extremely reliable and so, in the end, intelligible[12] – the patterns are too deeply systematic for chance or random influences to lie at their basis. This leads us to:

Fact 5. Offspring virtually invariably share their specific character (are *homogenē*) *with a pair of parents, and vice versa*: more fully, (a) with a few

10 Explicit purposes with respect to the future and memory with respect to the past are found only in those animals that can perceive time, *de Mem. et Rem.* 1 449^{b}28–30.

11 It is a consequence of this that the living substances can be discussed *at the level of* the so-called infima species, the usual practice in Aristotelean biological writings. "The ultimate species are the substances (sc. with which we deal); the individual specimens, like Socrates and Coriscus, are not further differentiated (*adiaphora*) with respect to species", *PA init.* 644^{a}23–5 (a much contested passage). – Another outcropping of the "substance means a this" problem, cf. p.§8, pp. 61–62 Cf. also D. M. Balme (1972), *PAGA I, PA*i 1,639^{a}16 n., pp. 73–4, Düring (1943), p. 105, Driscoll (1981), p. 143, n. 54.

12 A formula stating the complete formal nature of an animal species is known technically as a "*definition*" (*horismos* or *logos*), and that which is formulated by such a definition (better, from our standpoint, by the definiens) goes by the name of "*essence*" (*ti ēn einai*); in those terms, Fact 4 is our first encounter here with the possibility of getting understanding of the essences of living things by deep and careful study of the living specimens. See §3, note 4, and next §11.

explicable exceptions, the existence of an animal is *invariably* traceable to a pair of parents specifically identical with it; (b) with a few explicable exceptions, a pair of animals that generate offspring at all are *invariably* specifically identical with one another and generate offspring specifically identical with themselves. This fact is perhaps the most remarkable of all: "Human being begets human being", as he repeatedly reflects,[13] *never* horse or squirrel or ant; from which can be immediately gathered with great probability that there must be a *copying mechanism*, highly reliable and very accurate, guaranteeing the transmission of specific nature identical and intact from one generation to the next.[14] Remarkable, to say the least.

Fact 6. These natural types are profuse in number and of enormous diversity; the biosphere presents literally thousands upon thousands of species, representing all sorts of extremes of morphological and functional variation; and the variety reflects a corresponding range of habitats and of choices of function – in fact, so amazingly prodigal is Nature with species, and so extreme, even bizarre, are the capabilities of functional adaptation, that it seems that hardly an ecological space or "niche" is to be found that some queer creature or other doesn't flourish in.[15]

Fact 7. These objects are subject to temporal as well as spatial limitations; even barring accidental misadventure, they invariably decline with time and eventually perish. That there seem to be no exceptions whatsoever to this phenomenon, of death, is another striking and surely significant fact of nature; why then is it, what can be learned from the fact, that living things apparently must have a specifically characteristic temporal as well as spatial size?

Our interest here is philosophical, and I have already disavowed the aim of furnishing a full-fledged independent treatise on Aristotelean biol-

---

13 *Meta.* Zeta 7 1032^{a}25, Zeta 8 1033^{b}32, Theta 8 1049^{b}25–9, Lambda 3 1070^{a}28, Lambda 4 1070^{b}31; *Phycs.* ii 1 193^{b}8, ii 2 194^{b}13, ii 7 198^{a}27, iii 2 202^{a}11; *PA* i 1 640^{a}25, 641^{b}26 ff., ii 1 646^{a}33; *GA* i 1 715^{b}2–4, ii 1 735^{a}21; *DA* ii 4 415^{a}28, ^{b}7 (cf. §16(ii) below); etc. Compare *CTB/PA* ii 6, 333^{b}7–9: "What's then the cause of *from man, man* (either always or mostly), and *from wheat, wheat*, and *not* an olive tree?", cf. *Phycs.* ii 4 196^{a}31–3.

14 The fact that the generation of animals *is*, normally, reproduction, is of course *no tautology*, but a very highly significant *a posteriori* truth. Its recognition inclines me to think that François Jacob is mistaken in saying, "Only towards the end of the eighteenth century did the word and the concept of reproduction make their appearance to describe the formation of living organisms. Until that time living beings did not *reproduce*; they were *engendered*." (Jacob (1973), p. 18, emphasis mine.) He may well be right about the word; but not the concept, which is prominent and explicit in Aristotle.

15 "For Aristotle, . . . this ordered diversity of living things *is a problem*", Pellegrin (1982), p. 161.

ogy.[16] It is also beside our main purposes to get into comparisons, favorable or otherwise, between Aristotle's attempt to put together a comprehensive and scientifically adequate explanatory rationale that would account for such "facts" as the foregoing, and our present-day understanding of such matters, such as it is. But two remarks are in order, one of which seems approximately self-evident, and the other, it is hoped, will be borne out by the ensuing discussion. First, it is evident that his questions – the quest for a causal account that would make sense of such phenomena as those just set out – had a certain rightness about them; to put it one way, any inquiry motivated by questions that good must be worthwhile. Second, while we are not primarily concerned with his biological theories, of which (as would be expected) parts are basically sound and other parts are basically completely mistaken, there are a number of points at which matters of substantive biology do seem to have an impact that is direct and considerable on the metaphysical theory of substance.

Let us then lay out a rapid summary of the overall structure of Aristotle's biological universe and the organisms that compose it.

16 The best and most comprehensive recent treatment known to me is Kullmann (1974), which thoroughly integrates a large body of previous literature, especially in connection with *PA* i (pp. 6–94). Some further references to more specialized studies are given as we proceed; but recall §0.

§10. Empedoclean infrastructure

For expository convenience we start with the most elementary materials and work "upward" to successive levels of formedness, but it should be emphasized that in an important sense it reverses the true order of things to proceed in this way. This is especially worth stressing in a contemporary philosophical/scientific setting in which the idea of all things' being "built up" from elements into which they are ultimately "reducible" has wide if not universal currency (even though this is not the same as acceptance). It had some currency in Aristotle's time also, and his attitude towards it is thorough disapproval. The basic Aristotelean intuition, of course, is one of a form's informing a matter; but this should be thought of more in terms of a form "reaching down" into the matter than of the matter being "built up" into the form. It must never be forgotten that when Aristotle speaks of form as a kind of *cause*, he is speaking literally and in earnest, and not of something that can be reduced away.

(i) 1st level: the simples (ta hapla). The ultrasimples deferred

The world is wholly saturated with Empedoclean matter, ranging from extremely dense to extremely fine; nowhere is there any 'void'. The simplest types of 'body' – according to the *Physics, ta hapla tōn sōmatōn*[2] – are the four elements, Earth–Water–Air–Fire; although according to an

---

1 As already emphasized, this sketch of Aristotelean morphology (in a schematic and nontechnical sense of the word) is anything but definitive. Some important expositions of the subject are those of Peck (1961) and (1965), Le Blond (1945), Düring (1943), as well as Kullmann (1974), already cited (§9 *fin.*).

2 *Phys.* ii 1 192^{b}10. It should be reiterated that here and throughout this work I am concerned only with what goes on in the sublunary realm, i.e. within the moon's orbit or so-called "sphere", thus ignoring for the most part all such matters as the aitherial element, planets and stars, Unmoved Motor, etc. My (weak) excuse for this (in the end, indefensible) curtailment is stated in §0.

extremely ingenious theory put forth in the work *On Coming-to-be and Passing-away* (ii 1–4), these four only appear to be simple (they are *hapla PHAINOMENA sōmata*, 330^{b}2), but in reality are 'mixed' (*mikta*, 330^{b}22), breaking down into combinations of the two pairs of contraries *moist* v. *dry* (*hugron*, *xeron*), and *hot* v. *cold* (*thermon*, *psuchron*); then

$$dry + cold \quad = Earth$$
$$cold + moist = Water$$
$$moist + hot \quad = Air$$
$$hot + dry \quad = Fire.$$

This last analysis, reaching what may be called the very deepest-lying "ultrasimples" of the world, is not directly relevant to or required for understanding of biological objects and processes, for which the four elements are as deep as we need go; but I will return to it later, in §22(iii). For the "ultrasimples", as such, represent Aristotle's view of that which is the most ultimate matter of things, or "prime matter" as it is sometimes called. This has been a focus of furious scholarly contention over many years, but I shall suggest that his actual position on it, as lofted in the *CTB/PA*, is quite a bit cleverer and more interesting than any of those which the scholarly contenders have attributed to him.

These four elements, then (hereafter sometimes EWAF) are the most basic to figure in the explanation of biological phenomena; sometimes in the biological works they are called *dunameis* ("potencies", "powers", "strong substances").[3] At *PA* ii 2 648^{b}9 they are the "origins of the natural elements", *arkhai tōn phusikōn stoikheiōn*.

At this level it is a world of *masses*, of stuffs and quantities thereof, and its logic a mass logic (cf. §9, pp. 69–71). The kind of *unity* that comes in is not the more advanced kind that goes with counting, but the cruder one characterized as a sense of *hen* in the paragraph of *Meta.* Delta 6 where

the subject isn't differentiated in kind (*tōi eidei adiaphoron* – not differentiated by a species?), where not-differentiated means that the kind (species?) isn't divided-off according to perception (= in a perceptible way), . . . e.g. *wine* is 'one' in this sense, and *water*, and all juices (lit. = things poured), like oil, and wine, and things (that are or can be) melted down – these because the ultimate subject of them all is the same; for they're *all* water or air . . .   (*Meta.* Delta 6 1017^{a}17–24)

Here a straightforward attempt to formulate the minimal amount of "unity" (in the sense that interests us) that comes with a mass term, is at

---

3 Cf. *PA* ii 1 646$_a$15, and Peck (1961), pp. 30–31, Peck (1963), pp. xlix–li. For earlier occurrences of *dunameis* in the old medical literature, the *Timaeus*, etc., cf. also Peck (1931), p. 31 n. 7.

the end crossed with an interjection of Aristotle's own physical speculation, about what everything (if I may say so) boils down to.[4]

Each of the elements, taken in itself and disregarding the further
reduction proposed in the CTB/PA, is "homogeneous" and "uniform", in
the sense that a quantity of Water, for example, divides into parts that are
also Water; any part of it is of the same nature as the whole and as any
other part. In accordance with this intuition, Aristotle's word for something with this kind of uniformity is *homoio-meres*, "of *like parts*". And
although the term is used by him and by later writers (Aetius, Diogenes
etc.) in explaining theories of Eleatics, Anaxagoras, and Empedocles,
there is every indication that the term itself, and the developed technical
distinction of the uniform *versus* the *nonuniform*, or *an-homoio-meres*, where a
whole is composed of parts "un-like" each other and/or the whole,
originates with Aristotle and not earlier. (But the germ of the idea is once
stated clearly by Plato.)[5]

(ii) 2nd level: compounds (suntheta)

These basic material elements combine in various ways and proportions
to form more complicated compounds (*suntheta sōmata*, *PA* ii 1 646[a]17,
etc.), but the latter are still *homoiomerē*, uniform and "having like parts"
from a molar standpoint. *Examples:* (from the *Meteorologica*) "metallic
stuffs (*metalleuomena*, lit. = stuffs dug out of mines) – bronze, gold, silver,
tin, iron, stone & other suchlike" (*Meteor.* iv 10 388[a]13ff.); other examples
would be wood, glass, coal, wine, honeywater. These are compounds that
can exist as such (= as wood, as gold) *on their own, kath' hauta*, and
accordingly by one criterion[6] could be termed "substances": namely,
being "what they are" on their own rather than by way of being part of
something else, and as opposed to the cases where "what something is"
connotes being part of an organic whole – cases to be encountered in §11.
But as already noted, such compounds are elsewhere rejected as substantial candidates on grounds of failing the individuative test;[7] and to the

---

4 Anything meltable is water; Delta 4, 1015[a]10; 24, 1023[a]28; *Meteor.* iv 8 *fin.*
5 *Protagoras* 329d4–8, "You mean (that Virtue has 'parts') as the parts of a face are parts –
mouth & nose & eyes & ears? Or like the parts of the gold, which don't differ from one another, or
from the whole, except in size?" And a related idea clearly underlies the distinction between a *pan*
(which is an unstructured aggregate) and a *holon* (which is a structured unity), as "bravely" but
unavailingly maintained by Theaetetus against Socrates' browbeating at *Tht.* 204[a]8–205[a]7. For
homoiomeres as applied specifically to the four elements as understood by Aristotle, *Meta.* A 9
992[a]7. 6 That of *Meta.* Delta 8, 1017[b]10–11, 13–14, 23–4; recall above, §6, p. 51.
7 *Meta.* Zeta 16, 1040[b]8–10; cf. again §6, p. 51 above.

extent that the substances are the individual *animals*, it is Aristotle's explicit and emphatic contention that the existence of such objects as these cannot so much as be intelligibly described, let alone explained, solely in terms of Empedoclean material elements – even together with cosmic forces driving the processes of their commingling and separation, i.e. so-called "efficient" or "moving causes" – whether Love and Strife, as Empedocles maintains, or something thermodynamically more standard. Rather, the present level is the upper limit of what, according to Aristotle's view, can come-to-be or can *be* at all by the agencies of *matter* and *force*; to get beyond this point requires the further agencies of *form* and *end*.

Details of Aristotle's criticism of Empedocles are deferred to §12(iii), for it falls in the category of moral-drawing rather than exposition of the Aristotelean biological universe itself; but it must be noted that an important divide is transited here: that is, since these complex individual units with their complex parts do exist, in no chance or erratic fashion and in great profusion over and above the "heaps", the inference is inescapable that constitutive substantial forms must be systematically at work in the world; at the next level upward we see the lowest traces of their agency.

§11. From mass to individual: anatomy and physiology, the Parts of Animals

(i) 3rd level: uniform parts of animals (ta homoiomerē)

Now, there are also "uniform" compounds that come about as part of the formation of living things. *Examples*: (from the *Parts of Animals*)[1] blood, serum, lard, marrow, semen,[2] bile, milk, flesh, also bone and sinew (but those typified by these last two introduce complications, see "4th level" to come). These compounds, however, unlike those of level 2, *cannot* exist as such, as "what they are" (= as blood, etc.) on their own; rather, apart from their functioning *as* part of a complete living organism, they cannot be these things (= blood, etc.) except homonymously, by a mere ambigu-

---

1 Though the *Meteorologica* list also includes a number of these, as do other passages throughout the natural writings. Citing here *PA* ii 2 647^{b}10 ff

2 But he changed his mind about this one's being a "part" in the *Generation*, on important theoretical grounds: cf. i 18 724^{b}23–31, and §14 below.

ity, merely in name.[3] Why is this? A complicated matter of which there will be more to say, but briefly and partially: because their nature, their being "what they are", includes fitness to a certain function or *work* (e.g., 641^a3, 655^b18–21), something not true of (say) *rock*, or *water*. Not only are these parts not that (= blood, etc.) apart from the body of which they are parts, but in addition, the moment the body of which these uniform parts are parts ceases to be enpsyched by a psyche (see §16 on this), these parts, like those of levels 4 and 5, cease to be that, and all that is left is EWAF.

(ii) 4th level: uniform to nonuniform

Now we are at a very delicate point; for about here begins an interface between the mass-system prevailing below, and the count-system prevailing above.

For there are certain sorts of "part" that on one hand consist of a *single* nonuniform nature, and for this reason divide into "like parts" and thus seem even as wholes to meet the condition for the uniform, yet on the other hand simultaneously have some further structure and form to them, hence partaking of the nature of the nonuniform as well. Such bi-polarity is first called to our attention for

certain of the Viscera, which on one hand are complexly structured (*polumorpha tois skhēmasin*), yet, consisting of a body that's uniform, also are in a manner of speaking simple;   (*PA* ii 1 646^b30–34)

soon thereafter we learn that the Heart is also like this:

the Heart divides into homoeomeries, just as does each of the other Viscera, but owing to its shaped configuration (*morphē tou skhēmatos*), it is also anhomoeomerous.   (ii 1 647^a31–33)

In such cases, of which (a) Vein (*phleps*)[4] is another example,

in one way the part is homonymous[5] with the whole, for example a part of Vein is Vein [as with the uniform], but yet in another way it's *not* homonymous [as with the nonuniform – i.e., a part of a Vein is not generally a Vein].   (ii 2 647^b18–19)

3 A frequent theme: of the nonuniform parts, e.g. *PA* i 1 640^b34–641^a3, but extended to all parts 641^a3–6, 18–21; cf. *Meta.* Zeta 16 1040^b5–10 – as opposed to inorganic parts (fire and earth) of (e.g.) flesh; cf. Zeta 17 1041^b12–16. A like consideration figures interestingly in discussing the formation of semen in *GA* i 18 722^b33–723^a1.

4 I adopt "Vein" for *phleps*, rather than "blood-vessel" as Peck and Platt, just because it seems better to reflect the required ambiguity as between the uniform, *vascular stuff*, and the nonuniform, *thing with a structure* (viz., "a Vein"); to me at least, "blood-vessel" too strongly suggests the latter.

5 Pellegrin (1982) cites this passage as marking the connection of Division and Differentia and with reason calls it "very difficult to translate" (188); but a very important concept lurks in

It may sound odd to us; but it seems we are being told that certain "parts" are *proto*-structural, of an intermediate nature or at an interface between uniform and nonuniform: the same nature somehow doubling as *stuff* and as *structure*. In *PA* ii 9, something of the same sort apparently is intimated about Bone, but the bi-polarity here seems to be between the uniformity of "bony stuff" (i.e., as we shall see, the $E_2W_2A_0F_4$ of Empedocles, cf. §12(iii) below) and a nonuniformity that is seen not so much at the level of "*a* bone", as it is at the level of the whole "system of bones", the skeletal structure of the whole animal (the entire chapter should be studied):

654^{a}32 The case is similar between the nature of the Bones and that of the Veins. For each of them is a connected system originating from one thing; and there's no *bone* itself by itself,[6] but either as a connected part or else attached and bound into it [= the "connected system"], so that nature can make use of it (654^b) both as one & continuous and as two & divided, for flexing. Likewise there's no *vein* itself by itself, but they're all part of a unity. ^{b}3 For if a Bone were something separated, it couldn't do the work for whose sake the nature of bones exists – for it couldn't be the cause of either any flexing or any straightening, being not connected but at a remove –, it would even be harmful, like some thorn or projectile lodged in the flesh. ^{b}7 Again, if a Vein were something separated and not connected with the origin, it couldn't preserve the blood inside it, for the heat from that origin prevents its congealing, as appears when separated blood goes bad. ^{b}11 The origin of the Veins is the Heart, and of the Bones is what's called the Spine, in all animals that have Bones, from which the nature of the other Bones is continuous; for the Spine is what holds together the length of the animals and makes them straight. ^{b}14 But since the animal in motion must flex its body, (the Spine) is *one* because of the continuity, but *polumer* by the division of the vertebrae.

After some more about the integration of the "system of Bones", the "unity" of the skeletal system (654^{b}16–655^{a}4) and related matters, some of which will concern us below, the discussion returns to the theme of bi-polarity between uniform and nonuniform, and puts the idea with great clarity:

655^{b}2 Very close to the Bones in their feel are also these sorts of parts, such as Nails, and Hoofs and Talons and Beaks, i.e. those of birds [as opposed to the

it. Evidently, "homonymous" here has to mean merely having the same name, and not also to entail (as it does in the *Categories*) that the formula or definition must be distinct. Thus this use of "homonym" does not exclude homonyms from being also some kind of synonyms – as in this instance they certainly are (see on Hoof and Horn below); the *Categories* sense of "(merely) homonymous" corresponds here to *homōnymon MONON*, e.g. *GA* i 19 726^{b}24. Similarly *Meta.* Zeta 9 1034^{a}22. (In the final analysis of this case they will actually turn out to be a new and different kind of *paronyms*: see §20(ii).)

6 Cf. *HA* iii 7 516^{a}10, "no such thing as Bone all on its own".

snouts of swine, which *rhunkhē* also covers?]. Animals have all these for the sake of defense. [b]5 For *the complete structures composited out of these and synonymous with the parts – e.g., the complete Hoof, the complete Horn –* have been contrived for the self-preservation of each of these [creatures]. Of this kind is also the nature of Teeth ... [b]15 related parts are Skin and Bladder and Membrane and Hairs and Feathers and parts analogous to these ... [b]21 in all these (which strictly are nonuniform), nonetheless *the parts are synonymous with the wholes.*[7]

A mass-versus-count ambiguity is being exploited here, of the kind that exists in English in (Quine's example) "Mary had a little *lamb*" (followed her to school one day, *versus* for supper one evening). We might say, e.g., that the mollusc's shell is made out of shell, or the pearl out of pearl, even if we are not inclined to say with Aristotle that the complete horn is made out of horn, or the tooth out of tooth (i.e., horny or toothy stuff).

In any event, it is at this level in the upward sequence that the formulation passes to, and remains with, the count-system.

Once this transition-point is formulated, it is available for exploitation with great vividness: the "system of Bones", the structure, is analogized to the armature used by modellers in clay – the framing that "subserves", he says (and "is for the sake of") the fleshy parts that are built around it.[8] Similarly with the "system of bloodvessels", the articulation-out (*diarthrōsis*) of which also plays a significant role in his account of early embryonic development, as we shall see in §14.

These transitional semistructural "parts" too are defined in part through their function ("work"), which is the reason why even being a portion of Bone, or Vein – the uniform pole of the ambiguity – really and truly so being, that is, requires being integrated into a *system* of Bones or Veins – the nonuniform pole of the ambiguity.[9]

(iii) 5th level: nonuniform parts of animals (ta anomoiomerē)

Head, ears, limbs, digits, organs of all kinds, external and internal (in fact, *ta an-homoiomerē* = *ta organika*, flatly, at several points).[10] Here the

---

7 The same point recurs for Horn at *HA* i 1 487[a]8–9: certainly *not* "an unimportant parenthesis" (Thompson), *nor* "secludenda" (Peck). Pellegrin (1982), p. 22 note 26, on *PA* ii 9 654[b]12: "Here again Aristotle has *chosen* a point of view that is not ours" (his emphasis).

8 654[b]27–34. As for Veins, see *HA* iii 5 535[a]34 ff., *GA* ii 6 743[a]2.

9 By "viscera" (*splankhna*) is meant the so-called bloodlike viscera (heart, liver, spleen, lung and the like); they are all *haimatika*, 647[a]35, [b]7–8, 665[a]29, 667[b]3, and Peck on *PA* iii 4 (page 232 n.); LSJ[6] also opposes them to *entera* (intestines). It would be tempting to think of *phleps* (Vein) as centered on the uniform side and *splankhna* (Viscera) on the nonuniform; but the ambivalence is too pronounced: see respectively 647[b]17–19 and 647[a]31–[b]9.

10 *GA* ii 1 734[b]28; i 18 722[b]30; *PA* ii 1 647[a]4. At the outset of *HA* (486[a]5),

whole part has the name, and its parts in turn not at all. The germ of the conception, we have seen, was known from Plato's day (cf. the "face" case in the *Protagoras*); Aristotle's remark shows the transition complete: we can go either way with Vein, which in one sense has 'like parts' – but what about with Face? Is part of a face a face? *Oudamōs*, "no way" (*PA* ii 2 647^{b}21; cf. also *Cael.* iii 4 302^{b}25).

Yet still as before, these parts too do not "have their names", are not "what they are" (= hands, etc.), except as operating according to their fashion in a functioning living being; separated from it, or if the animal dies, these parts may still look like "what they are" in their (superficial, here) "outward configuration" (*morphē tou skhēmatos*), but they no more really *are* these things than a carved hand, or a painted one.[11]

(iv) 6th level: animals (ta sunestētoka hola)

Finally the nonuniform parts are found assembled, organized and integrated into the complete living organism, the individual this or that. (For "this or that" naturally substitute his species, cf. §8.) The migration-barriers in the species take the form already sketched, that Socrates' (say) coming-to-be-Man is identical with his coming-to-exist, and when he ceases-to-be-Man, that individual ceases-to-exist (dies, presumably; for as field zoologists – as opposed to metaphysicians – we have no thought of, having never observed, such bizarre modes of extinction and genesis as were imagined in §7). When Socrates does die, what remains is not a man: "the corpse has the same superficial outward configuration [*scilicet*, as did the living being with which it is spatiotemporally continuous], but all the same it is *not* a man",[12] no more than the doctor in the drawing can be said to heal – at best, homonymously. And as already noted, this homonymy extends to the deepest of the underlying "parts": the nonuniform organs are no longer organs, the intermediate Bone(s) and Vein(s), etc., no longer Bone and Vein, and the uniform Blood and Bile, etc., no longer Blood or Bile.

---

asuntheta = *hosa diairetai eis homoiomerē*, e.g. *flesh*,
suntheta = *hosa eis anomoiomerē*, e.g. *hand* and *face*.

Many writers point out the similarity of the uniform–nonuniform dichotomy to the nineteenth-century physiologists' distinction between "tissues" and "organs".

11 *PA* i 1 640^{b}34–641^{a}3, ^{a}18–21, etc., *Meta.* Zeta 11 1036^{b}30–32, and of course "finger", *Meta.* Zeta 10 1035^{b}11, 24, "eye", *de An.* ii 1 412^{b}20–2, etc. We can, though, *know* it's a head or a hand without knowing whose head or hand it is, *Cat.* 7 8^{b}15–21.

12 *PA* i 1 640^{b}34. At *de Int.* 11 21^{a}23, though not that I know of in the biological writings, "dead man" is actually called self-contradictory.

§12. First principles of matter

Now we are in a position to do some philosophical anatomy and physiology on the concepts that are involved in Aristotelean anatomy and physiology of animals. For the concept of *form/matter* that figures in the integrative assembly of Aristotelean biological individuals, as just quickly sketched, involves several quite interesting points of theory.

(i) Hierarchical organization

One is this: the construction of an individual (ontologically speaking)[1] is by way of a hierarchical structure of stages, each of which is thought of as underlying the next as a "matter' for an "enmattered form" – thus the primary elements for the compound masses,[2] these for the uniform parts, etc., all the way up;[3] each stage is also described as existing "for the sake of" that above it (e.g. *PA* ii 1 646^{b}10–12), and all "for the sake of" the complete individual.[4] Such talk as this last, I would suggest, is not so

---

1 This is to allow for the divergence at certain points between the hierarchy as discernible in the finished product and the *temporal* sequence of stages in embryonic development – in which the earliest "parts" to articulate out (*diarthrousthai*) are actually the ontologically intermediate transitional or "interface" semistructures (level (iv) in the enumeration of §11), principally the primitive embryonic cardiovascular system. So far as possible, developmental topics and the biological ramifications of Fact 5 will be dealt with in §14; but owing to the many points of overlap with topics of structure and the ramifications of Facts 1 through 4, embryological matters inevitably creep in to a degree prior to them. For Aristotle on the methodological correctness of dealing with "being" before taking on "coming-to-be" (thus morphology before morphogenesis) cf. *PA* i 1 639^{b}11 ff., 640^{a}10 ff.

2 *Mixis* or *krasis* is already a rudimentary species of "form" (cf. §9, note 3): *Meta*. Eta 2 1042^{b}16, 23, *CTB/PA* i 10 238^{a}6–15, etc., and note 17 below. A good concise summary of the many-levelled aspect of Aristotelean matter is in Peck (1953), pp. 114–15.

3 *GA* i 1 715^{a}9 ff., *PA* ii 1 646^{b}5 ff., etc. Cf. *CTB/PA* i 5 321^{b}19 ff., where each of the "parts" is *ditton*, "double in its nature", both matter of what's over it, and form of what's beneath; also Joachim's (1922) note thereon, pp. 129–30. Also *Physics* ii 2 194^{b}9: "Matter is a relative term: to each form there corresponds a special matter" (after Hardie and Gaye).

4 At *PA* i 5 645^{b}15 ff. the whole *body* exists "for the sake of some complex (or complete) activity", *praxeōs tinos heneka polumerous* (or *plērous*). Cf. also Bonitz *Index* 62^{a}23 ff. (s.v. *anomoiomeres*), and §16 below.

much teleological as it is functional: beyond the inorganic compounds like wine and the like, which can be "what they are" *kath' hauta*, the nature of the uniform and nonuniform parts of animals invariably includes fitness to a "work", i.e. a specific contribution to the life of the total organism, separated from which the part no longer retains that nature or "is what it is" except by ambiguity; the "for the sake of" terminology is a variant on the same idea.[5] And regarding the terminology just now of "all the way up": in the vertical depiction we are sketching, the direction of "matter-to-end" can be represented as upward, but the direction of *formal* "causation" is *downward*: specific form determining overall organization, through the nature of the nonuniform structures so organized, "all the way down" through the particular sorts of uniform matters required to support those structures.[6] We shall return to this shortly (§12(ii) *fin.*).

(ii) Complexity of matter

Beyond this, however, we need mark also both a complexity and a degree of theoretical abstractness or attenuation in the form/matter notion, particularly in the notion of matter, in this biological theory that go considerably past anything in Empedocles, Aristotle's matter-concept's nearest ancestor – especially once we are past the interface between mass and count (concerning which there is shortly more to be said also). An aspect illustrative of this, which has many further ramifications also, is the following.

Beginning at the most primitive level, the "stuff" or "oatmeal" stage, we are used to the matter/form notion's intuitively including the idea of certain forms' *entailing restrictions on the sort of matter that will "take"*, as we say, *that form*: at the crudest level, where matter = stuff and form = shape, we know that a statue of Socrates, say,[7] can be formed from such materials as wood, marble, soap, bronze, snow, clay; whereas candidates like olive oil, air, dry sand, wine, mercury will infallibly frustrate even the craftiest of Moving Causes. So much is plainly *endoxon*, unquestioned lore ("can't make a saw out of wool or of wood" – *Meta* Eta 4).[8] But now beyond this,

---

5 The etymological derivation of *organon, organikon*, etc. from *ergon* and their accordant sense of "instrumental", has been frequently remarked; cf. also on *energeia*, §24(iii) below. "Nature seeks adaptedness (*to prosphoron*)", *HA* ix 12 615[a]25–6.

6 Kosman (1984), p. 143, appreciates this point, from a slightly different vantage.

7 Taking it that to be a statue of Socrates is pure-and-simple to be an inanimate solid having a surface conformation resembling to a sufficient degree the surface of Socrates (what is "sufficient" is of no concern here), and is independent of sculptor's or modeller's intent, circumstances of production etc. (Here "solid" excludes e.g. clouds; "inanimate", e.g. Socrates' lookalike twin Xocrates.) Cf. §20(i) on *Meta. Zeta* 3.   8 1044[a]29. Likewise *Phys.* ii 9 200[a]10, [b]5.

at the higher, more complicated stages, where matter = successively more complex structures and form = function or "work", an analogous relationship continues to prevail: the uniform tissues and nonuniform structures must be adapted to their functions and not only will not just anything do, but the requirements become exceedingly exacting and detailed: – if a function is *in-* and *di*-gestion, for example, then teeth and esophagus and stomach(s) need to be thus-and-so constructed; again, some structures are required to contribute to more than a single function (as teeth, for catching, for chewing, for defense); again, if an animal's specific manner of reproduction is of this or that kind, the requisite reproductive organs are accordingly restricted in their potential variety; again, the innumerable particular varieties of self-propulsion impose requirements of a very precise kind upon the structural layout and articulation of the skeletal and muscular systems involved; and so on indefinitely.[9] At the level of the finished product, that of the completed individual animal body, it too underlies as "matter"[10] a "form": the total life-style lived by individuals of that species, their total range of function; and thus constraints exist on the body as "matter" as a whole:

Take an illustration: A hatchet, in order to split wood, must, of necessity, be hard; if so, then it must, of necessity, be made of bronze or of iron. Now the body, like the hatchet, is an instrument; as well the whole body as each of its parts has a purpose, for the sake of which it is; the body must therefore, of necessity, be such and such, and made of such and such materials, if that purpose is to be realized.[11]

As is easily seen, a number of important strands come together at this locus or "topos" – namely, the idea of forms' either explicitly specifying, or else implicitly placing restrictions upon, the type of matter in which

9 Thus *aduneton badizein aneu podōn, GA* ii 3 736ᵇ24. These forms of explanation so permeate the works on animals that detailed references would be either interminable or largely random; for some further interpretive comment about them cf. §13(ii) below.

10 *DA* ii 1 412ᵃ16 ff., cf. §16 below. I speak typologically of the "life-style", meaning that complex set of capacities *for* the various activities, so-called "first actualization".

11 *PA* i 1 642ᵃ9–13 (Peck); cf. note 10 above. Also *PA* i 3 643ᵃ24–7.

12 The case of a form's restricting, without explicitly specifying, the type or the properties of the matter is discussed at numerous points in the biological writings in the terminology of "conditional" or "hypothetical necessity"; cf. the use of "of necessity" in the passage just quoted, and Peck's note thereon with further references; also *PA* i 1 639ᵇ21–640ᵃ9, and Balme (1972), pp. 76–82). The difficulty of the distinction between explicit and implicit restrictions by form on matter is all but too apparent in the notorious *Metaphysics* chapter devoted to the problem What Sorts of Parts Belong to the Form, and What Sorts Aren't Parts of the Form but of the Compound (*Meta.* Zeta 10–11). And the critical importance of the problem is of course attested to by (among other things) Aristotle's well-known morbid preoccupation with the snub nose – no fetish, but in this context illustrative of a serious crux: *concavity* carries no restrictions beyond surfaces in general, perhaps even including immaterial (= geometers') ones (cf. *Meta.* Epsilon 1 1025ᵇ28 foll.), but *snubness* has to be concavity in a nose, and thus becomes a persistently-

they are to be, can be, embodied; the unraveling of these strands is one of the central businesses of Aristotelean metaphysics.[12] To that we shall attend; but we cannot so much as commence unless it is clear that in speaking of "matter" in the present theoretical context, Aristotle can no longer be counted upon to mean the simple sort of thing we familiarly understand, lumps of rock, quantities of Water or Earth. – Rather, depending on the context the relevant "matter" may be, or include, something as complicated and highly organized as a complete organic system (cardiovascular, gastrointestinal, respiratory, skeletal-muscular, etc. ad lib.), or, ultimately, may be one of those most remarkably intricate total objects, against whose biological description in detail (even yet to be given) Aristotle issues that poignantly terse paper draft (even yet to be cashed), "an organized body, potentially having life in it".

The point is not difficult in principle, and would not require such emphasis here were it not for a pair of mutually opposing factors: on one hand the importance of the point in the actual application of the form-matter analysis to the biological objects that are the substances, and on the other a tendency among interpreters to stoutly persevere in reading "matter" as *stuff* or oatmeal or "goo", wherever encountered and regard-less of level; to instance only one distinguished interpreter, Sir David Ross in an otherwise laudable note on an important paragraph in *Meta.* Theta 7 (which we too shall examine – cf. §§20(ii), 23(i)), abruptly compromises the central intuition in his final clause:

The difference which Aristotle here points out is that between two levels at which the cleavage between substratum and attributes may be made. You may distin-guish accidental attributes from their subject, and in this case the subject is a substratum containing certain essential characteristics [= in *Categories* language, is a primary substance; cf. §§4, 6, 8]; or again you may distinguish the essential characteristics from the substratum to which they belong, and in this case the substratum is *bare unqualified matter*.[13]   (*AM* ii 257 (1049[a]26 n., my italics)

Not in the least: the idea involved is neither scientifically so simple-minded nor philosophically so disreputable as that last suggests (in my view there is in this theory no such thing as "bare unqualified matter" –

returned-to study object, for the very good reason that according to the theoretical framework that Aristotle is endeavoring to elaborate (*Meta.* Epsilon 1 *ibid.*) "*all* the natural things 'are said' (or 'are called [what they are]') like the snub, e.g. nose eye face flesh bone, and generally *animal*; and leaf root bark, and generally *plant* – for the formulae of none of these things are independent of movement but always include a matter" See §23(iv) for an effort to shed some light on these issues.

13 Both the basic mistake and a step in the direction necessary to correct it are made just earlier, *AM* ii 256, 1049[a]24–7 n.

nor, for all of that, in any other theory known to ancient Greek thought prior to Stoic physics – unless it be, possibly, Anaximander's).[14] Not that it cannot ever be simple; it is simple enough with the bronze and the statue, or the letters and the syllable, hence their usefulness as study objects. But with the biological objects that are the real substances, it is always exceedingly complicated, and terminology like "featureless" or "unqualified" in the connection with the concept of a matter is at very best unhelpful.

Another way of seeing the question is this. We can think of an individual organism as built up by way of the series of stages just described – though, as was cautioned at the beginning of §10 and just now in §12(i), what we are really looking at is the "reaching down" of the specific form as a whole. That is a determination of the whole nature of the organism: of all its "parts", through the nonuniform, through the semistructural, all the way to the uniform. Of course, at the base of the hierarchy, the organism is composed of E and W and A and F – everything in our sublunary region is so composed; the elements are not "used up" when the animal comes-to-be (for more about this aspect, see §20(iii)). But recall that all the *organic* parts (in our sense of "organic", i.e. "living") are tied to the existence of the whole (no blood or bone or hand except as parts of a living whole), and *all the "matters" above the EWAF are tied to their being informed by the whole form* – when death occurs, not only is the whole no longer (e.g.) an individual sheep, but with it disappear the organ systems and the organic matters, everything that was *"ditton"* (footnote 3). Looked at in this way, the entire hierarchy is within the form, and disappears from the matter as a whole with the form, and what is left is as close as we can get in Aristotle to "bare unqualified matter".[15] This is one of the points at which the "metaphysics of the biology" is more subtle and complex than the "metaphysics of the *Metaphysics*": for the organic matters that are *"ditton" do* come-to-be and pass away, whereas e.g. *Metaphysics* Zeta 8–9 says flatly that matter does not come-to-be or pass away; the reason, of course, is that Zeta 8–9 is thinking of simple matters like bronze. (It is even wrong about that, since bronze, an alloy of copper and tin as was known to the ancients, obviously is creatable and destructi-

14 Certainly Earth, Water etc. are not "bare and unqualified". And what is taken as "prime" is itself relative to the context of inquiry: in the context of biological objects, Aristotle more than once nominates for "prime matter" (however tentatively) the "natural constitution of the catamenia", *GA* i 20 729ᵃ33; cf. *Meta.* Eta 4 1044ᵃ34–5. Also *PA* ii 1 646ᵃ34; Peck (1963) (*GA* (Loeb)), pp. xi–xii, 110 n.

15 This may not be quite right as it stands; for although the dead body has none of the parts or materials of the *living* body (except EWAF), it might well be thought to have more form to it than *just* a heap of EWAF. There is no science of necrology, in the requisite sense, to which to appeal for an answer to this.

ble. When he wrote his theory of interelemental change in the CTB/PA, Aristotle even believed that EWAF could come-to-be and pass away.) We shall be back to this topic a number of times (§17(iii), §19, §22, §23, §24).

(iii) FORM needed to get above the 2nd level. Criticism of Empedocles

We saw in §10 that the material elements under the influences causing mixing and unmixing can build up in the way of "compounds" to compound *bulks* or masses – what Aristotle calls "heaps" – of a primitive order of differentiation, but no farther. Let us try the thought-experiment of imagining with Aristotelean imagination what the sublunary world would look like if the Empedoclean elements and the forces ("moving causes") driving their mixing and separation were all that there was. Those agencies could build up to rocks and rills, templed hills, puddles, ponds and oceans, earth and sky, the minerals and other materials *in* the earth, the clouds and other ephemera *of* the sky. (In fact, the Empedoclean elements and the efficient forces could very likely build up to the condition of the pre-biotic Earth, much as it is nowadays believed that it would have looked to the unaided vision of a time-traveller or other visitor, perhaps over 3×10^9 years ago, or to the condition of present-day Mars.) But that is the limit to what can be achieved by the "mixing together" and "distilling out" of homogeneous masses; in Aristotle's view, if there were no constitutive properties in the sense of §8, the sort of world described thus far in this paragraph would have to be all that there was: not a bad sort of world, with a certain amount going on in it by way of both "alteration" and "coming-to-be and passing away":[16] transform-

---

16 As Joachim pointed out long ago ((1922), pp. xxxvi f.), the work CTB/PA is in fact mainly concerned with generation and destruction at this level, of *homoiomerē*, and thus at most in a preliminary way with substances in our sense. The distinction between *genesis* and *alloiōsis* in i 3 uses an anti-migration condition (319b6 ff.) not supplemented with a condition concerning individuativeness, and the examples in the ensuing discussion oscillate between "the body" (which might imply such a condition) and "the bronze" (which presumably does not). It is stated that it is the *material* cause that is being sought (318a2, 9–10), and the governing sense of *ousia* in the work is stated in ii 8 to be one in which Earth is *contrary* to Air, and Water contrary to Fire, *hōs endekhetai ousian ousiai enantion einai*, "in the sense that a substance can be *contrary* to a substance" (335a5) – in evident conflict with *Cat.* 3b24, were the explanation not to hand, that we are dealing with the material substructure of the organic world and not with the complex organic substances themselves, as "composited by nature" (*hai phusei sunestōsai ousiai*, ii 1, 328b32; cf. Joachim's note thereon, pp. 191–3). (On the "contrariety" point, Joachim follows Philoponus' rationale: that the opposition involved is that of the deeper-underlying "moist versus dry", etc. – 331a1–3 n., 218, and §22(iii) below.)

ation of compounds, seasonal changes, lunar, solar and planetary motions, weather, erosion, et al. (think again of present-day Mars). But the leap is immense from here to such phenomena as Fact 1 (a world swarming with sharply defined biological individuals), and Fact 2 (having intricate specifically determined development, form and function), and Fact 3 (their demonstrated degree of complexity and organization), a jump that to Aristotle plainly requires a further and higher-order type of explanatory rationale than "mixing" and "unmixing"; hence the hypothesis of a distinct type of causal agency, called form,[17]

That this is indeed Aristotle's outlook comes out especially clearly in his reaction to Empedocles' own attempt to account for the building-up of the natural world-as-we-find-it, using a theoretical framework having only the four material elements and the two forces, Love and Strife, that drive processes of commingling and separation. His story is of *evolution*: according to it, in the portion of the cosmic cycle leading down to our own day,[18] the four elements began by being wholly Mixed together (we may call this *Phase E-1*), under the total ascendancy of Love, as undifferentiated as possible (DK frr. 27, 29). Then (*Phase E-2*) Separation began to occur, owing to Strife (DK frr. 30, 31), and different regions of the cosmos began to have different local mixtures of elements – that is, mixtures differing in the *ratio* or *proportion* of elements; at this point (*Phase E-3*) the influence of Love was found in local regions where elements were *drawn* together to form compounds, both inorganic and (*Phase E-4*) organic, such as Bone, whose formula (for this see below) is (fr. 96):

$$E_2 W_2 A_0 F_4.$$

The next evolutionary step (*Phase E-5*) was when these bits of organic matter, as commingled at E-4, in turn mixed up into miscellaneous animal 'parts' on their own ("faces without necks", "arms without shoulders", fr. 57); these 'parts' then in turn (*Phase E-6*) mixed up into random combinations, or "Scrambled Animals" ("ox-kind with human faces", "of human form with ox-heads", fr. 61, 59). Most of these monsters were of course functionally mal-adapted and did not survive, or even if otherwise successful, died off because unable to reproduce (fr. 61.3–4). But (*Phase E-7*) in a very small fraction of cases, creatures were thus "mixed together" that happened to be both well-adapted and

17 Recall that *mixis* or *krasis* is already a primitive species of "form", note 2 above.
18 In order to get on with the account, I pass over in silence a number of difficult and controversial issues in the interpretation of the "Cycle".

reproductively viable; these are those that have survived, and their progeny are among us – and *include* us – today.

The key to this account is of course the idea that compounds and complexes of elements are defined by the *"formula"* or *"ratio"* or *"proportion* of the mixture", *logos tēs mixeōs*; it is uncertain whether the actual phrase is Empedocles', for it is found earliest in allusions by Aristotle.[19] But there is no question that the idea is active in the *Peri Phuseōs*; the statement of the formulae of Bone and of Blood (fr. 96, 98) is explicit, including the assignment of numerical values. On what ground, then, does Aristotle, departing from his usual levelheaded language, call Empedocles' theory such immoderate names as "inconceivable", "clearly impossible", "absurd", "fantastic"?[20] *Not* because it is evolutionary, deviating from the true view that present-day species are eternal, did not come-to-be, have always been and will always be;[21] the problem is more fundamental: the account evinces *no* appreciation of the difference between *mixture* and *structure*.

We can accept for argument's sake (though it is clear from §11(i) that it is more complicated than this) that the Blood of some species of animal, say, Horse, is, in part, accurately defined by an Empedoclean formula, of the type $E_xW_yA_zF_w$; there is an understandable sense in which that *is* a simple mixture of elements, in the proportion x-y-z-w (even though, to Aristotle, that is *not* what blood *is* – i.e., the point that nothing can be blood that is not enpsyched by the psyche of a complete living thing. Leaving that aside, then): such a compound can be called homogeneous (or with Aristotle, homoeomerous), in no particularly technical way but in the sense that any portion of it is much like any other portion – as a consequence, a small sample of it will serve as an adequate representative of the whole mixture (this is why a "blood sample" is all that is needed to diagnose the condition of *all* the blood of a given horse).[22] Mixture, the same throughout, is all there is to it, and Empedocles' analysis is adequate (so far as the present contrast is concerned, not that Aristotle has no further objections, see §11).

But when we come to deal with a complete animal, that is something

---

19 *PA* i 1 642ª18–24; *DA* i 4 408ª13–18; cf. *Meta.* A 10 993ª17–18.

20 These epithets being variously drawn from *GA* i 18 722ᵇ17–30, *Phys.* ii 8 198ᵇ34, *Cael.* iii 2 300ᵇ25 ff. Observe that in the last, *dunaton ē* should be omitted in line 26, as it is by the OCT and Budé, and is not by the Oxford translator. The words, which are in neither MS E nor either the lemma or the paraphrase of Simplicius, in any case subvert the sense.

21 *GA* ii 1, *DA* ii 4; cf. §16 – reference is to the gennetic capacity of individuals *as* a sort of threptic capacity of the eternal species.

22 *Pace PA* ii 2 647ᵇ33–35. (Here I am ignoring the thesis that "drawn blood is not blood".)

else. A *horse* is obviously more than a mixture, and not homogeneous at all: it has a *structure* without which the same elements in the same proportions certainly do not add up to a horse. This is easily seen by the simple if distressing expedient of putting the horse through a large grinder, and carefully preserving all the material coming out the other side – whereby are obtained exactly the four elements composing the original horse, in exactly the same ratios as before; but no one will mistake that quantity of matter for a horse. For the *structure* has been destroyed. In this sense the horse is *heterogeneous* – consisting of diverse parts, that have to be organized in a particular and very definite manner. This is a higher-order compound than a mixture. (There is no such thing as a "horse-sample", on the order of a "blood-sample".) A similar point holds for such "parts" of animals as head, neck, thorax, leg – these are structural also, not just mixtures like blood.

The point of belaboring the obvious at even this little length is that this difference, between mixture and structure, is evidently entirely unapparent to Empedocles, who goes straight from *blood* and *bone* as material mixtures of elements, to *heads* and *legs* as further material mixtures of elements, to *whole organisms* are still further material mixtures of elements, without seeming to notice the conceptual difference and added dimension of complexity that comes in with the latter type of case, and certainly without making it explicit.

This is the point of Aristotle's severe and even vitriolic criticism: Empedocles' scheme of *elements* and *ratios* is the earliest clear pre-figuring of the scheme that Aristotle means to exploit to the uttermost, of *matter* and *form*. But Aristotelean *form* means *structure* – that is, *biological* structure – and that concept is altogether lacking in Empedocles.[23] As long as simple "mixing" is all that is recognized, Aristotle argues, there is no rational explanation of the repeatable "complete organic structure", *hē holē morphē*, of "subcomponents and substructures", *moria kai skeuē*, the "composition and substance of the whole", *hē sunthesis kai tēs holēs ousia*.[24] The *"logos* of the mixture" is only the crudest beginning.

In sum, to fail to realize that causal agencies beyond the mixing of uniform elements are required to explain the most basic features of the biosphere, is to miss completely the significance of Facts 1 through 3. Beyond this, Empedocles' theory of generation and animal development fails to come to grips with Facts 4 and 5:

23 At least, from the evidence we have – but also, from the evidence Aristotle had, which presumably was more than we have. It is plain that he went through Empedocles' verses thoroughly, looking for that concept, and that he did not find it. And he knew what he was looking for.   24 Thus *PA* i 1 640b22–9, i 5 645a30–6 (whence the quoted expressions).

So, Empedocles was wrong when he said that many of the characteristics belonging to animals are due to some accident in the process of their formation, as when he accounts for the vertebrae of the backbone by saying, 'the fetus gets twisted and so the backbone is broken into pieces': he failed to realize (a) that the seed which gives rise to the offspring must have within itself the appropriate type of power; and (b) that the producing agent was pre-existent: it was prior not only in formula, but in time: that is, *human being begets human being*, so that it's because the former is such as he is, that the latter's coming-to-be goes as it does.[25]

(There is a notable parallel between Aristotle's physico-biological argument against Empedocles, and the argument for "forms as causes" at *Phaedo* 96–102. Both operate in the framework of a broad contrast between moving/material "causes" on one hand and formal/final ones on the other; and for both, the two are related as "the real cause" (here, form) and "that without which the real cause couldn't cause" (here, matter) (cf. *Phaedo* 99b, and §19(ii)).)

25 *PA* i 1 640$_a$20–7 (partially after Peck).

§13. First principles of Form

(i) Uniform and nonuniform: a closer look

A conspicuous feature of the succession of stages that are descried in the constitution of a biological object is the advent of "non-uniform parts". Now we must look a little more deeply into the concept of "non-uniformity", the an-homoiomerous, for it is at the core of our concern.

Aristotle nowhere addresses himself to a full-scale analysis of this important idea, being apparently content to convey its gist with schematic intimations of the form, "such as resolve into parts unlike the whole", together with examples (of the kind already cited in §11). From his practice, however, we can make out some of the features that seem to figure significantly in his understanding of it. (1) The simplest and most obvious feature of something non-uniform in Aristotle's sense is *spatial* heterogeneity or regionalization: differences among its spatial portions; in the case of higher organisms as wholes, animal bodies tend to be organized, and component organs tend to be distributed, along geometrical axes of orientation with respect to which they display characteristic symmetries and (especially) asymmetries – (a) an antero-posterior axis, for the most part associated with the direction of locomotion and orientation of the digestive apparatus, along which animals are generally asymmetrical with respect to fore and aft, (b) a dorso-ventral axis, for the most part associated with the direction of gravity, along which animals are generally asymmetrical with respect to top and bottom; finally (c) a plane of (for the most part) bilateral symmetry, right and left.[1] Similar geometrical characteristics are found in the various organic parts, although some terminological conflation is evident in Aristotle's discussion of this instance between the bipolarity of any linear axis and the bilateral symmetry of certain organ pairs (Kidneys, et al.) or of organs that tend to come in halves (Brain, et al.).[2] For both organic parts and organic wholes, however, such geometric distributions are highly pervasive, and are in natural objects one source of the fact that dividing the object results in "parts unlike the whole".

(2) Closely connected with this in anything nonuniform is the presence of properties that are in various ways irreducibly structural, in the sense of originating in the way in which parts are organized or distributed or related or composed, and not attributable to the same parts in a different arrangement, nor dependent directly (though almost always indirectly or mediately, cf. §12(ii) above) on the more elementary materials involved. It is this aspect which Aristotle, unlike ourselves perhaps, seems to conceive of as coming in stages or degrees: there are the fully structural nonuniform parts of animals ("Head, Hand") which resolve into parts different not only from the whole but also from one another; then there are the semistructures ("Bone, Bloodvessel") which, according to him, have parts that *are* like one another and that (for that reason?) can be said "in a way" to be like the whole as well.[3] In either event, the further factor that is invariably present in any nonuniform entity (of whatever "grade") – whether it be arrangement, organization, composition or (in biological cases) some highly complex "form" consisting of a number of these, is not yet another part, but goes to the integration of the parts – in Aristotle's language, not another "element", but a "principle". It comes in enormous variety ("there are *many* differentiae", *Meta* Eta 2 1042^{b}15–25), and is of course *the* central preoccupation of the metaphysics.[4]

---

1 Bipolarity with respect to each of three axes (Aristotle calls it being *diphues*, or *dimeres*), *PA* iii 5 667^{b}31–4; iii 7 669^{b}18–21; *IA* 2 704^{b}17 ff.; symmetry and asymmetry, *HA* i 15 493^{b}17–25. Cf. *isophues*, *HA* i 13 493^{a}23. Not all forms manifest these differences along all three axes, e.g. the radially-arranged sea-urchin, *PA* iv 5 680^{b}9; cephalopods are variants with respect to up and down, *GA* ii 6 741^{b}33; and the first two axes are interchanged in Man, who walks erect, *HA* ii 1 498^{b}11 (more accurately, of course: the other forms deviate from the organization in Man, which is the most natural, *PA* ii 10 656^{a}10–13). (I continue to leave aside plants, cf. §9.)

2 *PA* iii 7 669^{b}13–670^{a}7.

3 Cf. §11(ii), and the passages from *PA* ii there cited (646^{b}30 ff., 654^{a}32 ff., for "Viscera", "Vein", "Bone").   4 See §24, and §13(ii) *fin.* below.

(3) A third conspicuous aspect of the nonuniform as manifested in higher organisms is specialization of various regions or tracts of animal bodies to furnish highly specific adaptedness to specific functions: different "parts" being given over to locomotion, ingestion, digestion, reproduction, sensation and so forth, each in a very definite and particularized manner according to the species in question. The phenomenon is that of *differentiation*, and Aristotle's knowledge of the gross features thereof accessible to megascopic anatomical and physiological observation in a great variety of species is vivid and detailed. (He is quite unaware of the underlying cellular basis of *cyto*-differentiation, knowing, as he does, nothing of cells themselves, and equally unaware of the evolutionary mechanisms involved in bringing about the phenomenon in its currently observable state in the animal kingdom, knowing nothing of organic evolution as well.) His interest in the phenomenon is twofold. Chiefly, first, to understand the "causes" responsible for these observed facts, *why* it is that the organic parts subserving the various functions in the various particular species are shaped and formed just as they are, and *how* it is that the functional differences of habitat, life-style, diet, methods of reproduction and so forth in each species are causally related to the manner of construction of the whole body and its parts of the animal of that species and to one another. A second interest is differentiation in the embryological sense: the processes of generation, by which pairs of species members produce offspring that are specific replicas, differentia by differentia, of themselves; this motivates a study of the course of events in embryonic development through which the offspring gradually assume specific form over time from conception to completion, and a theoretical inquiry into the "causal" factors that must be at work here also, *why* it happens thus.

Not everything that eventuates from Aristotle's pursuit of these two subjects is germane to our philosophical purposes here; those points which are so will occupy the remainder of this and the following two sections. Also, the biological topic of differentiation itself is exceedingly deep and complicated; if we are to avoid drowning in the depths and wandering among the complications it is necessary that we restrict our attention to a few essential points of principle. On that understanding, however, it is useful to pursue the topic a little further; for the fact is that Aristotle does apparently come to conceptualize what he calls "differentia" in a way that is comparable (as well as contrastable) with the concept that is current today in speaking of the differentiation of tissues, tracts and organs, meaning specification and specialization of function through adaptive-in-effect articulation and diversification of structure, and this fact has a consequential impact on the advanced metaphysical theory of substance. It also seems as if the Aristotelean notion of differentia may have undergone some noteworthy changes, as between its character in such more programmatically-oriented works of his as the *Topics* and *Analytics* and the (maturer, very likely) form in which we are considering it; failure to appreciate these developments can foster some troublesome and persistent interpretive misconceptions that need to be circumvented if we are to proceed.

(ii) Something important has happened to Differentia

The idea of differentia is, if not commonplace, familiar; it goes away back before Aristotle to the Academy and the method of Dichotomous Division, according to which by importation of successive qualifying characters a generic kind is subdivided and subdivided again, resulting finally in smallest kinds of which the whole procedure is thus supposed to constitute an analysis or "definition". It needs no chronicling here that this technique is discussed, refined and elaborated at length by Aristotle in the Organon, and that his celebrated resulting theory of definition and classification, *per genus et differentiam*, passed down through his own text and the influence of Porphyry, the Greek commentators and the medieval tradition, heavily influenced the classical systematic taxonomy associated with Linnaeus that is widely familiar in natural-history connections today. Partly for this reason perhaps (abetted, in this century, by the Jaegerian *Entwicklungs*-scenario and his accompanying chronology of the treatises), it has frequently been thought that a main objective of Aristotelean biology must have been systematic taxonomy too, and the biological treatises the record of its beginnings at ordering, classifying and cataloguing the natural-historical data. However, recent work on this topic, dating from 1960 to the present, points in a quite different direction; and this provides a useful setting for the hypothesis I wish to pursue, that there may have occurred a considerable transformation in the Aristotelean concept of differentia itself, from its original provenance in the Academy and its aspect in such early contexts of discussion as the *Topics* and *Analytics*, to its employment here.

(The reader unfamiliar with these recent developments in the interpretation of Aristotle's biology is here forewarned that a crucial issue is precisely whether in Aristotle the technical terms *genos* and *eidos* themselves always, *or even ever*, bear the senses associated with *genus* and *species* in European biological discussion since the sixteenth century. Of course, given the unquestionable historical affiliation abbreviated in the previous paragraph, it would be at least implausible to contend that the two pairs of terms had no meaning-overlap at all. But it is very important to sustain the awareness that the theoretical context in which Aristotle adapted and reshaped these Platonic inheritances of *genos* and *eidos* was basically very different from that in which the modern concepts of *genus* and *species* have developed. Although in the discussion that follows I will not altogether refrain from "genus" and "species" as translations, the fact should be borne in mind that their meaning is by no means a closed issue.)

According to the standard discussion of differentia in the Organon, a highest genus (e.g., Animal) is divided by differentiae into pairs of subaltern genera,[5] each of which is further divided and sub-divided, forming a series of subordinate ranks (*genē hup' allēla*), until the infimae ("lowest") species are reached. Before such a division can be carried out the genera must be correctly recognized through a process of collecting the species: the species must be examined for common characteristics and thereby grouped in genera; these genera are then grouped under higher genera, and so on up to the summum ("highest") genus. In collecting, attention has to be given not only to traditional groupings recognized in common language, but also to any other cases in which common characters occur. Finally, the differentiae must be taken in the right order in the final division; if so taken, the last differentia will express the infima species.

As interpreters have studied the biological writings for applications of this program, as just described, to the classification of animals, they have soon discovered that these are rarely to be found. First to be abandoned is the insistence on exclusively pairwise or *dichotomous* division, for reasons thoroughly spelled out at the outset of PA (i 2–3);[6] much more fundamentally, the notion is also evidently dropped that something has gone radically wrong if the same differentia should show up at more than one branch of the tree – rather, as it proves, the facts force us to countenance a distressingly large extent (for a believer in Division) of *epallaxis tois genesin*, crossover of types (*GA* ii 1, 732^{b}15 ff.), thoroughly at variance with the strict and orderly structure envisaged in the Academy and those more "programmatically oriented" discussions of Aristotle's just mentioned.

In fact, since the early nineteenth century the impression has grown that, looked at from a systematic standpoint, the employment of the many hundreds of differentiae that figure in the biological discussions is so

5 Here I draw freely upon the clear account of the method in Balme (1960).
6 We shall return shortly to the sense in which Aristotle "rejects dichotomy".

disorderly, inconsistent and at variance with Aristotle's own theory of classification as to be, on the kindest estimate, something of a shambles; and this fact has occasioned much puzzlement among students of the zoology operating on the assumption that systematics must indeed have been one of the main objectives of the treatises. By all odds the foremost of these until recent times was J.B. Meyer,[7] who argued that the great majority of characteristics brought in as differentiae were not meant to form parts of formal ("artificial", *kunstlich*) divisions or definitions of kinds, but were intended as descriptive characters (*Merkmale*) guiding an informal, inductive grouping; the effect of the argument was to try to save the system by greatly reducing the number of characters supposed to figure in it as "essential", and at the same time to give better weight than the traditional approach to Aristotle's oft-repeated insistence that *many* lines of differentiation, and not the single one that is developed by a Division, are needed to characterize animal specimens (thus any real animal kind will be defined by many and various characters, never by a single one).[8]

Meyer's attempt was valiant and his view probably the best along this line that could be hoped for, but many problems remained. The number of groups that survived on his account as genuinely defined genera of species was exceedingly small, and those few still shot through with inconsistencies.[9] And Meyer's would-be distinction between differentiae that really belong in the definitory "essence" of a specific kind and those that are merely descriptive, does not seem to be anywhere supported in the text (although the idea of many simultaneous lines of differentiation certainly is).[10] The effort to make sense of Aristotle's employment of differentia in biology on the premiss that he was out to construct any sort of taxonomic or classificatory system remained almost wholly unsuccessful, and continued to remain so for more than a century after Meyer's gallant campaign.[11]

This entire situation has now been greatly clarified, in two main directions, negative and positive. The negative stage began with the pioneering work in the 1960s of Balme,[12] who made a thorough case that

7 Jürgen Bona Meyer (1855) (*Aristoteles' Thierkunde*). This high estimate of Meyer's work is not eccentric: cf. Balme (1960), p. 201 (in Barnes, Schofield and Sorabji (1975), vol. 1, pp. 185f.); Pellegrin (1982), p. 14, note 11.

8 Meyer (1855), pp. 76–111, 330 ff.; cf. *PA* i 3 643^b ff. This is what *Meta.* Eta 2 calls the "*manyness of differentia*", and is very important; below, pp. 102–104, §24.

9 Balme (1960), 202–5 (in Barnes, Schofield and Sorabji (1975), vol. 1, pp. 186–8).

10 Thus also Balme (1972), 101–9; below, pp. 102–104.

11 The best account and critique of the leading taxonomic interpretations of Aristotle in modern times is that of Pellegrin (1982), ch. 1.

not only are the groupings of animals in the Natural History not intended as systematic classifications or "Divisions", but that they *could* not serve such a purpose, for a basic reason frequently pointed out by Aristotle himself: they will not form a taxonomic *hierarchy*, any attempt at a hierarchical arrangement of the classes or "kinds" on the basis of division, will go down to defeat by the *epallaxis*, the criss-cross nature of the cuts.[13]

Subsequently, Balme sharpened this interpretation when he recognized that the focus of the criticism of *PA* i 2–3 really is not Division as such at all, but what Aristotle *calls* Dichotomy, and that in a quite special sense. The wisdom of Balme's revised view cannot be condensed:

. . . [Aristotle's] criticism holds not necessarily against division *into two* classes as such, but against division *by one differentia at a time* – whether into two classes or more. Instead he recommends dividing at the outset by many differentiae simultaneously, then further differentiating all these differentiae as required. His method is to be contrasted with any kind of division made by single differentiae, whether dichotomous or polychotomous.

. . . The method that he proposes instead is itself another form of division. It seems more likely therefore that his purpose here is to apply the logical technique of division to zoology, and to show that it must be conducted by multiple differentiae if it is to work.

Aristotle's aim in using division, then, does not seem to be classification, but definition. The first sentence [of *PA* i 2] states this aim – "to obtain the particular", i.e. to grasp, mark out by attributes, and so reveal the essential nature of a given *infima species*. This is always his aim in division.[14]

There is more to say about these positive suggestions concerning "multiple differentiae", but let us first deal with the rest of the negative aspect of the matter, that Aristotle's project is not taxonomic. Enlarging upon Balme's work, Pellegrin has made a case for this that seems to me definitive and final.[15] It is not that Aristotle does not classify – to the

---

12 Balme (1960), later revised in Barnes etc. (1975), and Balme (1962). A conspectus partly based on Balme's work is also given in Peck (1965), v ff.

13 E.g. *HA* i 6 490^{b}9; ii 1 501^{a}22; *GA* iv 6 774^{b}17; ii 1 732^{b}28 (cited above); cf. citations in Balme (1960), 206 n. 25; cf. 209 n. 33. As Pellegrin dryly remarks (p. 146), a taxonomistic Aristotle "obviously could not have left this problem alone after having pointed it out".

14 Balme (1972) (*PAGA I*), 101, 105.

15 Pellegrin (1982) (*La Classification des Animaux chez Ar.*). Here a bibliographic (or bibliogenic?) aside is appropriate, because the independent origin of some interpretive theses of Pellegrin's and my own, which are on the whole quite harmonious, might be considered as contributing to them some, perhaps small, probative value. Of Part III of this book, §§9–15(ii) was largely complete in its present form in 1976; §§10–13 was discussed (with a preface from §9) at the Princeton conference of December 1976 mentioned in §9, note 6, as well as various later venues. As I labored onward with the later portions of the book, I was aware of the appearance of Pellegrin's work, but did not register its fundamental contribution to the matters treated here in

contrary, "Aristotle classifies the animals, and he classifies them well" (195, E159), but his groupings are various, diverse and obviously not directed at a unitary system because they are occasioned by different investigative purposes at different places; they are "not taxonomic, because rather than distributing the animals into the compartments of a unique and fixed construction, they are orderings occasioned by the circumstances [*conjoncturelles*], adapting their extension and their rigor to the needs of the exposition under way" (141, E115).[16]

Balme and Pellegrin have also made a convincing case that *genos* and *eidos* in Aristotle's biological treatises really do not fit the pigeonholes of the modern *genus* and *species*; rather, *genos* is used for any kind that is subject to further division, and the *eidē* are the kinds into which it divides, which may themselves be subject to further division, and thus themselves be *genē*. (Since the same kind may on this footing be both, it is small wonder that interpretations proceeding on the assumption that *genos* and *eidos* should always denote fixed positions on a taxonomic tree should quickly lead to chaos.) The lower limit to this is of course the *atoma eidē*, which cannot be further divided.[17]

The details of that (the negative) part of the case can be pursued in the works cited; but the basic question remains: "What then *was* he doing," as Balme asks, "with all these differentiae?"

The answer seems to be threefold. The simplest part has to do with method: he uses the differentiae to group the animals in various ways because so many of the phenomena to be discussed are common to many forms; to try to discuss each animal *in toto seriatim* would be impossibly lengthy and repetitive.[18] Beyond this, however, there are two further aspects to the matter of a more theoretical kind, one of which is discussed by Balme, the other of which Pellegrin has in part brought into focus, and is what I am calling the apparent change in the Aristotelean concept of differentia already once or twice alluded to.

First, as Balme went on to argue (in my estimation correctly), a broad

§13 until this was forcibly called to my attention by Lennox's review (Lennox (1984)). At that point I acquainted myself with *La Classification*, a most agreeable experience, and added the portions here that refer to it (and sundry other references where germane). Then as the final copy of my book was being prepared for press, I learned that an English translation of a revised *La Classification* was in preparation by A. Preus for the University of California Press; through their kindness I have seen that translation in proof and have thus been enabled to add some page references to the English edition (marked "E", though my own bumpy translations are mostly unaltered).

16 For the argument, see Pellegrin (1982), 139–48 (E113–20).

17 Pellegrin (1982), 90–9, E63–9.

18 E.g. *PA* i 4 644ª23–ᵇ15; cf. i 1 639ᵇ1–640ª9. Cf. Pellegrin (1982), e.g. 39–40 (E24).

and basic purpose of Aristotle's detailed discussion of combinations of differentiae found in the various animal species, largely missed by the taxonomists, is to ponder the *causal* significance of these combinations: the systematic interrelatedness of the differentiae constitute a valuable clue to the real nature of the species in the sense of its specifically typical manner of interactive functioning ("doing business") with its environment. Examples illustrating the method in operation can be followed up in the concluding part of Balme's paper;[19] here let an imaginary example convey the general idea in principle: a certain (species of) animal (i) lives in a habitat that offers food of such-and-such a kind, (ii) his dentition is adapted to masticate such food, (iii) his dentition as a consequence of (ii) is unsuited for defense, (iv) he has horns for defense, (v) the food of such-and-such a kind is difficult to digest, (vi) he has two stomachs and is thus adapted to digest such food, (vii) as a consequence of (vi) he is bulky and slow, (viii) his feet, broad and flat, will support a heavy body weight, etc., etc. – It is not my aim here to pursue the particulars of the various causal connections that Aristotle looks for among the numbered characteristics in this type of instance, and I have accordingly used "consequence" or "thus" only in a couple of obviously noncontroversial clauses. The present point is that Aristotle is convinced that the various differentiae, both of structure and of function, *are* causally interrelated with one another in a highly sensitive way in every species and that the study of their combinations can thus lead the zoologist to an understanding of what the relevant causal influences are in each case.

The other aspect to differentia in the biological connection is this. The original, "logical" concept of differentia is basically that of a "difference from";[20] suppose Number as a genus divides into Odd and Even as species,[21] then the differentia of Even (say, Factorable By Two) represents a difference of Even *from* Odd, something that distinguishes this *from* that co-ordinate kind. It is in this meaning, of contrariety or opposition, that differentia is appropriately seen as "a sort of otherness";[22] and the idea goes over naturally to the case of the animals: a differentia would be a respect in which this type of animal is different *from that* one. Here we are close to the original idea of "definition", as a quasi-literal "drawing of boundaries" that will in principle "include" what is defined and "exclude" all else; also related is the notion of obtaining definitions by the

19 Balme (1960), pp. 209–210; in Barnes, Schofield and Sorabji (1975), pp. 190–1.
20 Cf. Pl. *Tht.* 208c foll., et al. 21 Pl. *Euthyphro* 12c, *Topics* 142b10.
22 *Meta.* Gamma 2 1004a21; cf. Bonitz, *Index* 192b23 ff. (s.v. *diaphora*). (Cf. also the everyday use of "variety".) The "otherness" connection is pursued at length using *Meta.* Iota in Pellegrin (1982), ch. 2.

"dividing" (*diairesis*) or "cutting" (the *tomē*, though not necessarily *dikhotomē*) of kinds; and indeed in some early works of Aristotle the concepts of both "definition" and "differentia" are more or less equated with that of Division.[23]

Now, in the writings with which we here have mainly to do, this intuition, of so-to-speak *horizontal*, interspecific, differentiation of co-ordinate kinds, "this from that", certainly is not lost. But I think it is also joined by a new and so-to-speak *vertical* dimension, in which it bears something nearer its modern sense, namely what we are calling adaptive-in-effect articulation and diversification of structure: it connotes a manner in which relatively undetermined, only generically characterized structures are variously specialized and specified – in this sense the focus is accordingly upon what a given differentia is a difference *of*: here, of *an underlying generic potentiality, and the differentiae are the particular manners in which that potentiality is found to be restricted or reduced.* Accordingly, the notion of differentia has moved somewhat, from its older association with ideas like "dividing" and "cutting" with respect to kinds, toward something more like an "articulating-out", "articulation" (*diarthrōsis*) of a specifically typical structure in a specifically typical organism, from a lesser-defined substrate potential receiving that finishing-off as final form. Differentia comes to connote determination as well as discrimination, shaping as well as sorting. Cloven-footed is differentiated *from* not-cloven; but both are differentiae *of* foot.[24]

This shift in the central focus of differentia, from being basically a classificatory concept to being one of construction as well, is of considerable import and needs to be borne steadily in mind. (Yet it is no complete surprise in principle. It was already foreshadowed in a point made about "constitutive properties" in §8 – we do not in this theory assume automatically to hand a stock of completed individuals that are just "there", for us merely to "sort"; rather, there is a problem about how such things are built up, it is necessary to understand their construction as well as their discrimination. The later concept of differentia comes to be a key factor in the theory of "Formal Causation" meant to deal with this requirement.) Looking ahead momentarily to the advanced stage of

23 E.g., *Posterior Analytics* ii 13; cf. the Oxford translator's note on 97ª1.

24 *Meta.* Zeta 12, 1038ª14–15. Difference not otherness: *Meta.* Iota 3, 1054ᵇ23 foll. Genus as *underlying* the differentiae: *Meta.* Delta 6 1016ª25–8. Cf. Gould's (1976) vivid evocation of structure/form *versus* flux/process in nineteenth- and twentieth-century biology. Also Pellegrin (1982), pp. 45–6.

My allusions to the vertical or constructional moment in differentia as "new", "advanced" and the like are not to be taken as speculative chronology or a hypothesis about Aristotle's "development"; recall §0 on this.

development of the theory represented by *Metaphysics* Eta 2, the constructional or organizational moment in differentia is quite marked:

Evidently though, there are *many* differentiae, e.g., (i) some things are constituted
[lit. "are said"] by a composition of the matter, as are such things as are
constituted ["said"] by *blending*, like honeywater, (ii) others by *tying*, like the
bundle, (iii) others by *gluing*, like a book, (iv) others by *nailing*, like a box, (v)
others by more than one of these, (vi) others by *position*, like a threshold or lintel
(for these 'differ' by being placed thus-&-so), (vii) others by *time*, like dinner and
breakfast, (viii) others by *location*, like the winds, (ix) others by the affections
[proper] to sensible things, like hardness & softness, and density & rarity, and
dryness & wetness, and [of these], some by some of these [affections], others by
them all, and in general, some by excess, others by defect . . . Of some things the
'being' (*to einai*) will even be defined by all of these [marks], in that some [parts]
are mixed, some blended, some bound, some solidified, and some employing the
other differentiae, as are Hand, or Foot.   (Eta 2 1042^{b}15–31; cf. §24(i).)

As this critically important passage also makes clear, the "manyness of
differentia" is not only inter-specific, but *intra-specific*: each atomic form is
determined by a large multiplicity of determinations – to take the gross
structural ones alone, there are those of Head and Limb and Esophagus
and Lung . . . And it is this aspect of the phenomenon that is the real
reason for the rejection of dichotomy, as the criticism thereof in *PA* i 3
explicitly states ("Each of these (kinds) has been marked off [*hōristai*,
defined] by *many differentiae*, which dichotomy cannot do", 643^{b}12–13).
As Pellegrin observes, "ultimately, it is this one-dimensional character of
dichotomy that is its fundamental vice, from which all the others flow",
and he aptly sees an Aristotelean multi-differential definition as "closing
in on a reality from several sides" at once, as "*poly-gonal* in the proper sense
of the term". What I have been calling a "line of differentiation" seems to
be the same as what Pellegrin calls an "axis of division".[25] And my
emphatic attendance to what I have been calling the "constructional or
organizational moment in differentia", finds a most harmonious counter-
part in Pellegrin's calling attention to divisions and differentiations as
importantly focused upon the animals' *parts*.[26]

By laying such heavy emphasis on the structural character of
differentiae I do not mean to suggest that all the differentiae Aristotle
discusses are morphological; he devotes much attention as well to func-

25 Pellegrin (1982) analyzes and discusses in detail *PA* i 3 643^{b}9–19: pp. 41–8 (E26–32),
and makes the connection with the problematic of Zeta 12 ("how can a complex essence, with
many differentiae, be *one*?") which will occupy us in §23.
26 Pellegrin (1982), pp. 62–3, 125, 143, 153–4, 188–9 (the "moriologie étiologique").

tional and ethological characteristics, "differentiae with respect to manners of life and dispositions and activities" (*kata tous bious kai ta ēthē kai tas
praxeis*) (*HA* i 1 487ᵃ10, etc.) – habitat, nutrition, socialization, breeding
characteristics, etc., etc. – the whole range of complex behavior that so
sharply distinguishes the zoological objects from everything else in the
world (cf. Fact 3).²⁷ But the structural ones are primary, the functional
ones presuppose them, and he frequently points out the dependence of
animals' behavioral works and deeds, *erga* and *praxeis*, upon their possession of the requisite highly diversified nonuniform "parts" with which to
perform them.²⁸

(iii) Note on the examples

Here it is appropriate to interject a notice that is not so much substantive
as advisory, viz., that Aristotle's own *examples* of structural differentiae
should not be taken unduly seriously – better, should be considered early
way-stations on a program intended to be much further elaborated. We
have seen that by such differentiae (in the biological connection) he
understands the whole, many-lined cumulative hierarchy of stages through
which the basic elements or "prime materials" are worked up into the
highly structured organic unit that is the individual specimen of the
species. In the light of this total apocalyptic understanding, the actual
examples can seem somewhat paltry and inadequate, e.g.

blooded – bloodless,
footless – footed – twofooted – fourfooted,
amphodont (incisors in both jaws) – karcharodont (jagged teeth, as the
    shark) – chauliodont (projecting teeth, as the crocodile),
solid-hoofed – cloven-hoofed,

and suchlike. To a degree the inadequacy is one of language, com-
pounded by Aristotle's sometimes reluctance – in marked contrast to the
theoretical boldness of the conception as a whole – to venture in practice
far beyond the distinctions made by common parlance.²⁹ In fact, he does

27 By "sharply" is meant strikingly, not that there are not gradations of "activity" between
the most active species and nonliving things, cf. *PA* iv 5 681ᵃ12, esp. *HA* viii 1 588ᵇ4–589ᵃ2. Also
Balme, *PAGA* I, pp. 81, 97

28 *PA* i 1 646ᵇ12–17, 22–5. Plants have fewer such "organic" parts than animals do because
they do fewer things, animals possess more and more varied such parts and a *polumorphoteran idean*,
PA ii 10 655ᵇ37–656ᵃ8. The "active faculties" (*poiētikai dunameis*) have to be located in the
nonuniform, *HA* i 4 489ᵃ27; *GA* i 2 716ᵃ23 ff, i 18 722ᵇ30; *DA* ii 1 412ᵃ28; Balme, *PAGA* I,
pp. 88–9 (*PA* 641ᵃ17 n.). We shall enlarge on this in §16.

29 Cf. Thompson's somewhat impatient note on *HA* viii 2 589ᵃ11. On the related matter of
the validity or viability of ordinary groupings for Aristotelean purposes, see Pellegrin (1982), 43
n., 66–7, 106–7.

enlarge on the available ordinary vernacular with more extended descriptions of particular differentiations, not reducible to single adjectives; but even then the characters described are all of a kind readily accessible to gross observation and can of course be claimed – even by him – to constitute only a minute fragment of the specific nature of any animal kind. Thus it would be absurd to claim that such accounts of differentiae as are given in the biological writings come within sight of actually defining any animal (still less that this is accomplished by such a formula as *zōion pezon dipoun*, Animal That Travels On Two Feet, frequently alleged in the corpus as definitory of Man). Nor, for that matter, are we ready to do so today. A *good* definition of Man might be a million pages long, perhaps a length of the order of that of the program by which Nature *constructs* a man;[30] briefly, it would have to be the *cash* to meet what we have already called the enormous paper draft on such a definition, contained in the words "organized body potentially having (human) life in it". Until we have it, I think our attitude to *pezon dipoun* and the like has to be temporary methodological suspension of disbelief.[31]

(iv) The place of Genus

The suggested perspective on Differentia has consequences for the concept of Genus as well: if differentiation is understood in terms of a sequence of stages discernible in a biological object, between the basic materials of which it is composed at the one extreme and the object as a completely differentiated (lit., specie-fied) individual at the other, *genus* in this scheme represents: *the upper intermediate range of the sequence.*

Because such a characterization is somewhat nonstandard and may be at first sight even of doubtful intelligibility, it may be helpful to come up

30 Crick half-seriously calculates (in his popular lectures published as *Molecules and Men*, Seattle, 1966, p. 59) that the information stored on the DNA of a single human haploid germ cell could be written out, letter for "letter" (the letters being, say, A, T, G, C, and the "letters" the corresponding nucleotide bases), in "about five hundred large volumes – all different". Of course, although the original is in some sense intelligible to Nature, the written transcription would be gibberish to us; thus a descriptive that we could follow (laboriously and in part) would be presumably many orders of magnitude longer, arguably as a whole altogether beyond our conscious comprehension. There are some interesting morals to be developed along these lines, but they lead much too far afield to be pursued here. Note, however, that it is a fixed point of Aristotle's scheme that however long the definition of Man may be, it *cannot* be *infinitely* long; *APo* i 22. ("The formulae aren't infinite", *Meta* Eta 3 1043^{b}35.)

31 Cf. §12(ii) above. And whatever else may be said about *dipoun*, Aristotle does not regard it, either, as wearing its meaning on its sleeve: for example, he cautions that its meaning is different (as of course it must be) in the formulae of Man and of Bird, *PA* i 3 643^{a}3, iv 12 693^b ff. This is connected with the point at the end of §2 (and note 15 of §2) about the same character as substantial differentia and nonsubstantial quality; cf. also §20(i) *fin*. Pellegrin (1982), 44, 64.

For "organized body potentially having life", and the reading thereof as a "paper draft", see further §16 below.

on it gradually by way of some concrete examples. Calling in a few familiar zoological kinds and confining ourselves for simplicity to a few very obvious surface characteristics, we may regard, say, an American Bison and a Tibetan Yak and readily discern in both (or "abstract", if you prefer, or "prescind") a common underlying generic nature that in each is differentiated in slightly different ways: both are large, heavy-bodied ruminants, having horns (in both sexes), a long tufted tail, and muzzles that are naked and moist; but the Bison has a larger hump, a broader head, and shaggy neck and shoulders; whereas the Yak is larger overall, has shaggy flanks, and his tail is bushier. If now we compare both Bison and Yak to a Hartebeest, we find further differences: the general ground-plan is similar, but the Hartebeest is smaller, shorter-haired, his horns are ringed and differently shaped, his face relatively longer and his muzzle not naked but hairy. Now comparing the three to an Asiatic Gazelle, there is again an underlying similarity on which are played variations: she is smaller still, more delicate, much speedier, and being a female of her species she lacks horns. We may proceed in the same way through Sheep and Chamois, Ox and Oryx, Gemsbok and Gnu, perceiving – and, subject to the limitations of language and portraiture, recording – between the members of each pair, "part" by "part", the relationship called in Aristotelean terminology "excess and defect" or "more and less":[32] the varying specifically typical restrictions or reductions of an underlying (in this case, bovine) generic potentiality, as (to take as simple as possible a case from our example above), horns in the Bovidae, where they occur, are found to be large or small, straight or curved or helical, ringed or smooth, deciduous or permanent, et cetera. Now, in line with the point urged in §13(ii) concerning the vertical as well as horizontal dimension in differentia, a similar feature is to be seen in the relationship of "excess and defect": in part it is a horizontal, interspecific relationship, one which obtains between Yak and Bison with respect to, say, horn size (the Yak's are larger) – in this dimension, it is the relation "specifically different, generically the same".[33] (In this form the idea is closely akin to the present-day concept of homology.) But the relationship is also vertical, that of the specific determinate form, "excessive" or "defective" as the case may be (large horns or small, straight or curved, etc.) to the potentiality of which it is a particular expression – in this instance, I suppose, *horned*, though ordinary language does not furnish us with such

32 Some significant aspects of this theme are pursued in Lennox (1980).
33 Thus *Meta.* Delta 7 1016$_b$31 ff., etc.

terms with anything approaching the profusion or appropriateness that the theory would require (a point noted by Aristotle as well).[34]

If we imagine this vertical relationship, between this or that particular determination among the range of generically permitted possibilities (Yak-horned, Ox-horned) and that potentiality of which they are particular determinations (*horned*, let us agree for argument's sake), now to be generalized over the total extent of specific characters that are presented by a specimen of any species, we have a rough approximation to the relationship of species to genus.

The vertical and horizontal dimensions are co-ordinated in a further sense: if we now proceed to forms manifesting greater differences from the preceding cases than the preceding cases have from each other, e.g. comparing Yak with species outside the class of Bovidae, say with Horse, then with Lion, then with Whale, the progressively increasing horizontal distances between the members of the comparison pair correspond to progressively greater vertical depths that one must go to to obtain a generic similarity. When we get so far as pairs of individuals that share no commonly-accepted "kind" short of simply Animal, the horizontal relationship comes to be called "generically different, the same by analogy – the relation, among "parts", of nail and hoof, hand and claw, feather and scale, bone and fishspine;[35] such is the case between Yak and bird, or shark, or fish, or coelenterate.

As serious science all the foregoing is, to say the least, rudimentary indeed; but several aspects of the concept of genus that is involved are of considerable interest and do not seem to be widely understood. First (i) is the notion that genus here really represents a level (in the vertical dimension) of potentiality: to take another simple illustrative case, a level at which e.g. a head of a certain overall conformation (dub it *bucephalic*) may be broader as found in the Bison, or narrower as in the Yak, or longer as in the Hartebeest, or smaller as in the Gazelle, and likewise through the rest of the organism, in the various sorts of manifestation that "excess and defect" may assume. Further, (ii) the potentiality should, it seems, be seen as *multi*-levelled, each upward determination of which restricts the range of possibilities open to further determination: in terms of the illustration just introduced, *bucephalic* as a cephalic conformation could be

---

34 For a conspectus of *genē anōnuma* see Bonitz, *Index* 69b2 ff.

35 *HA* i 1 486b18, etc. A particularly arresting case is that of the Blooded Animals, "all" of which have four feet. This statement can stand because "instead of" (*anti*) front feet, Man has hands (*HA* iv 10 687a7), and Birds have wings (*HA* iv 12 693b11) – the relation of analogy. See Pellegrin (1982), 181.

understood as coordinate with other, similarly specifically determinable conformations (*equine, feline, canine,* etc.?) that are themselves restrictive determinations of a still deeper or "more generic" potentiality for which no name (*cephaloid*?), happily no doubt, is in common circulation – and once again, likewise through the rest of the organism.[36] It is very likely unrealistic to expect any sort of definitive systematics of this hierarchical structure, if only because there must always be many alternative ways of ordering the sequences and also because the phenomenon is plastic in character and not naturally amenable to drawing of precise categories; as a consequence it is also likely that the expectable scientific utility of the scheme is by more recent standards limited in certain ways.[37] The important point is that of principle: genus means the generic capability of taking whatever more specific form is not yet excluded at that generic level, and this is the reason for its characterization above in terms of an "upper intermediate range".

It also follows (iii) that on this view genus is radically relative to species, meaning that what we regard as generic and at what generic level depends on the range and variety of specific differentiations of it that actually are found to exist: if many and multiform it lies deeper, if few and of little diversity it lies shallower. If none, it must be specific itself. (At this point, as will be seen, we intersect once again – very solidly – with the Population Problem;[38] there is also an important embryological connection, cf. §15(i).) Thus a genuine generic character is a potentiality *as seen through the particular specific differentiations by which in various species that potentiality is reduced*; normally this is the only way in which it can be seen at all, because normally genera are not found except as so reduced in one way or another – in Aristotle's language, are not found *para ta eidē*.[39]

A final backing-off to regain perspective. We have been pursuing here some important theoretical implications for genus of a way in which Aristotle seems to have come to think of differentia, but as with differentia, genus does not thereby come to lose its prior associations. It (more accurately, *genos*) continues to bear its central connotation of *kind,*

---

36 An attempt at rendering the metaphysics of this is made in §24(i).

37 An intriguing glimpse of a possibility of quantizing essentially this phenomenon is in Gould's (1976) appreciation of D'Arcy Thompson, pp. 87–91.

38 Cf. §7; the "definitive reformulation" that resolves the question touched on here is given in §21(i).

39 *Meta.* Zeta 12 1038ᵃ5 ff. "Normally", not as Aristotle there suggests, "absolutely" (*haplōs*) – fooled by a maladroit choice of example, *phōnē* and the *stoikheia*, he forgets his own theory of *terata*; cf. §15(ii), §21(i), and §23(iv). This also connects with *DA* ii 1 and the "organized body" as discernible only in the *living* thing – see §16(ii), controverting Ackrill (1972–3) on "Aristotle's definitions of *psuchē*".

of things *akin*; in fact, as Balme pointed out, in the biological writings the terms *genos* and *eidos* very frequently do not even carry the technical meaning of "genus" and "species" at all, and are often used with no more theoretical loading than our ordinary English idioms like "kind of crane", or "form of salamander".[40] Thus what we are pursuing *are* implications, particularly that the constructional or vertical moment in differentia implies a precisely converse moment in genus; but those implications are not pursued by Aristotle in his biology. They are metaphysical, and surface explicitly in his metaphysics. But their provenance is biological, and had to be traced to that source.

40 See Lennox (1984) for reference to *tode ti* being relative in this way.

§14. From mass to individual: embryology, the Generation of Animals

There is more to say about morphology and we shall be back to it, but certain of the further points to be dealt with are easier taken in when some relevant details are understood about the manner of the actual coming-to-be of biological substances. So it is time to look into some embryological concerns.[1]

It of course scarcely needs saying that the salient phenomenon facing any embryological theory is Fact 5: the fact of cospecificity between forebears and offspring; any would-be such theory that furnishes no explanation of this phenomenon, and in particular of its virtual invariability throughout Nature, is obviously of little use from the outset.[2] The Aristotelean embryology faces this problem squarely; the phenomenon is recognized and its fundamental importance understood, a number of further pertinent observations about the course of development of animal offspring over time are added to the picture, and a causal mechanism is adduced that explains the total observational given and reduces it to an intelligible pattern. Judged by our contemporary standards, for what those may be worth, the observations are in large part remarkably accurate; the adduced causal mechanism presents a more difficult case, for it is factually almost completely wrong and yet in certain

---

1 A primitive version of §14 and §15(i)(ii) was distributed to the members of the Society for Ancient Greek Philosophy and was discussed at its meeting in New York in 1975.

2 The history of the problem of the resemblances between parents and offspring in Greek thought prior to Aristotle – in Presocratics, Hippocratics, and Plato – is a very large and complex topic which there is not space to treat adequately here. The best general account known to me, which is particularly notable for its insight into Aristotle's difficulties over the role of the sexes in generation (§15(iii) below), is Erna Lesky (1950) (*Zeugungs- und Vererbungslehren der Antiken*); it also treats extensively the various ancient theories about the nature and origin of "semens", including the "pangenetic" theory.

matters of fundamental principle so completely right that it is something of a wonder how it can be simultaneously both.[3]

Before proceeding, however, a very serious caution. I have just asserted that the "salient phenomenon" facing the embryology is that of the cospecificity of parents and offspring, and as we shall see (§15(iii)), the evidence is that that is for the most part how Aristotle sees the problem in *GA* prior to iv 3. However, in interpreting the *GA*, one should keep in mind a deep ambivalence, much too little noted, in that work as to the *phainomenon* it is supposed to explain. That is, is it that of *species identity* between parent(s) and offspring, or is it that of offspring's *resemblance to its particular parent(s)*, the likes of Windsor chins and Hapsburg noses? The difference between these as *phainomena*, which is crucial, never gets sharply conceptualized in Aristotle's embryological discussion, an omission which has important consequences. It is my reading of the *GA* that the main preoccupation of the first three books in this area is with the former question, that the main features of the theory of generation are worked out in that context, and that the bringing to bear of the theory upon certain evident facts about heredity (and in particular, resemblance between offspring and female parent) in Book iv is basically a new – and unhappily belated – concern, and not even a central one at that (it arises in connection with teratology and the explanation of the sex of the offspring). This is perhaps the most critical issue at the juncture of the biology and the metaphysics: it is the embryological side of the individual-form versus specific-form issue. We shall develop it further in §15(iii), when the theoretical setting has been sufficiently laid out.

(i) Overview

Let us first look at the general idea that Aristotle deploys to deal with Fact 5, and then attend to some of the relevant details. According to the theory of *GA*, the specific form of the species is stored, in a very special way, in the semen (*sperma*) of the male parent. The female parent contributes a material mass of partially "concocted" (*pepemmenon*) "residue"

---

3 Needham (1955), writing, characteristically, from a contemporary perspective: "The depth of Aristotle's insight into the generation of animals has not been surpassed by any subsequent embryologist, and, considering the width of his other interests, cannot have been equalled", p. 42. See also the previous note.

Some recent extended treatments of Aristotle on animal generation are Peck (1963), Preus (1970), (1975), Kullmann (1979), Morsink (1982).

(*perittōma*), more or less identified with the menstrual fluid (*katamēnia*) of higher mammals and something analogous in other species, and also (in most cases) the place in which the fabrication of offspring is to occur. The generation of animals is then a process in which the form as stored in the semen is read into the matter as represented by the catamenia, by way of a pre-programmed sequence of mechanical and chemical operations (which are understood in a general way and for which several analogies are provided, but of which the full concrete details are not available). In the course of development the offspring-to-be passes from the condition of a relatively inchoate catamenial mass, through a series of intermediate phases as progressive differentiation takes place under the formative influence of the semen, until the final phase is reached, that of the "completion" or "end product" (*telos*): one or more fully specified miniature individuals co-specific with the parents. At the earliest stage the embryo (more accurately, the *kuēma*, "fetation" – Peck) is plantlike in its nature (an early event is its driving a "root" into the uterine wall),[4] but it is not yet actually, although it is potentially, an animal. Subsequently, as the parts articulate out, it becomes recognizably animal, but it is not yet actually, though it is potentially, any specific type of animal. Full specific form is acquired last, and only then do we have *a man* or *a horse*:

For it's not simultaneously that *an animal* and *a man* come-to-be, nor *an animal* and *a horse*, and likewise in the case of the other animals (= types of animal); no: the end-product or completion (*telos*) comes-to-be *last* of all, and the most distinctive character (*idion*) of each thing is (comes at) the completion of its genesis.[5]

Thus the development is one in which the original matter is successively articulated through more generic phases to more specific ones, until the final, "perfected" (*teleion*) phase is reached. The role of the semen throughout is to articulate, form, shape and set the developing animal as it passes through these phases toward fully specific form; it contributes no material part to the offspring, and influences only the offspring's form by way of its causal agency. When differentiation is complete, the semen's function is accomplished and it dissipates and disappears. In some cases considerable further *growth* of the offspring may take place after differenti-

---

4 *GA* ii 3, 736ᵇ; ii 4, 739ᵇ33, 740ᵃ24. The general description given here applies most directly to the higher vertebrates (or, roughly, "blooded" animals, Ar's *enaima*); many variations and refinements, homologues and analogues, are described at length in both the *Generation* and the *History*.

5 *GA* ii 3 736ᵇ2–5. Needham (1955) points out the affinity between this account and the "recapitulation" idea of more recent embryology, *op. cit*, pp. 40, 49; cf. "the embryo attains the point of being definitely not a plant before it attains that of being definitely not a mollusc but a horse or a man", 49.

ation is complete; such increase in bulk occurs through the intake of further material nourishment – e.g., in the case of vivipara (who bear live young), first *in utero* by way of the placental "root" up to the time of birth, and subsequently as the offspring takes nourishment from without.

It may be observed that on this theory, it seems a much sharper and deeper distinction must be made between the processes of embryonic or kuematic *differentiation* and of *development* than we are accustomed to today. Differentiation is a process at the end of which the completed offspring exists (see §15(i) for more on this); development is more like growth, a metamorphosis of an offspring already existent.

So much for the general idea. Now let us focus on some particulars that are apposite to our concerns here, as usual leaving aside much detail that is highly interesting in itself but dispensable for the purpose of substance theory.

A striking aspect of Aristotle's account is the certainty and clarity of its appreciation of the fact that the biological phenomena require there to be *two different ways in which specific form occurs*: one the way in which it is exemplified by specimens of the species, and a different way that figures in the copying process from forebear to offspring. Because the recognition that the second way must indeed be different is perhaps Aristotle's most remarkable single insight, biological or otherwise, let us orient our progress through some of the embryological particulars with that object-ive in view.

(ii) Preformation and pangenesis

This is in fact no simple matter.[6] The most natural – and in Aristotle's day, it would seem, quite widespread – primitive conceptualization of embryonic development is the idea (now known as "preformation") that the offspring grows from a "seed" that is itself a minuscule but fully developed specimen of the species – the well-known "homuncule" or "animalcule" that even microscope-equipped observers thought they could see in human and other animal spermatozoa as late as the eight-eenth century,[7] so powerful the influence of the idea still was even then. A second prevalent view of Aristotle's time, having indeed the authority of the Hippocratic author,[8] clearly arose from early attempts to come to grips with Fact 5: it explained the resemblance, part for part, of offspring

6 For the complexities, cf. Lesky (1950) (note 2 above), and note 3.
7 See e.g. Meyer (1939), ch. v.
8 Though it is not clear whether Aristotle knew this; cf. Needham (1955), p. 42.

to parents by suggesting that the "seed" must contain portions drawn from each part of the parent that supplies it, thus being in effect a kind of image of the parent at the point in time when it was formed – a feature that enables the view to explain the inheritance of acquired as well as inborn characteristics, something supposed possible both by Aristotle[9] and by Darwin when he tentatively hypothesized a nearly identical theory to the Hippocratic and called it "pangenesis,"[10] a title we may as well adopt.

These two views, preformation and pangenesis, are logically independent of one another, but in their ancient form, at least, they have an underlying link: the idea that the "parts" of the eventual offspring have got somehow to be from the beginning *in* the seed from which it grows (preformation is the idea that they are so, pangenesis is an idea of how they get there). Aristotle in the *Generation* is clear and definite that this is not the case. Against pangenesis he turns a number of pertinent observations suggesting that not *all* the parts, at any rate, supposedly represented in the "seed" could have been derived from the corresponding parts in the parent (parts the parent has not yet itself developed, cases where inheritance skips generations, et cetera – *GA* i 18 722^{a}1–16); he has also a deeper line of argument based on the distinction between uniform and nonuniform, which shows the notion in effect to crumble under analysis once the distinction is introduced:

Suppose the seed is drawn from both (uniform and nonuniform parts of the parent – the possibility of its being drawn from either type alone has earlier been ruled out),[11] then (the question is:) what can be the manner of the generation? For the nonuniform consist of the uniform parts in a composition, so that 'to come from the nonuniform parts' would have to mean, *coming from the uniform parts together with their composition.* – It is just as if something 'came from' a written word: if it came from all the word, it must come from each syllable, and if from these, it must *come from the letters together with their composition.* – And so, if indeed *flesh,* and *bones,* are composed of fire and that sort of thing, the seed would rather have to be 'from' these elements (= letters),[12] for how can it *come from the composition?* And yet, without the composition, there wouldn't be the resemblance. So if something sets

---

9 E.g., "the man from Chalcedon who was branded on the arm", *GA* 721^{b}32–4; cf. §15(iii) below.

10 Darwin (1868), *Variation of Animals and Plants under Domestication*, ch. 27. Darwin's version of the theory, if it need be said, is far more sophisticated than the ancient variety criticized by Aristotle.

11 For the argument in full, see the further analysis in §15(iv).

12 Reading *mallon* not *monon* in ^{a}35; otherwise, tr. "these elements alone" (cf. Peck).

to work later, to bring the composition about, then *that* would be the cause of the resemblance, and not 'the semen's coming from all the body'.[13]

$$(GA \text{ i } 18 \text{ } 722^a27-^b3)$$

The implications of this argument are highly remarkable; they are better left to our next spate of "moral-drawing", and accordingly will be considered in §15(iv). For immediate purposes, it is clear that the parts, and particularly the nonuniform parts, cannot be thought of as literally drawn into the parental semen from the corresponding parental parts; nor does the idea withstand scrutiny that such parts are literally in the semen at all; for they do not become manifest in the embryo or *kuema* all at once, nor in the manner that the preformationist theory postulates:

As for simultaneous formation of the parts, our senses tell us that this does not happen: some of the parts are clearly to be seen present in the embryo while others are not. And our failure to see them is not because they are too small; this is certain, because although the lung is larger in size than the heart it makes its appearance later in the original process of formation.

$$(GA \text{ ii } 1 \text{ } 734^a20-5, \text{ tr. Peck})[14]$$

(iii) Epigenesis

Instead, the manner of development is not simple augmentation of pre-existing parts, but epigenesis: the laying down of structures in temporal succession of which each is a basis for the next.[15] It goes somewhat as follows (as before, let us instance the case of a higher mammal like man or horse):

As we have already observed, the process of *sunistasthai*, of integration into a *sustasis* or *sustēma*, begins with a stage that is plantlike in character (ii 3 736^{b}10);[16] it drives a root into the uterine wall (ii 4 739^{b}33 ff., 740^{a}24–8) for its nourishment;

---

13 For more on the implications of the "nonuniform", cf. §15(i) below, as well as the further analysis of the present argument in §15(iv).

14 "This passage demonstrates that Aristotle had opened hens' eggs at different stages, and was well acquainted with the appearances presented there as early as the third day," Needham (1955), p. 47.

15 Epigenesis is not an Aristotelean word, and his own use of *epigignesthai* is in the normal Greek meaning of Be born after, Come after, Follow. It is used occasionally however for form "supervening upon" matter: e.g., *Meta.* Zeta 11, 1036ª11–12, ^{b}5–7. A thorough treatment is in Kullmann (1979), sec. 5.

16 The present displayed section is as much paraphrase as direct quotation; references are embedded rather than footnoted to minimize the to-and-fro for the reader inclined to pursue them. References are to *GA* unless otherwise indicated.

as an entity now 'separate' from both parents it is in that sense "managing for itself'", like the son that has left home and set up on his own (ii 4 740–ᵃ5–7). Accordingly, it already possesses metabolic (so-called "nutritive") psyche (*threptikē*) – it has its own *arkhē* (ii 3 736ᵃ).[17] Next, the parts begin to articulate out: first, and most important, the heart,[18] which is the *arkhē* of all (blooded) animals in the sense of both "beginning" and "first principle" of all the parts, uniform and nonuniform, *prōton hē kardia phainetai diōrismenē. arkhē gar hautē kai tōn homoiomerōn kai tōn anomoiomerōn* (ii 4 740ᵃ17–19).[19] Next, from the heart, the vascular system: the main blood vessels, and the umbilical circulatory arrangement to the placental "root" (740ᵃ33–5). Nature "traces out" (*hupegrapsen*, 740ᵃ28) the vascularization like a "framing" (ii 6 743ᵃ 1, cf. *HA* iii 5 515ᵃ34 ff); then the *trophē* oozes through the vessels and their walls to "set" into flesh (as it is solidified by cooling) and the beginnings of other uniform parts (ii 6 743ᵃ8 ff). The general course of development is from inward to outward – as against certain thinkers who had thought the opposite, e.g., Democritus who is criticized more than once on this score (ii 4 740ᵃ12 ff., ii 6 741ᵇ25). It is here in the "primary stage of construction" (*en tēi prōtēi sustasei*, 744ᵇ28, 745ᵇ4) that the skeletal system also begins to take shape: bones and sinews (ii 6 743ᵃ17ff., 744ᵇ27, 745ᵇ5), also an armature or "framing" (*PA* ii 9 654ᵇ27–32 – cf. also §11(ii) above).

The upper parts of the embryo articulate-out, *diarthrountai*, ahead of the lower, while the lower are relatively *adioristotera* (ii 6 741ᵇ27–9, 743ᵇb18), a clear recognition of the phenomenon later known as "cephalic dominance".

The *kuēma* is originally "plantlike", only potentially animal and specific type of animal. In the course of development it moves through successive actualizations – through being *threptikon* (lit. having *psuchē threptikē*, 736ᵃ35) to having *psuchē aisthetikē* (736ᵇ1), *kath' hēn* it's *zōion* or at least beginning to be; subsequently it becomes "perfected to the point of being now an animal potentially locomotive" (ii 4 740ᵃ24–7, tr. Platt) – in other words, becomes successively more specialized and specific.[20] Fully specific form comes last in development, as was already

17 See footnote 19 below.

18 This is one of the two chief points on which William Harvey, whose familiarity with and admiration for Ar.'s *GA* were deep and avid, was unable to reconcile his findings with Ar.'s account. He saw, in the white of the hen's egg, a "red pulsating point" (*punctum rubrum saliens*) (Harvey (1653), tr. Whitteridge, p. 241), just as had Ar. ("a point of blood, it beats and moves as though endowed with life", *HA* vi 3 561ᵃ11–13). But Ar. identifies this straight off with the heart; Harvey sees the succession as first blood, then the pulsating vesicle, then vascular fibres, and lastly the heart (Harvey, *ibid.*). Cf. Thompson (1913), 22–3; Lesky (1950), 145–6.

19 Peck (Loeb ed., p. 194) thinks that at this point "the fetation is definitely constituted – it is an individual – it *exists*, and that which exists can correctly be said to have an *arkhē*". But the text, although it certainly gives "exists" (he is right to retain *on* in 740ᵃ21), and has previously given "separated" (*apokrithēi*, 740ᵃ6), significantly does *not* give "individual". For some important further developments along this line, cf. §15(i).

20 It should be noted again, as at the beginning of §12(i), that the phases of development do not exactly correspond to the levels of organization there discerned within the finished product; some nonuniform parts appear before some uniform ones are laid down – the phases are determined by the species, the specific character of the end-product-to-be (v 1, 778ᵇ1 ff.). "Both (= uniform and nonuniform) come-to-be at once", ii 1 734ᵇ27.

indicated in the quotation above (p. 112); and the attainment of this state may (as in the case of man or horse it does) considerably antedate the time of viability of the new offspring, the intervening period thus being given over to considerable growth, from the size at which differentiation is complete to the size at term.

(iv) The storage of form in the semen

What then does this account of embryonic development tell us about the manner in which the form of the offspring must be stored in the semen? The actual parts themselves are not in it, not even in miniature, they appear in their final, finished form quite late, and can be seen to be developing toward that form prior to then, and definitely are not there at the beginning. Yet it appears that the form of the offspring must be there in *some* sense – otherwise, why Fact 5?

Aristotle's hypothesis is that there is in the semen, not the form itself, nor any portion destined to become the form,[21] but the power of constructing new individuals *of* that form. The nature of this power is informational (thus it is frequently referred to as a *logos*, a formula). It is the *logos* of a pre-determined sequence of physical and chemical formative activities ("movements" and "concoctions") which, given catamenia to work upon, will effectuate a corresponding sequence of changes in the catamenial substrate, each change presupposing those before it, *via* the postulated physical and chemical mechanisms (as "efficient" or "moving causes"). Thus the semen is several times referred to as having it in the "logos *of* these movements",[22] for which various analogies can be found elsewhere in the natural world, but whose operation here is nevertheless *sui generis*.

Briefly, the natures of semen and catamenia are as follows. All 'blooded' organisms (*enaima*) engage in the taking-in of nourishment (*trophē*) and the refining ('concocting', *pettein*) of it into residues (*perittōmata*), various uniform organic compounds that subserve various organic processes (cf. §11(i)) – the whole process is one of the kind we call metabolism, and thus may be called *threptic* (from the adjective from *trophē*) in the broad sense of metabolic.[23] The first stage of this process, in the

---

21 This is very important; cf. the final paragraph of this section, and footnote 27 thereto.
22 Cf. *GA* ii 1 734^{b}33, 735^{a}2; ii 4 740^{b}32; iv 3 767^{b}20.
23 The activity of 'threptic psyche', and its role in the overall 'being' of the organism, is further enlarged upon in §16 below. Strictly speaking, the threptic process (i.e., the refining of nutrients into 'useful residues') is our 'anabolism'; our 'katabolism', resulting in waste-products (Aristotelean 'useless residues') would correspond to the process he calls *suntēxis*, resulting in a *suntēgma*. At least, this is Platt's suggestion (in his Addenda to the Oxford translation of *GA* (i 18 724^{b}27 n.)).

117

alimentary tract, is digestion. The second stage, in the heart, results in the most refined of the threptic residues, namely blood; this is then pushed out through the bloodvessels to the various somatic tissues and organs which it sustains in their active 'being' and whose growth it also brings about (i.e., for which the blood is both 'threptic' and 'auxetic' in the sense of §16 below). Thus much, at this point, for metabolism. However, in the heart a small quantity of blood gets further concocted into the most refined residues of all, the 'generative residues': catamenia in the female, and semen in the male. Of these, catamenia is the more inert and passive, and semen the hotter, more kinetic and more active; and it is the particular characteristic activity of the semen, in accordance with the specific "*logos* of the movements*", that imposes the specific form of the male parent[24] on the catamenia furnished by the female.

In discussing the mutual operations of these two *arkhai* in generation, it is useful to separate certain issues of general principle from questions relating to the particular types of causal mechanisms that Aristotle theorizes as being involved. These mechanisms, according to his account, are briefly as follows:

The semen of the male parent, as has been observed, does not itself contribute any matter or constituent or part to the developing conceptus or *kuēma*; rather (a) it is *hot*, being a "foam" (*aphros*) whose base is Water but whose active ingredient is *pneuma* (= very hot air, the "heat" being not the ordinary sort, which is that of Fire, but something more like a "vital" heat; cf. GA (Loeb), Peck's introduction, pp. lii ff, and further references); (b) the semen is *active* and formative in character, being pre-programmed with a variety of highly intricate "motions", which "shape" and "set" the catamenia in stages as development advances.[25] Two comparisons are used to illustrate the activity of the *pneuma*: (1) the craftsman's tools (in this case "Nature" occupies the rôle of craftsman): they shape the wood, but nothing of the tools themselves remains in the finished product: "nothing passes from the carpenter into the pieces of timber, which are *his* material, and there is no part of the art of carpentry present in the object which is being fashioned: it is the shape and the form which pass from the carpenter, and

24 This is the preponderant view of the *GA* prior to *GA* iv 3. For complications and details, see §15(iii).

25 This is the other point (cf. footnote 18 above) upon which Harvey could not verify Aristotle. Looking for the 'inchoate mass', he dissected does (= female deer) taken by the royal hunting-parties in King Charles I's forest preserves at various points shortly after coition in the rutting season, and "could never find in the cavity of the uterus or its horns any semen or blood or trace of any other thing" (see Harvey (1653), 351–4). Six to eight weeks after mating, he found something: "resembling a membranous and mucilaginous coat or empty wallet . . . this elongated little sack is spun out over the whole cavity of both horns and of the uterus between them" (355). This is since called the blastodermic vesicle (A. W. Meyer (1936), 109–17). Thereafter a recognizable fetus quickly appeared (Harvey, 359–60).

they come into being by means of the movement in the material" (*GA* i 22 730^{b}12–15, tr. Peck), and so it is with the *pneuma*, Nature's tool. When its "activity" is finished, the physical material of the *pneuma* dissipates and disappears (ii 3 737^{a}11), still being itself no part of the offspring. (2) Another comparison is the action of rennet or figjuice in the curdling of milk: milk is the matter, rennet has got the *arkhē* that makes it coagulate and "set"; *hē puetia gala esti thermotēta zōtikēn ekhon, hē to homoion eis hen agei kai sunistēsi*, "rennet is milk that has vital heat; this integrates ('works into a unity') the homogeneous stuff, and 'sets' it", ii 4 739^{b}24. Sometimes the action of yeast is instanced along the same lines. So, too, the *pneuma* "sets" the *kuēma*.

As has already been observed, much of this account is factually incorrect: it is a mistake to suppose that only the male parent makes a genetically significant contribution to the specific form of the offspring (on this see §15(iii) to come), and Aristotle's idea of the causal influence that is exercised by this genetic contribution, literally "shaping" and "forming" the matter, is by present-day lights quite crude and childlike compared to the actual mechanisms involved, which are more complicated and more indirect as between the nature of the genetic material itself and the form manifested in the eventual offspring. The account has these deficiencies, among others. On the other hand, the correctness of these ideas on some significant matters of principle is notable also. The genetic material carries specific form, not by containing little whole animals or parts of animals, but as *information* that under the proper circumstances can proceed to direct the stepwise construction of co-specific offspring; this affects the form of the offspring not by developing into any ordinary constituent part of it, but by its influence on the physio-chemical processes that bring the construction about; it is also not consumed in the process, but is passed on intact (though stored on different material parcels in distinct individuals) from generation to generation. The affinities with some more recent findings in this area are quite striking.[26]

---

26 The noted molecular geneticist and Nobel laureate Max Delbrück, in an amusing but not entirely facetious little paper entitled "Aristotle-totle-totle", has suggested, mentioning some of the features of the account just enumerated, that the Swedish Academy of Sciences ought to award Aristotle a posthumous Nobel Prize for discovering the principle implied in DNA. (In Monod and Borek (1971), pp. 50–4.) That of course is too strong, chiefly because Aristotle, though very clear that specific form must be stored in the semen as information, is also very unclear about the nature of the language in which that information is written, which is the question that the DNA discovery answers so well. (Given his usual insistence that complexity of function presupposes, by conditional necessity, supporting complexity in the structure that functions (recall §13(ii) *fin.*), it is perhaps surprising that beyond an analogy or two, he does not inquire after the inner architecture of the physical stuff in the semen that works these amazing results. It is technically a "foam", as just noted (p. 118), which "consists of the tiniest particles, so small that each individual bubble cannot be detected by the eye" (ii 2 736^{a}15–16,

It is also interesting to note that so far as the principle is concerned, the *Generation* is not at all tentative or aporematic, but asserts the point with confidence and power: the *logos* that's in the semen directs the fashioning of the offspring, but it is itself *not* a *tode ti*, nor itself anything "finished" or "completed" (*tetelesmenon*, ii 1 734^{b}17–19); that is not its manner of being, nor is it anything but biological folly to look for any sort of resemblance between an animal part and the portion of the *logos* in the semen that codes for that part – "that part of the semen *is* sinew (?!!) – the statement's utterly beyond us" (i 18 723^{a}22). There is also considerable precision on the sense in which the semen is *potentially* (*dunamei*) this or that (i 19 726 ^{b}15 ff.): it is not that the semen is going to *develop* into this or that "with respect to its own bulk" (^{b}18), but rather that it has the appropriate "power" (*dunamis*) of moving the materials (i 21–2).[27]

after Peck).) There is also the debit mentioned earlier, his idea that the influence of the seminal form upon the catamenial matter is a simple, immediate and direct one of "shaping", whereas DNA's manner of expressing itself is not of this kind. On the other hand, these are points on which it is altogether inconceivable that Aristotle *could* have been right, and they probably in the end have little more force than to dilute "ought to" to something like "could appropriately". The essential point is the following: *he recognizes exactly the place at which a causal mechanism for a copying process is required, and what it is required to effectuate* (and then imagines a mechanism that will fulfill those requirements). See also §15(iv) below.

27 It is worth stressing this precision in *GA*, in view of the many places elsewhere in Ar., some of them important, where the cruder view is allowed (of semen itself as "potentially" animal, or "matter" for animal) – e.g. *Physics* i 7 190^{b}5, and *Meta*. Theta 7 1049^{a}1–3, 15. Ross comments on the latter, I think correctly: "he writes as if he accepted the popular view which treated the male and female elements as uniting to form the matter of the offspring. He is merely illustrating a general principle, and in such cases he often writes from the point of view of a common theory not his own", *AM* ii 155. Cf. Furth (1985), 135–6, and below: §20(iii), p. 197 on the (quite crucial) difference in "'out of' the *katamēnia*" versus "'out of' the *kuēma*", and §22(ii) on the effacing of this and other fancy distinctions (elsewhere clearly drawn) in *Physics* i 7.

§15. Specific form and specified individual

(i) What the embryology implies for the essentialism

Our vantage point from the biology is by now well enough established for us to profit from one or two perspectives it can afford us on the essentialism; let us take these in while the relevant portions of embryology are still fresh in our minds.

We first looked at the essentialism in a preliminary way in terms of "migration-barriers" in §6 and §8. In those terms, we observed, each individual or *tode ti* is thought of as coming in and constituted by a specific kind, in such a way that the coming-to-be of any individual *is* the coming-to-be of something of that kind, and an individual's ceasing-to-be something of that kind *is* that individual's ceasing to exist at all (as a consequence, it will be recalled from §7, occurrences of the type that we might be tempted to describe as an individual's changing from one such kind to another must be treated in one or the other of two ways, *either* the original individual has been destroyed and a new one generated, *or* the kinds involved are not substantial after all, *tertium non datur*).

The embryology has now invested the topic of the coming-to-be of individual living things, at least, with considerable concrete detail: we have seen how it views (say) *a man's coming-to-be* in terms of the progressive advent over time of specific form, as the original catamenial matter is differentiated through the series of intermediate generic phases to its final (*teleion*) fully specific phase. At what point, then, should we date the coming-to-be of *Socrates*, the individual man? At conception? But as we have seen, there is no *man* at conception, only "the first mixture of male and female" contributions called *kuēma* or "fetation" (*GA* i 20 728^{b}34). At birth, then? But by that time we have had a fully formed human being for several months, the semen has long since finished its work and disappeared, and all that has occurred subsequently is growth (cf. §14(i), (iii)). The only reasonable choice on this theory for the actual coming-to-be of *Socrates*, i.e. *the individual man*, seems to be: *the point at which differentiation becomes complete.*[1] Accordingly it looks as though we should regard the conceptus from the phase of the catamenial mass through its incompletely formed generic phases *not* as Socrates, but as matter in a process of formation that is potentially Socrates, and if all goes according to plan will become Socrates – just as it is potentially a man but as yet actually only animal, though if all goes according to plan it will become a particular species of animal, namely man. I call this choice the only "reasonable" one, and say "looks as though", because I can find no explicit statement of Aristotle's that directs us to fix the date of Socrates' actual genesis at the time I suggest (nor also, however, any explicit statement that directs us otherwise).

Of course, dating the history of an individual from the completion of differentiation carries with it a few practical difficulties; for example, that event is unlike other moments such as conception and birth in not being precisely fixable by conventional and universally understood criteria. Thus for legal purposes, occasions for commemorative celebration and so on, dates like that of birth or conception should no doubt continue in common use even were such a view as this adopted in theory. Indeed, it might well be that the time when differentiation is completed is not *precisely* fixable even in principle, we might never reach a position of scientific comprehension of the factors involved that would enable us to establish, or give us any *reason* to date, the commencement of Socrates any more narrowly than, say, within an interval of a week or two.[2] None of these considerations of course cast doubt on the theoretical satisfactoriness of the suggestion (which is not to say it could not be open to objection on other grounds).

This intuition about the commencement of biological individuals can now be extended a bit. It has been seen earlier (§14(iii)) that the onset of form in embryonic development is gradual and not instantaneous; starting with the catamenial mass, which relative to the final product is

---

1 It must be borne in mind (as mentioned in §14(i)) that this account presupposes that *differentiation* becomes complete at some point, i.e. when the matter is fully informed and the offspring organism is fully specific (= a man, a horse, as the first quotation of §14(i)), while *development and growth* may have a much further course to run.

2 Across the animal kingdom there is also much variation in the time of completion relative to the time of being cast-forth (parturition and its analogues), both earlier and later; the great classification into vivipara, ovovivipara, ovipara, etc. of *GA* ii 1 is itself a "clearly defined scale, the stages of which are determined by the degree of 'perfection' to which the parent is able to bring the offspring before parting with it" – Peck, *HA* (Loeb), p. xv. Even in some higher animals, according to Aristotle, differentiation is not complete until some time subsequent to birth: at birth the young are *skhedon adiarthrōta*, "still quite unarticulated", *GA* iv 6, 774^{b}5–775^{a}4, iv 4 770^{a}32–6, *HA* vi 30 579^{a}21–5 – cf. Peck's note ("On Licking Bear-cubs Into Shape"), *HA* (Loeb), vol. ii, p. 376.

inchoate and "heap"like,[3] the form comes on by degrees, of which the later intermediate stages (relative to the final stage) are the generic. And just now, we have seen reason to date the beginning of the existence of *an individual F* at the moment (or longer time-interval, if preferred) at which that process is complete, i.e. the matter completely informed, i.e. at last fully *F*. Prior to that, we don't yet have *the individual* that is to be named with the proper name for which he is eligible when *he* commences to exist, but a matter that is destined upon full differentiation to become that individual.

I now want to make a suggestion that at first sight may appear somewhat strange: that prior to full differentiation we not only do not yet have *the individual F*, "numerically one and the same" as that which subsequently is born, passes through childhood, adolescence, adulthood and so on along life's way: *we do not as yet have an individual, in the Aristotelean sense, at all*. Instead, from the time of the original mass to that of the final product we have something intermediate between "heap" and individual "this": something not only potentially but not yet actually Socrates, but also potentially but not yet actually a "this". On this view, the advent of individuality is *pari passu* with that of form, in being gradual rather than instantaneous, in coming by degrees, and one is complete only when, and because, the other is.[4] My suggestion is that according to Aristotle's view of these events, the developmental process that takes matter into specific form and the process that takes catamenial mass into discrete individual are one and the same process, and that our two ways of stating the result are quite unnatural for him to distinguish from each other. This is the ultimate source, I think, of the perplexing oscillations on "substance means a 'this'", which were noted in §8 and signs of which were already evident at the "surface of the solid" in §4, as the idiom of *tode ti* apparently wavers back and forth in application between *Socrates* and *man*: my hypothesis is that for him, the individuativeness property and the specific form property (which in this version of the theory is what "essence" comes to) of substantial kinds are in the end such as to coalesce.

Such a suggestion naturally calls for a closer look at what is understood

3 "Relative to the final product" is important; the catamenial mass of course is not *wholly* formless, but to the contrary – relative to the primitive materials or "simple bodies" – represents an extremely rich and specialized potentiality, even as much as a plant, perhaps (*GA* ii 3 736ª32 ff); the male *dunamis* could not produce anything with only Earth and such to work on. See §14, and §15(iii) below.

4 "And the product on the one hand comes to be of-a-particular-sort (*poion ti*), and on the other hand simultaneously also a particular 'this' (*tode ti*), and that's the substance" – iv 3 767ᵇ34, reading *hama* ("simultaneously") for *alla* ("but"), after Rackham and Peck. For the context see the Appendix to §15(ii) (pp. 129–32).

here by "individuate", which our morphologic-morphogenetic stand-point may now be helpful in undertaking. Here is the "heuristic and approximate" account, as it was called, that was given of the notion in the context of the *Categories* in §4 (p. 30):

> . . . the predicates naming the substantial kinds are *individuative* predicates, in the sense of terms marking off objects severally by way of a criterion of individuation that is part of their meaning: terms of the type today sometimes called "count terms", as opposed to "mass-terms" like *blood* and "adjectival terms" like *blue*. Thus they pick out individuals as wholes, and accordingly accept numerical modifiers and form plurals: the property remarked by Frege in those "concepts that isolate what falls under them in a definite manner", the only type of concept which a finite *number* can belong; and connected is the fact that, because such terms *F* are true of each member of their divided or distinguished reference as discrete *wholes*, the result of splitting an *F* in two will generally not be two *F*'s.

That was the (admittedly not very good) best we could do at the "surface"; now let us try to see farther in. We saw in §13(i)(ii) that the biological substances are strongly marked as wholes by the type of organization that Aristotle calls "nonuniform" in connection with their parts: the character of "resolving into parts that are unlike the whole", which we spelled out at some length in terms of structural properties, geometrical regionalization, divergent differentiation of parts, and the characteristic symmetries and asymmetries that mark the construction of animal bodies. Now, it is this fundamental characteristic of the living substances, I think, as thus partly analyzed, that carries with it the consequence for our concept of an animal kind *F* that what counts as *one F* is strongly and uniquely determined, as unmistakably distinguished from any part of an *F* or aggregate of *F*s, and from any other assemblage of parts than the type of assemblage that occurs in *F*s. (We shall see that this is one of the ideas that Aristotle expresses by saying that substantial "being" goes with "unity" or "being one".)[5] It is in this currency, I think, that the individuative notion for Aristotelean substantial predicates, as evoked by language like "marking off objects severally by way of a criterion of individuation that is part of their meaning", is in the end to be cashed: the animal species carry with them an exceptionally clear *criterion of unity* (= "what counts as *one F*") which is ultimately founded on the nonuniform organization of the specimens, a respect in which the animal kind notions significantly differ from other natural kind notions like *bronze* or *rock*. A well-known passage points in this direction:

5 Cf. §17, §23, *al.*

It's evident that even of the things supposed to be substances, most are [really] potencies, – both the parts of animals (for none of them exists separately; and when they are separated, then too they 'are', all, [only] in the sense of matter), and earth & fire & air; for none of *them* is a 'one', but they're like a heap, until they're worked up[6] and some kind of unity comes-to-be *from* them . . .

(Meta. Zeta 16 1040^{b}5 ff.)

Since the criterion for counting things of any kind is logically dependent (as Frege remarked) on such a criterion of unity, it follows that in this sense the count-property of the substantial predicates ultimately flows from the same source.

This is not, of course, to suggest that nonsubstances cannot be counted. The distinction between a *full* "unity", like a cat, and a *mere* "heap", like a pile of talcum powder, obviously admits of a large range of intermediate cases or degrees, in many of which (even most, whatever that might mean) a sufficient criterion of unity is present for counting purposes. The point is rather that on Aristotle's conception three things seem to merge together: (1) the degree to which a kind of thing is "formed", (2) the degree to which that kind of thing is "unified", and (3) the degree of *clarity* of the criterion by which things of that kind are to be counted. (This moral can be applied to "splitting an *F* in two" in the above quotation from §4, which of course means simple division into two sub-wholes and should not be confused with conceivable phenomena of a quite different kind like budding or twinning: if Socrates "divides in two" by, say, developing a dorso-ventral fold between right and left sides along which the halves proceed to separate, the left side developing a new right and the right side a new left, the penultimate phase before final separation being like a pair of Siamese twins – each one-half Socrates-sized? – joined at the little finger, there may be no objection to saying that the end result *is* two human beings. But then this is no mere "splitting". See further §21 (iv).)

This, then, is what I meant by suggesting that in Aristotle's mind the individuative property and the substantial form property of substantial kinds seem to coalesce: substances are *most* formed, and *pari passu* are *most* individuated and least heaplike. They are also, along the lines just indicated, "most countable", though by no means the only countables. Returning to the embryology, it follows that the sense in which the unfinished *kuēmata* simultaneously developing within the maternal parent of a multiparous species can be counted (as they obviously can)[7] is a

---

6 *pephthē*, lit. "they're *concocted*", as in the metabolic "concocting of residues" among animals; cf. Ross, *AM* 1040^{b}9 n. (ii 219), and pp. 117–18 above.

7 "They can be seen lying in a row; this is clear from the dissections", *GA* iv 4 771^{b}32.

sense in which certain heaps can be, with perhaps the additional rationale that unlike most heaps they are destined to become fully determinate individuals if Nature's plan is fully executed. By the same token, the name they bear at that period (say, "animal") is technically speaking not a fully individuative expression (as are "man", "horse" etc.), designating as it does entities not yet fully formed into individuals, but still to a degree masses or heaps. These consequences of Aristotle's apparent view, like the view itself (as I take it to be), at first sight no doubt appear somewhat strange; but the mindbending required of us to take it in, if undertaken sufficiently gently, does not seem seriously damaging.

(There is a related line to that of the criterion of unity, which will be followed up next in §16. It was seen in §13(ii) that Aristotle thinks of animals' complex *activities*, works and deeds (*erga kai praxeis*)) as presupposing the diversified nonuniform structures requisite for carrying them out;[8] in this way the nonuniform organ-ization of animals is related to transtemporal or diachronic individuation, both prospectively and retrospectively: prospectively, it relates to the "future-oriented routines" mentioned in §9 (as part of Fact 3) and the teleological dimension of the analysis; retrospectively, it contributes also to a *principle of agency*, the fact of ascribable self-initiated behavior. This line again leads to Fact 3, and beyond to the ethics.)

The case of multiparous species raises one further embryological point of some ontological interest. Consider a dog: one mating and she produces, e.g., four pups, another and there follows a litter of six, etc. Why this variation? Well, clearly there was a better supply of catamenia available the second time, hence more offspring. But then if quantitative variation of catamenia occurs, if there can be a lot, why does it have *this* effect, what is the explanation of the fact – Aristotle asks, "why on earth doesn't the semen just turn out *one great big animal*, in the way of the fig-juice (instead of several smaller ones being generated, from that residue)?"[9] A very intelligent question. The answer: built into each specific form, along with *footed* and *winged* and so on, is a *specific size-range: esti ti pasi tois zōiois peras tou megethous*, "for all animals there's a particular limit to their size";[10] one offspring may be somewhat bigger or smaller than

---

8 Thus the "active faculties", *poiētikai dunameis*, are located in the non-uniform, *HA* i 4 489ᵃ27; *DA* ii 1 412ᵃ28; *GA* i 2 716ᵃ23ff., i 18 722ᵇ30; cf. Balme, *PAGA* I, pp. 88–89 (*PA* 641ᵃ17 n.). (Also partly referenced at note 28 of §13, p. 104.)

9 *GA* iv 4 771ᵇ24 ff., as supplemented by Scot's Latin translation, cf. Peck, Loeb edition, 434 n.

10 *GA* ii 6 745ᵃ5; cf. iv 4 771ᵇ33 ff., and above, §5, p. 44 (for the "particular size-limit"). *DA* ii 4 416ᵃ16–18 says that the limits belong to psyche and logos, not to "fire and matter".

another, but not beyond these limits. The female has a certain amount of catamenia. If there is enough for $1\,^1/n$ $(n > 1)$ within the limits, the semen "sets" one and the remainder is discarded; if enough for $3\,^1/n$ it "sets" three and the rest is thrown away.[11] (Thus here the comparison with rennet and milk breaks down, as Aristotle has to admit.)[12] Hence it appears that with animals, *the count-property* still is lodged ultimately in the specific form, although the *number* comes from the matter!

(ii) Instructive morbidities and irregularities: teratology

As with any machinery, function is often especially well revealed through dysfunction: one finds out how something works by seeing the kind of thing that can go wrong with it. This is markedly the case with the theory that is advanced in the *Generation* of abnormal productions, or *terata*.

It is not hard to see from the account of animal generation sketched above in §14(iii)(iv) that the offspring is not simply a read-out of the genetic information stored in the semen, but instead represents the resultant of two opposing moments: the formative, "moving" and "setting" and "heating" and "shaping" influence of the male contribution, working against the resistance of the cooler and relatively inert[13] catamenia. Aristotle devoted considerable attention to the sorts of outcomes that can result from the collision of these "principles", one active, the other passive, for therein lies the answer to an obvious question raised by his general view: namely, what is its explanation of the fact that every animal offspring is not an identical duplicate of its male parent?

In the limiting, extreme case, in which the catamenia was wholly and completely pliable, it seems that the offspring would exactly resemble its male parent. In the vast majority of cases, "what acts also gets acted upon by what's being acted upon" (768^b16), and divagation occurs. Aristotle's discussion of the leading features of this process is not completely coherent, and is best given in his own words; a literal translation of the portion of GA iv 3 in which it is explained is appended to this section, and it will be examined at some length in §15(iii) below. Briefly summarized, according to it the "motions" of the *pneuma* may be modified in either of two ways in the process of being applied to the original catamenia or the developing kuema: (a) they may weaken and "relapse", the substrate being too resistant to take the bit of form it is their function to impart, and in such a

---

11 See *GA* i 20 729^a13–20 for how the male contribution gets "divided up" (*merizomenon*) in such cases, similarly here 772^a8 ff., *diairoumenōi tōi spermati*, [a]11.
12 771^b23 ff., 772^a22–5   13 But cf. note 3 above.

case the offspring will resemble the female rather than the male parent in that particular respect. (Why this last should follow, i.e. resemblance to dam, over and above difference from sire, is one of the points on which the explanation is puzzling: as can be seen in the appended translation, Aristotle seems to be saying that *maternal* as well as paternal "motions" are involved, thus apparently, though without saying so, throwing overboard the official view developed earlier in the work.) Or (b) they may "depart from type" into their opposite, the most striking instance of this being when the male "principle" is insufficiently hot and powerful to "master" the cooler contribution of the female, and the result is a female offspring. (The fine details of this process also are by no means clear; for discussion see again §15(iii) below.)

Such in outline is the treatment of the two vectors whose product is the new species member. Their respective contributions are even more vividly evident in the abnormal cases (in Aristotle's terminology, cases "contrary to Nature") where the result is *not* a new species member but represents *parekbasis ek tou genous*, deviation from type.[14] He is confident that such cases are assimilable into the causal schematism just outlined, and are explicable precisely as breakdowns thereof: so-called *terata*, whether "deformed" in a mild way, such as a female of the species,[15] or in a more drastic way, such as a mule (ii 8), all the way to the monsters and freaks and prodigious births of rustic legend and archaic imagination – in Nature (as opposed to imagination), all without exception are cases in which the "natural" process of development, which is towards being a male species member resembling the sire, has been *blocked* at some intermediate stage, the greater the deviation from type, the earlier the development must have been arrested. There is *no* such thing as development switching tracks from one species to another, and *no* such thing as an animal of one type gestating in another, and stories suggesting otherwise are merely a sloppy way in which people talk:

The end result, when the 'motions' [from the male] *relapse*, and the matter [from the female] does not 'get mastered', – there remains that which is most general, and this is just *animal*. People *say* that the product 'has the head of a ram', or 'of an ox', and in other cases likewise 'of some other animal', like 'a calf having a child's head', 'a sheep, that of an ox'. But all these things occur owing to the causes that have been discussed above, and none of them is as people say, but those are merely resemblances – which indeed come about even when no deformation is

14 iv 3 767ᵇ7. Of course *genos* here means type or kind, and cannot be thought to bear the technical sense that is opposed to *eidos*.
15 ii 3 737ᵃ27; iv 3 767ᵇ8 (Appendix below); iv 6 775ᵃ15.

involved. Hence it is that humorists often compare persons not fair of face to a 'fire-breathing goat', others to a 'butting ram'. And there was a physiognomist who reduced all faces to those of two or three animals, and often carried people along. However, it is *impossible* that a *teras* of this sort should come-to-be, i.e. one animal gestating within another (as is made plain by the greatly differing time-periods of gestation of man and sheep and dog and ox; it's impossible for any of these to come-to-be, except in its own proper time-period).[16]

(iv 3 769[b]11–25)

It follows from this analysis, together with the suggestion already made in §15(i) about the dating of the onset of full individuation at the point at which differentiation is complete, that a *teras* is not a full-fledged Aristotelean individual, because its differentiation, relative to the specific norm, has never been completed; it too is heaplike to a degree. The relativity to the specific norm is important – if we were to treat *animal* as itself a species, e.g. treating possible transitions from being *a dog* to being *an ox* as allowable migrations that numerically one and the same individual could survive, then there seems no reason not to regard the relatively undeveloped entity which, as things are, we call a *teras*, as a full-fledged individual – indeed, while metamorphosing from dog to ox, that "numerically one and the same" individual we just momentarily imagined might look just like that.[17] This relativity of the generic to the level at which the specific is taken to be fixed has been touched upon from another side already (§13(iv) *fin.*), and has many and deep metaphysical reverberations (§21).

Appendix to §15(ii): GA iv 3 767[b]23–769[a]6[18]

767[b]23 I mean by "each *dynamis*" the following: the progenitor (*to gennōn*) isn't just *male*, but he's such-and-such a male, as Coriscus or Socrates; and he's not just Coriscus, but also *man*. And so in this way some of the things belonging to the progenitor are nearer, some remoter – according as he has the generative power (*katho gennētikon*), not as what he may just "happen" to be, like the male progenitor being grammatical, or someone's neighbor. [b]29 And what's *peculiar* (*idion*) and *particular* (*kath' hekaston*) exerts the stronger influence on the genesis. For Coriscus is both man and animal, but man is nearer to what's peculiar than is animal. Both the particular and the kind (*genos*) generate, but more the particular; for that's the substance. As a matter of fact, the product (*to ginomenon*) indeed comes-to-be of-a-particular-sort (*poion ti*) – but simultaneously[19] also a particular

16 This does not mean that hybridization is impossible: ii 7 746[a]29–[b]20.
17 *Meta.* Zeta 8 1033[b]29–1034[a]2 (Furth (1985), p. 27). 18 OCT text. 19 Cf. note 4 (p. 123)

this (*tode ti*) – and that's the substance. [b]35 For which reason it's from the *dunameis* of *all* these sorts of things that the motions in the semens are constituted – potentially indeed from (the *dunameis* of) the earlier ancestors, but more especially from those of the one which in each case (768[a]) is closer to some particular – I mean by particular, Coriscus, or Socrates.

768[a]2 Now, when anything *departs from type* (*existatai*), it goes not into any chance thing but into the opposite, and so too in generation, what isn't mastered necessarily departs from type and comes-to-be the opposite with respect to the *dunamis* with respect to which the generator and mover didn't get mastery. [a]5 If, then, it's *qua male*, what comes-to-be is female; but if it's *qua Coriscus*, or *Socrates*, what comes-to-be is a likeness not of the father but of the mother; – for just as in general (*holōs*) mother is opposite to father, so the particular female progenitor (*gennōsa*) is opposite to the particular male-progenitor (*gennōn*). And likewise with respect to the next *dunameis* down the list; it [= the "motion"] always shifts over (*metabainei*) more to the next in line of the ancestors, both paternal and maternal. [a]11 Some of the motions are present *actually*, others *potentially*: actually those of the male progenitor and of the universals such as *man* and *animal*, potentially those of the female and those of the ancestors.

[a]14 Now (a) the thing departing from type (*existamenon*) shifts-over toward the opposites; but (b) the fashioning ("demiurgic") motions *relapse* [*luontai*, "slacken"?] into ones that are near them, e.g. should the motion of the male progenitor relapse, it shifts-over first by the minimal difference into that [i.e., the motion][20] of his father; [if a] second [time], into that of the grandfather; [a]18 and in fact in this way also among females, the [motion] of the female progenitor [shifts-over first] into that of her mother, or if not into that, into that of her grandmother; and so on up the line.[21]

[a]21 Most of all what naturally occurs is that [the male motion] does its mastering and getting-mastered, *qua* male and *qua* father simultaneously: for the difference is small [between male and father?], so there's no big job in their both occurring at once; for Socrates *is* a particular male of such-and-such a sort (*anēr toiosde tis*). [a]24 This is why for the most part the males resemble the father but the females the mother, for the departure from type (*ekstasis*) has occurred towards both respectively at the same time; *female* is opposite of *male*, and the *mother* is opposite of the *father*, and the departure from type is into opposites.

[a]28 But if the motion from the male *does* get mastery but that from Socrates *doesn't* get mastery, or the latter does but the former doesn't, then what occurs is the coming-to-be of males resembling the mother, or females resembling the father [respectively].

[a]31 But if the motions *relapse*, then [a] if the one *qua* male stands fast but that

---

20 The motion, not the type, thus Lesky (1950), p. 152, as against Wimmer.

21 The first explicit mention of motions emanating from the female's residue; cf. Lesky (1950), p. 152, and 15(iii) below. The received text says, "in fact in this way both among males and also among females"; Wimmer and Peck would omit the entire phrase. I follow OCT.

from Socrates relapses into that of his father, then there will be a male resembling the grandfather or some one of the other earlier ancestors, according to this account; [a]34 [b] if it gets mastered *qua* male, then there will be a female and for the most part one resembling the mother, unless this motion relapses too and the likeness is to be to the mother's mother or another of the earlier female ancestors, by the same reasoning.

768[b]1 The same scheme holds for the various parts; for of the parts some will very frequently resemble the father, others again the mother, and others still various of the earlier ancestors; for the motions of the parts, too, are present some actually, others potentially – as has often been stated.

[b]5 But it's necessary to take hold of the *general principles* ["general hypotheses"], First: the one just stated, that some of the motions are present potentially and others actually; but in addition two more; [Second:] that what *gets mastered* departs from type, into the opposite, but [Third:] that what *relapses* passes into the motion that's "next" to it: relapsing a little, into a near motion; more, into one that's farther away. [b]10 Finally [the motions] so run together that it doesn't resemble any of its household (*oikeia*) or kindred (*sungenē*), rather all that's left is what's common [to all], and it's [simply] man. [b]12 The reason for this being that this [= what's common] goes with *all* the particulars; for *man* is universal (*kath' holou*), but *the father*, Socrates, and *the mother*, whoever she may be [!], are particulars (*kath' hekasta*).

[b]15 The cause of the motions' *relapsing* is that what acts also gets acted upon by what's being acted upon, as what cuts gets blunted by what's being cut and what heats gets cooled by what's being heated, and generally what moves (except the first mover) gets moved by some motion in return, e.g. what pushes is pushed back in some way, and what squeezes is squeezed back; [b]20 – sometimes, it's even acted-upon altogether more than it acts, what heats may get cooled, or what cools get heated, sometimes not having acted at all, sometimes [having acted but] less than being acted upon. There is discussion of these matters in *Acting and Being Acted Upon*, where it's explained in what sorts of things acting and being acted-upon occur.

[b]25 What's acted upon *departs from type* and doesn't get mastered, either [a] owing to deficient power in what's concocting and moving, or [b] because of the bulk and coldness of what's being concocted and defined. But since it gains mastery *here* but fails to get mastery *there*, it makes what's being composited (*to sunistamenon*) turn out diversiform (*polymorphon*) – the way it happens with athletes through eating too much (*polyphagian*) [b]30 . . .

769[a]1 The cause of all the following has now been explained:
[1] Why males and females [offspring] come-to-be;
[2] Why some resemble their parents,
    [a] females [offspring] resembling females [parents], and males resembling males,
    or conversely,

[b] females resembling the father, and males the mother;

– and, in general,

[3] Why some resemble their forebears, and others resemble none of them; – all of which with respect to the whole body, and with respect to each of its parts. [a]6

(iii) The underlying and interesting source of the sexism

In the section of the *GA* just quoted, in which the official theory of generation as developed earlier in the work is for the first time confronted with some fairly apparent facts about heredity – particularly, resemblance between offspring and female parent – the evident result is, if not a rout, something of a disorderly retreat; nothing (or next to nothing) has been heard earlier of "motions" actively occurring in or coming from the female material in its own right, and the constantly reiterated theme, that it is only the semen of the male that has the *arkhē kineseōs* and that the female's contribution is *hulē monon*, has been last repeated only a page before the confrontation and consequent rout/retreat begins (766^b12–14). And beyond its inconsistency with the earlier explanation, the *GA* iv 3 account does not make very good sense in its own right: are the female "motions" *of* the catamenia (as instrument), or *in* the catamenia (as substrate)? If the former, then *what is being worked on*? If the latter, then *what is working*? Certainly the comparison of 768^b15, with hatchets getting blunted or warmers getting cooled, is not enough to support the suggestion of 768^a18, that there are female motions adequate to shape the *kuēma* into a facsimile of mother or mother's mother. It is worthwhile, therefore, to look a little farther into Aristotle's account of the respective roles of the sexes in generation – what factors can they be that have caused him to cling so stubbornly to the male-motions-only view, when his own observations (not to say anyone's observations) point so plainly to its untenability and it must be unceremoniously dumped as soon as they are brought up?[22]

---

22 Such review of recent literature as I have made, which is anything but comprehensive, indicates that apparently my view of *GA* iv 3 as a collapse of the earlier explanation, though not unshared, is not widespread. Thus Balme (1980), p. 2, equably epitomizes:

> If the sire's movements fail to control the foetal matter, the next most effective determination comes from the female's movements which are present in the foetal matter (blood in the uterus). If they too fail, movements inherited from ancestors exert control in turn . . .

The discussion of resemblance in Preus (1975), pp. 101–104, evinces no alarm on this issue. Pellegrin (1982), pp. 134–5, is not concerned with this problem (his focus is on *parekbasis* as a case of the "plasticité" of the human *genos*). Morsink (1982) calls the introduction of female movements "an important qualification of the form–matter hypothesis" (pp. 138, 141, cf. vi), and argues diligently in its defense against its critics and against sundry defenders of the un-"qualified" theory (pp. 141–3):

Charges of inconsistency and incoherence are a serious matter, particularly as regards a theory as brilliant in so many other ways as that of the *GA*, as well as one that has been so thoroughly studied over the years. I shall proceed by (a) establishing the extent of the surprise that *GA* iv 3 presents to the reader who has assiduously taken in what comes before, and then (b) offering an explanation for Aristotle's persistence in the male-chauvinist form of account until it inevitably crashes in that chapter. For I think that besides the conjecturable social and political bases for this cast of his thought, there is a theoretical source of much greater interest. (Some readers will as soon skip the details of (a).)

(a) The inconsistency

(1) Does generation transmit parental and not just specific form before GA iv 3? As briefly mentioned as early as §9 and again in §14, there is some considerable ambivalence in the *GA* over whether the phenomenon to be "saved" is that of offspring's resembling parents in specific form, or is resemblance in point of particular parental characters (the example was Hapsburg noses and Windsor chins; let "H-W" be acronym for this).

Certainly striking in *GA* iv 3 as just rendered is the claim that the male's formative contribution to generation is *multifold*: he generates *as* man and as animal, but also *as* Socrates and as male, in the form of seminal motions for all of these natures, both general and particular. Furthermore, the strength of the respective motions is said to be greater as the generative nature is more peculiar (*idion*) and particular (*kath' hekaston*); thus, according to this section, the most powerful contribution is that of Socrates = such-and-such a male (767^b25) = the substance $(767^b33-$

The qualifications made in Book IV do not conflict with the initial hypothesis, but bring it into line with some facts that would otherwise be its downfall.

Kullmann (1979), p. 52, likewise employs the language of "modifiziert". Peck (1953), p. 17, seems to think of *GA* iv 3 as an 'extension' and not a contravening of the earlier account. As far as I have found, only Lesky (1950), pp. 152–4, adequately appreciates the extent of the inconsistency between iv 3 and the earlier treatment; she too is struck (p. 153) by the oddity ("merkwürdig" is her word) of its overlooking by previous accounts – though she does cite (*ibid.*) a criticism of this part of Aristotelean theory from Galen (*de sem.* IV 602f., the following a tr. of Lesky's tr.):

. . . because they assert that it is the power of the *sperma* that develops and forms the germ, but a little later forget about this and quite fail to notice that they ascribe exactly the same powers (or even more) to the material, that they had previously assigned to the fabricator [Werkmeister], i.e., the formative power of the semen.

– Apart from questions of consistency with the account earlier in *GA*, I have not found company in regarding the iv 3 explanation as defective in internal coherence (cf. above), nor in tracing Aristotle's persistence to the last ditch in the "male motions only" theory to the theoretical difficulty of dividing the form (cf. below). It seems doubtful that the renegade remarks of *Meta* Zeta 7 1032ᵃ28–32, Zeta 9 1034ᵇ4–6, have much bearing on this issue.

35) = *tode ti* (767^b34-5) = the father (implied 768^a21-31, explicit 768^b14-15). A lesser kinetic influence is wielded by the specific form, Man, and the least is that of the genus, Animal (767^b29-32).

What then has been heard of H-W parental resemblances as theoretical *explanandum* earlier in *GA*? The answer is, not nothing, but rather little. Here is the evidence.

(1) According to the opening manifesto of *GA* i 1, which certainly should be accorded special importance, the phenomenon involves the sexes and homo-generic generation: *things generated by the sexual union of things of the same kind are of the same kind as those things, homogenē*. This is simply the fact that "generation *is*, normally, reproduction", i.e., Fact 5 of §9. (i 1 715^a22-4, $^b2-16$)

(2) In so stating the matter, the inquiry is leaving aside those cases of genesis (mainly of certain insects) which are "not *ex homogenōn*" because they are spontaneous, from decomposing matter (i 1 715^b27), such as fleas and flies (i 16 721^a8, i 18 723^b4), clothes-moths from wool (iii 9 758^b23), etc. Here there are no 'particular parents' to which resemblance would be an issue.

(3) In the great Scala Animalium of *GA* ii 1,

Some animals work up to completion and expel into the world something like themselves; . . . others engender something less articulated, which has not yet taken on its own shape, . . . an egg, or a scolex. (ii 1 732^a25-9)

In this scheme, which is repeatedly returned to, there can be no possible doubt that *homoion heautōi* and its cognates means specific resemblance; the more perfect offspring, *teleōtera* (733^a32 ff.), obviously are to be understood as *homogenē* or *sunōnuma* in that sense, that is, as contrasted with a scolex, *i.e.*, a pupa or grub (cf. i 16 721^a2-7, i 18 723^b3-9). In this context, the concept *tēn oikeian morphēn lambanein* (ii 1 733^b20-1) has to mean "assuming the form that is specifically peculiar or unique", not a familial or paternal "form" in any more exclusive sense. It is routinely so glossed in explanations: e.g. *egennēse to sunōnumon, hoion anthrōpos anthrōpon* (ii 1 735^a20-1), that is, man begetting man, *not* Alexander begetting Alexandrovich or Alexandrovna.

(It should be noted more generally that allusions to "resemblances to the parents", *homoiotētes pros tous gennēsantas*, are often to be cashed out in the same way, as specific, or at least are not automatically interpretable as (though they can sometimes be) likeness of particular "house and lineage", *sensu* Luke ii 4.)

(4) The discussions of results of cross-breeding (e.g. ii 4 738^b27-35) are

in terms of the specific types of the parents (though mostly factually wrong in this case; cf. Platt ad loc.); the same holds for the treatment of the mule (ii 8).

(5) That is fairly weighty on the specific-resemblance side. Contrarily, there is one section, totalling about one Bekker column, before iv 3, that *does* contemplate H-W resemblances. It is all in i 17–18, pro and contra pangenesis. (a) It is an argument for pangenesis that offspring resemble parents part for part as well as in the whole body (i 17 721^{b}21–4). As just pointed out, this language is not decisive of itself as to H-W resemblance, but in the surrounding context of (b) and (c) it is the likeliest reading. (b) The inheritance of acquired (*epiktēta*) and not just congenital (*sumphuta*) characters ("the man from Chalcedon", i 17 721^{b}28–34): clearly has H-W in mind. (Of course, this is later rebutted as an argument for pangenesis, i 18 722$_{a}$2 ff., etc., but we are talking about the *phenomenon*.) Similarly for the inheritance of mutilations (i 17 721^{b}17–20) (also rebutted, i 18 724^{a}3–7). (c) Likeness to remoter as opposed to nearer ancestors (i 18 722^{a}7–11) also seems to show H-W in mind.

From this review it seems fair to conclude that although there are indications both ways and obviously the issue has not been sharply formulated in the author's mind, the weight of the indications – especially in the globally important i 1 and ii 1 – is towards the theoretical explicandum's being the phenomenon of specific resemblance. Parental H-W resemblance mostly lies doggo, and maternal resemblance as a phenomenon is completely overlooked. In this setting the male-motions-only theory of specific resemblance is worked out in detail, and the embarrassing *denouement* of iv 3 is the inevitable consequence.

(2) Are the catamenia active and kinetic before GA iv 3? As to the idea that there are maternal 'motions' working through her catamenial contribution to genesis, this comes in iv 3 as a total surprise.

(1) We have discussed the formation of catamenia and semen in §14(iv); they are "generative residues" formed in the heart, from blood, which itself is the ultimate "threptic residue" that energizes and augments the various parts of the living body. Evidently the nourishing and growth-producing power of blood is also somehow kinetic in nature – it seems that the blood that is threptic and auxetic for e.g. the liver has hepatic motions, and that destined for the kidneys has nephritic motions; and at one point the threptic/auxetic activity of blood is explicitly claimed to be somehow continuous with the eidopoietic activity of the male's semen:

Semen is a residue that is moved with the same movement that is auxetic for the body when the final *trophē* is partitioned; coming into the uterus, it constitutes and moves the female's residue with the same movement wherewith it is moved itself.

(ii 3 737ª18–22)

Note that this *does not* mention a 'movement' that is peculiarly paternal as against specific: the portions or 'partitions' of blood that are threptic and auxetic for kidney and hand may be taken (for all this passage has to contribute) as so for *human* kidney and *human* hand, not necessarily Socratic or Callian. On the other hand, it *does* clearly ascribe a kinetic activity to the blood of the male, that is independent of and prior to the final refinement of that portion that becomes generative and seminal (and "comes into the uterus"). There seems to be no reason (gatherable from this passage) why the female generative residue, the catamenial, should not inherit such movements from her blood as well – but such movements are nowhere contemplated, let alone officially recognized, until iv 3. (Where, in addition, there is still the problem of detail unclarified even there (p. 132 above): movements *of* the catamenia, or *in* it? What is working upon what?) However, it should also be noted that the ii 3 passage quoted is confused on an important issue: the movements described are *auxetic* (growth-inducing), not *poietic* (formative), and the transition from auxetic movements in a threptic residue to poietic movements in a spermatic residue poses a serious problem to understand: if that transition is not very carefully negotiated, the "precision" of the account that we were recently admiring will collapse into the cruder version that we were contrasting with that.[23] Furthermore, even in iv 3, the image is still being maintained of the female residue's role as that of *resistance* to "being acted upon" (768ᵇ15 ff.); this is an indication that even in iv 3, the idea of activity on the part of the female residue still is not very clearly viewed.

(2) There are two further passages that might seem to suggest particular-parental movements, narrower than specific, but on close examination do not, still less maternal movements:

(i) The semen is a residue of the *trophē* that has become blood, that which is distributed into the parts [of the body] in its final stage. And this is the reason for its great power – for the loss of [such] pure and healthy blood is debilitating – and it is reasonable that the offspring come-to-be resembling the parents; for that which goes to the parts [of the body] resembles that which is left over.

(i 19 726ᵇ9–15)

---

23 §14 *fin.*, and note 27 thereto.

(ii) To recapitulate: we say that the semen 'underlies', as the final residue of *trophē*. (By *final*, I mean carried to each [of the bodily parts], and this is why that which is generated resembles that which generates; – it makes no difference [to say] 'comes from each of the parts' or 'goes to each' – but the latter is more correct. (iv 1 766^{b}7–12)

(The passage continues, The male moves, the female supplies only matter: ^{b}12–14.)

Thus there seem to be no attributions of catamenial activity or movement in the *GA* prior to iv 3.

(3) There are, however, a number of vague references to catamenia as 'spermatic' and 'potential', and it is possible that these may be intended as insinuating that catamenia can convey movements imposing maternal characteristics, if the seminal movements are weak.[24] Their weight as factors in the balance seems to me uncertain at best.

i 18 "Spermatic residues" in the uterus (but also in pudenda and breasts [?])
(725^{b}3)
i 20 Catamenia are semen that is not pure but in need of being worked on . . .
[comparison with plants] . . . when it is mixed with semen . . . then it generates
(728^{a}26–30)
ii 3 Female's a mutilated male, catamenia are impure semen – catamenia lack the *arkhē psuchēs* – so a wind-egg has parts of both [sexes][potentially?] [So Platt; what else can it mean?]
(737^{a}27–33)
ii 5 Wind-eggs have threptic psyche potentially, but can't complete the parts and the animal, without aisthetic psyche
(741^{a}23–8)

(The association of generation and threptic psyche in some passages also goes to a quite different point, relating not to an alleged spermatic power of catamenia but the generative power of the individual specimens being a kind of threptic power in the species: see §16(ii).)

(b) The interesting source of the sexism

The model of the nature of male and female that is taken for a starting-point at the outset of the *GA*, as *endoxon*, is that of male = what has the *arkhē* of movement, and generates in another; female = what has the *arkhē* of matter, and generates in itself (i 2 716^{a}5–7, 13–15); this is their "difference in *logos*", from which stem their differences in organic reproductive parts (^{a}23 ff.). When the actual theory of sexual generation is taken up in i 17, the discussion and refutation of the pangenetic hypothesis is the main

24 These, and this interpretation of them, have been suggested to me in correspondence by David Balme.

preoccupation of the next several chapters (17–21); and in the course of this, a suggestion of Empedocles' is considered as to how both the male and female parents might be thought to contribute to generation a genetically significant "semen":

Again, if [the semen] comes from all parts of *both* (parents) alike, there will come-to-be two animals; for it will have all the parts of each. Hence, if it's to be stated in this way, it seems Empedocles' view is in closest agreement with this one:[25] for he says that *in the male and in the female there is a sort of tally [i.e., complementary halves in each adding up to a single whole], but the whole doesn't come from either one,*
    "but sundered is limbs' nature, part in man's . . ."[26]
For [otherwise], why don't the females generate out of themselves, that is, if [the semen] comes from the whole body and they have a receptacle? But as it seems, either it doesn't come from all the body, or else it comes in the way that that one [= Empedocles] says – not the same parts from each, and this is why intercourse between the parents is required.   (i 18 722ᵇ6–17; also iv 1 764ᵇ3–20)

A modern reader can readily see that this suggestion (italicized in the quotation) is from a theoretical standpoint extremely promising: the "tally" (*sumbolon*) is, e.g., one-half of a coin or other conventional item which has been broken in two, one to be kept by each of two parties to an agreement, or their heirs or assigns, or one to be carried by a courier to validate, by matching with its complement in the possession of the recipient, the authenticity of his message.[27] But Aristotle does not follow it up, instead criticizing weaknesses in the way it has to be developed within the Empedoclean framework:

– But this is impossible too. For the parts cannot survive and be alive if 'sundered', no more than they can when they are large, in the way that Empedocles generates them in his 'time of Love':
    "where many neckless heads sprang up . . .",
and then, he says, grew together thus [as we see them]. Patently impossible! For not having soul nor some sort of life, they can't possibly 'survive', nor, if they are like several living animals, can they grow together so as to become one. Yet this is the sort of thing they have to say who say that [the semen] comes from all the body – as it went then in the earth under Love, so it must go for them in the body. For it is impossible that the parts be produced connected, and go off together into one

25 Following Peck, a few words that follow are deleted; but in any case they seem to have no bearing on the present issue.
26 Presumably this verse of Empedocles' (DK fr. 63, *q.v.*) continued with something like, ". . . seed, and part in woman's . . ."
Cf. Diels–Kranz (1966), i 336; Wright (1981), 219.
27 The same idea may lie behind Empedocles' admittedly obscure allusion to complementary "densities and hollows" in the respective male and female semens (DK fr. 92, from *GA* ii 8 747ᵃ35–ᵇ3), criticized severely and at length (747ᵇ3 ff.).

place. Then again, how are the top & bottom parts, and right & left, and fore & aft, 'sundered'? All these things are nonsensical.

$(722^b17\text{--}30, \text{ cf. iv i } 764^b15\text{--}20)$

Thus by the conclusion of the criticism of pangenesis, the initial model of *GA* i 2 is firmly set: the alternative to literal "parts (of the offspring) in the semen" has been established, namely "formative motions in the semen" – but the idea of a "female semen", which would have "motions" of its own, is still ruled out. The catamenia, it is explained, is analogous to the semen in every way, but because the female is weaker and cooler, the catamenia is less completely concocted (the discussion is summed up at i 19 $726^b30\text{--}727^a2$). The following completes the argument:

Since this [catamenia] is what is produced in females corresponding to the semen in males, but it is impossible that any creature produce two spermatic secretions at the same time [– where, one wonders, did *that* premiss come from?[28] –], it is obvious that the female does not contribute any semen to the generation; for if there were a semen there would be no catamenia; but as it is, because catamenia is in fact formed, it follows that semen is not. $(727^a25\text{--}30)$

It is in this way, then, that the conceptual bind comes about that leads to the inevitable collapse of this part of the theory in *GA* iv 3: Aristotle has clearly seen some potential merits of the Empedoclean idea that the offspring somehow pre-exists divided between the parents, in the way suggested by the "tallies" (722^b11); but that idea has had to be discarded, as having "nonsensical" implications ($^b30$). It should be noticed, however, that the implications criticized are *internal to Empedocles' account, which is preformationist*; something of merit obviously remains to the idea that is applicable to the dilemma Aristotle has fallen into.

In fact, the problem he faced was, and is, of major difficulty. Put in the terms of his preferred account of the matter, the problem is: *how the form of the offspring could be (could have been) divided into two (in the parents)?* Or, since according to him the form is imparted *via* "motions", *how the sequence of motions that shape up the offspring once the process gets under way, could be understood to have been directed by a formula ("logos") somehow pieced together from two half-formulas ("hemilogoi"?) emanating from the two forebears?* The twofold root of the problem is the exact nature of the halves or "tallies", and the manner of their combination into a single unity; and it can be thought of (purely heuristically) as a problem that *Nature* had to contend with long before science began trying to riddle out how Nature had done it. Indeed one way of appreciating its difficulty is to understand some-

28 Also noted by Platt *ad loc.* (Oxford translation).

thing of the way in which it is now thought that Nature solved the problem: by the mechanism of *meiosis* or *reduction division*, in which the form of an animal species (as carried in the chromosomal material) is reduced, for "spermatic" purposes, by one-half in each parent from a diploid to a haploid condition, and then recombined, diploided, complete, to constitute the genetic coding (the "formula", in Aristotelean language) for the offspring.

As a consequence, it seems that the male-chauvinist cast to Aristotle's account of generation may not be wholly, though it undoubtedly is partly, ascribable to unexamined biased assumptions concerning the nature of the sexes.[29] It is true that the model of the sexes assumed as *endoxon* is never seriously challenged, and that once the doctrine of concoction of generative residues and the theory of the generative seminal "motions" are worked out, the corollaries of female "powerlessness" (*adunamia*) (e.g. i 20 728^{a}18, iv 1 765^{b}8–15, etc.) and even "defectiveness" (*pērōsis*) (ii 3 737^{a}18, iv 3 767^{b}8, iv 6 775^{a}15, etc.) fall out with unfortunate ease. On the other hand, the analysis here points to another source as operational also: that *he was unable to see a way in which the form, i.e., in the context of the general account, the "motions" conferring form, could be divided.* When, in iv 3, "maternal motions" make their sudden and entirely unprepared (although, as *we* can see, well-enough motivated) appearance, nothing is said on this – obviously critical – point, and the account suffers from the incoherences already mentioned. But the extreme difficulty of the problem in his theoretical terms goes some way in partially explaining both that deficiency and the overall sexist cast.

In fact, it has occurred to me that there *was* an answer available, in his terms, that he might have, though he did not, hit upon. There is one "division into two" in Aristotle's idea of the distribution of form, that could have been theoretically utilized in this desiderated division of form of offspring between *female* and *male forebear*; and that is the division between *genus* and *species or final differentia*.

Here is one way the story could have gone, in which as much of the account as possible is left unchanged. The account of the role of the male remains pretty much as the *GA* gives it. The female contributes a catamenia, also as before. However, the female is further capable of concocting a small amount of her catamenial residue into a formative semen of her own. Because of her cooler nature, as before, however, this female semen is not as powerful as that of the male, and that in two ways.

29 Aristotle receives a severe lashing on this latter account in Horowitz (1976); he is judiciously defended, to the extent possible, by Morsink (1979).

First, male semen is required to start the generative process (this is obviously a point that any theory has to preserve; *ta thēlea ou gennai ex hautōn* (722^{b}13), "the females don't generate out of themselves"). Second, female semen lacks the vital heat that is necessary to bring the generation all the way to the ultimate perfection of final differentia; it has a *generic* formative capacity, but falls short of the fully specific. Thus, the male contribution is required to begin the process and to finish it, but between these extremes, *en tēi mesēi sustasei*, the two semens are in generally equal combat as together they vie to shape the product. (If grandparental motions, etc., are to be brought in, this is also the place for them.) Because both semens are kinetic and poietic in nature, rather than themselves literally *merē-ekhonta* or "part-containing", the outcome of their collision at each point is *one* "part", perhaps resembling one or the other parent; there is no danger of the "double parts" of the sort that repeatedly loomed on the pangenetic/preformationist basis.

The sole purpose of this little sketch (which it should be emphasized is neither history nor science but sheer fabrication) is to illustrate the point that in the scheme as Aristotle gives it, there *is one* place at which Form *does* divide in two in a way that could be theoretically useful in extricating him from his difficulty: and that is between the "uppermost" parts of the generic structure or "chassis" as laid down in the chronological sequence of formations, and the final differentiation via ultimate specific form. We know that he exploits such a relationship in other connections, such as solving the so-called Unity of Definition problem (§23(iv)), and explaining the "most rightful" sense of both *being* and *one*, that involving an actuality's being-predicated of that whose actuality it is (§16). But all the evidence is that the idea of correlating 'the *arkhai* of male *versus* female', not with 'active *versus* passive', but with 'specific *versus* generic formative activity', which could have resolved this vexatious quandary in a way basically congenial to the overall view – and when he really needed it – never occurred to him. And so, he had to accept a male-chauvinist consequence, and did so. Like a man.

(iv) Reflections on the a priori argument against pangenesis

Having had to deal with the ramifications of so important a break-down of part of the theory of generation, it is appropriate to conclude our moral-drawing from it by considering one of its more impressive successes.

In §14(i), it was claimed to be "perhaps Aristotle's most remarkable single insight" that

the biological phenomena require there to be *two different ways in which specific form occurs*: one the way in which it is exemplified by specimens of the species, and a different way that figures in the copying process from forebear to offspring.

(p. 113)

Subsequently we have reviewed the arguments, both empirical and theoretical, that the *GA* deploys against the prevailing theories that tried to postulate little parts of animals or little whole animals (thus carrying the specific form in the way of specimens) in the parental 'seed'; and the alternative account which Aristotle proposes, according to which the form is transmitted by way of the seminal "*logos* of the movements", has been laid out at some length. I wish now to return to the theoretical argument against pangenesis which was briefly considered in §14(ii), and whose implications were singled out as being particularly remarkable (p. 115).

Let us begin with a restatement of the whole argument:

722^{a}16 Again, whether [the semen] is only from the uniform parts, from each one, as from flesh & bone & sinew, or also from the nonuniform, as face and hand?

(a) ^{a}18 If from the uniform only, ($_p$ then there ought to be resemblance to the uniform only $_p$), but in fact it's the nonuniform parts that more resemble the parents, [$_{LP}$ the nonuniform ones, $_p$] e.g. face & hands & feet $_L$]. Therefore at least if the nonuniform's resemblance isn't because of the semen's being from all, why should the uniform's resemblance be because of semen's being from all, and not some other cause?

(b) ^{a}23 But if from the nonuniform only, then it is not from all parts. But it ought to come from the uniform, since they are prior and the nonuniform are composed of them; and just as what is generated resembles in face and hands, so also in flesh and nails.

(c) ^{a}27 But if from *both*, then [the question becomes]: what can be the method of generation? For the nonuniform consist (*sunkeitai*) of uniform parts in a composition, so that to 'come from the nonuniform' would have to be, coming from the uniform *and* from their composition (*suntheseōs*). – It's just as if something came from a written word: if it came from all the word, it must come from each syllable, and if from these, then it must come from the letters (*stoikheia*) *and* their composition. – And so, if indeed flesh and bones are composed (*sunestasin*) of fire and those sorts of thing, the seed would rather have to be from the elements (= "letters") – *for how can it come from the composition?*[30] And (722^b) yet, without the composition,

30 As will be seen below, this crucial question should *not* be taken as rhetorical. Or rather, there is a rhetorical taunt here ("the pangenesists I am talking about can't answer this question,

there wouldn't be the resemblance. So if something sets to work later, to bring the composition about, then *that* would be the cause of the resemblance, and not the semen's coming from all the body.[31]

I take the point of the foregoing to be as follows. The pangenetic theory aims to furnish a model of how a miniature replica of the parent may be produced (in the semen, or for all of that, in the left knee or in a bassinet or flower-pot, it makes little difference) by drawing representative samples from each part of the parent's body: let the process be called *replication by reduction*.

For an analogy to the pangenetic model, think of a large half-tone black-and-white photographic print, in fact a portrait of Abraham Lincoln, composed of dots which for argument's sake we may imagine to range through ten discrete intensities of darkness from o (white) to 9 (blackest). 'From; this there is to be 'drawn' a replica, say 1/100th or 1/1000th the size of the original, by taking every 100th or 1000th dot.

However, to accomplish this aim in such a case, some rather obvious conditions must be met (in the spirit of an *a priori* argument, we may call them "the abstract requirements").

(1) The dots have to be taken in a representative way: suppose the print is square and 10,000 (or 10^4) dots across, thus consisting of 10^8 in all or 100 million, then in 'drawing' one for every hundred, it will not do just to take the first million starting from the top; rather, the sample must be spread through the whole in some systematic way.

(2) But beyond that, what is needed is not only a 'sample' of the original in the sense of a blood or urine sample, a fair representation of the dots' intensity distribution from a statistical standpoint; obviously it is not enough to 'draw out' a representative jumble of dots. We do not get a *replica* unless they are also mutually arranged as they are in the original, retaining their relative position. (Note that this thought also connects strongly with the anti-Empedoclean considerations of §12(iii).) Conversely, however, if whatever mechanism may be postulated for carrying out this task includes a means of preserving the spatial relationship between each 'drawn' dot and its 'drawn' neighbors, then we have a simple model that comes as close as seems possible to what Aristotle calls, "being drawn from the elements *and* their composition".

because they simply haven't thought this issue through"), but behind it a real question ("think the main issue through: *what is* the process of *copying the composition?*"). Peck's discussion (Loeb *GA*, pp. 56–7) altogether misses the central point.

31 722[a]16–[b]3, my version adapted from both Balme and Peck. "(p . . . p)"=add. Peck (Loeb), "[L . . . L]=del. Drossaart Lulofs (OCT).

The biological case of "replication by reduction" is qualitatively exactly the same, and differs only in the nature of the 'elements', in involving greater complexity and much larger numbers, and in an additional spatial dimension. (Undoubtedly there must also be great differences in the 'drawing' mechanism, but since that is left entirely unspecified in both my account of the photo-copying and the ancients' accounts of pangenesis,[32] that difference may be ignored.) The parental body is a three-dimensional analogue of the large original half-tone, and corresponding to the various darkness-intensities of the dots in the half-tone are the various sorts of uniform materials in different parts of the parent: here a bit of Bony stuff, here a bit of Vein, here a bit of Brain, etc. Now, without needing to go into the details of any concrete physical process by which the 'drawing' of these into a minute replica of the parent may be supposed to be carried out, it can be seen from the start that it will have to meet both of the above "abstract requirements":

(1) it must get its 1/100th or 1/1000th of the uniform parental 'bits' from a proper distribution of parental somatic regions, not, e.g., just taking 1/1000 bits that are all Brain and then stopping.

(2) It must also get with each bit, *a notation of the place that that bit is to occupy with respect to its neighbor bits in the replica*; as with the half-tone, a jumble of bits statistically representative of their ratios in the parent is not a replica of the parent. In other words, the mechanism, whatever it may be, has got to preserve, for each bit, the *positional information* that specifies what sort of bit lies above and beneath, before and behind, to right and to left, of it – thus an *ordered sextuple* of positional information, which is not the most complex sort of information imaginable, but is clearly more complex than what is needed for the jumble, and is clearly needed if the *structure* of the parent is to be replicated by the process ("the elements *and* their composition"). (No doubt there is redundancy in the requirement as described, which Nature in her mathematical cleverness will find and eliminate, since she does nothing in vain. But it must *accomplish* all that is described, there is no eliminating that.)

In fact, look at what the abstract requirements, once merely spelled out, imply: *a pangenetic mechanism that actually is powerful enough to accomplish its purpose, must either have already in it, or else have the means of keeping straight as it picks up or 'draws' the bits, all the information necessary to assemble a replica structurally identical to the parent*, regardless whether it gets the bits from the parent's body, or from some other source, or for that matter fashions them

<hr />

32 As noted, sarcastically, by Aristotle: "*How* are the parts 'sundered'"?, 722b28 (§15(iii), p. 139).

out of catamenia. The importance of actually 'drawing the bits from the parent' is only as great as the extent to which the program that directs the process takes the information from the bits are they are 'drawn' (is 'soft-wired', as we say nowadays), as opposed to being 'hard-wired' – as it is e.g. in the semen according to Aristotle's own account. In any event, it can be seen that the *logos* directing the process has got to be informationally powerful to a degree in comparison with which the source of the bits' being the parental body is relatively trivial at most. In other words:

So if something sets to work later, to bring this composition about, then *that* would be the cause of the resemblance, and not 'being drawn from all the body'.

And that, I think, is the moral of the *a priori* argument against pangenesis, and the basis for calling it "remarkable".

It suggests to me that Aristotle saw the real weakness in the preformationist/pangenetic hypothesis, altogether beyond its failure to square with the observed facts of gestation, or to account for female offspring, and the rest: *the preformationist/pangenetic hypothesis is fundamentally a complete evasion of the issue of accounting for the copying process.* Its vacuity may most easily be seen by exaggerating the direction of "explanation" it provides, in the following lampoon of a theory of generation. According to the Lampoon Theory, the male spermatic secretion contains a male animalcule, and the female secretion a female animalcule. In copulation, the male and female secretions are mixed, and the male and female animalcules are brought into contact, within the body of the female parent. There, *the male and female animalcules copulate*, and behold, the new offspring is begun!

§16. Substance, psyche, and threptic psyche.[1] The *de Anima*

For a last word about the contribution of the works on technical biology to the theory of substance, let us look at what Aristotle has to say about the substances that are animals in the *de Anima*. For even apart from its discussions of matters like perception and the intellect (which go into more detail about these than do the other treatises, but which mostly lie off our path here), the *DA* also contains both some sophisticated theoretical apparatus and some indications of attitude on Population questions, that are most germane to our substantial concerns and do not occur elsewhere in Aristotle's biology. (It is extremely fortunate that he wrote a work on the psyche, and that it survived; had he not, or it not, no 'restorer' – in the spirit of §0 – could supply it, nor should dare to try even if she thought she could.) Thus although we shall have to return to it later, for some subtle psychosomatic metaphysics that we are not now ready to deal with, this is the right place for a first look.[2]

One crucial point of interpretation must be out in the open at once: we have been proceeding from the first on the understanding that what Aristotle standardly means by the form (the *eidos*) of a substantial

---

1 The associations of the English word "soul" seems to me to render it ridiculous as a rendering for Aristotle's *psukhē*, and "psyche" is better as a regular reminder that what is in point here is a highly idiosyncratic theoretical concept. Since English has no adjectival form of "psyche" corresponding to Aristotle's *empsukhon*, we shall have to invent one: rather than "ensouled", we shall say "enpsyched", and for a verb form, that the psyche "enpsychs" the body ("animates" would do, but let us be horrible consistently). Thus "psychology", as used here, means the theory of the psyche, as mentioned here.

§16 was read and debated at a conference on Aristotle's philosophy and science held at Florida State University in Tallahassee in January 1983. I am indebted to the organizers of the conference, Jaakko Hintikka and Russell Dancy, for the occasion, and to my co-conferees for comment and criticism.

2 In accordance with the focus on substance in this work, the discussion here will be entirely in terms of the psyche as a capacity for life, rather than as something specifically pertaining to consciousness and thought (for the distinction, cf. S. Mansion (1973)).

individual is the specific form that it shares with the other members of its species; this is the basis for the translation of *eidos* AS "species", where appropriate, as well as for his own expression, *homoeidē*, "things of the *same eidos*", for the many distinct individual species-members. As we have also seen, the area is controversial, there being signs of some ambivalence between this view and the view that he ascribes to each individual a form of its own – for the most recent example in the present treatment, some trace of this was evident in *GA* iv 3 (§15(ii)(iii)), though not much previously in *GA*. As will immediately become apparent in the sequel, for living things, form is psyche. On our standard understanding, it follows that *the same psyche is repeated in the distinct individuals of the same species*. And indeed, I believe that this *is* the view of the *DA*, which is like the treatises of biological research in operating at the level of the *eskhata eidē*, very much in the spirit of Fact 2 and Fact 4 of §9 – a spirit according to which individuals are studied for what they can reveal about the species-specific nature they embody. Hence whatever constitutes the uniqueness or idiosyncrasy of *this particular individual living thing*, as distinct from its *homoeidē* (a focus of preoccupation that to me seems very un-Aristotelean), it is *not* its Aristotelean psyche. The great depth of the difference between Aristotelean psyche and both Platonic psyche and medieval anima is, I think, not always well enough appreciated.

This is also the place to intercalate an important element that has had relatively cursory treatment since it was first noted in §9 in connection with Fact 3: the *teleological* aspect. For the connections between transtemporal individuation (§§4, 6, 9, 13(ii), 15(i)) and psyche at all its levels, but particularly the "threptic", as a capacity for what in §9 were called "future-oriented routines", are many and deep.

Of course, the account is not confined to human psyche (as *DA* i 1 402b3–5 makes plain), any more than the *GA* is confined to human generation.

(i) Schematic definition of psyche: de Anima ii 1

The pivotal section of the work is Chapter 1 of Book ii. There can be no better narration of the ideas involved than the way in which they are stated there; the interpretation I recommend will be given as we proceed.

412ª3 As for the views handed down by our predecessors concerning the psyche, let that suffice. Let us start again as if from the beginning, trying to determine what is psyche and what would be the most-fully-shared *logos* of it. ª6 Now, we say that one particular kind of the things that are is *substance*, and of that, there is (1) the aspect of matter, which of itself is not an individual something-or-other (*tode ti*), (2) the aspect of shape and form, in virtue of which it (= the substance) is then said to be *tode ti* . . .

(Note again, as most lately in §15(i), the suggestion that form confers individuality as well as essence.)

ᵃ9 . . . and (3) what is 'out of' these. And matter is potentiality, form is completedness (*entelekheia*) – and that last in two ways, (1) as knowledge is, (2) as theorizing is (= the exercise of knowledge).

ᵃ11 It is bodies that are most of all thought to be substances, and of these, most of all the natural bodies, *ta phusika sōmata*; for these are sources (*arkhai*) of the rest.

The last sentence is an important statement on the Population Problem: for with those words (at least, taken at their face value), at one stroke, out go the artefacts as substances. The intuition is that the "bodies formed by nature" are "sources" of the artefacts in that, after all, it is we human beings who make the *houses*, *statues*, and so forth, which we are wont to proffer when instances of *objects* are asked after, and likewise it is the bees and birds and beavers and spiders who make the *hives* and *nests* and *dams* and *webs*, about which they no doubt feel the same. To misapply a verse of the *Categories*, but to a pertinent effect: if you form a class consisting of the substances and the artefacts, then "if the substances did not exist, then none of the other things could exist".[3]

The next couple of dozen words have now to be both rendered and pondered with the greatest care, for simple and straightforward as they may appear, in fact they afford a glimpse of great significance into one of the *principles* guiding Aristotle's judgements about Population:

412ᵃ13 Of the natural bodies, some have life and some do not; and it is *self-nourishment* (*tēn di' hautou trophēn*) and *growth and decay* that we speak of as life. Hence, every natural body that partakes of life would be a substance; namely, a substance in the sense of the composite.

The notion of "self-nourishment", we shall see as further developments unfold, has a great deal more to it than (though it certainly includes) getting oneself fed. For the moment, in the interests of getting on, let it be

---

3 Artefacts are the products of what *Meta.* Zeta 7 calls "makings" (*poiēseis*); and even if they are substances, as pointed out below (pp. 159–60) their form must pre-exist in the psyche of the "maker", the form of the web in the psyche of the spider just as surely as the form of the house in the psyche of the housebuilder. The PA makes a similar contrast to the above, between artefacts (*tekhnasta*) and "the real things themselves" (*auta ta pragmata*), though without pronouncing explicit doctrine on the Population issue (641ᵇ13–14). We shall make a last disavowal of the artefacts as substances at the metaphysical level in §19(iii), though they will continue to be with us as illustrations, as they are (for better or worse) throughout Aristotle.

summarily stipulated from its brief introduction in §14(iv) that *trophē* (nourishment, nurture, maintenance, tending) and its modifier form *threptikon*, and the verb *trephesthai* in the middle voice, centrally connote the activity of an organism in maintaining itself in existence by the acquisition, ingestion and processing of nutrients, called *trophēi khrēsthai* (cf. ii 4 415^{a}26); wider than "food" or "eating", the idea translates into our vocabulary more in terms of *metabolic self-sustenance*.[4] Temporarily forestalling all further complications, what is portended in 412^{a}14–15 ("it is *trophē di' hautou* and *auxēsis kai phthisis* that we speak of as life") is that for living substances in the real world, *what constitutes the continuity of numerically one and the same individual substance over time (what has earlier been dubbed "diachronic individuation") will be whatever that continuity of "metabolic self-sustenance" may be empirically found, by the scientific investigation of Nature, to consist in.* Scarcely anything is said yet to fill in this bare indication any further, beyond the phrase "growth and decay": as for that, typically, the continuous life-history of an individual substance (once it has commenced to exist, cf. §15(i)) will be marked by metamorphic stages of development, usually including (a) growth and maturation, into a form regarded as (b) "adult", the arrival at a point of (c) completest development and maximum flourishing (called "peaking", *akmazein*, i.e. reaching the *akmē*),[5] and finally (d) a concluding phase of senescence and decline, ending in (e) natural destruction (for all of this recall §9, esp. Facts 2(b), 7). Yet, as vivid in the foreground as are these phenomena of "growth and decay" in practice, the *de Anima* is clear and emphatic that the phenomenon of "metabolic self-sustenance", *trophē di' hautou*, is theoretically much the more fundamental. We shall be back to this later in (ii) below (cf. p. 159).

The chapter proceeds with the project of "trying to determine what is psyche and what would be the most-fully-shared *logos* of it" (412^{a}5–6 above). The project is pursued in a sequence of four schematic definitions,[6] each complicated from the one before by the incorporation of new elements introduced in the intervening discussion. The exposition here is as magisterial as anywhere in the extant corpus.

412^{a}16 Since [the natural body in question] is indeed a body of such a kind – for it is one having life – the psyche would not *be* body, [but rather would be form,]

---

4 For this wide sense: The *eskhatē trophē* is *blood*, and constitutes the basic material of the body as a whole, *PA* ii 4 651^{a}13–15. In French it can be called "autotrophie" (Pellegrin (1982), 158).

5 In Man, by the way, "the body 'peaks' (*akmazei*) at from 30 to 35 years of age; the psyche, at about 49" (!) *Rhet* ii 4 1390^{b}11.

6 Of course the sequentiality of the fourfold definition has long been recognized; cf. e.g. Owens, "Ar.'s definition of soul", in Owens (1981).

for the body is not something [predicated] 'of a subject', but exists rather as [itself a] subject and a matter. Necessarily, therefore,

^{a}19 [1] *the psyche is substance, ⟨in the sense of form⟩, of a natural body potentially having life.*

– But substance [in the sense of form] is completedness (*entelekheia*). Therefore,

^{a}21 [2] *the psyche is the ⟨completedness⟩ of a body of this kind.*

– But completedness is spoken of in two ways, first as knowledge is, and second as theorizing is [= the exercise of knowledge]. ^{a}23 Then it is clear that [psyche is completedness] as knowledge is; for both sleep and waking depend on the existence of the psyche, and waking is analogous to theorizing, and sleep to the having but not the exercise of knowledge.

With this last clause, the very important provision is made that will allow enpsyched organisms to⋅ have *resting phases* with respect to their polymerous activities and behaviors, without the consequence of ceasing to be. (For more on inactivity and being, see §16(ii)).

– But in the same individual, it is knowledge that is prior in genesis. Hence,

^{a}27 [3] *the psyche is the ⟨first⟩ completedness of a natural body potentially having life.*

– But of this kind would be the sort of body [that is termed] *organic, having-organs* [*organikon*]. [412^b] – Even the parts of plants are organs, although extremely simple ones, e.g. the leaf is a covering for the pericarp, and the pericarp for the fruit; and the roots are analogous to the mouth, for both take in *trophē*. ^{b}4 – If, then, we need to speak of something common to all of psyche, it would be that

^{b}5 [4] [*the psyche*] *is the first completedness of a natural body ⟨that is organic, that has-organs* [*organikou*]⟩.

In the last transformation, the fourth and final version of the schematic definiens is obtained from the third version through the replacement of the expression (modifying "natural body")

([3]) *dunamei zōēn ekhom* (potentially having life)

by the expression

([4]) *organikon* (organic, having-organs, being organ-ized).

Therefore, the expositor must regard these two expressions as identical in meaning. We have already seen that the *organikon* in turn is regularly identified with the *an-homoiomeres* or nonuniform (§11); the physiological concept of the nonuniform has been elaborated at length and connected with that of differentiation by multiple differentiae (§13); and some deep implications have been drawn from the embryology regarding the connections in this theory between these aspects and 'being one' in the sense of being unified into a composite individual, in both a synchronic and diachronic sense (§15(i)). Thus for a reader or hearer sensitized by the Aristotelean lore of §§11–15, the transition from [3] to [4] in *DA* ii 1 is loaded with significance as to the conceptions surrounding the deceptively simple words, "natural body".[7] As for "potentially having life", we shall shortly be back to that.

The next phase of *DA* ii 1 develops themes concerning the basically metaphysical concepts of substantial *unity* and of *essence* ('what it is to be', *ti ēn einai*), whose main treatment in the present work should be postponed for the setting-up of form-matter metaphysics (§§19–23); but it is so densely interwoven with distinctively biological concerns that it still must be considered at this point:

412[b]6 Hence too it isn't necessary to inquire whether the psyche and the body are *one*, no more than whether the wax and the configuration [*to skhēma*, impressed by the seal] are one, nor generally the matter of each thing and that [i.e., the completedness] whose matter it is. [b]8 For, while both *one* and *being* are predicated (lit., "said") in a variety of ways, the most rightful of ways is the completedness ['s being predicated of that whose completedness it is].[8]

[b]9 It has, then, been declared generally what the psyche is; for it is substance, namely the [substance] in respect of the *logos*. And this is the 'what it is to be' [*ti ēn einai*] for 'a body of *this* sort' [*tōi toiōidi sōmati*]. [b]11 It's like this: suppose some tool or instrument [*ti tōn organōn*], e.g. a hatchet, were a natural body; then its substance would be the 'to be for a hatchet', and this would be its psyche; and if this were separated from it, it would no longer be a hatchet – except homonymously. [b]15 But as things are, it is [just] a hatchet; for it is not of *this* sort of body that the psyche is the 'what it is to be' and the *logos*, but of a certain kind of natural body having within itself a source of movement [*kinēsis*] and rest [*stasis*].

This marks a further refinement, here not so much on the Population issue[9] as of the concept being developed: when the *empsucha* are characterized as 'metabolic self-sustainers', this by definition includes having a capacity for certain sorts of *self-initiated activities*. (It is most unlikely that the *kinēsis* and *stasis* of 412[b]17 is confined to 'local' movement and rest; the latter is regularly made explicit in the *DA* by *kata topon*, and in any case the intention certainly is not to exclude either sessile animals or plants.[10] In fact, *kinēsis* and *stasis* are related as second and first actualization or completedness.) Thus here we again intersect with a *topos*, namely: the

---

7 Pellegrin (1982) quotes Gilson on the connection between the nonuniform and the threptic, p. 34, n. 13.

8 We shall return to the metaphysics of Being & One ("Unity of Form"), §23(iv).

9 As at 412[a]11–13, cf. p. 148 above.

10 At *DA* ii 2 413[a]24–5, *kinēsis kai stasis kata topon* is itemized as a separate line item from a certain *kinēsis kata trophēn*. The passage is treated below with context (413[a]21–[b]1, pp. 157 ff).

uniqueness to biological objects of self-initiated, future-oriented behavior, which we first met in §9 as the second half of Fact 3, and have periodically revisited (recall, especially, §13(ii), §15(i)). The idea is roughly that of a type of entity that, though perishable, *tries to continue to exist*.[11] Hence the two criteria overlap, since much of the self-initiated behavior of animals, at least, is in connection with their *trophē di' hautōn*;[12] however, though deeply connected, the criteria are not co-extensive, and *a fortiori* not identical. We shall return to this in §16(ii).

It should also be noticed in the contrary-to-fact *hatchet* analogy of 412^b10–17 above, as in the more accordant-with-fact *eye* analogy of 412^b17–25 below, how the anti-migration "essence" condition (cf. §6, §8, §15) is phrased in terms of homonymy: "separate" the psyche or form from the hatchet, or let the eye "lose" the psyche or form, and the *thing* we call the hatchet or the eye disappears, whatever remains is not any longer 'what it was', and if so called, is so called homonymously. (Notice too, however, that these two paragraphs do *not* go quite so far as to *say* that numerically one and the same individual does not survive the transformation – it is compatible with them that *one* individual was earlier a hatchet and later a nonhatchet, or "tehctah", or earlier an eye and later a noneye, or "eye" (speaking of homonymy). We shall come back to this also.)[13]

412^b17 We must consider what has been said also as regards the parts [i.e., now, of an acknowledged *natural* body]. For, suppose the eye were an animal; then *sight* would be its psyche; for this is substance of an eye corresponding to the *logos*. $^b20$ The eye is 'matter' for sight, and if this [sight] is lost, it is no longer an eye – except homonymously, just like the eye in stone, or the painted one. $^b22$ Now then, what applies to the part must be applied to the living body as a whole; for as the part [sight] is to the part [eye], so analogously is the whole of perception [*aisthēsis*] to the whole perceptive body [*to holon sōma to aisthētikon*] as such.

There follows a terse but extremely significant gloss on the technical expression, "potentially having life" (412^a20, 28).

412^b25 It is not that which has cast off [or: lost] its psyche which is "potentially such as to live", but that which has it. The seed and the fruit are "potentially bodies of this kind".

11 There is a strong affinity of content, and I would speculatively hazard, a possible historical connection, between Aristotle's idea of an organism's natural propensity to maintain itself in existence – one aspect of "future-orientation" – and Spinoza's concept of *conatus* (see, e.g., *Ethics* iii 7). Stuart Hampshire's famous parallel between Spinozist *conatus* and Freudian *libido* is also apt (*Spinoza*, pp. 141–4); but for Spinoza, Aristotle could be a source. (Hampshire saw the affinity, p. 175.)   12 Cf. Bonitz, *Index* 775^{b}56 ff. (s.v. *trophē* 2(e)).
13 The point has some subtlety: cf. §21.

It is straightforward enough that the intended designatee of the expression "natural body potentially having life" is not the corpse. And it is also evident that "the seed and the fruit" *could* be meant by that expression in *some* sense that the words are capable of bearing (although in strictness that would conflict with the official doctrine of the embryology, at least as regards "seed").[14] What is slightly surprising about bringing up "the seed and the fruit" in the present context is, of course, that they do *not* exemplify the potentiality/actuality relationship that the chapter is trying to elaborate, which is a *simultaneous* relationship between body (as material subject) and psyche (as form and substance-of), and not a *prospective* relationship between something potentially such-and-such and the actual such-and-such that it is later going to come-to-be if "nothing hinders". – There is no way of telling by what lapse of composition or transmission this irrelevancy was introduced; but by way of advancing the discussion to better effect, two comments are in order at this point.

First, it seems that at least at the present state of scientific understanding of these matters (for "present", read "$+1987$" or "-322" pretty much indifferently, as you prefer), the only practical way of getting to see a "natural body potentially having life in it" is by mentally abstracting to it from some existing natural body *actually* having life in it, a mental operation that is supposed to be analogous to prescinding from the wax-seal-with-the-impression-in to just the wax, or generally from the matter-informed to the matter (cf. 412^b6–9 above). In no way can this be as simple an affair as looking at a corpse, or some fruit or seed. There is indeed something faintly quixotic about the operation: trying to pull the Organized Body out from under the First Actualization is a bit like trying to pull the Cheshire Cat away from the Smile (it has even occurred to me that the second image might have been meant in some small part as light mockery of the first). At any rate, if we are to be accomplished Aristotelean psychologists and somatologists, this is something that we have to practice and become good at.

Some people are bothered by the fact that, as 412^b25–27 points out, the only "organic bodies potentially having life" ("OBPHLs") are the ones that are actually enpsyched. It is thought: since the bronze of which the hatchet is composed is identifiable as a matter independent of its assuming hatchet form and could exist before and after assuming that form, is it

---

14 That is, the equine *kuēma* is potentially an animal and a horse, but equine *sperma* is not. Cf. §14(iv). As there pointed out, this is by no means the only place in the extant treatises where such misstatements occur: e.g., *Meta.* Theta 7, 1049^a14–16, cf. §20(ii). The finer distinction between 'out of' the catamenia and 'out of' the kuema recurs below in the metaphysical setting: see §20(iii), p. 197, and note 16 thereto.

not a problem that the OBPHL is not so identifiable and cannot so exist?[15] According to the line being developed here, it does not seem to be a problem. It has already been pointed out, in §12(ii) *fin.*, that *all* the "matters" of a living thing that are "double" (*ditton*), down to and including the uniform, are tied to being informed by the whole form, i.e., enpsyched by the whole psyche, and can only exist when the form is there – take away the form, and what is left is just elements and nonliving compounds. The OBPHL is just the general case of this; it is the total matter, top to bottom, almost all of it *ditton*. It comes-to-be in stages, in embryonic development, as the various grades of psyche enpsych it, the story we have just heard in §§14 and 15. (It is imaginable that it could cease-to-be in a kind of reverse order, although that is not usual in nature as we know it.)

To put it another way: there is a disanalogy as well as an analogy between the hatchet or statue on one hand and the living thing on the other; but the disanalogy should be seen as pointing up once again the weakness of the hatchet or statue as an exemplification of the concept, rather than the inappropriateness of the application to living things. It can never be too strongly emphasized that hatchets and statues are heuristic and protreptic, not paradigm cases.[16]

Second, as I understand the methodology of this topic: with the continuation of research (of the kind that Aristotle has begun) concerning living things, the accumulation of knowledge about their structure and functioning and the advance of detailed scientific understanding of them, it is to be expected that biologists will come to understand in a much more concrete, specific and detailed way than is possible for Aristotle himself, exactly what sorts of physical structures are capable of supporting the functions whose exercise constitutes *living* for a living thing – in other words, science can aspire to be able to enlarge upon the description "natural body potentially having life" by giving a description of exactly what sorts of body, in detail, "part" by "part", Nature has fabricated for the purpose of actually having life.[17] This is the view that Aristotle's phrase in the *de Anima* should be regarded as a "paper draft" redeemable

---

15 This is one of Ackrill's (1972–3) worries in "Aristotle's Definitions of *Psuche*".

16 Cf. §19(iii). The point is nicely made in Kosman (1984), pp. 141, 143.

17 DA ii 2, "[The psyche] is not a body, but something which 'belongs to' a body, and for this reason 'exists in' a body, and 'in' *a body of such-and-such a kind*. Not as our predecessors supposed, when they fitted it to 'a body' without any further determination of *what* body, and *of what kind*, – although it is clear that one chance thing does not receive another. But taken *thus* [i.e., in *our* way], it happens in a rational manner [*kata logon*]. For the actuality of each thing comes about naturally in that which is already such potentially, and in its appropriate matter." (414ª20–27)

by such a detailed description when biological understanding has advanced that far; indeed the view has already surfaced in our outline of Aristotelean morphology (cf. §12(ii), p. 87, §13(iii), p. 105). It does not seem to me that Aristotle must regard *his* biology (better, *his* psychosomatology) as a finished science.[18] What must be understood, however, is the *nature* of the many discoveries (anatomical, physiological, physical, chemical) that are yet to be made. They will not be discoveries about the details of how the material elements are 'built up' into living bodies; *they will be discoveries about the details of what the form does to the matter*. Also, of course, these details are not *microscopic*.

All of this last has been elicited by the little paragraph $412^{b}25$–7, on "potentially having life"; we may now proceed to the rest.

$^{b}27$ Just, then, in the way of the [hatchet's] cutting and the [eye's] seeing, in that way, too, the waking state is completedness, $[413^{a}]$ whereas the psyche is like sight and the potentiality of the instrument; the body is what is this potentially. $^{a}2$ But just as the eye is pupil [etc.] and sight, so in the present instance the psyche and the body are an animal.

$^{a}4$ Therefore, that the psyche – or certain parts of it, if its nature is divisible – cannot exist separate from the body, is quite clear ["not unclear"]; for the completedness is *of* some of the parts themselves. $^{a}6$ Not that anything prevents some [other] parts [of the psyche] from being able to exist separate, on account of their being actualities of no body. $^{a}9$ Beyond this, it *is* unclear whether the psyche is completedness of the body in the way that a sailor is of a ship.

Let this suffice as a definition and sketch in outline of the psyche. [End of ii 1.]

The last two sentences but one, $413^{a}6$–9, come as something of a shock: nothing in the preceding has prepared the hearer for the news that on this account of the psyche there is room for actualities that are realizations of no material potential; obviously the way is being (rather stealthily) laid for the mysterious Productive or Active Intellect in Book iii.[19] And the profession of uncertainty about the merits of the psyche : body :: sailor : ship analogy, if meant seriously, seems a retrograde step after some of the profound and intricate subtleties that have gone before.

18 No more need he regard his zoology as comprehensive in the sense of including *all* the specific kinds; Pellegrin (1982) is right to reject "encyclopedism" as an Aristotelean ideal (180–6).

19 About which I have little to add to the enormous body of discussion on this vexed and still poorly-understood topic. It would be in accord with the general tendency advocated here to regard the active intellect, like psyche generally, as the same faculty in all of us numerically distinct human beings who are credited with it (though perhaps not the same as for nonhuman intelligences, for which see below). But I have no confidence in the consistency of any interpretation of the matter. Ross, *DA* 41–8.

However, these matters are beside our present concern, which is to gather in the remaining most salient points of substantive biology in the *DA* that bear on the metaphysics of substances. And the chief such point to emerge from the foregoing is undoubtedly, *trophē*: that of a living body's necessarily harboring, as a condition necessary to its existence as the very kind of thing it is, a capacity of "metabolic self-sustenance", as it was called, *trophē di' hautou*. What more has the *DA* to teach about this?

(ii) Threptic psyche and diachronic individuation

The capacity is named *to threptikon* and, sometimes, "threptic psyche"; it is basically, as has been said, an organism's capacity for maintaining itself in existence as the thing that it is. But it is worthwhile to start by seeing it in the context of the whole spectrum of capacities with which it can in various life-forms be associated. These are understood as forming a kind of hierarchy, each one presupposed by those that come after in the sequence: threptic psyche is first and most fundamental, found without exception in every living thing – plant or animal – on the Earth (413^a30–3, $^b7$–8, 414^a32–$^b1$, etc.), and presupposed by all the others. Next is *to aisthētikon* or "aesthetic psyche", the most basic of whose diversifications is perception by touch, shared by all animals (413^b4–9), and of particular importance to the threptic function of animals (it is an *aisthēsis tēs trophēs*, 414^b6–7, and is the "most necessary" of all the senses, 414^a3, cf. *PA* ii 8 653^b22–7); also, touch invariably brings in its train a capacity for craving or desiring, called *to orektikon* or "orectic psyche" and including, among other *orexeis*, hunger and thirst (414^b11–16). On top of this, in certain higher animals, are found other varieties of aesthetic psyche such as sight, hearing, smell, taste; and in largely the same species, also the faculty termed *kinētikon kata topon*, "kinetic psyche", a capacity for locomotion. Finally, a small fraction of the living things, identified as "human beings and whatever else may be similar or superior" (414^b18–19), are favored with *to dianoētikon te kai nous*, intelligence and the capacity for thought; it is likely that the reference to nonhuman intellects is meant to incorporate those formidable eternal reasoners that move the celestial bodies, and the Unmoved Motor itself.

Redescending to the mundane and to the threptic: it was noted earlier (pp. 148–9) that for biological substances, the general operating principle for what counts as the persistence of "numerically one and the same" substantial individual through change across time, is, that which (as best we can scientifically determine) constitutes the continuity of metabolic self-sustenance, the *trophē di' hautou*, of an organic body. This is because the fundamental function, *ergon*, of a biological substance – the function presupposed by any other functions it may have, the "most prior" element of its definition – is *to live*, when and only when it ceases to live, then and only then it ceases to exist; and the capacity of psyche that is the capacity for (and, it follows, thus co-extensive with) life itself, is the threptic. The point is made in *DA* ii 2 in terms of plants, which are thought to have only the threptic level of psyche, so that the living-function can be seen uncomplicated by the aesthetic, orectic, kinetic, etc. capabilities of the animals:

413ª21 . . . the enpsyched is distinguished from the unpsyched, by *living*, being alive [*tōi zēn*]. But *living* is said in several ways, and we say that a thing is alive if but one of the following is present: intelligence, perception, movement and rest in respect of place, and furthermore the movement in respect of *trophē*, and both decay and growth. ª25 This last is why all things that [merely] grow [the thought is: plants, which do none of the other things just enumerated] are thought to be alive; for they evidently have in them such a power and principle [*arkhē*], through which they acquire both growth and decay – in opposite directions. ª28 For they do not grow upwards without growing downwards, but they grow in both directions alike and in every direction – this being so of *those that are constantly nourished [trephetai] and live through to the end, as long as they are able to take up nourishment [trophēn]*. ª31 This [level of life] can exist apart from the others, but the others cannot exist apart from it in mortal creatures. This is apparent in the case of plants ["things that grow", as at ª25]; for they have no other capacity [413ᵇ] of psyche.

It is important that what is being put forward here be clearly and sharply understood; for matters at this juncture are highly delicate. We are being told (1) that for living things, to exist is to be alive, and (2) that one function for which any organized body that is alive must have the capacity or 'psyche' is metabolic self-sustenance or *trophē di' hautou*, and (3) that the continued existence of such a living thing consists at least in the continuity of that capacity, so that for a specific kind *F*, being the same individual = being the same *F* = being the same *threptikon F*. To that extent, the statement is informative as to the principles guiding Aristotle's judgements about Population (cf. pp. 148–9 above); but we need to notice several things it does *not* tell us.

First, *as formulated it still does not yet instruct us how to decide particular cases, i.e. specifically what to call the continuity of what is "the same and numerically one"*. For example, recall the fantastic transformation, Socrates to wolf, that was imagined in §7: the question was, Is this a transsubstantiation, involving a true destruction and generation, or has one and the same individual undergone an unheard-of qualitative change? The statement just quoted tells something important about what to look for in deciding such a case: namely, look for continuity in the threptic capacity; but it does not tell us what that has to consist in, and we certainly cannot assume that the continued existence of one and the same individual is guaranteed by what *looks like* threptic continuity to the layman or tyro in biological matters. The problem may be biologically very deep (of course no such claim is made for our imagined case, which is biologically absurd). (Cf. §19(ii) below, and point "Third" following.)

Second, the "at least" in (3) above is also important: theoretically, there *can* be threptic continuity through substantial change, where it is overridden as a factor by other factors – e.g. discontinuity in higher capacities, such as the loss of intellect if such occurs, or so radical a change in the *mode* of exercising some capacity, such as, say, locomotion, that all other apparent continuities are held to be offset. Or factors may turn out to be involved that from a normal, practical standpoint would strike us as quite extraneous. (For further details, see the final wrap-up of the Population issue in §21 below.) If threptic psyche is the only psyche the organism has, then this kind of issue becomes much simpler – there can be no question that this is one reason Aristotle uses plants for his illustrative purposes at this point.

Third, the whole question of threptic continuity is complicated by the difficulty of distinguishing in the threptic case between first and second actualization. That is, whereas with respect to *perceiving* or *locomoting*, there is a sense patent to everyone in which sometimes we are active, and sometimes at rest though still capable. Indeed, that is one of the most attractive features of the schematic definition: by distinguishing "first and second entelechy", "as knowledge is and as theorizing is", the conception makes a natural place for organisms that are conceived as essentially active beings (recall the second half of Fact 3 in §9) to go into a *resting phase* with respect to an activity without this having to be understood as a *diachronic discontinuity*, like a temporary death of some sort. That much is obvious; and much the same holds for *trephesthai* insofar as that is *eating* or *digesting*; but in the wide construal of an organic body's *trophē di' hautou* that seems to be required for the needed generality, i.e. "metabolic self-sustenance", what is the continuity of the *capacity* that is not just *metabolizing*? The problem is that threptically, anything that is alive at all seems to be always "awake" – what would threptic "sleep" be like? Presumably the best line for visualizing this is some sort of "suspended animation" that would have to be strictly distinguished from death (it is uncertain whether Aristotle would hold that this was biologically – let alone medically – possible; but that uncertainty is obviously beside the present point).[20]

In the passage last quoted, as frequently, the threptic capacity is introduced in close association with the ubiquitous tendency among biological objects towards "growth and decay"; but as was mentioned earlier (p. 149), these are not the same, and in the usual biological cases, the threptic capacity is at the core of the diachronic identity of the living substantial individual in a way that its growth and decay are not. On a little thought this appears reasonable enough in itself, but Aristotle in ii 4 carefully goes out of his way to make it explicit:

416[b]11 *Being trophē* and *being growth-producing* [auxetic] are distinct; for it's insofar as the enpsyched thing is something of-a-size that [*trophē*] is auxetic, but it's insofar as [the enpsyched] is *tode ti* and a substance that [*trophē*] is *trophē*. [b]14 For [the enpsyched] *preserves its substance, i.e.,* [*kai* epexegetic?] *for this space exists, as long as it is fed* [*trephetai*]; and it can bring about the generation, not of that which is fed [= itself], but of something like what is fed; [b]16 for its substance is already in existence, and nothing generates itself,[21] but rather preserves itself. [b]17 Hence this sort of [threptic] origin of the psyche is *a potentiality to preserve its possessor as such, and the trophē makes it ready for activity;* [b]20 which is why, if deprived of *trophē*, it cannot exist.   (Cf. *CTB/PA* i 5 322[a]23–8, & *GA* ii 6 744[b]33–7)

In this way the threptic is firmly and explicitly linked to the preservation of *substance*.

It should be kept in mind here that all the powers of the psyche – aisthetic, kinetic, et cetera – are mobilized in achieving the many particular instrumental *telē* that are 'for the sake of' the main *telos* of self-maintenance and self-preservation.[22] Giving chase, taking flight, stalking, assuming protective coloration, spotting prey, spotting predator, gathering nest materials, . . . all future-oriented routines; as observed in §9, in the animal world most of them do not involve conscious planning and explicit purposes, that is just one variety (not necessarily confined to humankind) that can serve as an illustrative model. In the

20 Since writing the above, I have learned of the strange and exotic poison called tetrodotoxin, which apparently can have exactly the narcoleptic effect imagined in the text. It is implicated in, among other things, the "zombieism" of the voodoo culture of Haiti. For details, see Davis (1986).   21 *GA* ii 1 735[a]13.

22 Marjorie Grene touches upon this in relating the "teleonomic study of biological systems" to the "diachronic rather than the synchronic study of their form" (though I am not sure I understand her suggestion that the former is "probably reducible" to the latter). "Aristotle and Modern Biology", in Grene and Mendelsohn (1976), p. 20.

same vein, the form of the web is in the psyche of the spider as surely as the form of the house is in the psyche of the housebuilder; but neither Aristotle nor anyone else (but a storyteller) would hold that the spider *thinks* about it, as the housebuilder can.

Perhaps the most dramatic, even spectacular, indication of the significance Aristotle seems to see in threptic or metabolic self-sustenance as criterial for the temporal continuity of biological objects, comes in the location of the *reproductive* or "gennetic" faculty in threptic psyche, and the idea of *the gennetic faculty in the substantial individuals as a kind of threptic faculty in the substantial species.*[23]

The passage that seals the threptic-gennetic connection is this (ii 4):

415^a22 . . . We must first discuss *trophē* and *gennesis*; for the threptic psyche belongs also to the others [= other living things], and is the first and the most commonly shared power of the psyche, in virtue of which life belongs to them all. $^a25$ Its functions are reproduction and *trophē khrēsthai* [cf. pp. 148–9 above]; for it is the most natural function in living things, such as are perfected and not mutilated or do not have spontaneous generation, each to produce another thing like itself – an animal to produce an animal, a plant a plant – in order that they may partake of the everlasting and the divine in so far as [415^b] they can; for all desire that, and for the sake of that they do the things that they do, in accordance with nature. – $^b2$ But 'that for the sake of which' is twofold: there is the purpose for which [*to hou*] and the beneficiary for whom [*to hōi*]. – Since, then, they cannot share in the everlasting and the divine by continuous existence, because no perishable thing can persist the same and numerically one [everlastingly], they partake of them as far as each can, some more and some less, $^b6$ and what persists is not the thing itself but something like itself, not one in number, but one in *eidos*.

(Very much the same theme is heard in GA ii 1: the part about trying to share in the eternal (*aidion*) near the beginning of the chapter (731^b24–732^a1), and the part about collocation of the threptic and gennetic psyche near the end (735_a13–26), cf. also *CTB/PA* ii 11 *fin.*.)

Thus the "primary psyche", in which threptic and gennetic are conjoined, represents a twofold capacity of certain biological objects with regard to transtemporal persistence. The threptic, in the individual, is the basic faculty of self-*maintenance* across time, and works by metabolic

---

23 Sometimes when the collocation of the two powers in one psyche is under discussion, it is called "primary psyche", as at ii 4 416^b20–5, according to which there is:
to trephon, 'what feeds' = the primary (= threptic) psyche,
to trephomenon, 'what's fed' = the body having the primary psyche,
hōi trephetai, 'that by which it's fed' = the *trophē*,
and the *telos* of 'generating something like oneself' is also assigned to the primary (= gennetic) psyche.

exchange of materials with the environment, particularly the processing of nutrients or *trophē khrēsthai* (pp. 148–9 above, and the quotation just now); this is explicitly *not* a generative process (for "nothing generates itself", 416^{b}16–17, p. 159 above), but a preservative one – had there been a *Parva-Naturalia*-style work devoted to this topic, it might have been styled, "On Perduring and Senescing". The gennetic, in the individual, is the faculty of self-*duplication*; it works by the intricate mechanisms that have been described in §§14–15. But looked at at the species level (or *sub specie speciei*), the gennetic faculty of the individuals becomes, and the preceding quotation from DA ii 4 indicates it explicitly conceived as, a threptic capacity of that eternal being (*on*), the species: this capacity too works by a kind of metabolic exchange of materials with the environment – as little parcels of matter are taken up by specific form to constitute new bits, or "parts" in the appropriate sense, of this higher-level object, which persist as such for a while before breaking up again, always being replaced by new and younger cohorts ("parts"). At this level it is also not a generative process (the species does not reproduce), but a preservative one – the preservation in this case, however, being everlasting.

The whole notion is an interesting and somewhat remarkable case of impressing some rhapsodical Platonic themes – Symposian, Phaedrian – the eternality and perfection of form, the yearning and striving of the perishable for the immortal and empyrean and divine – into a vision that is immediately recognizable by us who look back as at once poetically rather inspired and scientifically altogether coherent.

IV. BIO-METAPHYSICS

§17. Three lessons from the biology

Now we are in a position to bring this inquiry home to the metaphysics: extracting the relevant points of intuition and theory developed in connection with biological objects as Aristotelean substances, in order to illuminate what he calls (*Meta*. Zeta 1) the central and most vexatious metaphysical question: What *is* substance? Let us first take stock of the more significant new aspects that have been introduced into our *aristotelische Weltauffassung* since we took leave of the *Categories*.

(i) The size and depth of the world

First, the little world of the *Categories* is seen from the biological perspective to be embedded in, to be a spatially discontinuous fraction of, a much wider and deeper universe: the total sublunary universe of Empedoclean matter.[1] This universe is wider, in having a great deal more in it than just the ("primary", *sensu Cat.*) individual substances and their cross- and intra-categorial paraphernalia: there is matter in many other states than as worked up into substances – such as the many piles (molar "earth"), jugfuls ("water"), breezes, conflagrations, etc. *ad lib.*[2] And this universe is deeper: for the "primary" substances of the *Cats.*, which in that work, as has been noticed already (§4), are atomic, opaque, and inscrutable, are now seen to be endowed with internal structure: as the semi-stable "knots"[3] that are open to the detailed analysis that goes in terms of Matter and Form.

Here we should recall to mind, from §9, the radical consequences for

---

1 "Sublunary" still, as since §0, §10 (note 2).

2 An alternative conception of the difference (to me, less attractive as a construal of the *Cats.*) would construe the bio-metaphysical universe not as "wider", but as possessing a more complex vertical structure in terms of which (in *Cats.* language) the category of things neither in a subject nor said-of a subject no longer has to coincide with that of the primary substances – e.g., a pile of earth may now be construed as belonging to the first but not to the second. Cf. §17(iii) below.

3 Here, a term of art: see §18.

this whole scheme of Aristotle's adoption of an Empedoclean concept of the basic material elements – as opposed to, say, an atomic theory – a view that takes the basic 'elements' to be stuffs, bulks, fluids, gases, whose 'combination' is therefore not structural but chemical in nature.[4] It cannot be too strongly emphasized that the occurrence of *structure* in the natural world is for Aristotle a *phenomenon that calls for explanation*, that challenges us to 'find the causes'; and the basic matter, as such, 'of itself' (*kath' hautēn*) cannot be it. It is in this context that he deploys, with full methodological self-consciousness, the hypothesis that there is a causal agency at work in the natural world, called Form.

For the present the point is this: the biological application in effect takes the universe of the *Categories*, immerses it in the wider setting of Empedoclean matter, and opens the way to using the concept of specific form (called in the *PA* "the differentia in the matter", 643ª24) to explain the shaping-up of the organisms into "thisses" exemplifying stable natures or "whats" across time. Shortly we shall return to examine this further from a metaphysical perspective.

(ii) Constructional interpretation or vertical dimension of differentia. "Intelligible matter"

Second, we now know from the biology that this matter-form analysis has about it in actual practice several distinct complexities that are not called into play by the usual stock examples, such as bronze statues and spheres. It has in the biological application a hierarchical, many-levelled character, building up (i) the elementary materials through sequences of stages of organization, i.e., (ii) material compounds, (iii) the "uniform" (*homoiomerē*) tissue types, (iv) the transitional, semi-structural systems, (v) the fully articulated-out "nonuniform" (*anomoiomerē*) organ systems and (vi) organic bodies as wholes, each level functioning as "matter" for those above it (recall *GA* 715ª9–11, *PA* 646ᵇ5–35, *CTB/PA* 321ᵇ16–22, etc., and §12(i)(ii) above), where the particular mode of organization depends on the species. And although the concept of *matter* of course applies to the basic material elements, and to such relatively elementary compound stuffs as bronze or stone, and to such relatively refined compound stuffs as blood or marrow, the concept of a matter is also expanded to apply in general to *that which is capable of (further) form, that which is subject for*

4 "Not like colored marbles", I recall once reading in some work on nineteenth-century science, "but like colored fluids".

(further) determination. In this sense a "matter" may be something already of itself formed or differentiated to a considerable degree. In particular, as was argued in §13(iv), a "matter" may be a *generically-structured conformation*, of which there are various more specific determinations that stand to it as alternative possible differentiae (in the way that we imagined the specific cephalic forms of Bison, Yak and so on as standing to the generic cephalic conformation called *bucephalic*), but which itself is an already quite-well-worked-up nature, underlying which in turn (along with its companion generic forms like, in the example, Equine and Canine) are yet deeper generic natures (in §13(iv), *"cephaloid?"*) of which it and the others are more specific versions, and so on as form is successively abstracted away. At the next-to-topmost level, the entire complex organized body is called "matter" for its first actualization, the psyche (§16). At each level, save the topmost, the nature that is there located is a "matter" in the sense of *something susceptible of those more specific determinations not excluded by the degree of differentiation it already incorporates*; in this way it is *ditton*, "double in its nature",[5] both matter for what it is further shaped up into, and embodying form to the degree it is shaped up itself.

Such a generalization and attenuation of the matter-concept also ties in closely with the "vertical" dimension and the constructional or organizational aspect of differentia and genus, where genus represents the upper intermediate range of the sequence of levels through which an animal type is differentiated into specific form, and differentia connotes the articulation-out of some specification of that lesser-defined substrate potential.

This brings us to a point where it is apposite to hazard a speculation regarding the occasional peculiar contrast that Aristotle draws between "perceptible and intelligible matter"; for although the terminology itself is not found in the biological works or indeed anywhere but the *Metaphysics*,[6] an idea is at work here that *looks* like one of those for which that language is used. "Perceptible matter", *hulē aisthetē*, on one hand, seems always to be the ordinary, homespun notion of material stuff, either basic, like Earth, or compound, like wood, or some marrow. "Intelligible matter", *hulē noētē*, on the other hand, is on any account more puzzling; sometimes it seems to mean a supposed "material element" of some supposed immaterial entity, such as the geometer's circle. Without pausing here to risk an assessment of the merits of that idea, it seems that it also

5 *CTB/PA* i 5, 321ᵇ19 ff., cf. §12(i), footnote 3.
6 Epsilon 1 1025ᵇ34, Zeta 10 1036ᵃ10, Zeta 11 1036ᵇ35, 1037ᵃ4, Eta 6 1045ᵃ34, 36. We are back to this at more length in §23.

sometimes has the application of the vertical relationship borne by a more generic *nature* to the more specific differentiations of it – the idea of what in the simple example of §13(iv) was called the *bucephalic* bovine head-conformation underlying as an "intelligible matter" the respective head-forms of the Yak and of the Bison as divergent final differentiations. Later it will be shown how this idea can be made somewhat more precise, when the analysis of substantial being is stated in detail; it will also be tied in to a line of thought that we know to be Aristotle's own, when the problem of the so-called Unity of Definition is looked into in the light of intervening developments.[7]

In §23 an artefactual analogue will be offered: consider a city-state, or a club, having an organizational (written or unwritten) constitution. The "perceptible matter" of such an entity consists of the members of the community in question, who thus comprise its "perceptble parts" as of any particular moment of its history. But it also has *the "parts" that are specified in its constitution*: officers, standing committees, a legislative body, a disciplinary body, or whatever: these would form the entity's "intelligible" parts or matter, and are in an evident sense more permanent to (possibly to the point of being essential to) the entity, than are the particular persons who occupy, i.e. rotate through, these constitutional-ly-specified positions at one time or another. It seems apparent that Aristotle's way of looking at biological objects involves a similar distinc-tion, between the matter ("perceptible") that is taken up by the specific form of a given individual at any particular moment of its life, and the range of generic-through-specific differentiation ("intelligible") that is determined by its specific definition – if you like, a kind of natural "constitution" (which is "written" in one way in the specimens, and of a deep necessity in a different way in the semen, cf. §14(iv)).[8]

7 For the integration into the analysis of substance see §24; for the Unity of Definition connection, §23.

8 Here we are at the heart of a densely tangled thicket, involving not only the Unity of Definition question but that of Parts of the Form versus Parts of the Compound (*Meta.* Zeta 10–11, cf. §12(ii), esp. footnote 12, pp. 86–87), and several others as well; it will be treated in §23 below. Reserving the complications for the moment, it seems that Ross voices something very like the suggested interpretation of *hulē noētē*, though he does not make out the biological connection, when he comments: "*hulē noētē* in its widest conception is the thinkable generic element which is involved both in species and in individuals, and of which they are specifications and individualizations", AM ii 200 (Zeta 10, 1036a9 n.). I think he is wrong, however, in supposing that "in Aristotle's view everything that has sensible matter has intelligible matter, while the converse is not the case" (*ibid.*); Zeta 10 1036a11, which he cites for this view, tells only ambiguously (the noetic matter adduced being that of the "objects of mathematics"). And Ross proceeds to a general conspectus of "matters" in Aristotle that is thoroughly misguided; the moral may be gathered from §22(ii), §23(i) *fin.*

(iii) Form and unity

A third metaphysical area, one of great difficulty, that receives some needed illumination from the biology, has to do with the deep link, even perhaps fusion, in Aristotle's thought between the notion of being *formed* and that of being *unified* or '*one*'.

Let us quickly review our collisions with this refractory topic up until now. As early as §4, Aristotle was found in *Cats.* 3^{b}10–21 struggling to articulate the idea that not only are the substantial individuals, as treated in that work, to be regarded as each a certain 'this' (*tode ti*) and as individual (*a-tomon*) and as numerically one (*hen arithmōi*), but that something similar is true of the substantial species and genera too, and then gamely but hopelessly, certainly in the end with singular unsuccess, trying to explain what that similarity might be – in *what* sense it is that a species is a 'this'. And in §8, we ran into (or stumbled over) the puzzling more general phenomenon of Aristotle's seeming to regard individuality or 'this'-hood alternately as belonging to the specimens of the species, like Socrates, and to the species itself, like Man; at that stage we could do little more than point up the problem, indicate the apparent multi-stability for him of locutions like

Substance means a '*this*', as we maintain,

separate off some related but distinct questions (e.g. is this the view that every substantial individual has a substantial form of its very own, beyond that which it shares with fellow species members?), and take note of the general confusion and despair prevailing among the commentators regarding the entire topic.

Then, in §13, the "vertical", organizational dimension of differentia (just now briefly rehearsed) was explored, and in §15(i), while relating the embryology to the essentialism, we found ourselves led to the "strange hypothesis": that in some way that may not be altogether easy for us at our remove to understand, it is the substantial differentiae, constituting a thing as a full-fledged specimen of a substantial species, that are also responsible for its character of being a full-fledged individual 'this', as distinguished from an accretion or aggregate or 'heap'. In particular, the embryological suggestion was that prior to full specific differentiation, the embryonic (e.g.) human-being-to-be is neither yet Socrates, nor yet a full Aristotelean 'this', but still rather of the nature of a mass, although when it has differentiated to the point of being – say – *actually Animal*, it has achieved sufficient form – including, now, much in the way of partly-articulated nonuniform structure – to possess much of the generic nature that will become a portion of the "intelligible matter" underlying the eventual specific form.

In the transtemporal dimension, we have attended to the important role played in the natural realm by *telē*, ends or completions, "for the sake of which" the myriad future-oriented activities and processes "are"; the great majority of these too are specifically determined as part of organic "form". The most fundamental ones, directed at transtemporal persistence or self-maintenance via *trophē di' hautou*, have just been discussed (§16).

That some such link between form and unity may be operative is also hinted at in the intuition – suggested in §8 and §10, and about to be elaborated in the intuitive overview of §18 – that it is in general the existence of specific form that is *responsible* for the occurrence of Aristotelean individual 'thisses' in the universe at all: the intuition that, passing up the *scala naturae* that takes us from the elementary Earth, Water, etc. at one extreme, to the humans and horses at the other, substantial specific forms are required to get us past the level of rocks, rills, templed hills, puddles, piles and so on (recall once more the comparison with present-day Mars at §12(iii)). Thus without them, the thought is, even Fact 1 (§9) would not obtain.

This hypothesis of the apparent coalescence in Aristotle's thought of the individuative and the essence or constitutive properties of substantial kinds, although to our minds perhaps quite foreign and peculiar, seems to me to be the only at all plausible explanation of the extreme ambivalence manifested by the relevant textual material, which we shall consider more closely when the general reconstruction of the theory of substance is further advanced.[9]

Before proceeding, however, a small manifesto. I have used the expression "coalescence" and related terms like "ambivalence" and "multistability"; but I am not calling, and I think it would be a mistake, or at least extremely premature, to call, this running-together on Aristotle's part of notions that we are accustomed to distinguish – and this at the very center of the theoretical edifice he was trying to elaborate – a case of *confusion*. Our ability to make a distinction does not imply that an ancient thinker who apparently lacks the means to do so is therefore succeeding only in "lisping" what we can pronounce; and there is no reason to assume that Aristotle would be interested in helping himself to our

---

9 :"The problem of the unity of form", §23.

distinctions, had he access to them. My view is that he was creating – inventing – a concept of unitary material individual that had not thitherto existed as an explicit theoretical idea at all, with the aim of making conceptual sense of a *phenomenon* – strikingly visible in the animal kingdom – in which (a) the existence of individuals, both synchronically "unified" in the sense that underlies countability (§15(i)) and remaining diachronically one and the same while undergoing change across time, and (b) the presence of stable specific natures which seem never to be exchanged by the things that possess them and even remain stable when transmitted by reproduction, seem to co-occur, in their strongest forms, in the same cases. It is natural that in the newly-forged concept of substance, the properties of (b) "forming" and (a) "individuating" should have been seen as deeply connected, merging in an overall notion of "unifying" that covers them both. If closer to our own time they have decoupled, as indeed seems to be the case, that fact should be taken account of; but I find no basis in that fact for criticism of the form in which they originated. On the other hand, if someone finds this line not firm enough, and insists that confusion *is* what is going on here and what it should be called, then for comprehension's sake I am willing to adapt my phrasing to that viewpoint, and agree that: very well, on that understanding, at the very center of the theory, there is a confusion; but then I will wish to add, that it is still an exceedingly *interesting* confusion.

§18. Where we are at. An intuitive ontology, and the Population Problem (§7) briefly revisited

He got far enough, into enough areas of enough contemporary interest, for a projectibility problem to arise for Aristotle that is more serious, I think, than for any other "historical" Western philosopher except possibly Spinoza. That is, which is right?

> *If Aristotle were alive today, he would lap up molecular biology, atomic physics, relativistic cosmology*

or

> *If Aristotle were alive today, he would expound the Four Causes, Four-Element Matter Theory, Unmoved Motor, etc.*

A sensitive line of inquiry, in which a natural hankering of sympathetical-ly-inclined adepts toward the former tendency must be balanced against the canons of scholarly extrapolative caution – and in the end, of course, the doubtful meaningfulness of the question itself. It can even be dangerous.[1]

On some points there can be little argument: e.g., his laws of motion are not tenable; again, he rejected the atomic theory and that is that. On the other hand, we have seen that in a number of instances his biological insight reaches considerable depth, indicating that he was reaching after some right questions and issues, and even sometimes coming up with right answers and formulations, at a time when the available theorizing was very largely speculative and *ad hoc*, and the available corpus of systematic observation (other than his own) virtually nonexistent. As was stated at the very outset in §0, my interest here is to explain and to motivate his later theory of substantial essence, existence and individuation – a philo-sophical theory; and it suits that interest best to look once more at the Population Problem (What things are substances?), in order to ponder intuitively, in the light of developments in the discussion thus far, how he, or modern counterparts like ourselves, might now look at that.

Here there are several points to be made, or reinforced from the foregoing. First, I have said that I see the universe of substances (with their forms, essences, accidents, potentialities, generations-and-destruc-tions, and all the other baggage that goes along with them) as a *subuniverse* scattered through the total universe, which also contains a great deal else to which much of the apparatus of substance does not apply – e.g. events, like earthquakes and cyclones; other states of matter, like puddles and piles; entities like rainbows, and cities, and the sky; and perhaps the quasi-substantial states of matter like rock, etc., etc. That is, I see no reason to insist, or for Aristotle to have to insist, that absolutely everything in reality has to be either a primary substance (*sensu Cat.*), or else *in* a primary substance, or else *said-of* a primary substance – forcing reality to fit that rack whether it bends or breaks; that attitude, however typical it may be of the more belligerent philosophical spirit,[2] seems thoroughly unreasonable. And it seems *prima facie* simply absurd to insist that if there were no primary substances (*sensu Cat.*) then nothing else could exist at

1 I am told of a noted American professor, who liked to demonstrate the philosophical up-to-dateness of the ancients, whose History of Philosophy seminar was nicknamed by the graduate students "How Plato Invented the Atom Bomb".

2 As in Robert Musil's apophthegm: "Philosophers are violent and aggressive persons who, having no army at their disposal, endeavour to bring the world into subjection to themselves by locking it up in a system."

all: suppose the mean temperature of the universe were 1,000° hotter than it is, or merely consider the surface of the Sun – it is easy to find regions where nothing like (what Aristotle considers to be) those primary substances could possibly exist, yet we shouldn't then say: there's *nothing* there. The dependency claim, if it is to be in the least plausible, has to be relativized to this special ontological subsystem, and interpreted to mean: the existence of what is said-of, and what is in, the primary substances depends on their existence (and even then we may have doubts about "in": what about the "particular colors" shared by certain primary substances, *and* entities of such doubtful primary-substantiality as rainbows or the sky?[3] But never mind that – in his phrase, "This, let's drop", *Meta.* Zeta 10 1034^{b}33). So as I say, I see Aristotle as providing a theory, logico-philosophically interesting and biologically desiderated, of a subuniverse embedded as a spatiotemporally discontinuous portion within the total universe, and not necessarily as trying to retail in his substance-theory the whole truth about absolutely everything. But I could be wrong; I admitted above that retrodicting the verbal behaviour of philosophers is a chancy and even dangerous game; he might today bitterly denounce my view as vile heresy, or schism. It would be disappointing if he were really as dogmatic as some of his followers.

Of course, that the universe be hotter than it is is not a possibility for him, and he regards the subuniverse of substances as a necessary subuniverse, one indeed for the sake of which all the rest of the sublunary exists at all. This part of the apocalypse does not transport so well, and I shall return to it shortly.

On a related point, as anticipated in §7 and on this point with greater confidence to be representing Aristotle rightly, I regard the (sublunary) population of substances as the living beings and that is all; the artefacts may go the way of *DA* ii 1 412^{a}11–13 (§16(i)). Thus to me (and, I believe, for Aristotle) there is little interest in debating whether chairs belong or not, nor with taxing oneself over the enduring identity of ships in which over time every plank is replaced, at least as discussed by philosophers. Basically, while it is frivolous to say (as Wittgenstein half-facetiously said he briefly did, cf. §7) that the Population Problem is "merely empirical", there is a good sense in which we can say it is very frequently a *scientific* problem, to be approached in a sober and sensible way: track the putative individuals involved and after careful observation and consideration decide what is the best bag for them. Important discoveries are made in

---

3 It has the look of sheer legislation to lay it down as the *Cats.* does that "all color is in body".

this way, as when we learn (or after carefully observing and considering decide) that tadpoles and frogs are not distinct species as we may have formerly thought. There will always be fanatical extremes of irresponsibility, as when (fictitious) Héraclite-*selon*-Platon insists that not only is the frog distinct from the tadpole we want to say it was, but *no* object is *ever* the same for even a millisecond; at the opposite fanatical extreme someone will maintain (Parmenides? Leibniz?) that *no* object *ever* comes into or goes out of existence, however it may look. Aristotle duly notes these wild and fantastic and far-out positions; but the *History of Animals* is his real testament on the subject, as to *how* such decisions should be made: what is qualitative and what metamorphic but not substantial change (*metabasis eis allēn morphēn*, *HA* 487^{b}4), what is growth and decline, and what is the generation and destruction of individuals. This part of his projectibility-question seems relatively easy.[4]

But of course most of it will not transport, as is; we *are* in the last analysis doing history of philosophy past. Which brings me to prepare our exploration of the more difficult problems of substantial metaphysics, by an intuitive overview, beyond what has been said about his biological ideas, of the overall makeup of the world according to him. It is, he thinks, an Empedoclean, finite three-dimensional mass, entirely filled with the four elements which everywhere interpenetrate one another in varying proportions, commingling-together and separating-out through time in accordance with physical laws. Passing by much general theory concerning astronomy, meteorology, physics and the like, and coming straight to our present concern, we now observe that scattered through this three-dimensional mass[5] there are innumerable *knots*,[6] regions where the matter is very elaborately and intricately worked up into an organic unity – some kind of animal, say (here a worm, there a snail) – highly convoluted but relatively stable eddies[7] in the general commingling-and-separation. Up until this last, this was more or less straight Empedocles. Now, it has been indicated how Aristotle thinks the "principle" he calls "form" must be brought in on top of the Empedoclean basis (§12(iii)), to explain the

---

4 Which is not to say that it is easy, or yet settled here how, to portion out among the great variety of factors that can be involved in particular cases, the proper weights to assign in deciding them. Cf. §21.

5 Ontologically speaking; physically, they seem to be mostly near the surface of the Earth, at the universe's center.

6 Only some time after writing this sentence did I happen upon the colloquial use of *sustasis* in this actual meaning: *kata xustaseis gignomenoi*, Thucydides 2.21, "Knots of men formed in the streets". (For *sustasis*, cf. §8 (61), §9 (70), §12 n. 16 (89), §14 (115), §15(ii) (Appendix) (131), §19 (iv) (185–6), §23 (iv) (241).

7 "Like eddies in rivers", *GA* iv 4 772^{b}8; cf. *PA* ii 1 647^{b}2–4.

stability of the knots and the complex specific character that they manifest as long as they last (which *we* observe as that migration-resistance in the species (§6), which our little forgery in §4, "*Cats.* *4^{b}19 ff.*", was a first essay at stating). Now placed in context in the wider universe, such a material individual (i.e., animal) is seen as a semipermanent warp or bend informing the local matter, which the matter flows through at various rates during the organism's life history (this is called metabolism), while the form imposes the continuity.[8] Eventually the knot always unravels and disintegrates (that is called death); so that each knot's continuous history is finite; but part of the self-sustaining life-styles of these things is the ability of each one (or of the males, in species that have sexes) to transmit his form to (or 'knit' it into) a new region of matter (that is called reproduction);[9] since this process is repeated endlessly generation after generation, the continuity of the formative kinds is in that way infinite.

In this way, we look out through the full material universe and see scattered through it the millions and millions of different knots, all the places where matter is twisted by form into an individual: That was our starting-point, it will be recalled (§9), *quod erat, atque etiam nunc est, explicandum.*

This then is how the subuniverse of biological units fits into the larger one: it is not all that there is, but it is the most complicated part of it and (Aristotle thinks) it is that "for whose sake" the less complex materials are to be understood as existing; in some way it is the most important, a kind of culmination. (Cf. *DA, init.*) How that idea fares in the projectibility stakes, I let the reader judge.

---

8 After writing *this* sentence, I found the identical image at *CTB/PA* i 5 321^{b}24–28, led to it by Anscombe's reference, *op. cit.*, p. 56. (Also the army re-grouping in *APo* ii 19 100^{a}10–14?)

9 "The poems called 'Orphic' say that an animal's coming-to-be is like the plaiting of a net" (*GA* ii 1 734^{a}20). We still speak of the parts' being "*knit*". (On "reproduction", recall the caution of §9, note 14.)

V. METAPHYSICS

§19. *Hupokeitai DIKHŌS*: the two-stage domain

The three very broad points of perspective reviewed in §17: (i) the size and depth of the world, (ii) the vertical, organizational moment in differentia and genus, and (iii) the connection of form and unity, are by no means exhaustive of the metaphysical morals derivable from the biology; but they are already sufficient to give the outlines of the kind of universe that Aristotelean metaphysics puts up to correspond to (or in contemporary terms, to serve as a "model" for) the distinction that was floated in §8 between "constitutive" and "characterizing" things-predicated.

It is a universe ("model") of two levels or *stages*.

(i) *Metaphysical framework: outline of the static picture*

The *upper stage* is that of the individual substances and their accidental attachments, inherents or "coincidences" (*sumbebēkota*); it is in most respects – though not completely – identical with the entire universe of the *Categories*.[1] Based as it is on a domain of well-distinguished substantial individuals, to which attach or "coincide" (or in which inhere) the various qualities and so on, it also bears some slight affinity, to that extent at least, to the sorts of structures that can be thought of as models for present-day formal languages analyzed in terms of standard first-order quantification theory that were mentioned briefly in §8, although the comparison is highly extrinsic, most anachronistic, and made at all only to point the contrast that follows.

The *lower stage* is that of the shaping-up of the individual substances through form out of matter, and accordingly it is matter rather than

---

1 Dancy (1975b), 372–3, writing from the standpoint of the *Cats.*, refers to the *Meta.* idea of a deeper-underlying subject than the substantial individuals of the *Cats.* as a "cloud on Aristotle's horizon" and portending "trouble". It is a complication, and problematic, but there seems nothing menacing about it.

discrete individual "thisses" that is cast in the logical-semantical role of subject of predication. But as can be expected from the foregoing and will be seen in more detail, "matter" in this setting must be read not simply as "material stuff", but in terms of the full range of vertical differentiation developed above. This lower stage is unlike any metaphysical structure of contemporary vintage that I know of.

This idea, that of the universe consisting of two stages of which one, so to speak, rests upon the other, is expressed quite directly several times in *Metaphysics ZHΘ* in terms of "two ways of being (a) subject" or "of underlying", in Aristotle's terminology, *hupokeitai dikhōs*;[2] it is put tersely in Zeta 13:

'Is subject', 'underlies', is twofold: either (i) being a 'this' – as the animal stands to the afflictions, or (ii) as the matter stands to the 'entelechy', = the actuality of the fully perfected thing. (Zeta 13 1038^b5–6)

somewhat more clearly and expansively in Theta 7:

The 'that of which' (*to kath' hou*),[3] or 'the subject' (*to hupokeimenon*), are differentiated in the following way: by (i) being an individual 'this', or else (ii) not being one. For example, (i) the subject of the *afflictions* is: *a man*, i.e., a body & psyche; while the affliction is pale or musical . . . [here occurs a refinement that can wait until later, see §23(i)] . . . – whenever it's like this, then, the ultimate subject is: *a substance*. But (ii) whenever it's *not* like this, but what's predicated is a particular form and a particular 'this' (*eidos ti kai tode ti*), the ultimate subject is matter, substance in the sense of a matter. (Theta 7 1049^a27–b3)

– This two-stage structure assigns two configurations of 'being' according as it is an individual (upper stage) or a matter (lower stage) that is conceived as subject of *predication*; both configurations are synchronic, i.e. to be conceived as at-a-moment or time-independent (which is the reason for calling this part of the exposition the "static picture").

In fact, quite a lot of information can be gleaned from the *Metaphysics* about the more detailed structure of the lower stage: the separation of the notions of substance and ultimate subject (which coincide in the *Categories*, as has been seen (§3 (p. 22), §4(28), §6(50), §8(61)), (Zeta 3), the

2 Recognized by Driscoll (1981), p. 152 (n. 74), Lewis (1985), pp. 63 ff. But Lewis interprets the "two ways" more strictly (I think, too strictly): "x is predicated of y (y is subject to x) only if *either* x is an accident of y and y is an individual substance, *or* x is a form and y is a parcel of matter". As I see it, form surely *can* also be predicated of the individual substance (as it obviously is in the *Cats*, and see §20(iii)), and accident *can* also be predicated of matter (see §23(i)) – but the predicative relations must be clearly sorted out (*ibid.*).

3 Apelt's reading, *to kath' hou*, is plainly required (as against *to katholou* of the codices and Alexander; cf. Ross, 1049^a28 n., *AM* ii 257).

special and *sui generis* subjecthood borne by matter to form in the lower stage ("thaten", Zeta 7, Theta 7), its cumulatively hierarchical composition (Eta 4, Theta 7, Lambda 3), and more. All this will be developed in §20. The important intuition to retain for the present is the role of specific form in the lower stage as shaping up the elementary materials (they cannot do it "of themselves", §17(i)), by stages through underlying generic phases into fully differentiated species specimens (§17(ii)), and *eo ipso* via the form/unity link, into individual "thisses" (§17(iii)); note the explicit impacting-together of form and "this" at 1049^{a}35, the end of the Theta 7 passage just quoted).

(ii) Outline of the dynamic picture

But before proceeding with that, there must be incorporated into the picture without further ado the implications of the fact that this is fundamentally a theory of objects that exist through time surviving alterations: being generated, developing, "perduring and senescing" (p. 161), declining, and ceasing-to-be; thus in addition to the "static" notion of matters versus individuals as subjects of *predication*, attention is needed to the "dynamic" notion of matters versus individuals as subjects of *change*. – It should never be forgotten that the persistence of substance through change is heavily underscored by Aristotle himself in the *Cats.* as "most distinctive" and even unique to it (cf. §4, pp. 33–4); as we shall see, the *Meta.* account of this is left in an oddly unfinished condition considering the topic's importance (cf. §25).

Matter is standardly the subject of transsubstantial change (*CTB/PA* i 4 320^{a}2), which we are not yet ready to deal with systematically and which involves some especially difficult interpretive problems due to Aristotle's having tacked to and fro among several different attitudes about changes supervening upon matters (cf. §22(ii)). But we are now ready to fix anew, in the present meta-biological setting, upon the phenomenon of *individuals'* changing through time while maintaining themselves as "the same and numerically one"; for in this setting this phenomenon looks quite different from its aspect in the *Categories*.

The point on which to fix is the role played by specific form in securing the transtemporal identity of the substantial individuals.

"*Cats.* *4^{b}19 ff." in §4 showed how to state in *Cats.* language the phenomenon of the continuity of the same individual's being linked to the same substantial kind's continuing to be said-of it. But of course no such statement is actually made in the *Cats.*, and "*Cats.* *4^{b}19 ff." is a forgery;

accordingly, I proceeded to cast about in §4 (pp. 37 ff.) for an explanation of Aristotle's extraordinary quietness about this in that work, and came up with the speculation that he could have wished to refrain from making audible such an essentializing condition, out of reluctance to get involved, there, in trying to explain such a causal dependency of the individuals upon the kinds. Here, however, we are dealing with a theory deliberately designed to deal with this problem, and I have already indicated how he seems to see the hylomorphic individuals of the biosphere as being at any moment (= synchronically) thus dependent on specific form, both for their characteristic sharply defined natures, and latterly even for their very character of being individuals or "thisses" itself. In these terms, it seems that the phenomenon of cross-temporal identity (= diachronically) "numerically one and the same while receiving contraries", this unique capability of the substantial individuals, must also be traced to the same source: it is specific form that is responsible for the continued identity of (e.g.) the individual F through change over time, in that its persistence as numerically one and the same is its persistence as the same F.[4]

As understood here, this linkage of continuity of individual (F) to continuity as same F is not the view that "identity is relative" in the sense at one time advocated by Geach;[5] identity and nonidentity remain absolute and the usual laws are not affected. The idea is rather to understand the impossibility handed down as dogma in "*4^b19 ff.", of a single individual's exchanging kinds, now as springing from a concept of *what an individual is*: just as an individual F's coming- and ceasing-to-exist *is* something's (viz.: a matter's) coming- and ceasing-to-be F, so an individual F's continuing to exist *is* its persistence as the same F (but here the place of matter is more complicated, cf. the forthcoming three paragraphs).

It is obvious but worth stressing about the phenomenon of individuals' perduring across time (particularly the sorts of individuals that primarily concern us here) that, for it, continuity of their constituent matter is clearly neither necessary nor sufficient. Clearly not sufficient, in that an animal may die, or a statue be recast into a bell, with its constituent

---

4 The intuition is strongly evoked in Hartman (1977), esp. pp. 59–67. But I am trying to formulate it without the appeal he makes to *individual forms* and his identification of individual substances with their individual forms: specific forms are adequate to individuating matter into individuals (cf. §15(i), §20(iii)), and the identification stems at least in part from a mistaken reading of Zeta 6 (cf. §23(iii)(iv)).

5 Geach (1962). A very large and ramified literature (by no means fully represented in the bibliography) has pullulated from this germ over the succeeding quarter-century; having more than I can deal with in Aristotle's theory, I have resisted the temptation to engage this body of recent discussion and it is mostly overlooked here.

matter meticulously conserved (stipulating the necessary Population assumptions in the latter case for example's sake; and there are some further refinements yet to be incorporated (§25) concerning the 'matter' of an animal). Nor necessary, in that *one* individual may over time change its bits of earth and fire, blood and bone, whereas its persistence as one and the same (if it does persist) stems from the continuity of the specific form, in there persisting one and the same *F* – *whatever in detail that may consist in, or our criteria for its satisfaction may be*.[6] At this juncture the application to biological objects is critical – for whereas it is largely not typical of statues and spheres to engage in metabolic interaction and exchange of material with their environments, such activity is (as Aristotle explicitly marks in the theoretical concept of threptic psyche, cf. §16(ii)) indicative and indeed practically diagnostic of living things, which in principle may over sufficient time undergo even entire exchanges of component sensible matter without disturbance to their continued numerical identities through the period; thus for such objects, an identity concept independent of sameness of matter is importantly involved and needs to figure in the explicit analysis.

Specific form, then, is linked to the "unity" of substances in the sense of their oneness through time – dynamically, as well as statically. In the terms of the intuitive view of §18, as now amplified by the two-stage domain idea, it is *by* being formed, folded, and twisted by specific form into semi-stable "knots", *that* the materials of the lower stage, whose own nature is to ebb and flow, agglomerate and separate, give rise to persistent individuals having traceable histories.

Thus to locate in specific form, as I am suggesting, the source of the continuity of 'numerically one and the same' individual through time, where such occurs, may seem to go counter to a long-standing interpretive tradition running back at least to Aquinas and unanimously recited in the textbooks, imputing to Aristotle a doctrine going by the title, "*matter* as the principle of individuation". This is not the place, nor am I the person, to examine the meaning of this idea for Aquinas, still less for the many others who (interpreting Aristotle or otherwise) have made use of such a notion; but, bracketing that without prejudice, I think

---

6 These words should be noted (and perhaps admired) for the artful way in which they dodge the Population Problem, pursuant to the policy adopted since §7 *fin.* of refraining from the usual practice of muddying the points of metaphysical principle by mixing them up with debates over the appropriate criteria, possible clashes among them, etc. There is much to be said about what the persistence of the same *F* consists in in particular cases, and the appropriate criteria therefor; but it comes from (and should come from) sources other than the metaphysical: biological (very possibly, deep-biological), ethical, legal, religious, other. The whole matter of "advice" on substantial population is rounded up in §21.

Aristotle's position at least can be clarified. He certainly holds that two distinct individuals not differing in species are nonetheless distinguishable in point of their distinct material components: meaning in this case, presumably, distinct parcels of "sensible matter" (§17(ii)), Earth and Air, flesh and bone:

> . . . when once the whole exists, thus-and-such a form in these here flesh and bones, that's Callias, or Socrates; and they're different on account of their matter – for that's different –, but the same in form (*eidei*) – for the form is indivisible (*atomon to eidos*). (Zeta 8 1034ª5–8)

That is straightforward, and reasonable: the same specific form is here seen to be impressed on neighboring but non-overlapping regions of matter, thus stamping out Callias and Socrates respectively; and the context makes plain (cf. *ēdē*, "when once", "now already") that Aristotle is thinking of these two as taken *simultaneously*, synchronically, and accordingly pointing to their divergent materials as of this moment. As already indicated, however, he nowhere implausibly suggests that Socrates' matter as of this moment, or any part of it, is a "principle" that "individuates" him in the sense of his having to consist of that matter as long as he lasts; we have seen that the whole weight and thrust of the biological cases – including the theoretical analysis of the *threptic* in *DA* ii – is to the contrary. What he does say is that matter is the source, not of the identity or the individuation of individuals, but of their *plurality*: of the fact that the same specific form *can* be impressed simultaneously into "neighbouring but non-overlapping" regions of a medium or *hupodokhē* – and in actual cases of generation, of the actual number of individuals produced, as was seen in §15(i).[7] Given a suitable pair of individuals, however, there is no reason of Aristotelean metaphysics why the very fire and earth that this noon composes Callias and distinguishes him from

---

7 Pp. 126–7 above. This connection of matter with plurality, in both directions, is quite pervasive. P→M: "All things that are many in number have matter", Lambda 8 1074ª33; cf. Delta 6 1016ᵇ31, Lambda 2 1069ᵇ30 (and Ross, *AM* i 176). More surprisingly, M→P: "In all cases where we see it's thus, where there's a substance in a matter, the *homoeidē* are many, even indefinitely many", *Cael.* i 9 278ª18. The latter is more surprising because it locks out the *possibility* of there ever being a species that had only a single material specimen. I imagine the thought is as follows: all material substances must be engendered and must cease to be (cf. §9, Fact 7, §16(ii), and *GA* ii 1 731ᵇ33–732ª1 in the Oxford translation with Platt's note). They must be engendered by *homoeidē* which pre-exist them, and they generate *homoeidē* which survive them; that is nature (cf. 16(ii)). Therefore, a species with only a single material specimen is impossible by nature. – By contrast, in the vertically restricted *Categories* universe, the "methodological opacity" of whose substantial individuals has already been noted (§4 (p. 28), §8 (63), §9 (67)), it seems that the numerical diversity of cospecific primary substances must be regarded as a simple brute fact, a *datum* not further reducible or explicable or analyzable. Regis (1976) seems to think that the individuals of the *Meta.* are in the same case.

Socrates could not, by a set of extraordinarily curious chances, twenty years from now compose Socrates – and vice versa too –, where yet Socrates then would nonetheless be deemable one and the same man as Socrates now, and Callias likewise, if the *customary* conditions for that relationship were deemed to have been met – whatever they may consist in, or our criteria for their satisfaction may be (cf. p. 179 above, and n. 6).

In sum: in the two-stage domain as outlined so far, specific form is seen to be the source of the unity of the substantial individuals in two dimensions, the synchronic and the diachronic. Form is "principle of synchronic individuation" in the sense that it warps or stamps out the materials into a multiplicity of self-contained unitary packages; the source of the *multiplicity* is matter ("they're different on account of their matter"), but the source of their *unity* is still form – as is vividly apparent in the case of multiparous reproduction, §15(i), and maintained in principle e.g. above in the passage from Zeta 8. Form is "principle of diachronic individuation" in the sense that it is continuity of form or psyche (same F, "whatever in detail that may consist in, or our criteria for its satisfaction may be") from which springs the transtemporal unity or atomicity of a single individual. By the same lights, just as it was noted before that (statically speaking) the form/matter device renders the substantial individuals, atomic and opaque in the *Categories*, now accessible to analysis in terms of their structure, so we can note here that (dynamically speaking) it is the continuity-of-specific-form principle that underlies the phenomenon, which was saluted in the *Categories* as "most distinctive" of substances but could not be explained there, of their capability of maintaining themselves "numerically one and the same" while undergoing change across time.

(iii) Why artefacts are bad examples

In fact, it can even be said, at the risk (which I will accept) of a little exaggeration, that this fundamental connection between the diachronic "unity" of a substantial individual and the continuity of its specific form entails a basic and too-little-noted inappropriateness in the stock illustrative examples (the statues and spheres; houses are slightly better) that litter the corpus; for in a significant sense they are not merely *just* examples, but *bad* examples. A full-fledged substantial individual is one whose "unity" is such as to persist through changes that may include change in its constituent matter; and the interactive metabolic exchange with its environment that typifies a biological object is paradigmatic of this, as most vividly eventuates in the *DA* as epitomized in §16(ii). By contrast, the "form" of a bronze statue or sphere is thin and exiguous indeed, merely the configuration of the surface that holds in the bronze; and any attempt to alter or exchange the constituent matter of such an object is necessarily external, invasive in character, and at least temporarily destructive. Between these extremes come the moderately elaborate artefacts like the ships and the houses, which, so our intuitions seem to say, can survive the (gradual, perhaps) replacement of their constituent materials or modular parts, and whose "metabolism" is that of maintenance and repair – yet it is easily seen that such processes, philosophically fascinating as they apparently are, still are artificial and externally-induced simulacra (for they are *not self*-maintenance, or *self*-repair) as compared with the natural and intrinsic type of change associated with the life-history of animals; and the intuitions involved are correspondingly less certain and more easily baffled (as the philosophical discussions perennially make plain).

We seem to intersect here once again with an idea that first became apparent in the embryological connection toward the end of §15(i): that substantiality, and with it form and unity, come in degrees.[8] At that point the suggestion was that a not-as-yet-fully-formed, embryonic, individual-to-be was also not as yet a fully individuated Aristotelean "unit", being still, overall, masslike in its nature, and that the achievement of final form and of full individual status were to be seen as not only simultaneous but identical. The aspect that eventuates here is related: the biological objects bring strikingly to our attention a variety of form that can hold together the temporal career of an entity through changes of state, size, condition, place, and constituent materials; form that determines down to very fine detail the structure of the continuant "knot" as it warps a region of the sublunary material ocean, by reaching deep down into the "noetic matter" in the fashion that was first noted in §12(ii) – for in an entity like a man or a shark, though the elementary materials change through time, and the various specifically determined substructures and subsystems

---

8 This does not, as might be thought, clash with the claim of *Cats.* $3^b33–4^a9$ ("Substance does not admit of a more and a less"); for that paragraph seems to teach only that a substantial *F* is not more or less *F* (i) now, than itself, or (ii) at one time, than itself at another, or (iii) than some other *F*. It does *not* say that certain appropriately chosen *F*'s cannot be more or less substance than certain other appropriately chosen *G*'s. – We cannot, of course, simply adduce $3^b34–5$ in support ("I do not mean that one substance is not more a substance than another – we have said that it is"), this clearly referring to the view, not safely exportable from the *Cats.* without at least some interpretive care, that takes the gradient of diminishing substantiality to be along the axis: primary substance > species > genus ($2^a11–14$, $2^b7–8$, 29–31, cf. §4, p. 29).

serving as "noetic matter" also evolve to a degree as the specifically characteristic processes of development and senescing run their course, still he must consist throughout of *bone* and *flesh*, *heart* and *bloodvessels* (as *Meta.* Zeta 11 firmly admonishes). It is as against this paradigm of substantiality, rich and complex as it is in the vertical dimension of differentiation, that examples like houses and ships appear as indeed displaying some useful analogies, but also a palpably lesser degree of form and therewith of the "unity" that can *resist* (persisting through) change over time – and as for statues and spheres, palpably lesser again: the vertical dimension of differentia is here almost wholly absent, the form (as was said) "thin and exiguous", the matter wholly "sensible" as opposed to "noetic", and we are but a hair's breadth from heaphood. In such a *scala substantiarum* it might occur to us today, beneficiaries of much subsequent technological evolution, to insert artefacts of more plausible substantiality than Aristotle's houses – to name but a single possibility, automobiles[9] – as coming somewhere between the houses and the animals; here there is a kind of built-in artefactual "metabolism" certainly of a higher order than the maintenance of ships; and the philosophical amusement of debating the consequences of installing new engines in old vehicles would at last find an ancient thought-counterpart, in trying to project what Aristotle would have made of cardiac transplants.

Once the weakness of artefacts as exemplar substances is understood, there is no harm, in itself, in using them as illustrative examples where such strengths as they enjoy may prove helpful; as will be seen, that is Aristotle's spirit in *Meta.* Eta 2, where it is roundly declared that none of the (mostly artefactual) items that have been introduced there to illustrate substance are really substances, nor any of the characters supposed to illustrate differentia really differentiae, but that they are admissible nonetheless, because

> . . . all the same there's something *analogon* (to substantial being) in each of them; and as among substances what gets predicated of the matter is the actuality itself, (so) among the other definitions too (*sc.* in our examples), (it should be what) most of all (corresponds to actuality).   (Eta 2 1043^{a}4–7, cf. §24(i) below)

It is both unfortunate and puzzling, however, that Aristotle's *Metaphysics* discussions are oriented so obsessively around artefactual study objects; for as a consequence, whereas some of the static features of the building-up of substances in the lower stage get considerably illuminated, still the paramount lesson of the biological substances – unity across time through

---

9 More on the automotive kingdom will be found in §23 (iv).

change, including change of matter – tends to get neglected in the general preoccupation with statues and boxes and houses;[10] and this is another side of the peculiar lacuna in the extant corpus: the fact that the project of actually working out the dynamic features of the two-stage *Metaphysics* universe is left unfinished at some highly critical junctures, requiring us restorers to fill in some highly critical points according to our own devices.

It may finally be noted here that as a result of our discerning variations of depth in the vertical dimension of differentia in different cases, the Population Problem acquires a bit of further subtlety than before; for it now has not only the form: Are these, and those, and the other things, substances?, but in addition: Are those *as much* substances as these, and these as much as the other things? This of course accords nicely with Aristotle's use of language like *mallon, malista* ("more", "most of all") for such degrees; and from our own standpoint it reflects our intuitions' now being guided – though still not compelled – by newer considerations coming to bear, which had not yet emerged when the Problem was initially stated. In fact we shall shortly find that the two-stage domain idea enables a perspicuous final reformulation of the Population Problem itself: in a word, that the substantial individuals are those entities lying at the interface of the two stages of the domain (§21(i)).

That concludes the initial statement of the metaphysical universe we are now dealing with. It will be helpful in assimilating the more detailed studies of different parts and aspects of it, which follow, for all concerned to pause and fix the overall intuitive picture firmly in mind. It is worthwhile to try to *visualize* this universe – it comes, with practice – to *see* the substances (and, according to one's view, the artefactual quasi- or pseudo-substances) that are the subjects for the characterizing things-predicated-of in what is here schematized in the upper stage, as shaped up and held together as continuants over time by the warping or eddy-creating factor that is constitutive form, whose subject in turn is ultimately the Empedoclean materials in what is schematized as the lower stage. ("Upper" and "lower" *are* meant schematically – in the vivid mental image which it is useful to have of the affair, it is probably better to think of the theater of matter's-being-formed in the earlier suggested topological terms (§18) of a uniform medium's being twisted into knots, than to try to press the metaphor of a sub-basement.)

---

10 Thus Hartman (1977), p. 58. Hartman points out the importance of the continuity-of-form principle and regrets that Ar. doesn't say more about it (p. 84); I have suggested that the connection of threptic psyche with this principle in the *DA* goes some distance in this direction (§16(ii)). But he is right about the *Metaphysics*. Cf. §25.

(iv) What is 'primary substance'? – From CATS. to META.

The large transformation of perspective between the *Cats.* picture and that of the *Meta.* has important consequences as to the controlling *criteria* for the 'substantial', in a sense that is quite distinct from the criteria that are applicable to Population concerns, but rather relate to a reordering of that which is 'posterior' and 'prior' in substance, and in particular that which is '*most* prior', or 'primary'. We shall be looking at this in more detail below (§23), but it should be sketched here in brief before we try to proceed further, for although it plays a major role in the strategy of *Meta.* Zeta–Eta, the stage-directions of Zeta–Eta do not play up the importance of the role as much as they helpfully could. The point goes considerably beyond terminology, and is worth restating from §8.

It has been many times remarked in the foregoing that in the *Cats.*, the controlling criterion for the substantial is *subjecthood*: being a substance is being a subject, a *hupokeimenon*, and the more of a subject, the more of a substance. On this criterion, as the *Cats.* makes very explicit, the 'first' or 'primary' substance will therefore naturally be that which is 'most of all' a *subject*, which in the *Cats.* is the likes of the individual man or horse (2^b15–17, 2^b37–3^a1), the *atomic substances* as they have been called above.

Now in *Meta.* Zeta, as we are about to see, 'being a substance' is forthwith decoupled from 'being a subject' (Zeta 3), and thenceforward is associated instead with *that which MAKES* the individual man (etc.) *to be what he is and a "this"*: we are looking for a 'cause'. The 'search' (1028^b3) for substance thereafter in Zeta is accordingly for something that will best meet this revised criterion; and it follows that whatever that something turns out to be, *it* (and not the individual man) will accordingly be the 'most prior', 'first', or 'primary' substance. In the course of Zeta, several candidates for this office are dialectically picked over and found insufficient (some high points are in §23, q.v.); and 'primacy' is regularly associated with each of them as long as they are under review ('subject' as 'primary', Zeta 3 1029^a2, 16; 'essence' as 'primary', Zeta 4 1030^a10, Zeta 6 1031^b14, 1032^a5, Zeta 11 1037^a28–$^b3$). Eventually (Zeta 17), the question is restructured as:

the *cause* (*aition*) is being sought, of a matter's being some definite thing;

this 'cause' is declared to be form, and this form is declared to be substance (1041^b7–9). The individual man is thus no longer 'atomic', but instead is a complex, a *sunolon*, composited (*sunistamenon*) 'out of' matter by form.

The conclusion is that *'primary' substance is form*:

> while some things aren't substances, still such substances (i.e., composites) as there are, are composited (*sunestēkasi*) in accordance with and by way of a nature of their own, and that very nature would appear to be substance (*of* them),
>
> (Zeta 17 1041^{b}28–30)

in the sense in which "the substance *of* each (composite) thing (= the form) is the *primary cause* of its 'being'" (1041^{b}27–8).

This relocation of the 'primary' in substance, from individual to form, of course comes as no surprise to us as adepts in the biological analysis of morphology and morphogenesis; but that background being somewhat muffled in Zeta, it is worthwhile to keep it explicit.

To round off this prospective sketch of the relocation, let us recall from §16 the metaphysics of *psyche* in the *DA*: (1) psyche is substance *in the sense of form, of* a natural body as matter; but "substance in the sense of form" means actuality, therefore (2) psyche is *actuality of* such a body as matter; but of actuality, there is that which is prior and posterior (in the sense illustrated by "knowledge" and "theorizing"), therefore (3) psyche is the *prior or 'primary' actuality of* such a body as matter (*DA* ii 1 412^{a}19–28); and it is in virtue of that 'primary' actuality, that the composite, i.e. the animal, is an individual or *tode ti* (412^{a}6–9, 413^{a}3).

But more on those profundities must now await exploration of the intermediate ground.

§20. Substructure of substance. The lower stage

With the overall framework in mind, we can return to the "static picture", in order to look more closely at the idea of an underlying *subject* of things-predicated, particularly as it occurs in the lower stage.

In fact, the result that the embedding of the *Categories* universe in the much larger metaphysical universe of matter and form immediately entails a new and more ultimate concept of 'subject', and therewith in effect a lower stage underlying the domain of substantial individuals, is the first significant result of *Metaphysics* Zeta/Eta, reached in Zeta 3; thus a reading of that chapter is in order.

(i) Substance versus subject. Metaphysics Zeta 3

The reading I suggest seems altogether straightforward; but there are controversies and a subtlety or two, and it must be done. In the *Cats.*, as has now been more than sufficiently noted,[1] the ultimate subject of all things-predicated, directly or indirectly, are the substantial individuals, the individual *F*'s and *G*'s: in one way or another, everything in that world in the end comes down to these, without which, it is repeatedly emphasized, "none of the other things" could exist (2^b5, etc.). It is natural, therefore, that, faced now with the question of *Meta.* Zeta/Eta, "what *is* substance?", the nimble-witted pupil of the *Categories* would think of taking precisely this fact about the substantial individuals in that work as their *defining property*: to suggest that to be a substance just *is* to be an ultimate subject (1029^a1), in the technical sense of "that of which (*kath' hou*) all the other things are said (= predicated), but never it of any other thing" (1028^b36) (recall that it was because they were subjects for all the other things that they were "called substances most of all" and "primarily", 2^b15–17, 2^b37–3^a1).

– If this is so, then it needs to be ascertained what sort of thing it is that meets this "subject" condition in the enlarged setting, and the method adopted is that of taking an arbitrary representative material object and endeavoring to abstract or conceptually detach from it everything that appears to have the form of a *katēgoroumenon*, of something predicated-of anything. If, when all that is predicated has thus been "stripped off" (1029^a11), something is left that underlies all else and itself is predicable-of nothing further, it will qualify as "ultimate subject" – and thus, if the trial identification of the two is sustainable, as "substance".

The specimen object under study is evidently a statue (1029^a5), whose "being that" is hence a relatively simple affair of being thus-and-so in visible external configuration (*skhēma tēs ideas*, 1029^a4),[2] a fact that I think proves important. We now reason as follows: the "stripping-off" of the *katēgoroumena* proceeds, detaching the statue's "affections, products and potencies" (1029^a13), and then its "length, breadth and depth" ($^a14$), until nothing remains but its matter (some bronze, $^a4$), predicable of nothing further, "the primary thing to which these (others) belong ($^a15$–16), accordingly qualified as basic subject.

That last conclusion is allowed to stand: what meets the technical condition for "ultimate subject" is the component matter of a thing; but, Zeta 3 continues, the conclusion is also sufficient to undermine the trial identification of such a subject

---

1 See most recently pp. 176, 180 (note 7), 185.

2 Cf. §12(ii), and note 7 thereto (p. 85). This is the same as the *morphē tou skhēmatos* that a corpse shares with a spatiotemporally contiguous previously living thing, which is *not* enough to make the former more than homonymously "man" (§11(iv), cf. §11(iii)). For a living thing it is a mere superficies; but it is about all there is to a statue; recall §19(iii).

and "substance", since a matter, like *some bronze*, "of itself (*kath' hautēn*) is neither said to be a particular thing (*ti*), nor so-much nor anything else by which being is determined, demarcated, marked off, given definition" (however one wishes to render *hois hōristai to on*, 1029ₐ20), hence lacking the intuitive requirement for a substance of being a well-demarcated and discrete individual "this" (*khōriston kai tode ti*, 1029ᵃ26–30).

The outcome then is that although a substance is indeed a subject, for some *katēgoroumena*, it is not the "primary" subject (1029ᵃ1) fished after in the chapter; and though matter proves to fill the latter role, it of itself will not make a substance; and the two are related in that "the others (= other categories) are predicated-of the substance (= of the statue of Socrates), but it (= being a statue of Socrates) of the matter (1029ᵃ23–24)" – the first adumbration of the double-stage theory just sketched out.

This dissociation of *substance* and *ultimate subject* in "post-Categorean" Aristotle is very basic; it is a consequence of the shift to a *causal* concept of substance just indicated in §19(iv), and will recur frequently – next, in (§21(i)) below.[3]

In fact, parenthetically, looking back on the thought-experiment, it now can be seen by hindsight that the transition in the "stripping-off" process from the upper to the lower stage – that is, from accidents predicated-of the statue to substance predicated-of the bronze –, which we know *must occur somewhere*, here must occur at the predications of "length, breadth and depth": namely the determinations of complex three-dimensional shape that in fact constitute the bronze *as* a statue of Socrates (rather than as a statue of Zeus, or as the sphere which is instanced in favor of the same moral as the present at *Phys.* iv 2 209ᵇ9–11).[4] For such as statues, detailed coordinates of "length, breadth and depth" are not mere accidents of size or "so-much" but are essential, and their airy dismissal as "particular quantities" in the dialectical unpacking of the trial identification (1029ᵃ14–15) should be regarded as by implication cancelled for this case in view of the outcome of the chapter.[5]

3 I do not see with Dancy (1978) that Ar. has to be "attacking a view of his own" (p. 373) in calling attention to this consequence of the Zeta criterion for substantiality over that of the *Cats.*

To put the contrast another way: on the *Cats.* criterion, the "stripping-off" routine would stop – cold – at the substantial individuals; Zeta 3 shows how in the wider and deeper setting it has to go well beyond that. It seems clear to me that all of this is evident and not especially problematic for Aristotle.

4 Like Stahl (1981), I do not think that Zeta 3 commits Ar. to the notorious *materia prima*, nor that that conclusion can only be escaped by supposing, with Charlton (1970), p. 138, that 1029ᵃ10–26 "are all a statement of an opponent's line of thought". My suggestions on the *materia prima* issue are in §22(iii).

5 See note 2 above. – Does this mean that a given character (as named in ordinary language) may be accident in one kind of substance and part of the essential differentia in another? The

(ii) Matter informed. Materiate ('upward') paronymy. Meta. Theta 7

An aspect of the form/matter configuration in the lower stage which both leads to some interesting ramifications and also is symptomatic of considerable clarity on some metaphysical points that are not entirely easy, is the way in which *paronymy*, familiar to us from its role in the upper stage as partially analyzed by the *Categories* (§2), also figures below in connection with matter.

The terminology is adapted and precised from an idiom of everyday language: when something Y is formed out of a matter X, Y derives from X a paronymic nature (or alternatively, Y derives from the name of X a paronymic epithet – as earlier, use-mention niceties are thoroughly ignored) of the form *X-en*, or *of-X*:

> The thing (Y) is not called *that* (X) out of which (it comes to be), . . . the statue is not called *wood*, but takes a derived term, *wooden* (*paragetai xulinos*),[6] and *bronzen* (of-bronze) but not *bronze*, and *stonen* but not *stone*, and the house is called *bricken* but not *bricks* . . .　　　　　　　　　　　　　　(Zeta 7 1033ª16–19).

More generally, extending through the vertical hierarchy of the lower stage:

> It seems that what we call not "*this*" but "*thaten*" – e.g.
>
> > the box is not *wood* but *wooden*, and
> > the wood is not *earth* but *earthen*,

and once again if the earth is likewise not another (*that*) but *thaten* – (it seems, then, that) always the *that* is, put without qualification (*haplōs*), potentially the adjacent thing up in the sequence. For example, *the box* is not *earthen*, nor (of course) *earth*, but is *wooden*; this (= some wood) is what's potentially box and what's matter of a box, i.e. *wood* unqualified of *box* unqualified, and of this box, this wood. But if there's something primary, which is such that there's not again a deeper (lit. "further") thing ("*that*") with respect to which it's called *thaten*, then this is a prime matter; e.g. if

---

answer is certainly yes; there is no avoiding this as soon as the scheme is applied to real cases. Whether it really is the same character in such a case is quite another matter; zoological research will be required. Cf. §2 *fin.* above; it will be seen that this consequence is actually much less odd than first may appear: §21 below.

6 The word "paronymy" is not used, but the idea is evident. *paragōgē* is a Hellenistic grammarians' name for "derivation", and Bonitz points out (*Ind.* 562ᵇ49) that *paragein* = *parōnumiazein* at *Phycs* vii 245ᵇ11. For the context, see §22 (ii), pp. 219–20.

earth is (not *air* but) *air-y*, and
air is not *fire* but *fiery*, and
fire is prime matter, which is not an individual "this" (*tode ti*).
(Theta 7 1049^{a}18–27)

Envisaged here, obviously in highly schematized and oversimplified form, is a five-tiered hierarchy with Fire at the ground floor and wooden boxes at the top (arrows in the schematism representing paronymy-transitions):

a box, which is wooden

↑

wood, which is earthen

↑

earth, which is air-y

↑

air, which is fiery

↑

fire, which is
prime, for nothing X lies
beneath it with respect
to which fire is X-en.

Here the oversimplifications are indeed many and gross, one being the designation of only a single element or compound at each level,[7] another the pretense that the constitution of earth, etc., could in fact (even by Aristotle's lights) be as described, another the fact that the scheme culminates in the composition of boxes, which hardly presents the order of difficulty that so powerful and all-encompassing an edifice as this could plausibly be thought to have been designed to address.

But some items of significant principle show forth also. One is the existence of a range of locations, between the prime matter at the lower extreme and the final differentiae at the upper, at which matter/form divisions can be made, and where precision calls for specifying just what fills the role of matter *at each point*, which will be, at any point above that of the prime, something *ditton* in its nature, already embodying form to some degree.[8] It is in this spirit also that we are frequently directed, in the case of matter/form descriptions of entire complete substances, to specify the "last" possible differentiae and the "nearest" or most "proximate" possible matter:

7 "If it's 'made of an element', clearly it's made not of one but of more than one, or else that one will be the thing itself", Zeta 17 1041^{b}22–3. 8 §12(i), §17(ii).

– What's the cause of a *man* in the sense of matter? The catamenia? [*Sc.*: No.] . . .
It's the *nearest* causes that must be stated; "what's the matter?" asks not for *fire*, or
earth, but the matter that's peculiar to the thing (*tēn idion (hulēn)*).

(Eta 4 1044^{b}1–3).

– [Again regarding the "matter" of man]: take *fire*, *flesh*, *head* [these stand
respectively for ultimate elements, uniform parts, and nonuniform parts – cf.
§§10–11]: all of these are matter, and the final one is [the type that's] matter of the
actual *substance*. (Lambda 3 1070^{a}19–20)

Likewise in the Fire-to-boxes case, the composition, though cumulative,
has stages whose relationships of nextness should be accurately charted
("the box is not earthen, but wooden".[9] This is no mere logical or
terminological nicety, for it is clear in addition from Theta 7 that it is
connected with the idea of stages in the physical fabrication process: earth
must first be metamorphosed into wood, for there to be what's potentially
a box, or alternatively into bronze, for there to be what's potentially a
statue (1049^{a}22, 17); thus:

It's not (potentially this or that) at just any old time whatever – for example, is
earth potentially *a man*? Or not, but rather when it's already become semen, and
perhaps not even then? . . . The semen's not yet (potentially a man), it's got to be
(cast) into another, and change its state; but when by way of its own moving
principle it *is* presently in this state, then it is at this point potentially a man.[10]

(Theta 7 1049^{a}1–3, 14–16)

(Here there is a connection with the analysis of substantial metamorphosis or transsubstantiation in terms of de-differentiation and re-differ-
entiation in e.g. *Meta. Eta* 5.)

A second item of principle is the pointing of *paronymy* to mark the special
and sui generis variety of subjecthood, that matter bears to form in the
lower stage. In the upper stage, as we saw (§2), the individual F (e.g., the
box of Theta 7) is said to be white$_a$ paronymously, from the whiteness$_n$ it
underlies as a subject in the sense of a *tode ti*. Here in the lower, it is said to
be wooden$_a$ paronymously, from the wood $_n$ that underlies its constitutive
specific form (box) as a subject in the sense of matter. Tying in the
metaphors of "subject" and "underlying", according to which this is

9 The "is not" of course means "is not strictly speaking" or "should not be called without
further elaboration (*haplōs*)"; it is not being claimed *false* that the box is in any sense composed of
earth, or a man of flesh.

10 Reading Ross's text. The ilustration is of course exceptionally – and quite avoidably –
loose, Aristotle not himself regarding semen as matter for the offspring, or "potentially man" in
that sense, as we have seen him at some pains to make clear in §14 (see §14(iv) *fin.*, and note 27
thereto (p. 120), with Ross's comment).

"beneath" (*hupo*) that and "on top of", "over" (*epi*) the other thing, with the notions developed earlier of the vertical dimension in differentia and genus, we can think of the *accidental paronymy as downward* and the *materiate paronymy as upward*, in relation to the individual substance in which they both terminate.

(iii) Informing, composing and becoming: fixing on form

What is interesting about this materiate paronymy, apart from its "direction", is that it seems to be symptomatic of clarity about some distinctions whose sedulous observance is much in order in a theory such as this. Since this order of clarity on this particular area is anything but consistently prevalent throughout the corpus, and indeed is absent in several of Aristotle's more important discussions, the opportunity should be taken here to pause and fix the intuitions involved, which will also be much made use of in what follows. Consider again, not the box of wood but the lately-much-maligned (§19(iii)) statue of bronze, and for a convenient schematism let us illustrate hylomorphic compounds of the form "*the M-en F*", where M = matter and F = form, in this way:

so that *the brazen statue* looks like this:

Note here that in the above context, the word "statue" does not designate *the statue*, but the form of the statue; what designates the statue is the entire expression

$$\text{`` } \underbrace{\overbrace{\text{statue}}}_{\text{bronze}} \text{ ''} .$$

Here the point (call it "A") should be marked, as highly important, that there are *three*, distinguishable, 'beings' in this situation: (1) the form, (2) the matter, and (3) that which is formed out of the matter by the form. I believe it is a serious mistake in Aristotelean metaphysics to identify the form with the formed thing (and likewise to identify the lack, *sterēsis*, with the unformed thing), as is done in some recent discussions.[11] To do this,

11 E.g. Charlton (1970) on *Physics* i 7, Hartman (1977), ch. 2.

first, undermines the 'central dogma' that form is a *cause* of the being that is the formed thing; it also goes against Aristotle's claim that the form does not come to be, and must always pre-exist (Zeta 7, 8). The form is form *of* the formed thing, the lack is lack of form *of* the unformed thing (normally, the matter). Note finally, however, that there *is* reason to use the same word *F* to name the form (*F*) and the formed thing (*the individual F*), a point that will be returned to shortly.

The other intuition (B) I wish to be sure is fixed here is this: by form must normally be meant specific form, not a form that is peculiar to the composite individual.[12] We have already seen this to be a topic of some ambiguity and ambivalence in the *Generation of Animals* (§15(ii)(iii)), and no one can claim (or at any rate, should claim) that the issue is clear-cut. There, it looked as if Aristotle mainly has specific form in mind until the radical shift that occurs in *GA* iv 3, where suddenly individual forms of the two individual parents come into play – inconsistent with the preceding, and incoherent internally, it was argued. The considerations favoring specific rather than individual form as the understanding of *eidos* in the *Metaphysics* are briefly these:

First, as just pointed out, the form is the 'cause of the being' of the composite (Zeta 17): and to play this role, it must be a distinct being from the composite that is effected or caused.

Secondly, form has always to *pre-exist* the composite (Zeta 8), which alone shows that it cannot temporarily coincide with it; the manner of its pre-existence and the details of how it comes to form a composite are elaborately spelled out, in general terms in Zeta 7–9, but more concretely and particularly in the *GA*, as we have studied in detail (§§14–15).

Thirdly, form itself *cannot* either come-to-be or pass-away, for reasons given in Zeta 8 and 15, whereas it seems that an individual form would have to do that simultaneously with the composite that it formed – though we shall go further into this aspect in the next paragraph.

Fourthly, there is the repeated explanation that there is a source, an origin (*arkhē*), of the fact of the many composites' – which are, after all, called the *homoeidē* – being formed by the *same* form: namely, matter (§19(ii)); this reinforces the impression that standardly there is *one* specific form (of sphere, for example), realized in the *many* bits of matter that are variously suited to 'take' it by conditional necessity (§12(i)(ii)) – that

---

12 In the present generation, the individual-form interpretation perhaps goes back to Sellars (1957). In response to Sellars a probing and thoughtful review of the evidence was made by Albritton (1957), finding the case for the interpretation not nil, but not proved. Since then, it has become widespread, and occurs in various versions in Charlton (1970), Balme (1980), A. C. Lloyd (1981), Whiting (1984).

there *is* a fact, which the given explanation explains, a *hoti* explained by the *dioti*.[13]

These are very important fixed points, consistent with which I can see only two potential ways around for ascribing individual forms to Aristotle.

(1) Aristotle might have held that the individual forms (or individual psyches, in the real case) do not come-to-be but are eternal, and are just enmattered or incarnated for the lifespan of what we (on earth, so to speak) call the composite. That would go some ways to meet the first three of the fixed points; but would also raise the awkward question how an Aristotelean form could 'be' when it was not materially instantiated. And while some such view may be attributable to Origen, there is nowhere a legible statement of such a doctrine in Aristotle.

(2) Aristotle does say that forms *are*, or *are not*, without their ever coming-to-be or passing-away (Zeta 15 1039^{b}24–6). By this he probably seems to most readers to mean, initially and plausibly: "the forms that *are*, like Man, *are*; and the forms that *are not*, like Goatstag, *are not*; and facts like these are eternal, can never change, since no form ever comes-to-be or passes-away". But perhaps that is not what he means: perhaps he has individual forms in mind, and is thinking as follows: "of course no form comes-to-be or passes-away, only the composite does that, but: at the moment the composite comes to be, its individual form *is* (though earlier it *was not*), and as soon as the composite passes-away, then its individual form *is not* (though earlier it *was*) – but without the individual form ever being generated or destroyed. Thus coming-to-be and passing-away are still as standardly analyzed in Zeta 7–9 and the *Physics*, in terms of the *hupokeimenon* and the lack and the form; and as Zeta 8 makes clear, the form itself doesn't do *that*. It just *is*, and before and after it *is*, it just *is not*."

Such a view would already be questionable on the "form as cause" and "form must pre-exist" counts; but there is a more fundamental difficulty with it. Namely, I cannot say whether Aristotle means this (or better, thinks he means it); but I hope he is not trying to mean this, for this is one of those things that it is impossible to mean. *If something earlier is not, and later is, then it has come-to-be: that is what coming-to-be IS, from the very meaning of the term, on any "is" and "is not" and on any possible account of coming-to-be.* Of course there are different *accounts* of coming-to-be, such as the Eleatic theory that it is impossible because not-being is impossible, and Aristotle's opposing theory that it is coherent because that blank not-being that so stymies the Eleatics is analyzable, into the substrate that is

---

13 In the sense of *APo* i 13 78^{a}22.

the matter and the lack that is the absence of the form from the matter.[14] But it makes no sense on any account to say that anything *is not*, then *is*, and then *is not*, but that it nonetheless has not come-to-be and passed-away.

Aristotle says plainly enough, I think, that form cannot come-to-be on *his* account of that notion, because if it did, there would have to be a substrate and a lack out of which it came-to-be, which he thinks leads to an infinite regress (thus Zeta 8 1033^{a}31–^{b}8). And when he says, further,

[Substantial form], then, either must be eternal, or it must be destructible without its ever being the case that *it* is being destroyed, and must have come-to-be without its ever being the case that it is coming to be,   (Eta 3 1043^{b}14–16)

and alludes again to the thesis of ungenerability of form (as already argued by him in Zeta 8), I take him to be stating that form is eternal because of the nonsensicality of the alternative. At least, the alternative really being nonsensical, the principle of charity recommends this reading.

Thus this way to individual form also does not, I think, get past the fixed points.

Back, then, to the exposition. We may now proceed to some modest philosophical analysis: both the bronze, and the whole statue (the "composite"), may in ordinary language be said to "have" the form, but this "having" is not at all the same in the two cases: the *bronze* "has" the form in the sense of taking or being shaped up by it; whereas the *statue* "has" it in the sense of exhibiting or exemplifying it. The relation of the statue to the bronze is precisely that which has been baptised as materiate or upward paronymy; it is a vertical relation, one of those (but decidedly not the only one) called by Aristotle *ex hou*, "from or out of which".

However, this very straightforward situation – at least in this very simple case – of the statue's (in static terms) "being", becomes a little subtler and more devious when tied in with considerations of its (in dynamic terms) "coming-to-be", and it becomes possible, perhaps even easy, to make metaphysical mistakes.

Suppose the bronze previously existed in a different form, e.g., that of a cubical block: then corresponding to the distinction just made in static terms, there is a difference in dynamic terms between regarding the *coming-to-be a statue* as something that happens to the *bronze*, and as

14 It makes no difference, as Ross seems to think (*AM* ii 188), whether the transition from not-being to being is instantaneous, or gradual as I take the embryology of *GA* to make it (§15(i) above). Nor does *form*'s coming-to-be make any better sense if it is instantaneous (*AM ibid.*).

something that happens to the *block* – a difference that is spanned by such an expression as "from the block of bronze", harmlessly enough, – as long as the bivalence is not forgotten.

(1) If "from the block of bronze" means, "from that particular entity, the individual cubical *block* (one that was *composed* of the bronze)", we have a case of *becoming*: here, *the block's becoming a statue*, an occurrence that may either be regarded as (A) involving one form's being exchanged for another (if the phrases be allowed, cubicity for socracity), or alternatively, may be thought of as (B) taking place within a more minimal form which the evolving entity possesses throughout – which of these alternatives we choose depending on and reflecting our attitude in this case regarding Population; if (A), the becoming is substantial; if (B), it is not. (Shortly, these alternatives will be distinguished as the "up" and the "down" options, respectively – see §21(i).) But in either case, if "from the block of bronze" is read in this way (= "from the block"), it does not mean that the statue *is made of the block*; the block has disappeared; rather, a horizontal (that is, trans-temporal) sense of *ex hou* is involved which is quite distinct from the vertical, connoting not *matter* but *origin*, and the situation is like this:

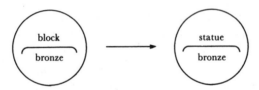

(This is the case in which Aristotle says that the 'out of which' 'doesn't remain' – *Meta.* Zeta 7, *Phys.* i 7. For the practice of keeping it vague whether a 'becoming' is substantial or not, see on the "polarities", §22(ii).)

(2) If, on the other hand, "from the block of bronze" means, "from that quantity of *bronze* (which happened recently to be conveniently identifiable as bounded by a blockish cubical surface)", the relevant relationship is the relative product of the vertical and horizontal *ex hou*, and we have *the bronze's being formed into* (NOT becoming) *a statue*, or:

statue [15]

15 The characterization here of "being formed into" will do for immediate purposes but is not yet in a definitive version; for a last refinement see §21(i) *fin.* below.

In the simple cases used in these illustrations, it is ordinarily the same matter that is the original matter and the contemporary matter; in the organic cases, of course, this cannot always be counted upon.

It was remarked (p. 192 above) that clarity on this topic is not consistently maintained throughout the Aristotelean corpus. When the territory has been made reasonably secure, we shall look critically at a couple of well-known discussions of it that seem to fall discernibly short of the Theta 7 standard: those of *Phys.*i 7 and *Meta.*Zeta 7 (cf. §21(ii) below).

In general, then, what (1) *becomes* a statue, as the block does, must be something that already "has" (= exhibits or exemplifies) a form, albeit minimal, which it (A) may or (B) may not lose in the process – it's an *object*. What (2) is *formed into* a statue, as the bronze is, is, as such, regarded as a matter and thus as independently of whatever form it may "have" (= be shaped up by); to the extent that it plays the role of matter, that quantity of bronze does not become a statue, nor, of course, is it accurate to say that the statue *is* bronze except in just the paronymous sense we are here concerned with: in this case, a degenerate paronymy (cf. §2) where "bronze" must mean of-bronze, bronzen.

These distinctions are not merely scholastic (in the generic sense): it is of both philosophical and extra-philosophical importance to recognize the *fundamentally different* "out of which's" (*ex hōn*) they are, by which the animal is (1) 'out of' the *kuēma*, and by which it is (2) 'out of' the *katamēnia*.[16]

It can be seen from this that materiate paronymy is considerably more than a grammatical trope, and represents a quite important sharpening of the theory of the lower stage. To epitomize: where F is a form and M a matter, the paronymic complex, *the M-en F*, represents a structure such that the matter M underlies or is subject to the form F, or "has" it, in the sense of being shaped up by it; the resulting individual – *the F* – "has" the form in the sense of exemplifying it. The idiom *M-en* signalizes that the individual F is *composed* of M, formed out of M considered as a matter, rather than as matter-in-some-other-form – so that although the matter M *was* no doubt earlier in some other form (*CTB/PA* i 5 320ᵇ17), still the

---

16 Recall (§14) that a *kuēma* from its outset is catamenia that has started receiving some form (thus a *kuēma* is 'catameni-en', at least for a little while), even when it is most primitive, as *to prōton migma thēleos kai arrenos* (GA i 20 728ᵇ34).

(*ex hou* #1:) "The parts are in the kuema *potentially*" (ii 4 740ᵃ2 ff.) – I have not found *ek toude* for *kuēma*, but *scolēx* is *ex hou* in exactly this sense (ii 1 732ᵃ31–2).

(*ex hou* #2:) "It's in the female that the matter is, [i.e., prior to copulation] *out of which* [is made] that which is fashioned" (i 22 730ᵇ1–2).

Ar. can be sometimes distressingly casual about the difference, e.g. *GA* i 18 724ᵇ14–19 (for which reason Peck, "vv. 12–22 inepta seclusi", cf. his note, Loeb ed., p. 76).

M-en idiom isolates the vertical – i.e. upward – as opposed to horizontal dimension of "out of which", *ex hou*, distinguishing e.g. *being formed from bronze*, the sense of subjecthood that concerns us, from *coming-to-be from a bronze block* – a related and a pertinent notion, but now plainly a distinct one.[17] (As already anticipated, we shall be back to some less-surefooted Aristotelean discussions of this area in §21(ii) below.)

These distinctions are indeed so crucial for any sort of accurate thought in this area that it is advisable to adopt at this point some fixed terminological conventions with an eye to keeping the various relationships thoroughly sorted out; of course, the canonical modes of talking about to be proposed should not of themselves be mistaken for *analyses*, but they can serve as a presystematic sorting of the analysanda – fixing of the relevant *ideas* – without which it is questionable whether genuine analysis could be expected to get very far.

(1) (*F–M.*) Regarding the brazen statue, then, there is first of all the relation of the form to the matter; for this let us pre-empt the word "informs", and agree to say uniformly that in this case the socracity,[18] i.e. the Socratic shape, *informs* the bronze, and thereby it is that there is a statue of Socrates. (Elegant variations include "shapes up", "overlies as form to matter", "actualizes" – and in the best and most interesting cases, of course, "enpsychs" (§16), or "animates".) Conversely, for the relation of the matter to the form, the bronze *is informed by* the socracity (also "shaped up by", "takes", "is subject to (as form)", "underlies (as matter)". It is probably best to avoid "has", which as already noted can mean either the present relation of matter to form, or the entirely distinct relation of individual to form; entire eschewal may not be possible, in which case "(has)-in-the-sense-of"-riders may be called for. It is this relation-cum-converse, of course, that is abbreviated " ⌒ "; hence recall once more that in contexts of the type

the terms in F-position designate the form and the context as a whole designates the individual as a whole; thus in

"   statue   "

bronze ,

---

17 Vertical idea clearly identified by Owens in *DOB*², see pp. 339, 341.

18 It should perhaps be made explicit that this nomenclature for the form of the statue is quasi-facetious and certainly not meant to be imitated. No more should the form of a man be called "humanity" or *anthrōpotēs*. Recall §3 on this.

"statue" designates the shape, not the statue, and the statue is named by the whole (to echo the *Categories*, by being called synonymously from the shape).

(2) (*F–I.*) That brings us to the second relationship, that of the form to the individual; for this let us employ the expression "is form of", *never* "informs" (thus "*man* informs Socrates" is henceforth ill-formed), and agree to say uniformly that socracity *is form of* the statue (not the bronze). Note most particularly that this relation *is not* identity, cf. point (A) above. (Here an acceptable variant is "constitutes". I would venture that the verb, "to form", also belongs here: the shape *informs* the matter and thereby *forms* the statue. But it may be better not to make a practice of the usage if there is any chance of conflating the F/I with the F/M relation thereby.)

Another important variant for the same relationship is when the individual is called a 'substance' and the form is called 'the substance *of*' that individual; this is not an elidible ambiguity, but of great metaphysical significance, which will receive some further elaboration in §23(ii).

Conversely, the relation of the individual to the form may be evoked as its *exemplifying* the form (alternatively: "is a specimen of", "comes in the specific kind . . ."). "Has" is, as above, preferably avoided altogether if practicable. I prefer not to use "instantiates". As the allusion to the *Categories* just now reminds us, what I have suggested be called "is form of" coincides precisely with the substantial cases of what in the *Cats.* is called "is said-of" (if it is stipulated that "is form of" may be used for part as well as all of the form. On the same stipulation, the I–F relation is the substantial case of "called synonymously after").[19] Accordingly, the material-mode sense of "defines" is also admissible here, along the lines of §3 (p. 23), and "demarcates", "determines" etc. (cf. the renderings of *hōristai* in Zeta 3 1029ᵃ20, p. 188 above).

(3) (*I–M.*) Then there is the third relationship, that between the component matter and the individual. This becomes slightly complicated, we shall see, in cases where numerically one and the same individual can survive *changes* of component matter – which have earlier been argued to be the paradigm cases of substance theory; and there are related complications connected with the division within matter of "sensible" and "intelligible" (§17(ii), §23(iv)); but for present purposes of fixing terminology, all of that is for the time being better ignored. Let us then

---

19 Thus Zeta 10 1035ᵃ7–9: "The form, and the thing *qua* having form, is to be called in each case ['so-and-so', e.g. *statue*], though the material just in respect of itself is never to be called [that]". Hartman (1977), pp. 72 ff., has trouble with the first clause of this, which may be attributable to his different rendering of the sentence (which is *not* about *identifying* the thing with the form as opposed to the matter).

agree to say uniformly that the matter *composes* the individual (alternatives include "is shaped up into", "is formed into", et al.). Conversely, the relation of the individual to the matter is that of *being composed of* ("consisting of", "being made of") – this of course is what Aristotle's preferred terminology calls *M-en*, the individual as an upward paronym from *M* as its vertical *ex hou*.

These three relationships – if converses are counted, these six –, as has been said, need to be kept strictly sorted out. It is to be hoped that the terminological conventions will assist in that discrimination.

All three (or all six) are basically synchronic in application: they figure in thought about the "being" of an entity formed out of a matter, either as of a moment, or if over time then nonetheless statically: various of the *relata* may disappear and be supplanted if changes of various kinds occur, but the relationships themselves are not temporal ones. Now, the introduction of change through time into the picture brings with it several diachronic relationships which call for terminological sorting as well; here it will be found that relatively little can be done at the level of fixing linguistic conventions before we are forced by the nature of the case back into the depths of theory. We shall see also that Aristotle's command of these points seems to be not unvaryingly firm.

Considered above were two different ways of regarding the arising of a statue: (1) *becoming*, its coming-to-be "from" the *block* into which the bronze of the statue was formerly cast, and (2) *being-formed-into*, its coming-to-be "from" the bronze, ignoring its erstwhile form as a "lack" irrelevant to this mode of regarding. Subject to the refinement that is still to be dealt with,[20] (2) presents the fewer difficulties – at least of terminology; this is the relative-product "from" or *ex hou* which was depicted:

and for this we can agree to say uniformly that the bronze *gets formed up into* a statue (or "gets shaped up into"); and conversely, that a statue *gets formed up out of* the bronze, where "up into" and "up out of" are supposed to evoke the vertical dimension and distinguish this case from that of becoming.

As for becoming, it was noted that *the block's becoming a statue* was itself

---

20 Cf. the end of footnote 15 above, and §21 (i) below (on the "up" and "down" analyses).

regardable in two ways: either (A) as a transsubstantiation, the individual block being one substance which perished, and the individual statue another, new and distinct substance which was generated, or alternatively (B) as a nonsubstantial metamorphosis undergone by a single substantial continuant, numerically one and the same through the two metamorphic stages. The choice between (A) and (B) was seen to be a typical instance of the Population Problem, and consequently (in accordance with policy) not pursued further while metaphysical matters were under consideration. However, now that some of the distinctions have been codified that separate the various factors involved in becoming and getting-formed, together with what has been learned in §19(i)(ii) about the subjecthood of matter to form in the lower stage, it is possible now to enlarge upon the remark toward the end of §19(iii) (p. 184) about the location of the substantial individuals in this overall two-stage scheme. This in turn will lead to a final and definitive perspective on the Population Problem itself, including on the alternatives that confront us in this case of *becoming*.

§21. Individuals at the interface, and related matters

This section is given to elaborating and refining the theory as developed in the foregoing. It has no references to texts of Aristotle, and it does some things with the theory that Aristotle would be most unlikely to do. Yet I believe that in content it is about Aristotle's theory, and that in method it is defensible.

(i) *Individuals: at the interface between the stages. Definitive reformulation of the Population Problem, and some corollaries for the Substanzbegriff*

As for the location of the substantial individuals in the overall scheme: *the individuals lie at the interface of the two stages of the domain.* The specific forms that form them *as* individuals of a given substantial kind, i.e. migration-resistant characters (§6(ii)) that numerically one and the same individual cannot over time lose and survive, shape up matter in the lower stage – the matter, M, with respect to which the individuals themselves are upwardly paronymous, *M-en*. The characteristics that an individual *can* transit into and out of possessing without terminating its existence, attach to individuals in the upper stage – an individual to which a characteristic X_n attaches thus being with respect to it downwardly paronymous, X_a. The concrete particulars of being-formed (morphology) and of getting-formed (embryology) have been extensively reviewed.

But which characteristics are which? Which are the forms, the substantial differentiae, and which are the accidents? How has the discussion since §7 contributed to resolving questions of the type, *Are F's substances?* (for particular values of *F*)? If something appears to change in some radical or hitherto unheard-of way, are we any better placed to state the necessary and sufficient conditions under which it nonetheless may be held to remain the same individual? – The answer to the latter two questions is: To some extent, but the benefits are mostly indirect. As first suggested in §7, in most of the *real* instances, it is not metaphysics, but *the close and accurate study of Nature* that must resolve questions of Population, in case after real, particular, case. – Then what about the hypothetical changes that philosophers debate with such tireless zest and zeal: changes from being of-wood to being of-steel, brain transplants, the ship of Theseus, Jekyll/Hyde transformations, spatiotemporal discontinuities, strange divisions-in-two, etc. etc.? – Here again it is apposite to recall the suggested wisdom of §7: it can be useful to consider fantastic cases, not mainly (as some of the literature might suggest) in order to astound and bewilder the readership by posing questions that are (by design) unanswerable on ordinary intuitions, but because "there are several important methodological morals, concerning the apportionment of weights in Population decisions between metaphysical and nonmetaphysical factors, that can be more sharply and quickly pointed using specially-crafted fantastic cases than in any other way" (p. 58). As to the hypothetical changes just instanced, I shall argue in (ii–iv) below (see esp. pp. 208–10) that the considerations relevant to their resolution, too, must come largely from nonmetaphysical quarters – depending on the case, sometimes from biological quarters, or legal, or practical, or humanitarian, or even religious. In any important case, the relevant considerations are far *too* important to be left to metaphysicians.

So let us develop the perspective of the individuals at the interface by introducing it to some actual and possible changes, in order to see what the relativism of the metaphysical theory on Population can concretely come to. That will incidentally enable us to tie up the thread about *becoming* that was left hanging at the end of §20(iii) above.

On the view officially adopted in §7, then (that it is not up to the metaphysical theory to dictate sides on the question What things are substances): if, on one hand, someone (in the spirit of §20(iii), call him or her B) were to consider a transition from *man* to *gorilla* or *wolf* as, in his or her estimation, an allowable migration transitable by a single individual, or if, on the other, a fetishist (A) concerning, say, *pallor* (a leukomaniac) were to regard this property as a genuine differentia of the genuine species, *pale man*, and thus held that a day at the beach meant the extinction of the individual who began it (and the birth of someone new and inferior) and that sunlamps were assassins' tools – on the official view, it would not be the task of Aristotelean substance theory to correct the peculiar views of such exponents. Since §7, the deepening and refinement of the applicable intuitions that was intended to be effected by educating them with Aristotelean biology, should exert a beneficial influence upon such decisions; anyone familar with the paradigms of the animal kingdom should do much better than such as exponents A and B.[1] However, the theory as we now have it does furnish a way to formulate what they (A and B), along with the rest of us who hold saner views, are doing in making the judgments they make. Exponent B, in assigning the dramatic and indeed absurdly gothic changes – to us, *prima facie*, substantial – that mark the transition from *a man* into *a wolf*, to the status of mere phases in a single life history, is in effect drawing (or finding – i.e., claiming that Nature draws or finds) the interface between upper and lower stages of the domain a great deal *lower*, in this instance, than most of us are normally accustomed to. Exponent A, on the other hand, the leukomaniac, in holding that *pale man* constitutes a kind, such that what others see as a superficial exchange of accidents is actually the generation and destruction of individuals, is in effect seconding *pallor* into the category of substantial differentia and form, and in this way drawing (or finding – i.e., claiming that Nature draws or finds) the interface between the upper and lower stages of the domain at a level here that most of us would normally think of as abnormally if not absurdly *high*.

In general, for exponents X, *X's solution to the Population Problem*, whether grotesquely silly, like A's and B's, or sound and well-considered, like the reader's, *consists in the level at which in each case X finds the interface between the lower and the upper stages of the two-stage domain*, for in that answer is contained X's detailed conclusions as to which actual and possible changes should be analyzed as the adventures of individuals that perdure

---

[1] This is not to say that with such familiarity all the difficulties disappear; for some biologically conceivable but interestingly hard and instructive cases cf. (ii), (iv) below.

and senesce through time, and which as the generation and destruction of individuals by the differentiation and de-differentiation of matter. Picking up on the intuitive ontology of §18, the ultimate in the direction represented by A, placing substantial significance in to-us-trifling changes by raising the interface, is Heraclitus as cartooned by Plato and the Cratylan tradition ("*no* object is *ever* the same for even a millisecond"); the extreme in the direction of B, consigning to-us-drastic changes to the accidental by pushing the interface downward, is Parmenides or (bracketing all problems of interpretation) Leibniz ("*no* object *ever* comes into or goes out of existence, however it may look").

Between these extremes, the legitimate debate continues over the true location – or the just placement – of the migration-barriers, and therewith of the interface between the stages and the division between essence and accident, case by case (usually, type of case by type of case). In the course of it, the case may be encountered of *the block's becoming a statue*; and the alternatives that face us are now expressible as follows.

(A, or "up" direction:) If the becoming is substantial, that is because (in our new terms) the interface lies at *block* and *statue* – or, it may be, above; if so, how far above is still open – apparent transits from one of these to the other in fact cross migration-barriers and accordingly the individuals involved respectively perish and are generated; that which "underlies" the becoming lies beneath the surface in the lower stage, is a matter and "underlies" in the manner of a matter.

(B, or "down" direction:) If, on the other hand, the becoming is not substantial but is survived intact by a continuing individual, that is because the interface lies lower – how much lower is still open, but enough lower so that a single substantial form *F* connects the earlier block with the later statue as the same *F*, numerically one and the same individual through the migration; that which "underlies" the becoming lies *at* the interface and *is* that individual, and underlies in the manner of an individual.

In determining which of these two accounts is correct, it would be both appropriate and desirable to obtain the consensus of the natural historians of and the theoreticians concerning blocks and statues (the advice of steleology and andriantology); but that question need not be pursued further here.

Let us next proceed to confront the perspective of the individuals at the interface with those actual and possible changes that were spoken of, so as to ponder the apportioning of the factors involved between metaphysical and nonmetaphysical. But the viewpoint is already enough developed that we can appreciate how different in character is the Aristotelean substance concept in the *Metaphysics* setting, not only from that of the *Categories*, as has been explained, but from other, subsequent concepts that in various ways have descended from it. The difference has been building ever since the notions of *substance* and of *ultimate subject* were separated in reading *Meta.* Zeta 3.[2] The place of the substantial individuals at the interface of the two stages reflects an "ultimacy" quite different from the "substance" of Spinoza, or the *Tractatus*; for they constitute neither the ultimate subject of all that is nor the most elementary possible incomposite objects entering into the most "atomic" possible states of affairs;[3] and they are unlike the "substances" of Leibnizian monadology as well as the others in being not only impermanent but, on the cosmic scale, quite fragile; and they contravene the doctrine of the First Analogy by incessantly and in enormous numbers coming-to-be and ceasing-to-be without thereby inflicting the slightest noticeable damage on the Empirical Unity of Time.[4] Rather, as will be elaborated below, the concentration of the Aristotelean substances at the interface of the two stages, paronymic from both the overlying accidents or "coincidences" and from the underlying matter, ties in with the distinctively Aristotelean idea of *Meta.* Gamma: that of *being* (*on*) in general as a *focal* concept (*pros hen legomenon*), with substantial being, the being of substances, at the center or focus (cf. §23(i) below).

(ii) "Continuity of form": some further consolidation

It has been urged above that according to this theory, *being an individual* goes with *being of a substantial kind F*, and furthermore that *being the same individual* is to be understood as *being the same F*. In his commentary on "TSAS",[5] Alan Code pointed out that the second of these conditions does not follow from the first. That is a correct observation: there is a consistent view that would hold that to be an individual is to exemplify some substantial kind (or other), and that to continue to be the same individual is to continue to exemplify some substantial kind (or other), but perhaps different kinds at different times. Obviously the view I mean to attribute to Aristotle is stronger than this, and that is an important fact about it.

2 §6(i), §8, §9, §17(i), §19(i), §20(i).
3 Contrā Tractatum (5.4541): Complex sigillum veri?
4 The allusion is to the strange argument which is supposed to prove that if substances were generated and destroyed, there would have to exist a multiplicity of parallel times for them to do it in (*KRV* A 182–189 = B 224–32).
5 Code (1978b), commenting on Furth (1978).

Code went on to ask: What extra premisses could Aristotle add to the claim that "the advent of individuality is *pari passu* with that of form" (§15(i), p. 123) in order to derive this more exacting migration-resistance condition? That is worth exploring, though perhaps not as much in the present setting as in some others that have exerted some influence now and then. In saying this I have two things mainly in mind.

(i) The interest it has for some philosophers (I have no reason to count Code among them) derives from the picture of perduring objects that has them built up or logically constructed out of temporal, even momentary stages – the latter being basic or "given", and the problem being to give criteria under which two distinct entities called stages stand in the relationship of being stages of the same object or individual. I do not intend to argue here that this problem and the picture that lies behind it are misconceived, though I do think the picture puts matters back to front in some important ways. But it seems clearly not a good way of approaching Aristotle's view, in which (as I see it) it is the perduring objects that are the "given" vis-à-vis the pair, objects and stages; stages are discernible in them as, if one wishes, temporal parts, but parts *naturally* connected via the continuity of form (*q.v.* below), not of themselves "loose and separate" absent some metaphysically posterior connecting relationship or genidentity. In the intuitive terms of §18, the idea of form as a warping or "knotting" factor is meant seriously, as evoking this priority of continuous objects to their phases.

(ii) Beyond this, for our purposes here there is not so much interest in *deriving* this portion of the concept as in *elaborating* it.[6] We have now come far enough with the schematic "substructure of substance" in general to do some of that at this point, particularly with a view to heading off some unintended suggestions that might be encouraged by the expression "continuity of form". The remainder of this section is along such lines.

Code and I are of the same form or kind, since we are both of the kind Man.

Obviously Code and I are not the same man, nor are Code and Jimmy Carter, as Code himself has indeed publicly protested (*ibid.*).

Here we face a concrete Population issue. It has been sufficiently stressed above that the metaphysical theory does not settle such issues; so to deal with it we must look at the non-metaphysical considerations that can relevantly come into play in one direction or the other.

(1) First we may call up once again the fantastic case broached in §7,

6 Of course, deriving it is *one* way of doing that, as anyone long associated with the UCLA philosophical tradition is from time to time reminded.

where in a sequence of transformations there absorbingly described, Socrates is seen to become a wolf. It was asked, Is the same individual still there?; and it was seen that several opinions are compatible with the evidence, of which two should be singled out for attention here. In terms of the A ("up") and B ("down") tendencies as just distinguished:[7] (A) if *man* and *wolf* are Aristotelean substantial species, the answer must be No; Socrates has ceased-to-be and a new individual has come-to-be, which had better be named something else. (B) if it is wished to maintain (and we saw that there could be grounds for so doing) that the same individual *is* still there, then it must be denied that *man* and *wolf* are Aristotelean substantial species, and the same *F* that that individual is before and after the change is some deeper-underlying substantial nature that persists, which the man-*like* and wolf-*like* phases are metamorphic phases of.

There are, then, these two ways (generically speaking) of thinking of such a case.

(2) Now then, what of one individual man becoming another individual man? Certainly this is metaphysically possible, though biologically rather unlikely (but before jumping to hasty conclusions about that last, wait for the next type of case, (3)). It can be viewed as one pole of a contrast of the same genus as the A/B contrast just drawn, and can also usefully sharpen the notion of continuity of form. Consider the following fantastic eventuality: Socrates, before our eyes, begins to change in a different way from (1); and at the end of the thirty-minute transformation there stands before us a man (*no* question about that) who in appearance, character, recollections and every other imaginable respect would tempt us to consider as a possibility, even to suspect, the actual coming-to-be of Leopold Bloom. Is the same individual still there? As before, there are alternatives, and the Science of Being does not of itself choose among them for us. Philosopher A,[8] who says No, is most likely impressed with the discontinuities of memory and character and language-capability and so forth, and on this account pronounces this a new individual man (once again, generated in a most unusual manner). Philosopher B, who is a secret or closet *synechephile* (a "lover of continuity"), for whom consider-

---

7 These of course are *not* the "A" and "B" of "*Philosopher* A" etc. in §7; those *personae* emblemized *rationales* for one or another specific placement of the migration-barriers in the case there imagined, whereas these represent the tendency of momentum for downward and upward movement of the inter-stage interface of §21(i) above.

8 This means the philosopher of the A-persuasion as understood in the present section; cf. previous note. – In passing, I am assuming that it makes no difference whether the man at the conclusion of the change is under the impression that the year is 1904 or 1987 (if the latter, it may be that he also believes himself to be in his 120s).

ations of spatio-temporal contiguity override all others, declares this to be one and the same man, Socrates, regardless of the offsetting factors or whatever the poor wretch himself may protest.

More can be said about these alternatives, as well as others that may be left aside for present purposes, but the immediate moral to be drawn from this case is the following: in both the (A) and the (B) versions of the case, we have before us a *man* at each moment throughout – according to (A), one replaced by another, according to (B), the same at the end as at the start. Now, according to my understanding of the ("artful") expression "continuity of form, in the sense of there persisting one and the same F – whatever that may consist in, or our criteria for its satisfaction may be" (§19(ii), pp. 179, 181), of these two versions only the (B) version represents the continuity intended; and the weak sense of "our having before us a man at each moment throughout" that is compatible with the individuals' being distinct, at the end from the start, i.e., the (A) version as it turns out for this case, is not sufficient to qualify it as an instance thereof. Thus Code, Carter, Socrates and Bloom are of the same form, *man*; however, Code and Carter in the actual world as we all construe it, and Socrates and Bloom in our fantastic hypothetical case according to the (A) version, are certainly not *the same man* – though Socrates and Bloom would be so in our hypothetical case according to the (B) version, and odd as it may seem, Carter and Code could be so even under, and despite, all current indications to the contrary in the actual world (but the sort of construal that gives that result is better deferred for the moment – cf. (iv) below).

(3) From the clear metaphysical possibility of the (A) version of case (2), it can be seen that spatiotemporal contiguity, even accompanied by "having before us *an F* at each moment throughout", is not a sufficient condition for "continuity of form" in the intended sense, thus neither for *the same F*, and neither for the same individual. Let us explore a little further in this (A) or "up" direction.

Here are two cases readily imaginable, not even particularly "fantastic", in worlds enough like our own for us to want the Science of Substantial Being to be able to accommodate them. In the first case, there is a species Q of snake that periodically undergoes a process of moulting, which process popular natural history unhesitatingly regards *the individual Q* as surviving intact, the same individual. It is thus with some surprise that the microbiological herpetologists discover the process to include alteration of the chromosomal genetic material throughout the organism – minor alteration to be sure, but still of a magnitude at least as great as hitherto associated with descent from parent to offspring through several generations. The possibility must be faced that the process is fundamentally not a metamorphic but a reproductive one, a *generation of an individual Q* (and the destruction of its progenitor). (This is one type of case I have in mind in footnote 6 of §19 on the "artful" expression about continuity of form, and it illustrates the moral (p. 202 above) of some things' being too important to be left to metaphysicians, not to mention being altogether beyond their competence. There are in fact known biological phenomena that raise this sort of question.)[9]

In the second case, there is a society of human beings in an isolated part of the earth for whom the onset of puberty is regarded not as a "passage" with the "rites" familiarly associated therewith in our anthropological literature, but as literally the death of the child and the birth of a new individual, an adult. (It is important that this is no eccentric whim of theirs, but something they believe about *Nature*.) A funeral is held, followed by a baptism and appropriate celebration and merrymaking; there is an elaborate system of religious belief involving two separate Heavens, peopled by the departed souls of children and adults respectively; legally, the adult is considered the descendant of the child that gave its life that she or he might be born, thus inheriting its property, but although child marriages are common, the descendants not only are not thought to be married to each other but are discouraged from becoming so (this is because as descendants of the same married pair, they are *siblings*!). When told of our view, that the same human being survives from a state of being a child to that of adulthood, they marvel at our innocent acceptance as fact of so naive a fantasy, and write it off as wish-fulfilment, noting the consoling power of myth for the primitive mind.

(4) Nor is spatiotemporal contiguity a necessary condition for "continuity of form" in the intended sense, thus neither for *the same F*, and neither for the same individual. Let us explore a little further in the (B) or "down" direction.

Here are two cases readily imaginable, in worlds enough like our own for us to want the Science of Substantial Being to be able to accommodate them. As for the first, it is not a theorem, still less an axiom, of Aristotelean metaphysics that Socrates could not cease to be in 399 B.C. and recommence his existence in A.D. 1957 – or right here and now. (Of course, the metaphysical possibility should not be confused by the host of problems about whether we could be certain (or so much as believe) that

---

9 I am told of certain sporulating ferns whose cells pass from the diploid to the haploid state in successive phases of the life-cycle – or are they *not* phases of the life-cycle, but successive generations?

it was Socrates, whatever he might say, or whether he could know (or believe) it himself – interesting problems, without doubt, but beside the present point. And the metaphysical possibility of course is not a *real* possibility; cf. §21(iii) below.) If that is too hard to visualize, consider again the clubs and city-states that were brought up in §17(ii) (and will recur in §23(iv)) as objects well-suited among human artefacts to exemplify the contrast between "sensible and intelligible matter". Thus the Oxford University Shakespeare Society ceased to exist (= was dissolved) at a meeting at Balliol in 1867, and was brought back into existence – was reconstituted, new members of course, but one and the same club (its constitution had been found in a drawer) – at a meeting at Trinity in 1903. (The example is imagined, like the others.)

In the second case, it is my understanding (but if incorrect, I would contend it is still a coherent understanding) of the personage known as the Dalai Lama, that he does not die; but when the phenomenon occurs that in ordinary humans is called death, a search is undertaken throughout his region for that male infant determined to have been born as nearly as possible at the same moment (other signs being consulted in case of ties); that infant, once found, is considered and proclaimed to be the Dalai Lama – not the *next* Dalai Lama but the selfsame one. Here some effort and ingenuity may have to go into ascertaining the temporal contiguity which is indeed criterial for this particular perduring thing; but spatio-temporal contiguity plainly is not required, or for that matter very easily imagined.

(iii) Apologia pro modo docendi

Here a justificatory plea like that of §7 may again be appropriate. Obviously, not all of these examples present real problems awaiting serious investigation; but it is important to recognize that the principles they illustrate are not trivial. Let me be particularly emphatic that I have no thought of committing Aristotle *in propria persona* to the neutrality that I contend the Science of Substantial Being of itself must maintain on such questions: he certainly knows better than to think that you can generate a man in any other way than from parents, or that a man can have intermittent existence, or that the changes of adolescence are substantial (in his sense). The point is that his metaphysics of substance, as well as failing to apply to some possible worlds that we can think of,[10] also will

---

10 Cf. §18, and Furth (1986).

accommodate worlds in which nature works differently from the actual world as we are normally accustomed to construe it, and that to ring such changes through certain such worlds in a controlled way can illuminate the divisions and (sometimes) the overlaps between that which is fixed by the metaphysical structure, and that which, though deeply pervasive in things as we know them, yet flows from other sources. There is a wonderful statement of Wittgenstein's that I think points a not dissimilar moral:

> If someone believes that certain concepts are absolutely the correct ones, and that someone who had different ones would fail to realize something that we realize – then let him imagine certain very general facts of nature to be different from what we are used to, and other conceptual structures than the usual ones will become intelligible to him.   (*Investigations*, II xii)[11]

(iv) Form and spatio/transtemporal atomicity: some harder cases

I next wish to pursue some consequences of an idea that emerged at the end of the outline of the "dynamic picture" in §19(ii): it was seen at that point that Form was "the source of the unity of the substantial individuals in two dimensions, the synchronic and the diachronic", in ways that were briefly evoked (see p. 181). It will be recalled also that Matter entered that scene as playing the role of "medium or *hupodokhē*" in which Form is instantiated, and as required and responsible for any *multiplicity* of simultaneous instantiations, even though it is still Form that is required and responsible for pulling each of those quantities of Matter into a unified and in that sense atomic "this". Here a diagnostic tool that is particularly revealing of the apportioning as between metaphysical and nonmetaphysical criteria in Population allocations – as well as bringing into clear view some other subtleties – is the case of a world in which individuals can and more or less regularly do split into co-specific pairs, and such pairs can merge into one.

Suppose that Socrates does "divide into two" in the way that was briefly imagined in §15(i): by "developing a dorso-ventral fold between right and left sides along which the halves proceed to separate, the left side developing a new right and the right side a new left, the penultimate phase before final separation being like a pair of Siamese twins – each one-half Socrates-sized? – joined at the little finger" (p. 125); let that

---

11 The idea of this passage may already have been detected influencing the methodological strategy of §9.

description of the process stand. What is to be said of the identities of the entities that result from the process? Along the lines of the foregoing discussion, it is apparent that several rational reconstructions are compatible with the evidence as stated.

RR (1). Socrates has ceased to be, and two new human beings have come to be: they should receive new names (e.g. Roscrates and Guilcrates); neither being the same man as Socrates, it follows that Xanthippe is a widow. I think it will be agreed, after duly weighing the alternatives to come, that this interpretation is definitely preferable to all alternatives, on all of the relevant grounds – legal, moral, religious, practical and philosophical.

RR (2). Socrates, the right-hand "twin" of the pair prior to final separation, has produced a new individual, presumably a descendant, by a process called aristerogenesis or budding-to-the-left; in commemoration of the comparable occurrence reported in the second chapter of Genesis, the new production is called Evecrates (pron. "Eevcrates"). Socrates is one and the same man as before. If it is wondered why it is so certain that Socrates is the *right*-hand member of the pair, the answer is that a long tradition of Talmudic-style scholarship has grown up from study of the phenomenon, and authorities are agreed that the perduring continuant must be the one on the right owing to the inherent *betterness* of right than left.[12] Occasional deviations occur, however, here as everywhere, and courts of appeal have ruled that dexiogenesis or budding-to-the-right was an allowable interpretation under appropriate circumstances.

RR (3). Also possible, though peculiar in some ways, are interpretations under which Socrates has *not* ceased to be, but *has* become *two*. I can think of at least two important versions of this:

RR (3–i). There are now two distinct individuals, Socrates$_R$ and Socrates $_L$, numerically distinct from each other, each of which is numerically one and the same man as Socrates prior to "division in two", and Xanthippe is a bigamist. This version, it seems to me, has a certain intuitive coherence and appeal: the simultaneous Socrates$_R$ and Socrates$_L$ are diverse in the absolute sense of being composed of distinct parcels of matter going about their separate business, but both are the same as Socrates in the sense of being, both, later metamorphic stages of a single individual man at an earlier metamorphic stage, whom it happens

---

12 *PA* ii 2 648ª12–13, *PA* iii 3 665ª22–6, *IA* 4 706ª20–4, cf. *Cael.* ii 5 288ª2–7 (on priority of right to left), and *PA* iii 9 671ᵇ29–30, *IA* 4 705ᵇ18 ff. (on right as natural origin of movement). The best introduction to this rich subject is G. E. R. Lloyd (1962), esp. (for Aristotle) pp. 61–5. A classic source is Hertz (tr. 1960).

Xanthippe married. (Socrates$_L$, perhaps, may be supposed immediately after separation to have read and reacted with disappointment against the works of Anaxagoras (if *Phaedo* 97b–99d were historically credible), with a marked effect on his later intellectual development, and was subsequently declared by the oracle to be the wisest of all; whereas Socrates$_R$ became an orthodox Pythagorean and accordingly was thereafter submerged in the School and not subsequently heard of.) The only drawback to the interpretation is that, contravening as it does the law of transitivity of identity, it is logically impossible (at any rate, such would no doubt be the consensus of logicians); but except for that, it seems rather attractive.

RR (3–ii). Socrates "has become two", yet there is still a single individual, Socrates, numerically one and the same man as the normal-appearing human being that preceded the separation; but Socrates consists now of two spatially discontinuous portions (call them "halves", or more generally "parts"), each of which actually somewhat resembles that normal-appearing human being which, now, the pair of them collectively is one and the same man as. (Xanthippe's situation in this case, while certainly not bigamous, is otherwise probably better not elaborated on.) Of course, to call such a *pair* of anthropoid objects a "man", consisting of "halves", is a provocative and very likely in the end indefensible departure from convention (Aristotle would *buy* it no more than would we – cf. *Meta.* Mu 7 1082^{a}22, "two men are not some one thing over and above both of them");[13] but its demerits seem to me to stem from its conflict with our received concept of what belongs in the species-form *man*, and not from any felonious abuse of the concept of being numerically one and the same F as (save for the fact that here F *is* man).

This last case has instructive implications that are worth pursuing. It is not difficult to imagine a form of life (in Wittgenstein's sense) that would give it space to move in: for example, it would be selectively desirable for a warlike species like ourselves to have the capacity to split into "parts" in this way prior to marching off to war: one "half" of each "man" remaining at home; prodigious feats of valor could then be expected of the army, since the "fallen" could continue their domestic existence upon cessation of hostilities under no greater disadvantage relative to the "survivors" than the loss of a "part" – like an amputee.[14] The only

13 The quotation is actually not decisive on precisely this point, as it begs just that point by calling them "men"; but it shows where Aristotle's instincts would lead were he faced with it.

14 Much remains open here about the psychology of these split-into-halves individuals; perhaps it is best for the immediate purpose of the example to think of the halves as sharing a single consciousness, which may not make sense under every imaginable psychology. I regard the issue as not of too much relevant importance.

problems arise when the victorious though reduced host returns, and even then not if it is made a rule of the game that the returning "halves" must merge, and only with their complements, Callias$_R$ with Callias$_L$ and not with Socrates$_L$ (for example, it might be a fact of nature that attempted mergers of such "parts" as had not originated by splitting from each other were bound to fail by immune rejection, like an organ transplant from an unrelated donor failing to "take").

However, the consolations of immunology do not absolve us from considering the other metaphysical possibilities: suppose, then, that Socrates$_R$ has indeed fallen on the field, and that Callias$_R$ returns and perversely merges not with Callias$_L$ but with Socrates$_L$ instead. The situation then looks like this:

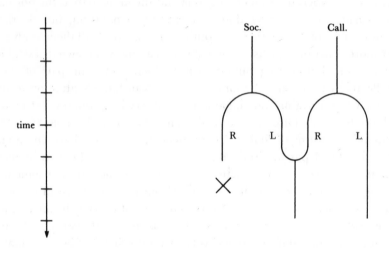

The question is, who (what individual) is the result of this promiscuous merger? As always with Population questions, the actual choice of answer is less important than the principles involved, and the case points to one principle that is important. The tidiest answer, as in RR (1), is that a new individual has been generated; there is no reason of principle to regard the promiscuous mergee as either Socrates or Callias (certainly the survival of Callias$_L$ is adventitious and extraneous to the question, and no reason to regard the mergee as Socrates); there are various inconveniences connected with calling it both; and in any case, bypassing all that, the interesting possibility that the case brings to light is that of considering the entire field of merger candidates for a given (partial-) individual like Callias$_R$ *as (parts of) a single individual* in exactly the same sense that RR (3–ii) originally assigned the role of "parts" to the right-left offspring of the splits – possibly, if the facts so prove, all the way out to the species. The case is instructive in pointing the moral that the distinction between what we regard as individuals on one hand and as flocks and schools and swarms and gaggles on the other is, while certainly not arbitrary (some quite powerful influencing considerations have now been built into this case), also not automatic, and in some perfectly realistic situations can be difficult and call for detailed analysis, whose results could well conflict with traditional understanding.[15]

15 Cf. §21(iii)(3) above, the case of the snakes called Q, pp. 208–9.

§22. Return to the lower stage: some further corollaries

(i) Note on the conservation of matter

Having recognized that divergence of views on a Population question can be conceptualized in terms of divergent placings, lower versus higher, of the interface between the stages of the domain – the lower the placement, the more minimal the form, assuming a constant level of change going on –, we can utilize an extreme case of this to deal with what otherwise might appear a puzzling problem. Namely, since the notion of diachronic individuation was introduced into the two-stage framework at §19(ii), repeated allusions have been made to "conservation" of matter through substantial change, to Socrates' matter today becoming Callias' matter in the future, and the like, all of which seems to presuppose the tracing of *matter itself* through time, in order to be thus (in principle) re-identifiable as the matter first of this and then of that, thus as itself in some sense "the same and numerically one" throughout. Yet it has also been contended at some length that numerical identity over time is linked to continuity of *form*, whereas a matter, as such (i.e. except as thus or thus informed) seems by definition devoid of form and is argued in *Meta*. Zeta 3, as we saw (§20(i)), to lack the nature of a "this" – from which it seems to follow that a matter cannot, of itself (*kath' hautēn*), admit the same concept as does an individual substance of being the same and one in number. In that case, how to make sense of its conservation and exchange?

It certainly does seem that we possess a concept of *this here quantity of bronze*, e.g., *the bronze of this statue*, regarded as an entity enduring through time, however differently cast or molded or struck, even when split into a discontinuous state such as 10,000 coins (if there seems a difficulty in principle about imagining such an entity as this traced across time – the practical difficulties are of course something else – then let the bronze in question be ineradicably perfused with a unique color, or somehow radioactively tagged (whatever that might mean for Empedoclean matter)). If we can indeed conjure up such a concept as this, it seems both natural and consonant with the foregoing to hazard that the possibility of our doing so equals the possibility of our thinking of the bronze under an *extreme* "minimal form", a form with little more to it than a blank check fillable-in by history, such that the bronze has remained informed by that form no matter what has happened to it (or perhaps the coloring or tagging did the trick). It is in this way, conceptually speaking, that quantities of matter can be tracked; it remains a fixed point that numerical identity over time is linked to form.

The possibility granted, I am nonetheless disinclined to turn that possibility into a Population decision; that is, outside the context of philosophical discussion, my inclination is not to countenance such a form as the above and *pari passu* not to recognize such an "individual" as that parcel of bronze; but as can be seen it is not from lack of wherewithal for the feat.[1]

Matter considered independent of even minimal form, I think, cannot be traced through time: bronze *as such*, not this quantity of bronze (which involves such a form) but just *bronze*, is a nature, of which any part is the same as any other (unless the partitioning involves form). (Thus there turns out to be a significant distinction between the substantial individual, a scattered one formed by an extremely minimal form, that is All the Bronze in the Cosmos, and just Bronze.) It is matter in this sense, presumably, that the vertical relations of form to matter (*informing*, recall §20(iii) above) and of individual to matter (*being composed of*) should be thought of as ultimately terminating in, as well as that diachronic notion of *getting formed up out of* that we have been at pains to distinguish fundamentally from *becoming*.

1 Such an attitude is reinforced, though not beyond appeal, by the consideration that, were the parcel of bronze to be given substantial-individual status in the way described, then the statue into which the parcel of bronze happens today to be fashioned would be on the *Metaphysics* theory *automatically* ruled out as a substance on the ground that "no substance is composed of substances", Zeta 16 1041ᵃ4, 1040ᵇ14, Zeta 13 1039ᵃ3 ff. (quite independent of any other scruples about artefacts). Frede (1978) reaches a similar view, see e.g. p. 37.

(ii) Three sometimes-neglected polarities, and two consequently weaker accounts of coming-to-be in ζeta and the Physics

The synchronic and diachronic picture of subjecthood, substantial persistence and change that has been pieced together in §19–§21 is a development mainly of three polarities:

(1) the 'twofoldness' of 'being a subject' (*hupo-keisthai*), as between (a) the matter-underlying-form and (b) the individual-underlying-affliction configurations, associated with the lower and upper stages respectively of the two-stage world (§19(i–ii)),

(2) the distinction between the ("horizontal") *ex hou* that is the origin of a thing, and the ("vertical") *ex hou* that is a thing's (an *M*-en thing's) own contemporary matter (M) (20(iii)), and

(3) The difference between regarding a given change as (a) the passing-away and/or coming-to-be of substantial individuals, by the de-informing and re-informing of a matter, and regarding it as (b) an exchange of afflictions by an individual that perdures, which has been phrased in the "neutral" language of migration-resistance and the placement of the divide or "interface" between the upper and lower stages (in the A-"up" or B-"down" directions, respectively) (§21(i–iv)).

All three polarities are unmistakably Aristotelean (though some of the "neutral" language is new), and each of them is found to be stated with tolerable clarity at one point or another in the text, as we have seen. However, in several of Aristotle's main discussions of change and coming-to-be, the poles of one or more of the polarities seem to be assimilated or impacted, one or more of the distinctions seem to be blurred; the consequence is interpretive confusion and dismay, and the attribution to Aristotle of views that are conflicting and sometimes quite odd. Two such discussions may serve as representative: that of *Meta.* Zeta 7, and the well-known "introduction of matter" chapter, *Physics* i 7.

Let us begin with the latter. It is possible that it was written (or alternatively, was meant to be read, or heard) before *Meta.* Zeta 3, for it closes with the profession that "whether the substance is the form or the *hupokeimenon* is not yet clear" (191^a19–20), a question that Zeta 3 is supposed to settle once and for all, as we saw (§20(i)).[2] In any case, the picture it draws is demonstrably less articulated and complex than that

---

2 It is possible, but I think unlikely, that a more sophisticated reading is intended of 191^a19–20: "we have not yet made clear how to distinguish (in the field, so to speak) the two sorts of cases: the ones where form informs matter (in which the substance is substance *of*, i.e., the form), and the ones where affliction afflicts individual (in which the substantial individual plays the role of *hupokeimenon*)".

which has now been conjured up from the Zeta and Theta passages considered in §20. The main strategic objective of *Phycs*. i 7 is to establish that in every case of coming-to-be, without exception, whether substantial (*ex allou allo*) or qualitative (*ex heterou heteron*) (189^b33, cf. Ross *AP* 491), there is an underlying subject of the change (190^a13–15, 33–4, ^{b}1–4, 9–10, 19–20, 33–4, 191^a4–5, 7–8 . . . 11–12). Possibly as a tactical device toward that strategic end, both polarities (1) and (3) are not sharply defined: (3a) and (3b) tend to be assimilated, as an unmusical man's coming-to-be musical (e.g., 189^b35) is run together with some unshaped bronze's coming-to-be a statue (e.g., 191^b13–17); similarly for (1a) and (1b), as when *matter* wavers indiscriminately between *the man* who 'underlies' the music and *the gold* which 'underlies' the shape (190^b23–5), and when *form* likewise oscillates between *the music* in the man and *the order* (*hē taxis*) that organizes the gold (190^b28, cf. $^b13$–17).

Likewise, polarity (2) between the two senses of *ex hou*, though present, is present in a somewhat muffled way. In the review of "what is said" about comings-to-be (190^a5–13, 21–9), variously described (189^b34–190^a1), it is remarked that when "it is said" that A comes-to-be B, it may or may not "be said" that B comes-to-be '*out of*' (*ek*) A. For example, both the man and the unmusical "are said" to come-to-be musical, but although it is "said" that the musical has come-to-be 'out of' the unmusical, we don't "say" that the musical has come-to-be 'out of' the man (190^a5–8); the explanation suggested is that what a thing comes-to-be 'out of', should be something that has been made to disappear by the change, not something that still remains (190^a21–3, 26–8). It seems to be this explanation that led one interpreter[3] to the astonishing conclusion that since in a substantial change something comes-to-be 'out of' matter, Aristotle must here be contending that the *matter* is made to disappear by the change (!). The merits of this interpretation have been adequately dealt with;[4] however, the foregoing discussion allows us to see that *Phycs*. i 7 starts off using the *origin* sense of *ek*; then, in the midst of the rehearsal of what we "say", the sense here called 'vertical' is suddenly introduced:

Although sometimes it's "said" thus in the case of things that do remain, for we say 'a statue comes to be out of bronze', not (that) bronze (comes-to-be) a statue[5] (190^a24–6),

3 Jones (1974). 4 Code (1976).
5 In the setting of the "somewhat muffled" articulation of Polarity (2) at this point, it is probably overreaching to take this "not" clause as marking the difference between objectual (horizontal) and materiate (vertical) source of a coming-to-be (cf. §20(iii) above, p. 195). In any case it should not be taken as Jones (1974) suggests (pp. 484–5), to mean "we do not 'say' that the bronze statue comes to be" on the ground (here quite mis-invoked) that statues are bronzen not bronze; cf. Code (1976), pp. 360–1.

without its being made explicit, or possibly even realized, that this is an entirely *different* 'out of'. It takes an intuition that is thoroughly versed in the Theta 7 concept of vertical *'out of which'* to see that it is the horizontal and vertical 'out of's that are being contrasted as "two ways of coming-to-be something" in the following:

So that it's clear from what's been said that that which comes-to-be as a whole is always composite (*suntheton*): there is
(1) something that comes to be,
(2) something that comes to be that, and this in two ways[6]:
  (a) the *subject* (*hupokeimenon*),
  (b) the *opposite* (*antikeimenon*)
– by *being opposed* (*antikeisthai*) I mean: the unmusical, and the absence of configuration (*askhēmosunē*), the absence of shape (*amorphia*), the absence of order (*ataxia*);
– by *being subject* (*hupokeisthai*) (I mean): the man, and the bronze, the stone, the gold. (190^{b}10–17)

(Here the running-together of the poles of Polarity (1) is particularly flagrant.)

Let us turn to *Meta.* Zeta 7, where the suggestion recurs that 'out of which' has a favored application to "the thing that doesn't remain":

As for that 'out of which' as matter they come-to-be, some are said, when once they've come-to-be, to be not *that* but *thaten*, e.g. the statue is not stone but stonen; and the man, i.e., the healthy man, is not said to be *that* 'out of which' (he has come-to-be (that). The reason is that he comes-to-be 'out of' both the lack and the substrate, which (latter) we call the matter – e.g., it's both *the man* and *the sick (one)* that come-to-be healthy –; however, it's really much more said to come-to-be 'out of' the lack, as 'out of a sick (one), a healthy', rather than out of man; which is why the healthy (one) isn't called sick, but is called a man, and the man is called healthy. But as for things where the lack is unclear or has no name – such as in bronze, (the lack of) whatever configuration, or in bricks & timbers, (the lack of) house, 'out of' these they (statue, house) seem to come-to-be in the way that in the other case (the healthy one comes-to-be) from the sick; which is why, just as in the other case the thing is not called *that*, 'out of which' (it comes-to-be), so here the statue is not called *wood*, but rather takes on a derived term, *wooden*,[7] and *bronzen* but not *bronze*, and *stonen* but not *stone*, and the house: *bricken* but not *bricks* – since it also isn't the case that 'out of' wood a statue comes-to-be, or 'out of'

---

6 There seems to be a minor reverse in terminology between 190^{a}2–3 and here at 190^{b}11–12: earlier, the "gignomenon" is that which is there at the start of the change, and what is after the change is "what it becomes"; here, it is that which arises as a result of the change, and what was before the change is "something that comes to be that". The ambiguity of "that which comes-to-be" in English parallels that of "to gignomenon". Cf. also Ross *ad loc.*, *AP* 493.

7 Recall §20, n. 6 (p. 189).

bricks a house, if one were to examine the question carefully, he wouldn't say it *simpliciter*, because coming-to-be requires a *change* in the 'out of which', but not that it remain. This, then, is the reason why it is said in this way.

$$(1033^a5-23)$$

This explanation is simply wrong: for two distinct *ex hou*'s are imperfectly distinguished. That is, as we now know,

(1) "The statue is 'out of' the bronze"

is the vertical relation of a thing-with-a-form to its own matter;

(2) "The well (one) is 'out of' the sick (one)"

is the horizontal relation of a thing-with-a-form to an earlier thing-without-that-form (or thing-with-a-lack).

(Whether or not the earlier and later things are the *same* thing in this latter case is, as we have seen, an entirely separate issue; cf. §20(iii), §21 (i).)

Thus the reason why

(1) *the statue isn't properly called bronze (but may be called bronzen)* is that the statue is, vertically, *of-bronze*, in the sense that has been discussed; and this is *not* the reason why

(2) *the well (one) isn't properly called sick (but may be called man)*, which is rather that the well (one) has ceased-to-be sick by way of coming-to-be well, thus the same *hupokeimenon* "remaining", horizontally, while it passes from one *antikeimenon*, which has disappeared, to its opposed *antikeimenon*, which has replaced it. Thus the two configurations are altogether different, in a way that the Theta 7 account renders altogether formulable, and this paragraph of Zeta 7 is by comparison something of a jumble.[8]

(At paragraph's end, as at the outset of *Phycs.* i 7, it is suggested that the locution "comes to be 'out of'" should be restricted to cases of type (2), where the 'out of which' 'doesn't remain'; there is nothing against making such a restriction on the expression *ex hou*, but it will not make the type (1) cases go away or diminish in importance – note that they are back on the scene, locution and all, immediately at the beginning of Zeta 8.)

What is the explanation of these retrograde treatments in Zeta and the *Physics*? It has already been suggested (p. 218 above) that the effacing of Polarity (1) in *Phycs.* i 7 may be understood in the light of the overriding strategy of the chapter, that of perceiving a *hupokeimenon* in all comings-to-

8 Owens (DOB²340–1) sees no problem – surprising, since he is clear about the vertical *ex hou* (cf. §20, note 17).

be, an objective whose value might offset the cost of temporarily ignoring other interesting considerations pointing in the direction *hupokeimenon legetai dikhōs* or *pollakhōs*; and we have also seen that Polarity (2) can be retrieved from the chapter, although there is initial uncertainty on the point and the language of *M-en* is not in sight. But in Zeta 7, where the language of *M-en* is present, Polarity (2) is muffed entirely. I can see no reason for ignoring so good a distinction once it had been clearly made; so I infer, with all due diffidence on so treacherous a historical issue, that when the last paragraph of Zeta 7 was composed, the distinction had perhaps not yet been clearly made.

(iii) *Return to the ultrasimples. Hupokeitai* TRIKHŌS, *and why Aristotle doesn't need a materia prima*

The thorough shaking-out that has now been given the various polarities involved in the theory's account of subjecthood and change, now puts us in a position to appreciate the ingenious story that is woven in the *CTB/PA* about the absolutely ultimate constituents (in the "vertical" dimension) of material reality: what in §10(i) were called the "ultrasimples".

It was pointed out in §10 that so far as the requirements of biological explanation are concerned, there is on Aristotle's view no need to go to any deeper vertical level than the Empedoclean Four Roots, and indeed we have seen a main burden of his account to be that the deeper one goes in that dimension, the less comprehensible the biological phenomena appear (thus §12(iii)).

In fact, the only phenomenon of any sort that would require any theoretical descent beneath the Empedoclean-style 'simples', would be the possibility of one such 'simple' changing into another. Empedocles himself held very firmly that such change was impossible, as we know from both the clear testimony of the fragments (frr. 11, 12) and from Aristotle's report (*CTB/PA* i 1 314^{b}23–4, 315^{a}4–6), although Aristotle proceeds to argue, by disingenuous misinterpretation of the "Cycle", that Empedocles cannot consistently rule such elemental change out of his theory (315^{a}3–15; I pass over the details).

Now, Aristotle for his part thinks that elemental metamorphosis is an observed empirical fact (e.g., ii 4 331^{a}8–12). Actually, it does not seem too difficult to save the phenomena he seems to have in mind, without resort to the idea of true elemental change: if it appears to us that Water changes to Air when evaporation occurs, or that Fire turns to Earth when flame is succeeded by ashes and soot, one might always consider Empedocles' own answer,[9] which is that in such cases one element is not *changed* into another, but simply *replaced* by it. Thus, in (say) combustion, a process occurs (presumably traceable back to the agency of cosmic Love and Strife) in which a region of the cosmos (say, a fireplace, or a forest burning away in summer) that at one time has a very high *logos*/ratio of Fire to other elements, later is characterized by a *logos*/ratio that is proportionately Earthier; no Fire has been destroyed, or Earth created, they have only been moved around, or "pushed":

> For coming-into-being from that which no-wise is is inconceivable,
> And that what is should be destroyed is impossible and unheard-of,
> For there it will always *be*, wherever one may keep pushing it.   (Fr. 12)

However, Aristotle does not follow Empedocles in this, and he also has theoretical as well as observational reasons for thinking that change of elements is real (cf. *De Caelo* iii 6–7). But since according to him all change requires a persistent substrate (see, e.g., *Phys.* i 7, the chapter just now considered), the question arises what it is that can serve this office in this instance. The answer, as retailed in *CTB/PA* ii 3–4, is most interesting.[10]

It is his discussion of this subject in this place, as much as anything else to be found in the corpus, that has encouraged interpreters to suppose that Aristotle believes there to be a single, featureless and completely indeterminate substratum or *hupokeimenon* underlying changes of this kind, which the tradition has called *materia prima* or "prime matter"; in the famous and oft-quoted description of this strange concept given by Zeller, this is "pure Matter, without any determination by Form . . . that which *is* nothing, but *can become* everything – the Subject, namely, or substratum, to which none of the thinkable predicates belongs, but which precisely on that account is receptive of them all . . . This pure matter . . . Aristotle calls *prōtē hulē* (= 'prime matter')".[11] And it has to be conceded that Aristotle's attempts at a general explanation of his theory of elemental change are much obscurer than his treatments of the specific changes themselves, and much more susceptible to the "strange", *prima–materia*, reading. Let us therefore attend to the clearer treatments first.

As in *Physics* i 7, so also in *CTB/PA* the "twofoldness of subject"

9 On Empedocles' denial of interelemental change, see Lloyd (1979), p. 142, note 87; Wright (1981), 29–30, 172–3.

10 Many of the points in the following reconstruction were arrived at independently and simultaneously by M. L. Gill, who discusses it in her Gill (forthcoming), "Laying the ghost of prime matter".

11 The quotation is from W. Charlton's useful discussion of the whole question in the Appendix to his Charlton (1970) ("Did Aristotle believe in Prime Matter?", pp. 129–45), reviewing all the Aristotelean passages that have been thought to insinuate such a belief, and arguing (with cogency, as I think) against the received interpretation. The chief contender against prior to Charlton was King (1956), rebutted on behalf of the tradition by Solmsen (1958). Charlton's own contentions have been controverted by Robinson (1974).

doctrine (our "Polarity (1)") is not consistently adhered to, and the idea that there must be a single *subject* underlying every change is thus frequently expressed in the idiom of there having to be a single *"matter"* underlying every change, even accidental change like change of place (i 1 314b26–315a3). This need cause no difficulty, as long as the great generality of the usage is borne in mind. Nor is there any great harm in the fact that the *CTB/PA* rather confusingly uses the word *element* (i.e., *stoikeion*) both for Earth, Air, etc. (e.g. 329^{b}23), and for the underlying Hot, Cold, Moist, etc. (e.g. 330^{a}30), though sometimes, more consistently, the former are "the *so-called* elements" (*ta kaloumena stoikheia*, e.g. 329^{a}16, 26). We may dispel that ambiguity by using "element" only for Earth, Air, etc., and referring to Hot, Cold, etc. only as the "(primary) contrarieties" (*prōtai enantiōseis*, 329^{b}17). These points stipulated, the theory of the specific inter-elemental changes is as follows.

The "primary contrarieties" are four in number: Hot as against Cold and Moist as against Dry (=H *v.* C, M *v.* D). Now, it is of the nature (*pephuke*) of the contrarieties to form pairwise "linkages" (*suzeuxeis*), of which six are mathematically possible ((4 × 3) ÷ 2); however, contrarieties that are opposed to each other do not by nature "link" (*ou pephuke sunduazesthai*), so that the "linkages" possible in nature are four: namely,

H + D (Fire), H + M (Air), C + M (Water), and C + D (Earth)

(ii 3 330^{a}30–^{b}7). Many elegant and pleasing symmetries and other relationships are described, among both the simples (*hapla*), and the "mixed" natures (*mikta*) that are the so-called elements (ii 3, 330^{b}21 to the end), which can be left aside for our purposes.

Now, when some Fire changes to some Air, the underlying structure of the change is that in a "linkage" joining H and D (i.e., in the Fire), the D is replaced by its opposite, the M, while the H remains as the persisting subject (thus the result, H + M, is the Air). (Sometimes this replacement is described in rather Phaedonian terms, as the D being "vanquished" or "overcome" by the M[12] (e.g. 331^{a}28, 29, 35), whereas sometimes the opposite that is replaced is said simply to "pass away" (e.g. 331^{b}1).) So the change looks schematically something like this:

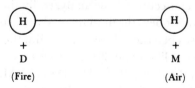

12 *kratēthēi* – the word is that also used for the "mastering and getting mastered" of the male's semen in *GA* iv 3, cf. §15(ii, and Appendix) above. Cf. also *Timaeus* 56c–58c.

The reason why Fire can change directly into Air in this way is precisely that they share a common contrariety, H, which can "link" with either D or M; the *CTB/PA* employs special technical terminology for this, saying that the component H is a *"reciprocally compatible complement"* (*pros allēla sumbolon*, e.g. 331ª24, 33–4) with respect to both D and M, and that a pair of elements thus sharing a component and accordingly capable of direct change from one to the other are *"consecutive"* (*ephexēs*, e.g. 331ᵇ4). "Complement" translates *sumbolon* (which may be remembered from Empedocles' speculations about each parent's contributing to animal generation a "tally", the pair of which then fit together to make the offspring, §15(iii) above); here the idea is that a contrariety is a "reciprocally compatible complement" with respect to both of the contrarieties, i.e. from the pair to which it does not belong, with which it can "link".

It is now easily seen that "the genesis of the (so-called) 'simple bodies' (i.e., the elements) will be cyclical" (331ᵇ2–3), by way of "consecutive" pairs; in the direction that is described in the work (331ª24–ᵇ2), namely, Fire to Air to Water to Earth, it will go like this:

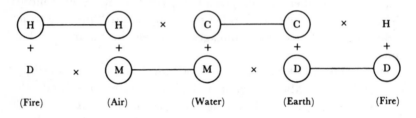

That is, Fire *can* and does turn into Water, and vice versa, or Air into Earth, but because those pairs are not "consecutive" (in the technical sense defined above), each such change must go through an intermediate stage, involving first one and then a second contrariety as the persisting subject; for this reason it is "more difficult" (331ᵇ6) and "takes longer" (331ᵇ11), whereas change between "consecutives" is "easier" and thus "quick" (331ª25, 24).

There are some further details that are not important here; the chief thing to see is the thoroughgoing radicalness of the idea. Restricting ourselves first to "consecutives": as analyzed by the theory of the *CTB/PA*, elemental change obeys the fundamental principle of all change, that all change requires a persistent *hupokeimenon*. But the 'subjecthood' of this sort of *hupokeimenon* is like none of the 'subjects' we have seen hitherto: when H persists in the change from H + D to H + M, it is (1) *not* 'subject' as individual is subject to accidents in alteration (it would be foolishness to suppose the theory to be saying that 'from' *being* dry, the H *'came-to-be'* moist, like the unmusical man who came-to-be musical). *Nor* is it (2) 'subject' as matter is subject to form (though as mentioned above (p. 223), the *CTB/PA* does use the *word* "matter", but this is just its way of saying "subject"; no one could seriously imagine the theory to be saying that dry and moist were two forms *informing* the H). Instead we have (3) a new and different deep configuration – a subject (*hupokeimenon*), indeed, but a subject in a third way, known as "a *'contrariety'* in a new *'linkage'*, or *with a new 'mate'* " – so that, as it may be put on behalf of the theory, "underlying is actually now *three*fold", *hupokeitai trikhōs*. Of course, there is no reason to expect a configuration that occurs only between ultrasimples to look like those more readily recognizable in daily life, like the musical man or the statue of bronze – and it does not; rather, it differs from the ordinary (two) configurations in a way slightly reminiscent of some more recent microphysical theories relative to the physics of ordinary life at the molar-object level. Here are two possible models for the "third type of subject" (in both, what is pictured happens to be Fire):

(1) A chessboard of four squares, and on it a single Rook:

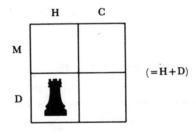

$$(=H+D)$$

The "consecutive" "linkages" are those adjacent *via* a single rook's-move; diagonal moves are forbidden by Nature, but the same result is accessible through successive "consecutive" moves.

(2) A four-pole double switch, where each lever can travel only in its straight groove, one between D and M, the other between H and C:

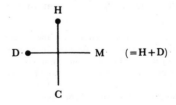

$$(=H+D)$$

I suggest as a good name for this theory, "*Aristotle's theory of contrariety confinement*". It is a much more interesting and sophisticated theory than that fathered on him by the scholars as that of "prime matter".[13]

So much for its clear statement in the case of the specific interelemental changes. We may now look at the attempted more general statement, which comes earlier than the details just summarized, and which has been thought to commit Aristotle to a single undifferentiated *materia prima*:

[1] 329ᵃ24 Our own doctrine is that there is indeed a kind of matter of the perceptible bodies, 'out of which' the so-called 'elements' come-to-be, but that this has no separate existence but is always bound up (or "confined"?) with a contrariety. [2] ᵃ27 A more precise account of the position has been given elsewhere (= *Physics* i 6–9). However, since the 'primary bodies' are also 'out of' the matter in the same way, these must be explained as well. [3] ᵃ29 We must reckon as an 'originative source' and as 'primary' the matter which is *hupokeimenon* for, yet inseparable from, the contraries: for the Hot is not matter for the Cold, nor Cold for Hot, but rather that which is *hupokeimenon* for the both of them.

Therefore, [4] ᵃ33 the 'originative source' is, firstly, that which is potentially perceptible body, secondly, the contrarieties (that are bound up or "confined" with the first), I mean like hotness and coldness, and thirdly, what's already Fire and Water and the like (that has come-to-be from the first two). For these (bodies of the third kind) (329ᵇ) *do* change into one another, and are not (immutable) as Empedocles and others assert, for otherwise there could be *no* alteration, whereas the contrarieties do not change ᵇ3.   (Adapted from Joachim)

It seems to me a fair assessment that this really is not a very clear statement of anything at all: *either* of a single-prime-matter view, *or* of a contrariety-confinement view like the one found in *CTB/PA* ii 3–4; so that a reading that tries to extract either meaning from it must resort to some degree of torture. Once again with due diffidence, then, the *lectio excrucians* I suggest is this:

[1] (329ᵃ24–7) We hold that even for the coming-to-be of the so-called 'elements' there is a *hupokeimenon* (as often, miscalled or at least misleadingly called a "matter" and an "*ex hou*"), but this *hupokeimenon* is of a special kind: it is a "*contrariety*", which means that it can only exist in a "linkage" in which it is "confined" with another contrariety.

[2] (ᵃ27–9) We are adapting the *Physics* account to this case, thus speaking here

---

13 Solmsen (1958) (p. 252) observes the tendency of the passages just analyzed, but takes it for variant phrasing along the lines of pre-Socratic ideas of "powers": "there are sections in our treatise [= *CTB/PA*], notably ii 4 (dealing with the mutual transformations), where matter is practically forgotten and the moist and the dry, the hot and the cold are allowed to fall upon one another in the good old hostile Presocratic way" – rather than, as I am suggesting, a bold, brilliant and highly original piece of physical theorizing.

in the way we do there of "matter" and "*ex hou*" in a highly generalized sense that spans Polarities (1) and (2) (and indeed, now that "underlying is *three*fold", Polarity (1) is stretched even farther).

[3] (ª29–33) Thus what counts as *arkhē* and *prōtē* is the *hupokeimenon* for (e.g.) *both* H and C in the coming-to-be of Water from Air or vice versa (M+H ↔ M+C),–that is, M–or of Earth from Fire or vice versa (D+H↔D+C)–that is, D.

[4] (ª33–ᵇ3) Thus we have got three levels of *arkhē* in our account of this sort of coming-to-be: (1) the persistent contrariety (called "the body that's potentially perceptible", because it is only actually seen, observed, within a "linkage"), (2) the contrarieties from the other pair that are alternatively bound up with it, (3) the so-called 'elements' that thus change into one another – for this does occur, whatever Empedocles may wrongly suppose, though the contrarieties themselves are immutable.

§23. Substance and substance *OF* in *METAPHYSICS* Zeta: some perennial cruxes

Now let us tie in the picture, as developed so far, with some further famous doctrines and difficulties of *Metaphysics* Zeta-Eta.

(i) Being as 'referred to one thing (pros hen legomenon)'. Zeta 1

Zeta 1 opens with the maxim: *to on legetai pollakhōs*, "*being* or *that which is* is said in many ways". We have seen something of the multidimensionality of "that which is" in the Aristotelean scheme: e.g., synchronic versus diachronic, the form–matter dimension of differential depth, the variety of "subjecthoods" and of "*ex hou's*" (or "*ex hōn*"?), the division between substantial and nonsubstantial metamorphoses. I wish now to concentrate more closely on Aristotle's idea that this entire complicated metaphysical congeries is built around the substances as a *center* or a *focus*. This can be set out in terms of notions already treated, as a redistribution of emphasis rather than breaking unbroken ground.

The first sentence of Zeta continues: ". . . as we went through earlier in our remarks 'on the number of ways' [*sc.* in which things are said]", where the title *ta peri tou posakhōs* evidently is a reference to the philosophical lexicon, *Metaphysics* Delta, here presumably to Delta 7 *s.v. to on*. However, as the rest of the paragraph proceeds to expound the primacy and priority of substance in the scheme, it becomes evident that the main idea being developed is one not found in Delta 7, but explained at most length in Gamma 2: that of "being", or "that which is", as *"referred to one thing and one certain nature"*, *pros hen kai mian tina phusin* (1003^a33).[1]

The stock example is the *healthy*:

Everything which is *healthy* is referred to (*pros*) health, one thing (1) in that it preserves [health], another (2) in that it produces [health], another (3) in that it is a symptom of health, another (4) in that it is capable of it. ($1003^a35{-}^b1$)

That is, *health* is a certain state, an excellence of body, which has a definition; let that be: A balance of hot and cold elements (*Topics* vi 2 139^b21), or Uniformity (*Meta.* Zeta 7 1032^b7). That body is healthy$_a$, paronymously, from that health$_n$ (this may be regarded as unchanged from *Categories*' inherence).[2] But many other things besides such bodies are also healthy$_a$, and not homonymously either; for example:

(1) Certain foods are said to be healthy$_a$, not because *they* are in the state of health$_n$, but as being preservative of such a state$_n$ of body.

(2) Certain drugs and potions and other medicines are called healthy$_a$, because they are restorative of health$_n$ in bodies that have lost it temporarily.

(3) A certain complexion, e.g. clear and glowing and ruddy, is healthy$_a$, as being indicative or symptomatic of health$_n$.

(4) Even an unhealthy$_a$ body, Aristotle thinks, can be called healthy$_a$, if it is capable of once again receiving health$_n$.[3]

The being-healthy$_a$ of these four different healthies$_a$ (i.e., things-that-are-healthy$_a$) is said to be *referred to one thing* (*pros hen*), namely the state of health$_n$ of the healthy$_a$ body.

According to Gamma 2 and, by reference, Zeta 1, *being* (or *that which is*) is analogous to healthy$_a$ (or that which is healthy$_a$), in that, just as all the healthies$_a$ are (that) with reference to health$_n$, so all the *beings* are (that)

---

1 This is the topic of G. E. L. Owen's famous classic, Owen (1957). He rendered *pros hen legomenon* as "having *focal meaning*" (I render "is (or "said as") referred to one thing"). His version was an evocative expression of Aristotle's idea; but it has the drawback that what has "meaning" in philosophical English is a word rather than a thing-that-is or *on ti*, whereas Aristotle's concern, as usual, is with beings. Similar misgivings apply to Owen's emphasis on ambiguity (which has to be of expressions), as opposed to Aristotelean homonymy (which is of the things named by the expressions, cf. §1). But Owen's "focus" and "center" are very apt, and I retain material-mode versions of them in this connection wherever possible.   2 Cf. §2, note 8 (p. 18).

3 Cf. Zeta 7 1033^a10?

with reference to substance.[4] At this point we should recall the intuitive picture of the two-stage domain with the substantial individuals at the interface between the stages, as conjured up most lately and in most detail in §21(i), for I take it that that universe is being described at this point in Gamma 2:

> So, too, *being* or *that which is* is said in many ways, but all are referred to (*pros*) a single origin; for some things are said to *be* because they are *substances*, others (1) because they are afflictions of substance, others (2) because they are a route towards substance, or (3) destructions, or (4) lacks [of substance], or (5) qualifications [of substance], or (6) productive or generative of substance, or (7) [productive or generative] of things that are said as referred to (*pros*) substance, or (8) negations of any of these latter, or of substance.   (1003^{b}5–10)

That is, just as with health: substance (or: a substance) is a certain kind of being. (There is more to unpack in that statement; see §23(ii) below.) But many other things besides substances are also beings, and not homonymously either; for example:

(1) Some things *are*, by "afflicting" substances: these are the *pathē*, of which one example is that very health$_n$ that figures as the *pros ho* or "with reference to which" in the analogue to the case of '*being*' which is the things that are healthy$_a$.

(2) Some things *are*, by being a "route toward" substance. *hodos eis ousian* is not too clear; but it might mean the not-yet-substantial *kuēma* of embryonic development, "on its way to" substancehood but still pre- or sub-individual in character as well as pre- or sub-specific (at least, this interpretation makes sense in the terms of §15(i)).

(3) Some things *are*, by being "destructions" of substance – the absence of form of the matter[5] after a substance ceases to be.

(4) Some things *are*, by being "lacks" of substance – the absence of form of the matter before a substance comes to be.

(5) Some things *are*, by being "qualifications" of substance. These certainly overlap the *pathē*, and probably with the *pathē* are not just inherents in the *category* of quality but the inherents of all the nonsubstantial categories, which otherwise would not get on the list. In

---

4 Here it should be remembered (cf. the afterword to §1) that the Greek etymology of *ousia* in relation to *on* makes this claim internally plausible in terms of the Greek language in a way that does not hold in English for the words "substance" and "being", so that the claim has to be taken by the Greekless strictly as a piece of philosophy.

5 This (as also in (4)) is a technical violation of the policy about "informs" versus "is form of" that was promulgated in §20(iii), but "absence of form informing the matter" seems unnecessarily awkward – if awkwardness is noticeable at all in such surroundings.

the terms of §§2–3 as updated in §21 (i), they are all the characteristics X_n attaching to substantial individuals, which latter become with respect to the former "downward paronyms", X_a.

(6) Some things *are*, by being "productive or generative" of substance. In the context of a list of 'beings' other than substance that 'are said as referred to substance' (*pros tēn ousian legomena*) this is a slightly puzzling claim, in view of Aristotle's usual emphatic line that it is *substances* and substances alone that make or generate substances; perhaps what is intended is the *being* of being a parent, or housebuilder.

(7) Some things *are*, by being "productive or generative" of things that *are* within reference to substance – e.g., of all the previous items on this list.

(8) Some things *are*, by being "negations" of (1)–(7) or of substance. As far as I can see, this must mean the substantial and nonsubstantial lacks and destructions, of which the substantial are already here as (3) and (4).

All of these are fairly readily assimilable into the apocalypse as already laid out of the two-stage domain, taken transtemporally as well as synchronically, as a series of ontological items all relating in various ways to the substantial "individuals at the interface" as focus or center.

However, there is one omission that is most surprising: no mention is made in the list of *the matter and the parts of a substance, which ARE, by being "for the sake of" the substance as a whole*. This omitted *pros tēn ousian* or "with reference to substance" is much more important than several on the list; it is the one that is canonized in the terms of *M-en* (§21 (ii)), which in turn abbreviates, in the real cases, the hierarchical, cumulative upward sequence of "informing" that lies at the core of substantial morphology (§§10–11). In the terms of §21 (i), it is all the material elements (and subcomponents and subassemblies) M that underlie substantial individuals, which latter become with respect to the former "upward paronyms", *M-en*. That the upward, as well as the downward, paronymic relationship is indeed *pros hen* is brought out by a portion of the Theta 7 passage previously examined in §20 (ii) which could not be appreciated at that point, in which the two (i.e., the upward and the downward paronymies) are treated as *complementary*: after the elaborate fire-to-boxes discussion of *M-en*, and the initial statement of *hupokeitai dikhōs*, the statement continues:

For example, [i] the subject for the *afflictions* is: *a man*, i.e., a body and psyche; while the affliction is musical, or pale (the thing is called, when the music$_n$ comes-to-be in it, not music$_n$ but musical$_a$, and the man not pallor$_n$ but pale$_a$, and not a walk$_n$ or a movement$_n$ but walking$_a$ or moving$_a$ – just as with *that-en*), – well, then, whenever it's like this, the ultimate [subject] is: *a substance*; but [ii] whenever it's *not* like this, but what is predicated is a particular form and a particular "this" [*eidos ti kai tode ti*], then the ultimate [subject] is matter, substance in the sense of matter. So, *it turns out to be the right result that "that-en" is said with respect to both the matter and the afflictions; for they're both in-definite [amphō gar aorista].*

$$(1049^a29-{}^b2)$$

This cements in an extremely valuable and important piece. The "particular form and particular 'this'" is the specific form, Man, seen as molding a matter into a specifically-formed parcel (a *man*) and into an individual unitary "this" (*a* man), in the merged-together way that we have been repeatedly encountering.[6] The composite thus formed, as an individual substance, lies at the interface between the stages. Both her afflictions and her matter, respectively from "above" and "below", characterize her, but *of themselves they contribute neither essence nor this-hood, for in those stakes they are "both in-definite", in both of the merged-together senses –* in contrast to the formative substance-of, which contributes both essence and this-hood as that "by which being is defined" (thus Zeta 3 1029^{a}21).

It can also be seen here that this additional bit of theory also allows for some *accidents* to inhere in the *matter* as opposed to the substantial individual; the difference between the A/M and the F/M configurations being that the form individuates or individualizes the matter, whereas the accident does not.[7] Accordingly, there are now five possible relationships available as analysantia for predication: F–M, F–I, A–I, the "M-en" configuration M–I, and now A–M.

(ii) *Being and the being of, substance and the substance of. Strategy of* Zeta

Again recall the opening motto of Zeta, *to on legetai pollakhōs*, "being is said in many ways". A different ambiguity (from the *pros hen*) in the Greek locution *to on*, which is paralleled in the English word "being", we have already circled about in this study more than once: between an application (A) to *that which is*, and (B) to the being *of* that which is. In the first case, the expression can be cast in the plural *ta onta*, *the beings* or *the things that are*, and is unmistakable; but the singular remains bivalent.

---

6 E.g. §§4, 6, 8, 12, 13(i), 15(i), 17(iii), 18, 20.
7 Recall §19, note 2 (p. 176) on F. A. Lewis (1985).

This distinction is of course not that between existential and predicative being, but cuts across that: it divides both (A) the existent from (B)
the existence of the existent, and also (A) the healthies, the whites and the
braves from (B) their being white and healthy and brave.

(*A short historical digression.* Historically, the imperativeness of observing
this distinction was first brought out, in effect, by Parmenides, who
showed, in effect, that the consequence of assuming, as he tacitly does,
that all there is to *the being of the things that are* is just *those things that are*, i.e.,
that all there is to (B) is (A) (together with one or two other assumptions
that are largely innocent), was the monstrous and absurd doctrine of
Eleatic Monism. (The most important lemma in the reasoning was to
show that on this footing, *not-being is impossible*.)[8] This was enough to
provoke the post-Parmenideans into analyses of "the being *of*" that, in
effect, avoided the misgotten identification. The point received its first
explicit methodological (or metatheoretic) recognition in the *Sophist*
(242b–245d), although accompanied by the mischievous and entirely
untrue insinuation that all the systems since Parmenides down to the
Stranger's analysis had been oblivious to it, and had confused *being* (B)
with *the beings* (A).)

In Aristotle, exactly the same ambivalence holds for "substance" (i.e.,
ousia): there is (A) the sense in which Socrates is a substance and Coriscus
another one, the sense made obvious in talk in the plural of "the substances", and then there is (B) "the substance *of*" the substances,[9] which
is elaborated in causal terms as that which *makes* a substance in the first
sense a substance, and answers the question *why* it is such. In the *Categories*,
substances (A) are called "primary substances", and substances (B),
without the causal association, are called "secondary substances". In
Metaphysics Zeta, substances (B) are called "primary substances",[10] and
substances (A) are called "composites". This shift in the location of the
"primary" is the immediate (and, I think, methodologically self-conscious) consequence of the change in the stated *criteria* for substance as
between the two works, made explicit in Zeta 3: from subjecthood to
causehood (thus §20(i), §20(iv), *q.v.*).

Metaphysics Zeta–Eta is, of course, an inquiry into the nature of substance in sense (B). Zeta 3, having split substancehood from subjecthood
and contended that substance-of cannot be matter-of, ends by observing

---

8 The story is retailed in Furth (1967).

9 Extensionally, the relationship of course has been with us all along, in the dress of
substantial "said-of" from §1, and in a multitude of other terminological variants for the "F–I"
relation since §20(iii).

10 Cf. Zeta 4 1030ª10, Zeta 6 1031ᵇ14, 1032ª5, Zeta 7 1032ᵇ1–2, Zeta 11 1037ª28, ᵇ3–4, Zeta
17 1041ᵇ27, and §19(iv) above.

that so far as the upcoming investigation is concerned, the substances (A), the composites, are to be "set aside" as "posterior and clear", and declares of matter that it too is "in a sense evident", and identifies "the form" (the *eidos*) and "the shape" as henceforth to be the focus of the inquiry, and as "most problematic" (*aporōtatē*) ($1029^{a}29$–33). Thus the identification henceforth of "substance of" (B) with "*eidos* of" is plainly signalled at this point.[11] Aristotle's problem is then to work out the actual, detailed analysis.

The analysis proceeds through three main further stages (making four in all, Zeta 3 having been the first). And as in Zeta 3, the method employed is to set up a trial identification, of the form "*substance of* equals X", whose implications are then unpacked and examined – or in an idiom of two generations earlier, elenkhed (meaning, subjected to elenchus). The suppositions subjected to this deep scrutiny are:

(II) whether substance of, i.e. *eidos* of, can be identified with "*essence of*" (Zeta 4–6); the eventual answer is Yes, but much refinement and elaboration of this thesis are required;

(III) whether substance of, i.e. *eidos* of, can be identified with any "*universal*", understood in a carefully hedged Aristotelean sense (Zeta 13–16); the eventual answer is No, but much valuable information is gleaned along the way of establishing the negative result;

(IV) the final construal of substance of, i.e. *eidos* of, in terms of final differentia informing generic matter (Zeta 17 and portions of Eta).

We shall discuss some main points about (II) in the following subsection, §23(iii), and about (III) in §23(v). (IV) requires a section of its own, §24.

Also woven into the dense and in places disorderly tangle that is Zeta-Eta are treatments of three associated topics:

(a) substantial and nonsubstantial coming-to-be (Zeta 7–9),

(b) the problem of parts of the composite *versus* parts of the form (Zeta 10–11), and

(c) the generalized case of that problem: the problem of the unity of essence or form (Zeta 12 and Eta 6).

The first of these has been largely covered in §20(iii); the second and third are addressed in §23(iv).[12]

11 There is disagreement about this; my view concurs with that of e.g. Ross, *AM* ii 159–60 (Zeta 1 1028a11 n.); it is rejected by e.g. Hartman (1977), pp. 59 ff.

12 It will be seen from this overall outlook on Zeta that I do not think its interpretation requires the scenario that Ar. was reacting against the problem of the Platonic Third Man Argument; in this I am in agreement with the view of Code (1985b), as against that of Owen (1965a), etc. See also Driscoll (1981), p. 156.

(iii) "Essence-of" as substance-of

In Zeta, subsequent to Zeta 3, the discussion is governed by at least two basic pre-analytic assumptions. First, as just noted above, it is assumed that the candidate category for substance *of* a thing will be an *eidos*, in the general-issue sense of a Kind, such as Man or Dolphin or Crane, and the argument is over the correct analysis, metaphysical sorting, and internal structure of a Kind that is to serve in that office. A second assumption is that each Kind *is* in fact open to analysis, *has* an internal structure, which is intelligible and subject to rational, scientific investigation. (Here it should be remembered from §9, Fact 3, §13(iii) and elsewhere that in any real case this analysis must be extremely complex.) Aristotle's standard name for such an analysis of a Kind is "definition"; and as a matter of technical terminology, standardly the "*essence*" of anything (the *ti ēn einai*) is *whatever is articulated by the "definition" of that thing*; this understanding evidently goes back very early, since it is already a basic ground-rule in the *Topics*.[13]

On this basis, it is natural enough that the first suggestion to be advanced about what the substance *of* something might be, subsequent to Zeta 3, is that "substance of X" in this sense equals "essence of X". Some pros and contras of this idea are mooted in Zeta 4 and 6, and many difficulties quickly arise.

One difficulty stems from the fact, also plain in the *Topics*, and already noted by us away back in §3 above in connection with the *Categories*, that nothing in the notion of "definition" would *confine* it to the category of substance;[14] and if this is so, one would expect the notion of "essence" to be applicable to nonsubstances also, which renders it unpromising as an explication of substance as such. As will be seen, an answer to that potential problem does emerge; but there is a prior problem, which has made much trouble for interpreters and, it may be, for Aristotle himself, and which will block further interpretive progress unless dealt with.

Consider again the two assumptions, that (i) candidates for substance-*of* are Kinds, such as Man or Dolphin, and (ii) each Kind has a definition, which formulates its essence, essence being (by definition, as it were) the content of a definition. Now, it seems also to be settled Aristotelean doctrine that (iii) "there is no definition of individuals".[15]

---

13 E.g. *Top.* i 4 101^{b}21, i 5 101^{b}38, i 8 103^{b}10, vi 1 139^{a}33 (and vi *passim*), vii 3 153^{a}15, vii 5 154^{a}31. *Metaphysics*: Zeta 4 1030^{a}7, Zeta 5 1031^{a}12, Eta 1 1042^{a}17.

14 In the *Categories*, the definitions of such nonsubstances as White(ness), Relatives, Triangle and Circle are mentioned with equanimity (*Cat.* 2^{a}33, 8^{a}28–35, 11^{a}5–14, recall §5 *init.*), and *Topics* vi is replete with such cases.

15 Thus e.g. *Meta.* Zeta 15 1039^{b}27–1040^{a}7, Zeta 11 1037^{a}27, Zeta 10 1036^{a}2–8.

From these it immediately follows that there are no essences *of* individuals, i.e., individuals do not *have* essences.[16] Can this be right? Yes, on the right understanding of "of" and "have" – there is no definition of Socrates, and hence no essence of Socrates that he "has" all to himself; on the other hand he certainly *is* thought to "have" those essential properties that he cannot cease to "have" without perishing, and so on another construal of "have" he may be said to "have" an essence after all. The problem is not merely terminological, as becomes highly apparent in *Metaphysics* Zeta 6. We therefore must now look at that, and then return to Zeta 4.

There are three things (more accurately, two things with three titles) to deal with here: (1) Man, which is what gets the definition, (2) the essence of Man, which is what the definition formulates, and (3) Socrates the individual man, who is not definable but who must *satisfy* the definition that (1) gets, whatever that is (on pain of perishing, indeed).

In Zeta 4 and 6, and frequently elsewhere, Aristotle uses the expression "essence of X" (i.e., of course, the Greek for this) *both for a relation between (2) and (1), and for a relation between (2) and (3)*. It is well not to assume that these are the same relation; indeed it is clear that they are not. For (1) and (2) stand in the relation of identity, in particular in the relation of a *specific kind* to *itself as definitionally analyzed*.[17] Whereas, the relation of (2) to (3) certainly is not identity; its *Categories* antecedent is the "predicability of the (specific) definition" of the substantial individual, and a variety of other names for it in the wider *Metaphysics* setting were suggested in §20(iii), as we have just now been reminded (footnote 9).

If the expressions "essence of" and "having an essence" are to be employed at all (and they are difficult to avoid in this theory), without risk of massive confusion,[18] they must be disambiguated so that the

---

16 "A well-known Aristotelian dilemma", – Hartman (1977), p. 81. Hartman thinks to resolve it by recourse to "*qua*", "the best – but clearly imperfect – solution" (p. 82). That certainly is sometimes Ar.'s way, but the evidence of Zeta 6 and 11 (which do not employ "*qua*") suggests to me that the alternative I sketch below is open to Ar. also. On it, the truth that "to know a thing is to know its essence" (Zeta 6 1031b20) is *not* for Ar. evidence for the falsehood that Socrates is the same as his essence (Hartman, *ibid.*).

17 As already noted at §3, footnote 4, this is so obviously a truth of reason for us, teethed as we are on the implications of identity, that it is most instructive for us to follow Aristotle's labors – heroic struggles, even – to work it out as Major Metaphysics. The watershed as far as identity is concerned is of course "Über Sinn und Bedeutung".

18 The main interpretive difficulty that commonly arises at this point seems to consist in first recognizing (correctly) that according to Aristotle
(1) Man is identical with essence of Man,
but then (not seeing the ambiguity of "of" in "essence of" – see text) inferring that
(2) Socrates is identical with essence of Socrates,
which does not follow from (1) and according to Aristotle (according to me) is not true (see text). A second difficulty ensues when interpreters, seeing (correctly) that

difference can be expressed between the sense of "having" and "of" in which *the kind Man* "has"$_{(1-2)}$ an essence, which is the essence "of"$_{(2-1)}$ Man (or, as a terminological variant, which is E(Man)), and the other sense in which *Socrates* "has"$_{(3-2)}$ an essence, which is the essence "of"$_{(2-3)}$ Socrates. (In §20(iii), some other names for "has"$_{(3-2)}$ were also proposed, such as "exemplifies", "is a specimen of", etc.)

Despite the perils of the ambiguous terminology of "has" and "of", the doctrine of Zeta 6 on the matter is clear and plausible (though the *arguments* of Zeta 6 are something else): that the relation "essence of"$_{(2-1)}$ between essence and kind *is* the relation of identity,[19] and that the relation "essence of"$_{(2-3)}$ between essence and composite individual *is not*. The second conjunct is not made explicit in Zeta 6, but it is the only plausible line to infer on the question, or sophistical elenchus, "whether Socrates and essence of Socrates are the same" (1032^{a}8). To which the answer plainly must be: No, Of Course Not.[20] For the essence "of"$_{(2-3)}$ Socrates is of course, precisely the essence "of"$_{(2-1)}$ Man. That essence certainly is determinative of Socrates in highly important ways, but it and Socrates cannot possibly be the same thing. The point is made fully explicit and general at the end of Zeta 11: "primary substances", i.e. substantial kinds, are identical with their essences,[21] "composites" are not (1037^{a}33–^{b}5), also Eta 3 1043^{b}2–4.

(In fact, the very problem of Zeta 6, "What things are identical with *their* essences?", in part feeds on the ambiguity of "their", which comes from the ambiguity of "have" in the essences they *have*".)

(3) essence of Man *is* identical with essence of Socrates
(but on different readings of "of" – see text), infer from (1), (2), (3) that
(4) Socrates is identical with essence of Man and therefore with Man.
Since the same reasoning also proves that
(5) Callias is identical with essence of Man and therefore with Man,
the interpretation is on the verge of reaching the result that
(6) Callias is identical with Socrates.
But (6) is absurd, and the interpretation is in bad trouble. Consequently, it is at this point that interpreters have recourse to those mushy senses of "is identical with", such that Socrates and Callias can both "be identical with" essence of Man without being identical with each other, which have so plagued the tradition, or alternatively (but it is of no help here) to an individual essence of Socrates such that (3) is false. If only Aristotle had *written out* the "obvious solution" to the sophistical elenchus at Zeta 6 1032a6–10! It would only have taken a sentence.

19 Cf. Driscoll (1981), *ibid.* (p. 156), Code (1985b), pp. 110–13, Furth (1985), notes on Zeta 6.

20 It may be that the failure of some to see this is abetted by a mistaken rendering of Zeta 6 1032a6–10. Aristotle does *not* there say that the questions (1) whether the things that are primary and said in respect of themselves (*prōta kai kath' hauta legomena*) are the same as their essences, and (2) whether Socrates is the same as essence of Socrates, "clearly have the same answer" (Hartman (1977), p. 63). He says that they are "clearly solved by the same solution", which is entirely compatible with their having opposite answers (as it is evident to me he thinks they do).

21 Here it is of course fatal not to realize that "primary" has shifted its application between *Categories* and *Meta.* Zeta-Eta; §§19(iv), 23(ii).

With this distinction clear, let us see what can be made of Zeta 4.

The opening move ($1029^{b}13–16$) is the claim that the essence of X is that which X is "in respect of itself", *kath' hauto*. This is the technical bit of Aristotelese that the medievals rendered "*per se*", and it has been as far as possible avoided in the present work up to now; but there is no getting through Zeta 4 without it. The "in respect of itself" in Aristotle is a disjunctive concept, which in its full extension takes in so much that hardly any intension is left to it; so in Zeta 4, as frequently, Aristotle must try to narrow down to the relevant sense that will give the expression some content.

In the canonical explanation of *Analytics* iii 4,[22] an item X can belong to or be predicated of a subject S in respect of $\#_n$ itself (i.e., in respect of $\#_n$ S), if either

($\#1$) X is in the 'what is it' (*ti esti*) of S
(examples: X = twofooted, animal; S = man),

or ($\#2$) S is in the 'what is it' of X
(examples: X = male/female, man; S = animal),

or ($\#3$) X belongs to S *because of* (*dia* + accusative or neuter infinitive) S
(examples: X = receptive of grammar; S = man,
or X = died; S = getting throat cut (*kath' $\#_3$ hautēn = kata $\#_3$ spaghēn = dia to sphattesthai*).

Thus, Twofooted belongs to Man in respect of $\#_1$ itself, Man belongs to Animal in respect of $\#_2$ itself, and Receptive of Grammar belongs to Man in respect of $\#_3$ itself. (That which belongs to S, but does not belong to S in respect of itself in sense $\#1$ or $\#2$, belongs to S *kata sumbebēkos*, accidentally or coincidentally. Hence things that belong to S in respect of $\#_3$ itself are the *kath' hauto sumbebēkota* or "*per se* accidents" of S.)

It can be seen from this that an explanation of the form

$x \ R \ y$ iff x belongs to y in respect of itself,

with un-indexed "in respect of" in the explanans, conveys exceedingly little information about the relation R, and for this reason several paragraphs of Zeta 4 ($1029^{b}16–1030^{a}2$) must be devoted to groping after the relevant sense for this application; in the end it seems that as regards "essence of", sense $\#1$ is intended.[23]

---

22 Also known as *Posterior Analytics* i 4. My phrasing in what follows is taken from Furth (1986), and is indebted to Code (1986), on which the former is a symposium commentary.
23 Particularly, $1029^{b}16–19$; for details, Furth (1985) $1029^{b}15$ n., pp. 105–6.

A second difficulty in the exposition is the effacing of the essence-of$_{(2-1)}$ *versus* essence-of$_{(2-3)}$ distinction (thus "essence of *you*", "in respect of *yourself*", 1029^{b}14–16). Thirdly, the aporematic design of the chapter sometimes makes it difficult to separate dialectics from doctrine. Fourthly, the use-mention problems, usual when *definition* comes up in Aristotle, are particularly horrific. With due interpretive caution, however, here is some doctrine that the chapter Zeta 4 seems to teach.

(1) Definition, as we would expect, takes the form of species, S, being analyzed by way of, and only by way of, an essence that has the structure of genus and differentiae, GD (1030^{a}11). (2) The definition is constructed as an equation in which the name of S appears as what is nowadays called definiendum, and an expression naming the essence (i.e., genus as differentiated) appears as definiens: thus an equation of the form, "S = GD" (or "S = GD$_n$D$_{n-1}$ . . . D$_1$".[24] If the definition is correct, then (3) what is named by the expressions on the two sides of " = " must be *identical*, and (4) the definiens (called "the logos of the essence", 1029^{b}20) must *explicate* ("formulate") the essential nature that is only *named* by the definiendum – and in particular, in consequence, the definiens may not contain an occurrence of the definiendum itself (these two requirements, in reverse order, are the gist of the following, in which use-mention considerations are as usual to be stoutheartedly ignored):

The formula, therefore, in which the thing isn't actually present, but which *formulates* it, this is the formula of the essence for each thing. (1029^{b}19–20)[25]

(5) A nearly equivalent rendering of the "S = GD" structure is "S = *hoper* G" or "S = just what is some G" (1030^{a}3–7) (this technical idiom was first encountered toward the end of §5 above). But there seems to be some uncertainty about what the "GD" structure is, because the definitions in question are said to be of entities that are "primary" (that is, of "primary substance" in the new, *Meta.* Zeta sense, where that is "substance *of*" (§19(iv), 23(ii)), and:

of this sort [i.e., "primary"] are such things as are said *not* by way of saying something of something *else* [*allo kat' allou*] (1030^{a}10–11). The essence is *hoper* some [genus]; but when something is said of some *other* thing, that is not *hoper* some this (1030^{a}3–4). The essence cannot belong to anything but the species [pl.] of a genus and to them alone (for these seem *not* to be said by way of a 'participation'

24 This way of thinking of differentiation as cumulative, which goes back to §13 and §17, is developed much further in §24 below.

25 This laborious enunciation of (3) and (4) is another good example of what looks to us like elementary identity theory turning up as ancient Major Metaphysics. Cf. §3, n. 4, §23, n. 17.

26 Furth (1985), pp. 111–2 (1031^{a}19–24 n., 24–8 n., 28 n.)

or 'affliction', nor 'as accident'); that is, there will be a formula of each of these other things also, [formulating] what each signifies – providing there is a name, namely [a formula saying] that *this* belongs to *that*, or instead of a simple formula a more exact one; but these *won't* be definition, nor essence either.   (1030^a11–17)

The implication here is that the relation of "species [pl.] of a genus" ($^a12$) is not any form of "this belongs to that" ($^a15$–16), nor that of any "participation, or affliction, or accident" ($^a13$–14), and that conversely, where there *is* a relation "this of that", it cannot be *hoper* and cannot be essence ($^a3$–4, $^a16$–17). And the question arises, if no nameable relation "this of that" holds within the specific form, as its interior, what its internal structure is supposed to be. This touches *the* major problematic of Zeta, and we shall return to it (§23(iv)).

The other main preoccupation of Zeta 4 is that mentioned earlier in this section: since the scope of "essence" is as wide as that of "definition", and since it seems that all sorts of nonsubstances are definable, what can be the case for *explicating* "substance of" *as* "essence of"? Zeta 4 addresses this by reconsidering the question what sorts of things are definable and (equivalently) have essences, and makes a significant change of doctrine relative to the *Categories* theory, such as it is, of definition.

The discussion is carried out without benefit of the distinction between "having$_{(1-2)}$" and "having$_{(3-2)}$" and as a consequence is confusing in places: for example, when the question about essence is raised in connection with *pale man*, it is not clear whether it is being asked if *the supposed Kind, Pale Man*, "has$_{(1-2)}$" an essence, or it is rather being asked if *a certain pale man, i.e. Callias*, "has$_{(3-2)}$" it (as we shall see (pp. 240–1), this particular confusion seems to afflict Aristotle himself in Zeta 6). That problem temporarily set to one side, to proceed:

To get around the difficulty that nonsubstances seem to have essences too, it is argued that *essence is pros hen*, "referred to one thing" (§23(i)), in just the way that *being* is: there is a primary sense in which substances have ($=$ have$_{1-2}$) essences and a derivative sense in which nonsubstances do, which emanates from and parallels the manyness of being (1030^a17–$^b3$). The primacy of substance as the *pros ho*, "referred to which", case of essence for all the lesser or satellite "essences" is seen in terms of the "*unity*" of substance (1030^b6–12) – here again we touch upon the central problematic of Zeta; see §23(iv). In these terms, (I) a substantial kind like Man, it is argued, has the best and foremost sort of essence, since its oneness is so paradigmatic that no interrelatedness of parts was discernible within it (as above); the "having" and "of" are 1–2 and 2–1 as discussed before. This is the same essence that an individual man "has"$_{(3-2)}$.

In a derivative way, (II) a nonsubstantial individual (like Chalk White$_n$) or kind (like Color$_n$) "has"$_{(1-2)}$ an essence; in this kind of case there is nothing corresponding to "having"$_{(3-2)}$, for the reasons discussed in §§2 and 5. (That is, because the ultimate nonsubstantial individuals are *themselves* the definables, which can "pluralize" further only by way of inhering (§5), and their definitions are not predicable of the individual substances (§2)). (Why should a substantial kind have more unity than a nonsubstantial kind? See §23(iv).)

Finally, (III) there is the cross-categorial accidental unity of the supposed kind, Pale Man (or Cloak); this "has"$_{(1-2)}$ an essence (or perhaps Pale Man *is* the essence "of"$_{(2-1)}$ Cloak), and *an individual cloak* "has"$_{(3-2)}$ that essence too, the weakest of the unities that are conceivably assignable an essence in any sense.

(Here, (I)–(III) epitomize 1030^{b}3–12.)

The overall result of Zeta 4 and 6, then, is this: it is true, and not false, that substance-of is essence-of (i.e., essence-of$_{2-3}$), but to say this is not yet to say anything very informative. Because the internal *structure* of essence is not yet made out, except negatively, in that supposedly it can't be of the form 'something of something else' (1030^{a}11), nor 'participation, or affliction, or accident' (^{a}13–14); it is 'species [pl.] of a genus' (^{a}11–13), where these form a 'unity' in some way not yet specified.

The main upshot of Zeta 6 has already been stated (p. 236): that which "has"$_{(1-2)}$ an essence is identical with that essence; that which "has"$_{(3-2)}$ an essence is not (the latter inferred from 1032$_a$8 but explicit in Zeta 11 *fin.*), although the essence "of"$_{(2-3)}$ the latter thing is determinative or constitutive of it, and for it to lose that essence does mean its demise and extinction. It is also argued that cross-categorial attachments are not identical with "their" essences, and this is the point at which the failure in Zeta always to sort out whether the 1–2 or 3–2 "their" is involved (p. 239) turns out to make a difference. For what would be parallel to the approach that is taken to (I) would be to fix upon the (supposed) kind or species, Cloak, and ask after the identity or nonidentity of *it* with its$_{(1-2)}$ (supposed) essence, perhaps Pale Man. Instead, the arguments purport to show the nonidentity of the (supposed) essence of$_{(2-1)}$ Cloak with *a pale man* (1031^{a}19–28).[26] But *this* nonidentity is hardly surprising or even in need of argument; after all, it is part of the teaching of Zeta 6 that even *the individual man* is not identical with the (approved) essence of$_{(2-1)}$ Man – at least, I am taking it so (as reaffirmed above). On the other hand, if the parallel to (I) is followed, and we suppose that the not-in-respect-of-itself

---

26 Furth (1985), pp. 111–2 (1031^{a}19–24 n., 24–8 n., 28 n.)

"being", Cloak or Pale Man, *does* have$_{(1-2)}$ an essence, then it is hard to see how it and its$_{(1-2)}$ essence could fail to be identical – they are *ex hypothesi* related as content of definiens and definiendum. Rather, the issue is whether for such "kinds" as Pale Man there is justification to speak of essence or definition at all, and the case certainly can be made for answering "No" to *that* question (indeed, if the question is whether such an essence was a substantial essence, it could be answered affirmatively only by the "leukomaniac" of §21(i)). The two questions seem to have got thoroughly confused with one another in Zeta 6, and the guess may be hazarded that the omission to distinguish the 2–1 and the 2–3 "essence of" is one source, and a main one at that, of the confusion. Looked at in one way, it *is* the confusion.

(iv) The structure of form and the problem of unity

In examining the rest of Zeta and Eta it will be pertinent to bear in mind the very fundamental point about the Aristotelean universe that has been emphasized periodically in the foregoing: the point that the occurrence in the natural world of "thisses", integral, highly organized structures or systems (the *sustēmata*, or *sustaseis*) with a high order of "unity", is itself a major explanandum, especially in the setting of his Empedoclean concept of basic matter. It is my contention that there is a strong connection for Aristotle between something's being *unified* and something's being *formed*, and that form is responsible, not only for a substantial individual's having$_{(3-2)}$ its permanent essential nature, but also for its *being* a unitary *tode ti* or "this", at all, as opposed to an accretion or aggregation or "heap". Let us review briefly the evidence in favor of this perhaps still strange-seeming attribution that has been discussed so far. It is basically of two kinds.

First are the many passages, long familiar and puzzling to all students of the topic, alluding to *form itself* as *tode ti*, even though Aristotle is in other places well aware that this cannot possibly be right as it stands (thus *Metaphysics* Zeta 8 1033^{b}19–26). As has been pointed out (§8), this is a serious crux. I think its resolution is that form is *cause* of the *tode ti*. As two indicators along this line: at *Metaphysics* Zeta 17 1041^{b}11 ff., as we noted in §8, form is responsible for the syllable's being not only whatever syllable it is, but being "one" as opposed to a heap. And at *de Anima* ii 1 412$_a$6–8, as we noted in §16, it is form "in respect of which" a substance is spoken of as *tode ti*. (Recall also Theta 7 1049^{a}35, "a particular form *and* a particular this", at p. 231 above and §19(i), pp. 176–7.)

The second evidential line for a strong form/unity connection comes from the account of embryonic (or "kuematic") development in the *Generation of Animals*, which has been discussed and moralized upon at length in §15.

There is a third connection between form and unity, this one highly problematic and very hard to be clear about, because there are signs that Aristotle himself has problems and is less than clear. This is the question of the unity or oneness of form itself. Many things come together here.

The oneness that is problematical is not that there is only a single form of Man, one of Dolphin, one of Crane, and so on. On this, I have argued (§§16(i), 20(iii)), it seems that Aristotle is quite definite: there is only one form of Man, which cannot come-to-be or cease-to-be, because by definition coming-to-be is *out of something*, *ek tinos*, as matter (thus Zeta 8, and cf. §20(iii)); what there are many of, and what come-to-be and cease-to-be, are the hylomorphic composites, and what is responsible for the possibility of their coming-to-be and ceasing-to-be, and their plurality, is their matter (Zeta 7, 8, 15, Eta 1, 4, 5, Theta 8, and cf. §8, §19(ii)).

No: the problem that Aristotle has is that *the form is complex*, for it consists of *many differentiae* (on this see §24 below), and a recurrent *aporia*, both genuine and serious, in Zeta and Eta is: *how is it that the many differentiae combine into a SINGLE, UNIFIED form, a form that is ONE?* Thus,

1. Zeta 4 1030^a3-4, $10-17$, $^b7-10$ (part of this was already encountered a few pages back, in 23(ii), pp. 238–9): definition or formula of an essence is of *one* thing, *not* something predicated of something *else*, *not* a 'participation', or "affliction", or 'accident', *nor* 'one by continuity', like the Iliad or things unified by being 'tied together', but *one* in some other, much stronger way than that.

2. Zeta 11 1037^a18: it is clear *that* the definition is one single formula, but *on account of what* (*dia ti*) and *by what* (*tini*) is the form that is defined *one* – since it has parts?

3. Zeta 12 1037^b10: I mean this *aporia*: that whose formula we call a definition (that's essence, remember), why in the world is this *one*? Take e.g. Man, i.e. Twofooted Animal – let this be its formula. Why, then, is this one and not many, Animal *and* Twofooted? 1037^b24: "the things in the definition have got to be one".

4. Zeta 13: "arguments" are given that lead to the *aporia* (1039^a14) that substance is incomposite in the sense of simple (or, perhaps, simple in the sense of incomposite), "so that there cannot even be a formula of *any* substance(!?)" (cf. §23(v)).

5. Eta 3 1043^{b}32: substance is like number: both are divisible, and into indivisibles ("for the formulae aren't infinite"), yet, like number, definition has to have something *by which* (*tini*) it is one, and not like a heap; it must be stated what *makes* it one out of many. Also, substance is one, not (as some allege) by being some sort of unit or point, but each is a "completedness" (*entelekheia*) and a kind of nature.

Evidently there is a problem here that impresses Aristotle as real and pressing and difficult, but at the distance we stand from his conceptual *milieu*, it requires of us a certain effort of imagination so much as to be able to see what it is. It need not be a problem that seizes *us* as requiring resolution in contemporary terms for us to understand it in his.[27] I believe it is this. We have seen reason to believe that he thinks of form as something that "unifies" a matter into a "unitary" *tode ti*, an individual. But if form is to do this, it must itself possess a kind of "unity" of its own; as the originative principle, *arkhē*, of internal coherence and connectedness, it must itself be "one". To put it another way, the type of form that Aristotle thinks must be supposed operative in nature if the phenomena that concern him are to be explained and understood, cannot be just a scatter of "properties" or "characters" or "afflictions", but a powerful *integrative agency* that is *cause* of the unity, both synchronic and transtemporal, of the natural, i.e. biological, individuals. The many differentiae must come together to make *one* form that forms the many *ones*. "The substance *of* that which is one, must be one" (Zeta 16 1040^{b}17).

Now, Aristotle has two main models for how entities or 'beings' can attach together to make a unity. One is that of an 'affliction' or a *pathos* 'coinciding' with a subject, as pallor attaches to (a) man; such a unity as (a) pale man is a 'coincidental' unity, traditionally, *per accidens*. As we saw in §23(iii), there are two ways of looking at this which Aristotle does not always distinguish: the attachment of pallor to Coriscus that produces the coincidental unity, *pale Coriscus*, and the combination of pallor and Man that produces the coincidental pseudo-Kind, *Pale Man*. This is paradigmatically too weak a unity for the present application (it is the usual example of a *contrast* to the present application, thus Zeta 12 1037^{b}13–18), as is indicated by the disparaging comparisons to things "tied together" or "one by continuity".

The other model is that of a form or actuality informing or actualizing a matter or potentiality. We have seen that this is evidently regarded as a

---

27 Thus I think it goes too far to hold that "Aristotle has set himself an impossible and probably unnecessary task" (Hartman (1977), p. 38).

powerful unifying agency with respect to the hylomorphic composites; but for this to be applied in explaining how the *form* is "one", it seems that in some way the actuality-potentiality or form/matter relationship will have to be re-drawn *within the form or actuality itself*.

This is exactly what he tries to do. The attempted conceptualization utilizes two different devices, whose co-extensiveness is not fully apparent; one is that of "genus as matter", the other employs a distinction between "perceptible" and "intelligible" matter (*hulē aisthētē* and *noētē*). Let us look at the second device first.

Only a little reflection on the general schematism of form-matter analysis is required for the usefulness of such a distinction quickly to become evident. Aristotle's own example of this in Zeta 10 is a spoken or written *syllable* as contrasted with a brazen *circle*: here as so often with his artefactual illustrations, it is easier to grasp the distinction independently of his example than by means of it; so let us come back to that. For a better analogue, consider social clubs or city-states with constitutions, written or unwritten. The *perceptible matter* of such a quasi- (probably pseudo-) substance is the members or the citizens; and it is to be especially noted that this matter can change over time, as club members are inducted and cancel their membership, or as city inhabitants attain citizen status and are banished or die, without affecting the continued existence of numerically the same club or city – an excellent analogy with the metabolic exchange of material nutrients and "useless residues" that is typical for the real, living substances. However, certain components of such an entity are specified for its organization by its constitution: there shall be a legislative body (or rules committee) chosen in such-and-such a way – an Assembly, a Council, there shall be magistrates, tax officials. archons, ten annually elected generals – *offices*,[28] which at any given time are occupied by some or other concrete persons, but which, as offices spelled out as part of the ongoing nature of the entity by its charter, are "parts" that are parts of the form; these are what is meant by the entity's "intelligible parts" or intelligible matter. There is no doubt in my mind that this is how Aristotle thinks of biological form:[29] the composite animal is the form that has "taken up" the matter (*suneilēmmenon*); his phrase, "by 'Substance without Matter', I mean the Essence" (Zeta 7 1032^b14), means the form with the matter drained away, the single intelligible form of the species

---

28 "Eponymous archon, king, polemarch, thesmothetae, secretary of the thesmothetae" – R. A. Sealey, *History of Greek City-States* (Berkeley, 1976), p. 204.

29 A powerful and extended statement of the connection is *Politics* iv 4 1290^b21 ff. A good discussion is in Pellegrin (1982), 148–63.

studied by the zoologist, down to the least of its intelligible parts. Of course, in *Nature* the form is found only as form of actual specimens (leaving aside fancy theory about how the semen carries form in generation); but the scientist who studies the specimens is interested strictly in the "substance without the matter" (cf. §9, Fact 4). As regards the "unity", the idea apparently is that as the perceptible matter is differentiated into a perceptible unity *by* the form, so the intelligible matter is organized into an intelligible unity *in* the form. At least, that seems to be how the model works in this case. Whether Aristotle has succeeded in answering his question, "*by what* is the form one – since it has parts?" (Zeta 11), seems less than certain.

His own example in Zeta 10, the composite spoken or written syllable and composite circle of bronze, seems to be thought of in the following way. The *circle* divides into segments, and the segments in turn are of bronze, now, "the segments are parts in the sense of matter [i.e., perceptible matter] on which [the form] supervenes – although they're 'nearer' to the form than the bronze is, when roundness is engendered in bronze" (1035^a12-14). The *syllable*, on the other hand, divides into phonetic elements, in just the same way (1034^b26-8), and the elements in turn are materialized as letters in wax, or movements in air (1035^a14-17); but in this case the phonetic elements into which the syllable divides, unlike the segments of the circle, are regarded as parts of the *form* of the syllable (1034^b26-7, 1035^a10), i.e. as intelligible rather than perceptible matter. Schematically, the contrast is supposed to be:

As regards the syllable, the intuition here is marginally apparent; it makes some sort of sense to say that for the syllable-type –LAB–, it is part of the essence or definition that it consist of those phonetic elements –LLL–, –AAA–, –BBB–, in the same sort of way that a certain city-type has to have an Assembly, or a certain animal-type has to have such-and-such a digestive apparatus. As regards the circle, it is less clear why the segment-types of the circle-type have to be sorted with the bronze, and not as something the circle-type has to have (and not just the brazen circle). However, it is bootless to pick further at the example; the principle is tolerably clear and obviously of topmost importance in any case of appreciable differential depth. We shall return to it once more in §25.

The other approach to the problem about Unity of Form utilizes the notion of Genus as Matter. Once again, Aristotle's syllable does not help us much (also, in this case, Zeta 12 1038^{a}5–9, it is analyzed rather differently from the other connection). So as before, in order to visualize things better let us have recourse to a different artefactual analogue: automobiles, better yet, American automobiles as they were built in Detroit in the 1950s when I and my contemporaries were auto-manic teenagers. Here the *species* were: for a start, Buick, Cadillac, Chevrolet, Oldsmobile, Pontiac, all species of the *genus* General Motors Product; then there were Chrysler, Dodge, Plymouth, falling within the genus Chrysler Corporation Product; finally the genus Ford Motor Company Product was differentiated into Ford, Lincoln, Mercury; and all of us young American males were adepts at perceiving the three underlying generic affinities, the three basic generic groundplans, that were diversely differentiated into specific varieties in each of these genera. (The *megiston genos*, biggest genus, as frequently happens, was *anōnumon*, without a name, for the three genera were just the Big Three. I am leaving aside irrelevant complications like the moneidic genus Studebaker, etc.) We did not know it, but in viewing the automotive kingdom in this way we were profoundly Aristotelean; for Aristotle's concept of genus in its biological application is very like this, as has been suggested already in §13(ii) and (iv). The automotive analogue is quite well suited to evoke what was there called (paraphrasing) "the vertical as well as horizontal dimension of differentia, having less to do with classification than with construction, in which it bears something close to its modern biological sense, namely, adaptive-in-effect articulation and diversification of structure: it connotes a manner in which relatively undetermined, only generically characterized structures are variously specialized and specified. Genus is an underlying generic potentiality, and the differentiae are the particular manners in which that potentiality is found to be restricted or reduced (end of paraphrase)."

In such a setting, the application to the problem about Unity of Form is fairly straightforward. As with the "intelligible matter" device, you start with the composite, and then prescind to the single specific "substance without the (perceptible) matter" (doing the "matter-drain" again). What you have at that point is the specific form, consisting of a generic component differentiated by a complex variety of differentiae. Its "unity" is, as Aristotle explains it in Eta 6, that of actualization (i.e., the differentiae) to potential actualized (i.e., the genus), that is, of actuality to that of which it is the actuality. It seems to be important that this potentiality/actuality relation be visualized as *within the specific form itself*; for only so conceived does it resolve the difficulty to which Aristotle repeatedly calls attention in the passages cited (pp. 242–3), about what the intra-eidetic structure can be that relates the "things that are primary" (pp. 238–9).

(v) Generality does not a substance-of make. Zeta 13

This is the place to see what sense can be made on the interpretive lines developed here of arguably the most difficult two pages in Aristotle: Zeta 13, which discusses "whether any of the 'things said universally' can be substance".

There are two keys to the chapter. To begin, we must understand that Zeta 13, like earlier chapters of Zeta starting with Zeta 4, is concerned with substance *in the sense of substantial specific kind*: not with Socrates and Bucephalus, but with Man and Horse, and the question concerns the 'composition' (*synthesis*, cf. 1039^a12, 17) of substances in that sense, or what it is that substances in that sense are 'out of' (*ex hou*, 1038^b24, 1039^a4, 8, 15, 16): the question debated is, can substantial kinds be regarded as 'composed out of' 'things said universally'? Thus the problem is closely related to the Unity of Form question.

The confusing impression that the question concerns substantial individuals rather than kinds is encouraged by the author's usage in Zeta 13 of the expression "substance of", which ordinarily takes as object an individual ("substance of Socrates"; cf. §23(ii)), i.e., what has earlier been called a "2–3" relation. Instead, here, it is used in a "2–1" sense,[30] just like "essence of$_{(2-1)}$" – and indeed, the two are actually equated at $1038^b14–15$:

> "things whose substance is one and whose essence is one are themselves one"

(where I take the "and" to be epexegetic, and to mean "i.e.". Of course, it is elementary and beyond dispute that things whose$_{(3-2)}$ substance is one and whose$_{(3-2)}$ essence is one do *not* have to be one, as witness Socrates and Callias.)[31]

The second key is that by "that which is universal" is meant, "that

---

30 Hartman (1977), p. 63, sees that this is the usage, but makes the wrong identification (that is, makes it a 2–3 relation).

31 This is the construal of "substance of" at 1038^b10, 12–14 (4x), 32. At 1038^b30, "substance of *two*" (*duoin ousia*) is of$_{(2-1)}$ Man *and* of$_{(2-3)}$ Socrates.

whose nature is to belong to more than one substance *in the sense of substantial specific kind*". In practice, this means (1) generic substantial kinds, and (2) nonsubstantial particulars and universals.[32]

On these understandings, the chapter makes the following sense. (It is well to bear in mind here that since the reasoning leads explicitly to a paradox, there must be something somewhere in the reasoning that Aristotle cannot consistently continue to maintain, and Aristotle must know this, though he need not yet necessarily know what it is.)

(1038[b]8–16) Substance in the sense of essence (2–1) is supposed to be *idion* to that of which it is the substance (in fact, as we have seen in discussing Zeta 6 and 11, it is supposed to be identical with it); whereas it is the nature of a "universal" in the mooted sense to belong to more than one substance. Suppose then that such a universal does belong to more than one, and is the substance of them; then it is *idion* to them (in fact, identical with them); it follows that they are all identical with each other. Ergo, a universal that belongs to more than one substance in this sense can't be the substance *of* them in this sense.

(1038[b]16–23) Question: "But what about the genus? It can't be substance in the way that the essence (2–1) is, but it is *part* of the essence, so isn't it part of the substance in this sense? Then a universal, i.e. the genus, will be the substance of *something*." Answer: Whatever it is substance of, it has to be *idion* to (that is, identical with), as before, so a genus still can't be substance of any of the substantial specific kinds of which it is the genus, or the same result will again follow as in [b]8–16.

(1038[b]23–30) It is of course out of the question that nonsubstantial universals be the substance of anything, in any sense.

(1038[b]30–1039[a]3) It follows that if e.g. Man is such a substance, and XYZ is the definition of Man, then neither X nor Y nor Z is substance of anything.

(Remember that according to Aristotelean biology as well as metaphysics, it is the fully specific form that has the highest degree of actuality, and that less specific and more generic form is associated with lesser definition and with potentiality.)

(1039[a]3–14) On the other hand, the substantial kind as an actuality cannot be composed out of component substantial kinds as actualities, for the substantial kind is a paradigm of *unity*, and two unities of that order cannot possibly fit together into a new unity of that order. Even Democri-

---

32 Recall again here the intuition called up at the end of §5, according to which even in *Categories* terms the species Man is *itself not a universal*, despite the fact that it seems to meet the commonplace characterization of 'that which belongs to a multitude of things'.

tus got this right, when he said that two of *his* 'atoms' could never become one.

(1039^a14–23) But if this is right, we have a problem ("the conclusion contains an *aporia*"), we have proved too much, for if the substantial kind cannot be composed of universals, either generic or nonsubstantial, and if it cannot be composed of component substantial kinds, [*and if these are the only alternatives,*] then it would seem that it cannot be composite at all, which would contradict the most axiomatic foundation of the theory, that the substantial kinds *are* open to analysis (p. 234 above), that "definition and essence" belong to the substantial kinds pre-eminently and paradigmatically, if not exclusively.

It seems that the stated conclusions of the chapter are accepted, for it is reiterated at the end of Zeta 16, "that none of the things said universally is substance, and that no substance is 'out of' substances, is clear". The moral has to be that these are not the only alternatives, since the compositeness of substantial form remains axiomatic. The only remaining option is the potentiality/actuality relationship within the form, which has just been discussed (§23(iv)). How that is applied in detail is the topic of Zeta 17 and Eta 2, to which we proceed.[33]

33 An excellent analysis of Zeta 13 along similar lines is in Shartin (1984).

§24. The analysis of substantial being

The foregoing intuitive review of the structure of the lower stage, including the positioning of the substantial individuals at the interface dividing the lower and upper stages (§21(i)), puts us now at a good vantage to assess what seems to be Aristotle's lattermost and maturest attempt to characterize the structure of essential predication itself. This is made in *Metaphysics* Zeta 17 and, particularly, Eta 2, and it stands in rather marked contrast with some less successful, possibly earlier, struggles with the topic recorded earlier in Zeta, some of which were looked into in §23. On the other hand, even the Eta 2 account, advanced as it is, still focuses entirely upon the synchronic aspect of substantial structure while ignoring the diachronic aspect altogether, and even the discussion of the synchronic has its problems – there is a momentary blunder in the exposition that is then hastily set right, and the exposition as a whole suffers from defects in the examples – some of them candidly acknowledged by Aristotle himself. Under the circumstances it seems best to proceed by first (i) carefully picking our way through Eta 2 itself, noting its successes and difficulties along the way, and then (ii) to enlarge upon the pregnant but sketchy indications of the chapter by outlining the analysis of substance it seems to be intimating, in the light of the foregoing biological discussions and the ensuing metaphysical framework. After that, an attempt can be essayed at extending the analysis beyond what Aristotle offers here, into the transtemporal dimension: the diachronic – a risky venture, even though kept as close as possible to what is known to be his view regarding those aspects of the matter which he does treat of.

(i) Essential predication: the analysis of Metaphysics Eta 2

There are two ways to formulate the main objective of the chapter. One way is to reach all the way back to the beginning of this study (§1 *init.*), and the *Categories'* audacious project of analyzing all the varieties of predicative being, of *X's beings Y* for all X and all Y. As counted off at the outset, two of those beings were (1) the individual man's (Socrates') *being* man or animal, and (4) (a) man's *being* (an) animal, – that is, under the regimentation of "predicated-of", the cases (1) of substantial species or genus predicated-of substantial individual, and (4) of substantial genus predicated-of species. As the *Cats.* treated it, these cases were cashed out in terms of the said-of relationship; in the larger *Metaphysics* world, the said-of relationship between species and individual that analyzes (1) in the *Cats.*, is represented in terms of the relationship of form to individual that it was decided in §20(iii) to call "is form of" (p. 199 on "F–I").

Eta 2 deals in the first instance with assertions[1] of the *being* of substantial individuals that look more existential than predicative: assertions like *(a) man exists, there is (a) man*; and as for how to handle *Socrates is (a) man* in the revised setting, we shall find that some additional complexities are involved for which we must go beyond Eta 2. The central idea is to show how such assertions of 'the being of a substance' may be subjected to a pattern of *eliminative analysis* in which the substantial term (like *(a) man*) is explained away in favor of a form and a matter – respectively, the characteristic specific differentia and the characteristic matter-informed in each type of case. Moreover, it also turns out – after an abortive first

---

1 It seems to suit the exposition here to shift temporarily to a formal-mode format.

attempt at framing the analysis more conventionally (1045^b25–8), which risks compromising the coming insight but is immediately abandoned – that the intended elimination is *contextual* in character, effecting not only a substitution of terms in the statement-forms under analysis – the analysanda – but a transformation in the structure of the statement-forms themselves. Thus the analysans in each case shows forth an underlying "deep" or "philosophical grammar" for the particular substantial being in question, that differs markedly from the surface indications of the ordinary-language analysandum. This is quite clear despite the near-misfire just mentioned, and despite the usual weaknesses of the examples, about which, as has been said, Aristotle himself is in this case unusually emphatic.

The other perspective in which to see Eta 2 is to realize that since the substances are pre-eminently the living things, and the paradigm of the form-matter relationship is the psycho-somatic relationship, *the subject-matter of Eta 2 is really the same as the subject-matter of DA ii 1–5*, as discussed in §16. The opening sentence of Eta 2 at 1042^b10–11 announces the topic of the chapter as "substance as *energeia* of perceptible things", *DA* ii 1 412^a21 identifies "substance [in the sense of form]" with *entelekheia* (cf. §16(i), p. 150). From this perspective, there is a threefold linkage between (1) the *DA* account of the psycho-somatic as the first *entelekheia* and the natural body potentially having life, (2) the Eta 2 account of final differentia and highest or proximate generic potentiality, and (3) the account of Theta 1 and 6 of *energeia* and potentiality for *energeia*, as opposed to *kinesis* and potentiality for *kinesis*. (1) has been treated at some length in §16, and we now proceed to (2); the (3) connection will be tied in in §24(iii).

1. 1042^b9–24 Manyness of differentia: some pseudo-substantial analogies

1042b9 Since the substance [that serves] as 'underlying' [*hupokeimenon*], *i.e.* as matter, is generally acknowledged, and this is the one that exists potentially, it remains to say of the substance as *actuality* of perceptible things, what it is.

Now Democritus, for his part, seems to be of the opinion that there are *three* differentiae [entering into the constitution of things] – for the body that underlies – the matter – is one and the same, but it 'differs',

either[a] by way of 'rhythm' – i.e. configuration [*skhēma*],
or[b] by 'turning'   – i.e. position [*thesis*],
b15   or[c] by 'mutual contact'– i.e. order [*taxis*].

– Here the method to be developed is first illustrated in what is probably its simplest possible scientific form, the building of molecules out of various types of atoms as "matter", where the molecular "differences" then consist in which atoms are how arranged, in respects that are claimed reducible to three: (a) which atoms lie adjacent to which, (b) how oriented with respect to one another (the example given elsewhere, *Meta.* A 4 985^{b}18, is a 'difference' of ninety-degree rotation, H as opposed to ⊏), (c) how sequenced in linear order (e.g., AN versus NA).[2] Now, whereas Democritus had the arresting idea trying to reduce the *entire* constitution of *all* things to just this "matter" and just these three "differentiae", Aristotle proceeds to argue by contrast that:

1042$_b$15 Evidently, though, there are *many* differentiae, e.g. [i] some things are constituted [lit. "are said" – are *defined?* cf. §3, p. 23] by a composition of the matter, as are such things as are constituted ["said"] by *blending*, like honeywater, [ii] others by *tying*, like a bundle, [iii] others by *gluing*, like a book, [iv] others by *nailing*, like a box, [v] others by more than one of these, [vi] others by *position*, like a threshold or a lintel – for these 'differ' by being placed thus-and-so –, [vii] others by *time*, like dinner and breakfast, [viii] others by *location*, like the winds, [ix] others by the affections [proper] to perceptible things, like hardness & softness, and density & rarity, and dryness & wetness, and [of these], some by some of these [affections], others by them all, and in general, some by $_b$25 excess, others by defect.

– In this panel of examples, mostly artefacts, a variety of characters is represented as playing the role of final differentiating form, and various corresponding underlying natures are cast in that of the underlying generic matter being differentiated. The examples range widely in their plausibility as substance-proxies, from the middling ("box") to the ludicrous ("breakfast") – as they are plainly intended to; for the intent of the passage is to point up the "manyness of differentia" for at least two of the several relevant sorts of "manyness". First, there is the enormous variety of potential *lines* of differentia[3] that are collected in the general category of "excess and defect", "more and less", the thousands of characters that can figure in the constituting of something substantial, as has been discussed with some emphasis in §12–13. Here the intent is not only to rebut the extreme Democritean reductionism (reduction to a mere three), but also to free up the hearer from the obsession with (i.e., from Academic "mental cramp" regarding) single ones, like *twofooted* or *rational*. Second and more important, the widely varying credibility of the

2 At this level of analysis it is not important whether the three 'differentiae' are exclusive, e.g. that the example given of (c) could be seen as involving orientation (i.e., (b)): a rotation of AN through the plane (which gives however ИA).

3 The importance of this in the biological connection was highlighted in §13, and is also brought out in Pellegrin (1982) in his terms of "axes of division" (see §13, p. 103 and note 25 thereto).

examples points up that the actual analysis of substance about to be given is *schematic*, that the examples are introduced as *analogies*, and that therefore the analysis itself is meant to leave wholly open, so-to-speak without prejudice, the question what particular things are substances – in the language of §21, it is to provide insight into the sort of structure possessed by the individuals that lie at the interface of the stages, without thereby prejudging the level at which that interface should be thought to be found. To make unmistakable this approach to the upcoming, for illustration's sake Aristotle will countenance taking even e.g. *position* (= at the foot of a doorway) as differentiating a certain matter (= a beam of wood or stone) into a substance (= a threshold) – although for anyone but an oudomaniac (cf. the leukomaniac of §21(i)), and certainly everywhere else in the corpus, position is paradigmatic of shallowest accident – and indeed, despite the outlandish and most un-Aristotelean consequences of such a supposition, namely that distinct substances are being rapidly slaughtered and created anew as the worker indecisively tries out the beam beneath the doorway (threshold), beneath the window (sill), at the foot of the pillar (plinth), over the window (lintel), under the floor (joist), and so on. The height of such absurdity is attained by the momentary countenancing of *time* as a possible substantial differentia, though its deficiencies in such an office are too obvious to need detailing, and nowhere else in the corpus is it straightfacedly suggested that (a) *lunch* is a substance, differentiated out of a baloney sandwich by consumption at noonday.[4]

2. *1042ᵇ25–8. False start on the analysis*

These promising opening moves are abruptly compromised in the next sentence, which attempts to set out a specimen analysis of the "being" of *threshold* and *ice*, misguidedly, before it has been settled what is to serve as the relevant "subject" as matter, thus threatening to bungle the enterprise altogether by suggesting that the *threshold* is "subject":

1042ᵇ25 Therefore it's clear that the *is* [of substantial being], too, 'is said' in exactly as many ways [as the aforesaid manyness of differentia]: a threshold *is*, in that it-lies thus [*houtōs keitai*], and the 'being'[5] means *its lying thus* [*to houtōs auto keisthai*], and *there being ice* means *being-solidified thus* [*to houtō pepuknōsthai*].

– Here disaster looms. If "threshold" is grammatical subject for "it-lies" in the first clause of the attempted paraphrase, or antecedent for "its"

4 Hartman (1977), p. 91, evidently takes the examples more seriously.
5 Or, "the 'being' for threshold" (*oudōi* suppl. Jaeger OCT).

(*auto*) in the second, then the would-be analysis is at best highly misleading, since rendered in this way the paraphrase fails to bring off – or so
much as suggest – the contextual *elimination* of the pseudo-substantial
term "threshold" that is the aim of the entire exercise.[6] The problem, of
course, is that the relationship called in §20(iii) *is form of*, a relationship of
form to individual, has surreptitiously – though only momentarily –
supplanted the relationship there called *informs*, a relationship of form to
matter, and the one needed for the eliminative analysis.[7] The misstep
here, if that is what it is (see note), is redeemed a little further on, when the
intended analysis is given correctly (1043^a7-12), but for some unknown
reason was never corrected here.

3. $1042^b28-1043^a4$. Manyness of differentia: gesture at some better cases

1042^b28 Of some things the 'being' will even be defined by all of these [marks], in
that some [parts] are mixed, some blended, some solidified, and some employing
the other differentiae, as do *hand*, or *foot*.

The *kinds of differentiae* [*ta genē tōn diaphorōn*], then, must be grasped, for these
differentiae are going to be the principles of [sc. substantial] being [*arkhai tou
einai*]; for example, the things [differentiated] by the 'more and less', or by 'dense
and rare', and by the others of this sort; for all these are [forms of] *excess and defect*.
And if something is [differentiated] by way of shape, or by smoothness and
roughness, all these are [differentiations] by [forms of] *straight and curved*. And for
still other things, 'being' will be *being-mixed*, and 'notbeing' the opposite. It's
evident, then, from these [forms of differentia], that if in fact the substance is the
cause of each thing's being, it's in them that it's got to be sought what the cause of
the being of each of these things is.

– This speaks for itself, being a forceful restatement of the principle of both
vertical depth and horizontal multiplexity of differentia, both of which
were made much of in §§12–13; the constructional and organizational
moment (as opposed to classificatory) in differentia, also celebrated in

---

6 The disagreement in gender between *auto* (neuter) and *oudos* (masculine) is not decisive in
Aristotle; cf. e.g. *touto* (n.) referring back to *ton desmon* (m.) at *Meta.* Beta 1 995^a30-1.

7 There is an alternative possibility: that *auto* does not refer to the threshold. Then there are
two possible interpretations. If in *oudos estin, oudos* is predicate, we then read "a thing is
[predicatively] a threshold", and *auto* is that thing. If *oudos* is subject, we understand "there is a
threshold" and *auto* is then some unnamed subject that underlies the qualification or differentia
of position. Taken in either of these ways, the intended *analogia* is saved. In support of the
alternative, it may be noted that the overriding structure of the explication from 1042^b15 has
been in terms of "things that are said *by a composition of the matter*", and that this is perhaps
supposed to be carried through the examples that follow: "by a blending [sc. of the matter]", to
"by a position [sc. of the matter]" in the first mention of the threshold case, and so on. (My
interpretation of this passage has been influenced by discussion with John Cooper.)

§13, is greatly in evidence also. Nonetheless the points are only ones of principle, it is not to be gathered that *threshold* or *ice*, or even *hand*, or *foot*, are being proffered as substances, as the next sentence makes plain.

4. 1043ᵃ4–7. Disavowal of the examples

1043ᵃ4 Now, *in fact* none of these[8] is [really an instance of] substance, [neither in themselves] nor 'coupled' [= with a matter], but all the same there's something *analogon* [to each other, and to real substantial 'being'] in each of them; and as among substances what gets predicated of the matter is the actuality itself, [so] among the other definitions too [*sc.* in our examples], [it should ᵃ7 be what] most of all [corresponds to actuality].[9]

5. 1043ᵃ7–12. Statement of the analysis

1043a7 For instance: if we had to define *threshold*, we'd say *wood or stone lying like THIS*; or *house: bricks and boards lying like THIS* – or again, the purpose [*hou heneka*] would go in too in some cases; and *ice: water frozen or solidified like THIS*; or *harmony: a mixture of THIS sort of high and low*; and the turn's the same in the other cases.

– To what has already been said (including by Aristotle) by way of impugning the examples used in this chapter, it may be added here that *ice*, for an alleged substance, possesses at best a minimal share of the individuativeness property (no more than *bronze* could it withstand the antistrophic argument of Zeta 3, cf. §20(i)); *harmony* has even less, and indeed appears wholly devoid of thinghood of any sort; the deficiencies of *threshold* have been adequately chronicled above; and of *house* in §19(iii). However, the examples need not be believed, only investigated for the "something *analogon* in each" (1043ᵃ5), and that is not hard to spot: in each case the "being" of the substance-proxy is broken down into the finishing-off (informing) by a differentia-proxy of a substrate subject serving in the office of a matter. Furthermore, it seems that in cases where there is any vertical depth to the differentiation involved, the differentia, represented by the differentia-proxy, should be as nearly as possible the "final" differentia, and the matter the "nearest" or "highest" matter – a point already encountered in §20(ii)[10] – so that what is called

8 "None of these differentiae" (Ross) is plausible, even likely, from a meaning standpoint; but *ouden* doesn't agree with *diaphora*. "None of these 'being's", perhaps. The whole clause means something like, "None of these is substance, [neither in the sense of the substance *of* anything, as is Man], nor 'coupled' [with a matter, as is Man to form Socrates]".

9 Cf. Ross's translation, and his note on ᵃ4–5 (*AM* ii 229).

10 Pp. 190–1, and the apposite advice to the same effect drawn there from *Meta.* Eta 4, Lambda 3, and the fire-to-boxes case of Theta 7.

"wood or stone" in the sample analysis of *threshold* should be understood in ultimate strictness as the *idiaitera hulē*, an appropriately shaped and sized beam, or piece, of wood or stone.

According to *Meta*. Eta 2, then, the general form of analysis of the *being* of a substance is as follows: where S is a specific substantial kind, *there being a S* means that a matter M (in a real case, generically-organized) is differentiated into *a S* by a final differentia D – or schematically, with analysandum at the left of the definitional equivalence and analysans at the right,

$$\frac{\text{there is a } S,}{\text{a } S \text{ exists}} \leftrightarrow D \text{ informs a } M \text{ (or some } M\text{)}.$$

This bare-bones of a paraphrase of course represents the merest of beginnings, and obviously calls for enlargement-upon, with the thought of bringing it to bear upon, not (or not only) the pseudo-substances that people the Eta 2 discussion itself, but the real thing – along lines of which by now some inkling has developed. Thus "D informing a (or some) M", though here illustrated with M's like "wood or stone" and D's like "lying like THIS", is open to being *understood* (I hypothesize, is meant to be understood) in terms of the cumulative and many-levelled hierarchy of differentiation, epitomized (and slightly caricatured) by the Fire-to-boxes schematism of *Meta*. Theta 7 (cf. §20), which in turn gets much of its intuitive force from the notion of cumulative, many-lined differentiation that has been conjured up out of the biological setting (§§12–15). It seems, then, that a great deal is packed into that "D" of Eta 2, which calls for unpacking and elaborating. Conversely, the hypothesis about the place of genus in the vertical hierarchy as the "upper intermediate range of the sequence", with the associated interpretive framework that has been looked at somewhat (§13(iv)), suggests that at least as much is crammed into "a M (or some M)" of Eta 2, and calls for interpretive attention too.

Before pursuing these implications, however, let us first follow Eta 2 to its end.

6. *1043ᵃ12–28. Consolidation and conclusion*

1043ᵃ12 It's evident, then, from these [cases? considerations?] that the actuality's different when the matter's different,[11] and the formula; for in some cases it's the composition, in others it's the mixing, and in others it's some other of the ones

---

11 This must mean the *type* of matter involved in the constitution of a particular *type* of thing, not Callias' flesh and bones as opposed to Socrates'.

we've mentioned. This is why, of those who give definitions, the ones who, asking *what is a house?*, answer: *stones & bricks & timbers*, are speaking of the-house-potentially, for those are [the] matter;[12] but those who proffer *a receptacle to shelter chattels & bodies*, or something else of that nature, are speaking of the actuality; but those who combine both of these [speak of] the third [kind of] substance – composed of the first two – for it seems that the formula that goes through the differentiae is of the form and the actuality, whereas that which consists of the components is rather of the matter –; and similarly for the sorts of definitions that Archytas used to accept; they are of the combined two.

[a]22 E.g.: *What is still weather?* Absence of motion in a large volume of air; matter is the air, actuality & substance is the absence of motion.

What is a calm? Smoothness of sea; the subject in the sense of matter is the sea, the actuality & shape is the smoothness.

It's evident, then, from what we've said, what perceptible substance is, and how it is: there's substance as matter, and again as shape and actuality, and third the kind that's composed of these.

(ii) Eta 2 analysis approximated to real substances

(a) Genus, Differentia and differential depth

Most of the concrete examples in Eta 2 are very simple entities in which the portion playing the role of material subject is just a stuff – the wood of a box, the water and honey of honeywater, etc. – although in a couple there is a minimal hint of vertical complexity, such as the threshold (a beam of wood or stone "informed" by position into a threshold, where the beam itself has got formed (up out) of the wood or stone, by coming to exemplify beamish shape). In the real cases, on the other hand, the final differentia D_n of an individual substance – an individual S – should be seen as informing, finishing off, bringing to perfection or "entelechy", an underlying generic substrate which itself already has (in the metaphysical, not necessarily the chronological sense of "already") full differentiation short only of the final; let this not-quite-specific nature be called G_1. On this understanding, the existence of the full-fledged individual S would look like this:

$$\text{there is a } S \leftrightarrow D_n \text{ informs (a) } G_1;$$

although the notation of the analysans which is the right-hand side of the equivalence, in terms of D_n and G_1, has various shortcomings some of

---

12 Note that the stones etc. *still are* the matter and potentiality of the house, even after the house has come into being – cf. the vertical relationship of §20(iii). (Also Owens, *DOB*[2], p. 239.)

which will be explained shortly and not all of which are remediable, it is still in some ways more serviceable to our purposes than such Aristotelean patois as "*twofooted* informs (an) *animal*". "Informs" of course must be read in the quasi-technical sense reserved for that word in §20(iii); it evokes the form-to-matter relationship and is a terminological variant on the paronymic complex of the type

$$\overbrace{\substack{D_n \\ G_1}}$$

which has been used since then to suggest verticality in hylomorphic connections, and will find use in this one also.

Relative to the reality, the paraphrase is absurdly oversimple: for example, in view of that many-lined character of differentiation, so much touted in §13 and just now underscored in Eta 2 itself (3. 1042^b28–1043^a4), that final differentia D_n ought theoretically to be notated as highly multiplex – along lines suggested by something like

$$\overbrace{\substack{D_n, D_n, \ldots, D_n \\ G_1, G_1, \ldots, G_1}} \quad,$$

though for several reasons not exactly that would do (for example, its suggestion that the correspondence between final differentia and nearest generic matter be one-one is misleading); but in the interest of sheer wieldiness it is better to maintain the fiction of a single final differentia in the vertical dimension – as the first such oversimplification in the canonical scheme under development and by no means the last, let it be called Fiction No. 1.

Now G_1 in its turn is "obtained", metaphysically speaking, from a further-underlying, more generic substrate G_2 as *its* vertical *ex hou* by the formative influence of a next-to-final, penultimate differentia, D_{n-1}, which should next be placed in the scheme – though by setting them apart in this way, it becomes apparent that another large idealization is operative, namely supposing it possible to separate out that portion of the total vertical differentiation assignable to D_n and D_{n-1} respectively, whereas in fact (as pointed out in §13(iv)) the actual phenomenon is plastic in character and thus to split into stepwise integral or discrete jumps, to digitalize the continuous, is to misrepresent it to some extent (thus, Fiction No. 2 – the Fire-to-boxes illustration in *Meta*. Theta 7 suffers from the same drawback). On that understanding, however, the scheme may be further evolved: the analysis of the "being" of the individual S now stands at two levels of differentiation with respect to G_2, or something like

$$\text{there is a } S \longleftrightarrow D_n \text{ informs} \begin{cases} \text{(a) } G_1 \\ \text{(a) } G_1 \end{cases} = D_{n-1} \text{ informs (a) } G_2$$

– or, in the at this point apter terms of upward paronymics,

$$\begin{aligned} S &= D_n \\ \overbrace{} \\ G_1 &= D_{n-1} \\ \overbrace{} \\ G_2 &= \text{etc.} \end{aligned}$$

It has already been noted that Eta 2 focuses mainly on simple pseudo-substances with little vertical depth to them, as well as omitting to attend to the diachronic dimension at all. Eta 2 tells nothing about the numerical sameness of substances while changing through time, nor about the particular case of undergoing exchange of component matter – partial or total, metabolic or artificially induced. When it is looked into how the theory ought to be extended to deal with this dimension and these sorts of cases, an immediate consequence is that need arises for some sort of distinction like that between the "perceptible" and the "intelligible" matter of a substance. This is because it is typically the perceptible matter – the literally component material stuff – that would be expected to be the medium of such exchange, whereas the hierarchy of substructures, sub-substructures and so on specified in the definition (or "Constitution") of the substance – the intelligible matter, by the hypothesis of §17(ii) and §23(iv) – should remain relatively constant throughout, though subject to the pattern of the species as to their evolution through processes of development, "peaking" and decay (§17(ii), p. 166, §19(iii), p. 183, cf. §16(ii) (*DA* on continuity of threptic)). As long as we remain within the synchronic limits in effect set by Eta 2, however, this distinction can be overlooked (as a "fiction" that is temporary so far as the present reconstruction is concerned). In these terms, then, the entire descending analysis of a substance S, from the ultimate or "final" differentia D_n, through the deepest-lying generic nature (or, in fact, intelligible matter), to the simplest or "prime" of the material constituents or perceptible matter, would successively unravel the structure of the differentiated "knot" in the general fashion of the following:

$$S \;=\; D_n \;=\; D_n \;=\; D_n \;=\; \ldots \;=\; D_n$$

$$\overbrace{\quad G_1 \quad} \qquad \overbrace{\quad D_{n-1} \quad} \qquad \overbrace{\quad D_{n-1} \quad} \qquad \overbrace{\quad D_{n-1} \quad}$$

$$\overbrace{\quad G_2 \quad} \qquad \overbrace{\quad D_{n-2} \quad} \qquad \overbrace{\quad D_{n-2} \quad}$$

$$\overbrace{\quad G_3 \quad}$$

$$\vdots$$

$$\overbrace{\quad D_{n-k} \quad}$$

$$\overbrace{\quad G_{k+1} \quad}$$

This picture goes a certain distance toward realizing some of the intentions of the Eta 2 analysis, but there are rather serious flaws in it as well, going to points of principle and more consequential than Fictions 1 and 2. Nor is it easy to see how to rectify them, at least in any notation that could be conformed to print and paper. One is this (Fiction No. 3): the scheme does not show forth (vividly, as would be desirable, or even at all) that each upward determination is a *restriction* of the generic nature underlying it,[13] to which, in principle at least, there are many alternatives that would lead, if selected at that level, to divergent specific forms (in real cases, unlike the threshold case as imagined on p. 253 above, almost invariably nonexistent forms); thus the entire upward sequence – as represented at the extreme right of the figure – can be thought of as a path traced by a certain natural "choice function" through an arboreal pattern of possibilities, tracing a line of actuality from the pattern's "trunk" to a point at its "top", none of which this notation notates.[14] A related defect is (Fiction No. 4): absent from the schematism, and hard to imagine how to supply, is any inkling that as the upper levels of differentiation approach D_n, the nature of the entire entity is approaching that of *a S, an individual S, a distinctly recognizable individual S*; in a better rendering (were it possible), just as one should be able to *see* the object itself as becoming recognizably more *S*ish with the successive accumulation of differentiae, so the connection between the terminology for the *S* and that for the *D*'s should be more evident than in this language-form, rather than

13 §13(ii), see pp. 102, 107.

14 Care is needed here to avoid misunderstanding from a modern viewpoint: Aristotle would *not* call the "alternative" unrealized natures *possible* natures, because it is his view that the only possible forms are the forms that actually *are* (on this, and the whole subject of Aristotelean modality, both logical and metaphysical, see Hintikka (1973)). Therefore, the real problem about Fiction No. 3 is that it fails to notate the exclusion of those alternative natures *as* naturally impossible, and the path of the "choice function" *as* naturally necessary.

stipulated, or supplied from intuition or general knowledge (a similar objection could possibly be directed at *twofooted* and *man*)[15]

Thus if, as someone is supposed to have said, "a good notation is like a good teacher",[16] it has to be faced that this one unhappily leaves out some critical lessons of the course. Yet it is unapparent how these shortcomings can be effaced, and were they, simultaneously, the notation could not remain even minimally surveyable; it would have to acquire many further dimensions and in any case the effort would lead far from the substantive (in the sense of *inhaltlich*) concerns of Aristotelean metaphysics. Weak as it is, the schematism still serves the pertinent purpose of highlighting some of the chief points at which the use of imagination and the suspension of disbelief are most in order in assimilating the analysis.

An aspect that can be incorporated, with a little effort, relates to the "strange hypothesis" flown in §15(i), as to the impacting-together on this theory of full individuality and full specific form; for from this it follows that only the complete Aristotelean substance, *the S*, incorporating all specific differentiae up to and including the last, is a full-blooded and fully-authentic individual, and the underlying stages have about them still (once again, metaphysical rather than chronological "still") something masslike in their nature, something partaking of the "*matter*-as-subject" character that is characteristic of the lower stage of the domain, to which of course they all belong. It will turn out that to this "strange" aspect an equally "strange" feature of the elaborated-upon Eta 2 analysis corresponds.

To epitomize what is being read out of – and from other points of our reflections on the corpus, read into – Eta 2: *the being of a substance* is understood as the differentiation of a generically characterized matter by a final differentia,

(1) there is a $S \leftrightarrow D_n$ informs (a) G_1,

where G_1, the "highest" genus, incorporates the entire range of vertical differentiation – save the final – in the manner described. Wherever G_1 is vertically composite (as here it is understood to be), the possibility is always in principle open of making the genus/differentia cut somewhere lower in the hierarchy, taking a leaner genus and a correspondingly fuller differentia; it is not necessarily actual error to do this; but taking the

---

15 There is an additional crudity to a modern eye in the representation of the contextuality of the "definition", in that (as we would put it) the same variables are not free on both sides of the biconditional. This can be justified to some extent: cf. (c) below.

16 Anscombe and Geach (1961), p. 131, *à propos* Frege's Begriffsschrift.

highest genus and final differentia is preferable in the spirit of "stating the nearest cause" (§20(ii), pp. 190–1, also pp. 255–6 above): it is the "best" on a scale where "least best" would be to sweep the entire range of differentiation into a single enormous differentia like *humanoid*, and assign the role of *G* to something very low-down, *an-idion*, "common to everything", like *fire, and earth*.

That and the foregoing is enough for now about D_n and G_1 in the analysans of (1), and we should turn to the other two ingredients of the analysans: the requisite notion of "informs", and the existential quantifier represented in the analysans by "(a)".

(b) "Informs" in the analysans

"Informs" in (1), as has already been emphasized (§20(iii), pp. 198–9), must be taken to be the relation of form to matter informed, a relation already noted important to be kept sorted out from the relation of form to individual – a point on which as we have seen there is momentary faltering in the midst of Eta 2 itself (2. 1042^b25–8). In this fact, that "informs" as opposed to "is form of" figures in the Eta 2 analysis, consists the critical difference between this analysis and that of the *Categories*: the true "subject", "thing that underlies", in *the being of a* (substantial) *S* is not *the individual S* but the matter informed by the form into an individual *S*. By the same token, as will shortly be seen, the true "subject", of that case of predicative being which is Socrates' *being* man (pp. 250, §8(pp. 64–5), §1 (p. 9)) is not *Socrates*, the individual man (but the Eta 2 analysis by itself, being wholly synchronic, cannot deal with all the ramifications of this case; cf. §25 below). This contextual reshuffling or *metarrhuthmisis*[17] is highly significant; it proves to have been the key to springing several of the most intractable locks in the earlier parts of *Meta*. Zeta (§23).

(c) The quantifier "(a)"

The left-hand side of (1) is a straightforward assertion of the existence of a certain sort of individual, in which a standard quantifier is applied to a fully individuative or count-type predicate *S*; its semantic interpretation in terms of whatever contemporary first-order logical framework may be preferred is unproblematic.

---

17 A nice word, indicative of grammatical/analytical transformations generally: cf. *Phycs* i 2 185^b28, Bonitz *Ind.* 461^a56.

The right-hand side of (1), however, is something else ("strange"): it is the Eta 2 *explication* of the existence of such an individual, in terms of the existence of an only-generically-defined substrate that is sufficiently formed to be a subject for the final differentia D of substantial species S, but of itself, as has been argued, falls short of full individual status. Accordingly the quantifier in "informs (a) G_1" has to be interpreted in a not entirely standard way, in that the variables it binds have as what comprises their range, not individual substances but something underlying individual substances, and not *individuals* underlying individual substances because there are no such individuals, but instead the sub-individual generically defined substrates that lie below the interface dividing the two stages of the domain. In other words, the analysans of (1) has to be regarded as governed by a quantifier binding variables whose range consists of things masslike rather than fully individuated in nature. And the paradigm to which (1) as a whole is thus seen as gravitating[18] is of the form:

$$\left(\begin{array}{l} \text{a (brazen) statue of} \\ \text{Socrates exists, or} \\ \text{there is a brazen} \\ \text{statue of Socrates} \end{array} \right) \longleftrightarrow \left(\begin{array}{l} \text{Socratic shape} \\ \text{("socracity", §20, n.18)} \\ \text{informs} \\ \textit{some bronze.} \end{array} \right)$$

Such a "mass" or "material" quantifier as that in the analysans of (1) needs to be notationally distinguished, however roughly, from any familiar idiom notating the standard quantification in the analysandum. The following vernacular ("strange", as promised) will suffice for our purposes: let the material quantifier "some" (as in "some bronze", above) be written "V_m", and let variables of the style $g_1, g_2, \ldots, g_{k+1}$ range over successively more ill-defined material masses at generic levels $1, 2, \ldots,$ $k+1$ beneath the level of the substantial individuals (the analogy with familiar first-order quantification thus weakening as lower levels are taken); then the analysans would assume this notational form:

$$(V_m g_1) \;\; \overset{\displaystyle D_n}{\overbrace{}}_{g_1}$$

where the intended parallel to the paradigmatic brazen statue is:

$$(V_m \text{ bronze}) \;\; \overset{\displaystyle \text{socracity}}{\overbrace{}}_{\text{bronze}}$$

---

18 *Philosophical Investigations* I, §385.

and where we also have, as reminder that we are still well within the reservation defined by *Meta.* Eta 2, the following total analysis of the being of a threshold:

$$(Vx)\text{threshold}(x) \longleftrightarrow (V_m \begin{array}{c}\text{beam of}\\\text{wood or}\\\text{stone}\end{array}) \quad \overbrace{\text{beam of wood or stone}}^{\text{positioned } \textit{thus}} \quad .$$

(In connection with the last, if we discriminate more *versus* less *idiaitera hulē* in the construction of thresholds (pp. 255–6 above), the existence thereof may be more elaborately analyzed as:

$$(Vx)\text{threshold}(x) \longleftrightarrow (V_m \text{ wood or stone}) \quad \overbrace{\text{shaped into } \textit{beam}}^{\text{positioned } \textit{thus}} \quad ;$$
$$\overbrace{\text{wood or stone}}$$

here there is a crude facsimile of the multi-tieredness characteristic of the real cases, although the "manyness of differentiae" in the horizontal dimension still is not well evoked by the case – Fiction No. 1 remains.)

If we restate the Eta 2 analysis in our present terms, then, it looks like this:

$$(2) \qquad (Vx)S(x) \longleftrightarrow (V_m g_1) \quad \overbrace{g_1}^{D_n} \quad .$$

The deficiencies of this rendering have by now been sufficiently dwelt upon; they are endurable if it does succeed in suggesting the main point it is meant to: namely, that the transition from left to right, analysandum to analysans, decomposes the substantial *individual S* into generic material substrate and final formal differentia, and in the process the predicative structure of the whole is basically altered, from the configuration *is form of* which relates species to specimen individual, to the configuration *informs*, which relates differentia to matter.

As has been suggested earlier, this (left-to-right) transition can also be thought of as that from the *Categories* to the *Metaphysics* conception of substance.

(iii) Psyche revisited: entelechy and energy

We observed early in §24(i) that Eta 2 can be seen as really having the same subject matter as *de Anima* ii 1–5, i.e. as an abstruse reformulation of the (vertical, in our current metaphysical terms) psycho-somatic relationship that was partially explored in §16. The *DA* formulation was in terms of potentiality (*dunamis*) and "completedness" (*entelekheia*); however, the potential is itself of two kinds, and it will help us to integrate this part of the picture to fit that distinction into it.

According to *Meta.* Theta, the twofoldness of the potential both answers to and (it seems) derives from the twofoldness in *energeia* or actuality.[19] The potential "in the strictest sense" (1045^b36) is potentially for "movement" (*kinēsis*), and this is contrasted with the potential for actuality in the *DA* ii/Eta 2 sense:

On the one hand, there are the cases where [actuality] is as *kinēsis* in relation to *dunamis*; on the other, the cases where it is as substance to a certain matter. (Theta 6 1048^b8–9).

The classic exposition is the following from Theta 6:

1048^b18 Since among actions that have a limit [*peras*], none is a completion [*telos*], but each is the sort of thing *relating to* [*peri*] the completion, – as e.g. slimming is to slimness; the [bodily parts] themselves, when they are slimming, in that respect are in movement, though those things which the movement is for the sake of [whose presence constitutes slimness] do not yet belong to them – these things are not action, or at least not complete, just because it is not a completion. $^b22$ But that [sort of action] in which its completion is contained is a [real] action. $^b23$ E.g., in the same moment one is seeing and has seen [= "knows" by sight], is understanding and has understood [= possesses understanding], is thinking and has thought [= "knows" by insight]. But if you are learning, it's not the case that in the same moment you have learned, nor if you are being cured, that in the same moment you have been cured. $^b25$ However, someone who is living well, at the same time has lived well, and someone who is prospering, has prospered. If that were not so, [the living well, e.g.] would have had to come to an end at a certain point, as it is the case with slimming [= when the state of slimness, of one's having completed an act of slimming, has been achieved]. But in fact it does not [have to do that in that way]; you are living *and* have lived. $^b28$ Of these [actions], then, one group should be called motions [*kinēses*], and the other, actualizations [*energeiai*]. For every movement is incomplete – slimming, learning, walking [= in the sense of walking to Piraeus, or taking a walk], these are movements and are incomplete. $^b30$ For one cannot in the same moment be taking a walk and have taken it [or be walking to Piraeus and have walked there], nor be house-

---

19 I will not try to sustain here a distinction between *energeia* and *entelekheia*, though I think there is one (for powerful authority to the contrary, see Ross *AM* ii 245 (1047^a30 n.), Bonitz *Index* 253^b46 ff. s.v. *entelekheia*). The terms are respectively formed from *ergon*, work or function, and *telos*, completion or end, and they respectively connote something whose work or function is *internal* to it (*Meta.* Theta 8 1050^a21), and something whose completion or end is *within* (cf. "that in which its completion is contained", 1048^b22 in the following quotation from Theta 6). The idea of *telos* as internal *vs.* external will be taken up shortly.

building and have house-built, nor be being moved [*kineitai*] and have been moved [*kekinētai*]; they are different, as [in general] are moving [*kinei*] and having moved [*kekinēken*]. ᵇ33 But at the same moment the same thing has seen and is seeing, and is thinking and has thought. This sort of thing, then, I call an actualization, the other sort, a movement.

In the terms we have been developing subsequent to §16, we can see that this contrast is between two sorts of actualization that can be thought of as respectively "horizontal" and "vertical".

A potentiality for a *movement* is actualized by that movement's getting under way; the movement has a "limit", that is, aims at a completion (*telos*) outside itself (the movement itself is *atelēs*, "incomplete"), with the attainment of which (i) that movement must by definition cease, and (ii) the potentiality for that movement is gone.[20] (There is a parallel here, though only a partial one, with the coming-to-be of the musical "out of" (*ek*) the unmusical, or the statue "out of" the block (cf. §20(iii), §22(ii)), i.e., the coming-to-be and the *ex hou* in which the completion of the coming-to-be destroys the *ex hou*.) Thus in this case there is (1) a *dunamis*, (2) the process of actualization (housebuilding, curing, walking to Piraeus) in which the *dunamis* is coming to be realized and the completion is being approached, and (3) the arrival at the completion (house built, cure achieved, Piraeus arrived at), whereupon the movement is over and the *dunamis* (for *this* movement) no longer exists.

A potentiality for an *energeia* proper is actualized very differently: the actualization is not a process directed at and terminating with the achievement of a *telos* external to it; when this sort of actualization gets under way, its *telos* is internal to it and is realized at the same time (*hama*) and by the same fact as the commencement of the actualization itself.[21] Furthermore, this potentiality and its actualization are not incompatible, as are movement-potentiality and movement-completion: to the contrary, the paradigm of the relationship is the first-to-second actualization relationship in the case of the psyche, where the ability to see is not "used up" or destroyed by the seeing, but made most manifest by it, completed

---

20 Kosman (1984), a treatment of this matter that is highly recommended, calls movements "kamikaze" actualizations: a movement is aimed at "a completion whose realization means the death of that very motion [= movement] whose purpose is to bring it about" (p. 127, cf. 131). For the above interpretation of "limit", see Ross *AM* ii 253 (1048ᵇ18 n.).

21 The four occurrences of "at the same time" (*hama*) (1048ᵇ23, 25, 30, 33) clearly connote "by the same token" (Kosman (1984) 127, "virtually one and the same thing").

or perfected. (Thus the partial parallel to this side from §20(iii), §22(ii) is the vertical coming-to-be of the statue "out of" the bronze as opposed to the block, where the bronze is an *ex hou* that "remains" and is not replaced.[22]) Thus in this case there is (1) a *dunamis*, and then (2) the sort of actualization of that *dunamis* which the *DA* calls "either not an alteration at all (being rather an advancement[23] and indeed into completedness), or a different kind of alteration" (Oxford: "an alteration in a quite different sense from the usual meaning") (ii 5 417^{b}6–7).

The long passage of Theta 6 quoted above also connects the contrast between actualizations proper and movements with what is known as the perfective aspect of verb inflection in Greek: for an actualization proper, "the sort of action in which its completion is contained", it is simultaneously true that *I am X-ing* and that *I have X-ed*, whereas in the case of movements, when *I have X-ed*, by definition I am no longer X-ing, and when *I am X-ing* it cannot yet be the case that I have X-ed. Here it is necessary to know that the idiom translated *I have seen*, for example, does not mean "I saw (in the past)", but "I am (presently) in the state of having completed (i.e. 'perfected') an act of seeing". It is in these terms that the *telos* of house-building, namely having-house-built, which means having finished the house, could not have started to 'be' while the house-building was still going on, and once the *telos* has started to 'be' entails that the house-building must have stopped; whereas having-seen 'is' at every moment when the seeing 'is'.[24]

With this we can make a connection with a theme going back to §16 and past that to §13 and §9: we can see the entire vertical hierarchy of the accession of form into matter in terms of actualization in the sense that Theta 6 has distinguished from movement. In the anatomical/physiologi-

---

22 Kosman (1984, p. 135) reads the presentation of Theta 6 1048^{a}30–^{b}8 as "chiastic", so that the examples of house-building and awakeness and seeing are actualizations proper and the examples of the shaped and the wrought are movements. If this is right (and I am not sure it isn't), then there may be another polarity-problem here like those discussed in §22(ii); for though "as the wrought is *to the unwrought*" (1048^{b}4) *could* mean (with some strain), as the statue is *to the block*, there is no way to make "as what has been shaped out of the matter is *to the matter*" (^{b}3) mean anything but, as the statue is *to the bronze*, which has to be the vertical actualization and not the horizontal replacement by a different or contrary being. On the other hand, if the presentation is *not* "chiastic", then the immediately ensuing statement of the actuality/movement contrast at 1048^{b}8–9, already quoted above, is not as properly motivated. I see no tidy way out, i.e., it looks as if the problem may be with Aristotle rather than with Kosman (1984).

23 The word is *epidosis*, an increase, a progress, an improvement, an advance. As a transitive verb, *epididonai* is to make a benefaction, give freely, bestow (LSJ).

24 Borrowed from Furth (1985), p. 135 (Theta 6 1048^{b}25 n.). Cf. Kosman (1984), pp. 123–7.

cal terms of §§12–13 and the psychological terms of §16, the hierarchy looks like this (here so many "Fictions" are crowded together that I will not even mention them further):

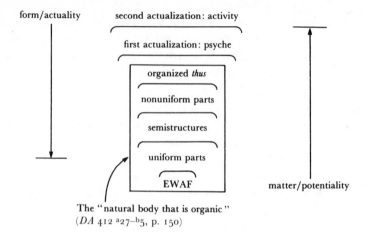

The "natural body that is organic"
(*DA* 412 ᵃ27–ᵇ5, p. 150)

§25. The analysis of Eta 2 extended to the diachronic dimension

(i) Persistent form and exchangeable matter

Finally I wish to try to understand how the scheme of Zeta 17 and Eta 2 might apply to the analysis of cases not provided for in those chapters, namely the cases of substantial individuals that persist over time while evolving or "receiving contraries" and in particular while undergoing exchanges of component matter. This will necessitate some speculative reconstruction, in the spirit of §0, and readers who consider such an enterprise illegitimate in the quest for the historical Aristotle may well wish to have nothing to do with it. On the other hand, it has already been pointed out more than once in this study that it is after all Aristotle himself who calls attention to the phenomenon of the transtemporal persistence of individual substances through alteration as that which is "most distinctive" about them, *malista idion tēs ousias* (*Cat.* 4ᵃ10); any analysis that may be attempted is necessarily speculative, but there is nothing anachronistic in calling attention to the phenomenon as something it would be reasonable to wonder about the Aristotelean analysis of. And I believe there are in fact quite a few indications of the way in which it should go, most of which have already come up here; there will be nothing especially radical about it. So at the risk of criticism, I will proceed.[1]

Our first need is to represent somehow the exchange of component matter within a continuing substantial individual. This will naturally be matter that is perceptible as opposed to intelligible matter, in the sense sketched in §23(iv). To notate this, we need a symbol that is like "⌒" in connoting *informing* and *being-informed-by*, but which is applied specifically to mark *the point in the vertical hierarchy of differentiation below which exchanges of matter are compatible with the continued existence of an individual of the substantial kind in question*; to this end, let us appropriate the emblem " ⋀⋁⋀ ", in contexts of the type

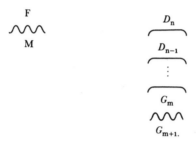

Thus we obtain a rough-and-ready schematic representation of differential depth where, in the right-hand column, G_m represents the deepest generic level in the constitutive nature that comes with the substantial kind of (of$_{(2-3)}$, cf. §23(iii)) the substantial individual in question, whereas G_{m+1} is matter that the substantial form happens to shape up, whether temporarily or (it may be) permanently, where yet exchange of this or lower matter would be survivable by numerically one and the same substantial individual. (What is above the " ⋀⋁⋀ " is the "knot" of §18; what is below is the perceptible matter passing through.)

In such a schematism, the continued existence of numerically one and the same S through time ("down through time", as the representation has it; but see below) will be representable along lines of the following sort,

---

1 There is some parallel between this way of proceeding here and my little fabrication in §4 (*4ᵇ19 ff.) of a paragraph of *Categories* 5 that Aristotle did not write. But there is also a large disanalogy, at least in my estimation. For I think (and suggested in §4) it is quite possible that the author of the *Categories*, when writing the *Categories*, was fully conversant with the fully Aristotelean thesis of *4ᵇ19 ff., but had reason to pass over making it explicit. On the other hand, the question why the nature of transtemporal continuity (or "diachronic individuation") is not studied, at length and in depth, in the form-matter setting of the metaphysical writings is to me a total mystery.

where "F" for the moment abbreviates the entire column of essential differentiations, and "M" the exchangeable matter:

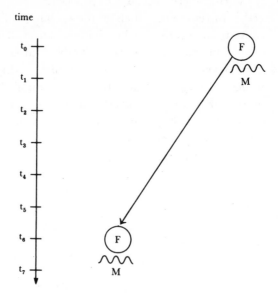

(In this representation, the "downward" direction of time has had to be pushed to one side slightly in order to accommodate the "downward" relation of form to matter. Later, when more differential depth is brought into the depiction of the form-matter dimension, the direction of time will have to be bent even further toward the diagonal. There is no way of getting all the dimensionalities consistently represented here without a greater talent for perspective in logical space than I possess.)

Before proceeding further, it is worthwhile to fix here the relationship between this first approximation of the diachronic structure of substance and the spectrum of alternative realizations of it that would result from alternative locatings of the line marked by "ᴧᴧᴧ"; the warrant for this thought-experiment is *Meta.* Zeta 10–11. For example, then: let the column

$$
\begin{array}{c}
\text{F} \\
\text{ᴧᴧᴧ} \\
\text{M}
\end{array}
$$

be Socrates, the individual man, and consider a simplified line of differentiation involving Socrates' *bones*:

– It might be held that their constituent Earth and Fire could change over time while Socrates continued, but that they must (by the definition of Man) always consist of that proportion of Earth and Fire called *Calcium*.

– Or it might alternatively be held that, although they happen now to be composed of Calcium, this is a mere consequence of Socrates' recent dietary practices, and Socrates could survive intact even were the proportion of Earth and Fire in his bones to be altered to that quite different ratio called *Silicon*.

– Or it might alternatively be held that it is only by way of resource availability, and not part of the definition of Man, that Socrates is made (in part) out of bones at all, and that human form could equally well be realized in a structure that was, say, exo- rather than endo-skeletal in nature, carapace instead of bone, and Socrates, the individual man, could survive as one and the same individual man a transit from one to the other of these.

– Or . . .

In each of these cases in turn, the dividing-line below which matter is exchangeable within a persisting individual – the line marked '〜〜〜' – is thought of as placed successively higher; in the last case indeed, if we may judge from *Meta*. Zeta 11, Aristotle would say excessively high:

. . . it's not right, it leads away from the truth, it makes one suppose that Man could exist without the parts, in the way that Circle can exist without the bronze, (1036^{b}25–8)

– where the context indicates that by "parts" is meant what we are accustomed to think of as human parts, like human flesh and bones.

No doubt Aristotle's judgment about this in *Meta*. Zeta 11 is a sustainable one; but in any case, whatever the most sustainable choice for the division between exchangeable and nonexchangeable (including intelligible) matter in the end may be, among the alternatives enumerated or others not stated above, it is one more liberating consequence of our relativistic methodology as regards the Population Problem[2] that we do not find further progress blocked until we can *decide* the question what matter-changes a certain kind of individual can or cannot survive, i.e. (in Aristotle's words), *solve* the very difficult problem of What Things Are Parts of the Form, and What things Aren't Parts of the Form but (only) of the Compound, either for particular cases like the above, or worse yet, generally. Rather, as things stand, the analysis can be pursued in schematic terms, just as it is in Eta 2, and questions about its application to various particular cases, both real and (if desired) imagined, can be sidetracked for subsequent treatment in the light of the view as a whole, together with, preferably, the relevant testimony of natural science.

2 §§7, 20(iii), 21, 22(ii).

Returning to the schematism, then, and assuming the Population of the universe to be fixed, in all its various dimensions including the placement of the division of exchangeable *versus* nonexchangeable matter, the total world-view of the substantial universe as thus far developed might be diagrammable as follows, where the various different substantial kinds are indicated by subscript indices "a", "b" etc. on the substantial schematic letter "*S*" (in particular, "S_b" indicates Man):

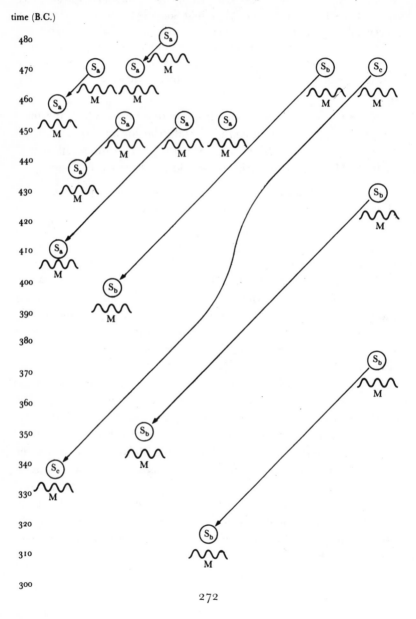

Though still to be improved upon, this even now gives a serviceable depiction of the role of continuity of form, (down) through time constituting this, that and the other individual S_a, S_b, and so forth as, in each case, the same S_a, S_b, etc. later as earlier in its temporal span. The three S_bs (individual human beings) illustrated, it may be noted, are shown as existing over the temporal spans 470–399, 427–347, and 384–322, respectively; but the present level of diagrammatic capacity does not yet reveal their peculiarities any further than their simply being S_bs whose existence is bounded by those temporal termini. As for the S_as, evidently they are shorter-lived substances (on the whole) than S_bs; they are individual lions. The middle-left-central portion of the diagram represents a litter of three S_as that came-to-be in 450; one of these ceased-to-be in 436, one lived to an unusually ripe old age (for a S_a) until 415, and the third met its end very shortly after its formation. The single S_c, extending from 473 to 341 or for the extraordinary period of 132 years, is an individual Galapagos tortoise.[3]

The temporal direction is shown as downward. Much better, but unsuited to print and paper, is to think of it as *backward*: in the sense of a cosmic cinematographic backward tracking shot, in which present occurrences become visible to our 180° peripheral vision, and therefrom recede before us steadily into the temporal distance – we see where we have been and are, but not where we are going. (It is in fact standard usage in Homeric Greek to refer to *past* and *future* with the words that mean "in front" and "behind" respectively[4] – our progress through time is that of oarsmen.) Within this overall apocalypse, the substances' temporal elongation is along the axis that is parallel to our temporal vision into the past; those whose nearer ends terminate within our field of view have ceased-to-be; whereas those still intersecting the backward-rushing plane of our 180° periphery are as yet contemporary. Thus much for how the scheme should be visualized; with print and paper, vertically is how it must continue to be drawn.

---

3 Or possibly a *phoinix*, date-palm (*de L. & B. Vitae*, 466ᵃ9–10).
4 Thus LSJ s.v. *opissō* (Epic for "behind"): "of Time, *hereafter*, since the future is unseen and therefore regarded as *behind* us, whereas the past is known and therefore before our eyes."
An example there given of future versus past is *Odyssey* xi 482–3 (Odysseus to Achilles):
seio d', Akhilleu,
ou tis anēr proparoithe markartatos out' ar' opissō
("No man more blessed than you, Achilles, neither in the past (lit. 'in front') nor indeed in the future (lit. 'behind')".
An example of future versus present, *Iliad* vi 352–3 (Helen to Hector):
toutōi d' out' ar nun phrenes empedoi out' ar' opissō essontai
("This man (= Paris) neither is now of sound sense, nor in future (lit. 'behind') will he ever be").
I am indebted to Robert B. Todd for the reference.

(ii) Interior of "the same S"

This method of representing continuity of form leads naturally to a symbolism for the circumstance of *something at t_{k+j} being the same S_b as something at t_k*: let the temporal indexes t_k, etc., be subscripts to the quantifiers, and let the possibly distinct sensible matters composing the same substance at the two times be styled with distinct material variables M′ and M″ (although, both clauses being closed, this is technically inessential and done only for emphasis); then, strictly in *Meta*. Eta 2 terms, *something is a S_b at t_k* assumes this guise:

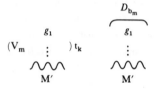

likewise for *something is a S_b at t_{k+j}*:

and their being *the same S_b* looks like this, the connection being by continuity of that range of differentiation from the final to wherever the divide is between form that must remain (including, where present, intelligible matter that must remain) and matter that may be exchanged, the divide represented by "〰〰":

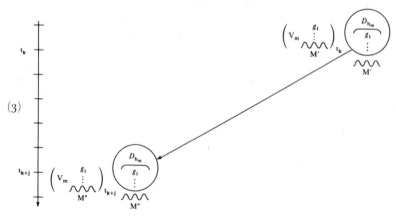

(3)

(Of course, the same circumstance is depictable in terms of the *Meta.* Eta 2 analys*anda*, perhaps in the form:

$$(Vx)_{t_k} S_b(x) \ \& \ (Vy)_{t_{k+j}} S_b(y) \ \& \ x = y.$$

But as would be expected, the Eta 2 analys*antia* afford a version that is more vivid and informative as to the structure of the situation itself – for recall that "is form of" is analyzed by "informs".)

Here, then, is something more of the finer detail that was left out of the sketch of the "total world-view of the substantial universe" a few paragraphs back (p. 272): particularly, beyond the representation of the continuity-of-form principle via

the variable-binding operators "$\left(V_m \ \begin{matrix} g_1 \\ \vdots \end{matrix} \right)_t$" quantify into the entire substantial context to pick out the sensible-and-generic matter of which the substance is composed at those points of its existence. (Why not, it may be asked, only the sensible matter, e.g. the Fire and Earth? Because I am taking the matter of the substantial individual – the entity at the interface of lower and upper stage of the domain – to begin with what underlies the *final* differentia, in our symbolism D_n, or, for a S_b, D_{bn}, thus to begin at the proximate-generic level. If that assumption is disputed, the possibility of restricting the reach of the operators is afforded by the scheme.)

On the other hand, the machinery employed in (3) is still entirely general, in the sense that it affords a means of expressing the temporally extended existence of *some individual S_b or other*, but it does not yet contain the type of handle that would enable us to pick out a particular S_b from his contemporaries – in the sense that Socrates is a particular S_b as distinguished from Callicles and Coriscus.

Because we are about to see how this scheme as extended from *Meta.* Eta 2 handles certain matters of *individual reference*, a topic which has been prodigiously discussed by philosophers in recent years and on which there has arisen a prodigious contemporary literature, it is well here to step back momentarily for a few reminders and some taking of bearings. For the conceptual setting in which such questions arise is very different in this theory from anything familiar today.

We are considering a metaphysical theory that responds to a question that is taken to be thoroughly serious and un-rhetorical, which is,

Why are there material individuals?

Now, in Aristotelean terms there is more than one question here: there is the question in which *why?* translates out as, *to what end?* or *for what purpose?, hou heneka?* – this suggests an answer along the broad lines, "because it is better (in this and that and the other respect, which must be spelled out for the answer to have content)". We have touched on this aspect of the matter in §16 (individuals reproducing "for the sake of" species), §18 (lower-down materiate entities in the lower stage of the two-stage domain "for the sake of" higher-up formed entities), and §23(i) (being as 'referred to' (*pros*) substance).

However, the main burden of the account thus far has been on the question, "Why are there material individuals?", in which *why?* means, *what causal agencies must be at work in the world to bring it about?*, and here the main lines of the explanation have been spelled out in some detail: that first (1), there is the "cause" called *specific form*, which is that in virtue of which matter is formed up into individuals and without which the world could only contain masses and "heaps" – thus §12(iii), §17(iii) (with earlier encounters going all the way back to §4). And second (2), there is the "cause" that *moves the materials into a state of specific formation*, which in the case of natural as opposed to artefactual individuals means the "motions from the *pneuma*" in the semen of the sire, which, we have seen, must carry the form not as the individuals do, but complementarily – thus §14, §15(i) (iv).

These are the elements figuring in the answer to the question, why there are individuals (that is, as the theory of substance construes it, individual substances formed out of matter by specific form) in the material world at all. Now against this background, let us consider what the sources may be of our interest in the theory's having the type of referential device just mentioned: "the type of handle that enables us to pick out a particular individual S_b from his contemporaries – in the sense that Socrates is a particular S_b as distinguished from Callicles or Coriscus".

After all, it is not automatic. To see this, let us first examine the matter from the perspective of what is 'evident relative to us' or *phaneron hēmin*, and then try to see it in a more cosmic vein in terms of that which is 'evident by nature' or *phaneron phusei*.

'Relative to us', that is, us S_bs, our concern with the identities of particular individual S_bs, one as opposed to another, certainly is connected with such deeply rooted facts about us as, e.g., our tendency to mate for life, or at any rate for longer than seasonally; our tendency to bring up our own offspring, who reciprocally tend to recognize their own parents as such – even going no farther than these, which perhaps are even built into our essential specific nature (though at most *hōs epi to polu*, "for the most part" – in view of the exceptions), it is not hard to imagine creatures not wholly unlike ourselves, perhaps somewhat more like the Guards of the *Republic* than human beings (which the Guards arguably are not), in whose form of life the identity of particular individuals is simply of zero importance, not so much as recognized: the nearest available member of the opposite sex will do for mating purposes; infants are offered and reciprocally take the nearest available lactating breast for nurturing purposes; naturally there is no such institution as private property (as indeed with the Guards, in this instance); and so it goes. Always pending, of course, the natural-historical research needed for the factual determination, it seems very plausible that the life-style of some real animal species is like this (cf. *HA* viii 1 588^{b}30–589^{a}2).

So it seems that in some sense it is our institutions, not necessarily sheerly conventional, possibly ones that we occupy by some necessity of our nature, that influence our interest in the particular identity of *Socrates*, whereas from a viewpoint more cosmic and less 'relative to ourselves', – the viewpoint of that *megistē*-natural-historian, the Cosmic Registrar – the difference between one S_b and another would be as insignificant as that between one ant and another in a colony of a hundred million. Yet, that comparison itself suggests at least two further considerations. First, the fact that it *is* a fact about *us* that individual differences do count, and that recognition is a given individual as 'the same again' is frequently of significance, automatically brings it within the ken of the Cosmic Registrar; for her, no doubt, the identity of a particular individual S_b has not the *subjective* looming-large that the identity of one's particular mate or one's particular progeny has for one of us S_bs, but nonetheless, S_bs being natural, 'relative to nature' it *is* a part of nature. Second, even in those species in which individual differences go unrecognized and are without epistemic significance 'relative to them', these normally will still be of consequence 'relative to nature'. This is evident from the practice of even the mundane natural-historian, who may not care in the least *which* ones of his mutually-ill-distinguished S_xs were exposed to the external environment influence whose action he wishes to study, and *which* ones were sheltered from it as controls, but who thereafter, following up the consequences, cares a great deal, in each case, *which* particular individual S_x is *the same S_x as* some particular S_x that did, or did not, get the exposure, as the case may be.[5] From this standpoint, it seems that even the Cosmic Registrar will wish to take note of the identity of particular individuals in her Register, if only to key each ceasing-to-be as that of *the same S_x* as one that previously had come-to-be.

To start, then, on the representation of the *being* of some particular S_b such as Socrates: we may first consider how the *Meta*. Eta 2 style of analysis would naturally go over to the explication of synchronic assertions of the form "*this* is a S_b", as made, canonically, in the presence of a human being to whom attention is meant to be directed by the demonstrative "this".

Understood along Eta 2 lines, such a statement would evidently be decomposed into a portion corresponding to the final differentia D_b, the relation *informs*, and a portion corresponds to the all-but-finally-shaped-up generic matter informed by the differentia as of the time of the assertion, all the way down to the component Earth and Fire composing "*this*" S_b at that moment. In other words, the explication of "this is a S" would differ from that of "there is a S" as given in (1) (§24, p. 261), in containing, rather than the material quantifier "(a) G_1", a *demonstrative* element picking out that particular generic matter, perhaps according to the pattern

(4)   this is a $S \leftrightarrow D_n$ informs that there G_1.

In fact, there is warrant for this approach in *Meta*. Zeta 17, where the question *What is substance?* is addressed in the form, *What makes something a substance?* e.g., *why is* (or, *what makes*) *this a man, and this again a house?*, and the correct logical form for this question is argued to be, not, why is this *man* a man (that is, "to ask why a thing is itself – which is no question at all" – 1041[a]14, 21–2; cf. §8 *fin.* above), but:

why *the matter* is some definite thing (*ti*),[6] e.g.:

---

5 I am trying to state the case carefully and non-anachronistically, in terms that are appropriate to *observation* but that do not imply a language of *experiment*.
6 The textual situation has difficulties; cf. Ross's a.c., 1041[b]5.

Q: why are these (= bricks and stones, cf. 1041ª27) a house?

A: Because there appertains what it is to be (a) house, *huparkhei ho ēn oikiai einai.*

Q: Why is this – or (better), this body, thus-and-so conditioned (*to sōma touto todi ekhon*) –, a man?

– So we're asking the cause – and this is the form – of a *matter's* being some definite thing (*ti*), and this is the substance. (Zeta 17 1041ᵇ5–9)

Here, I take it, the words "*these* (bricks and stones)", "*this* body, thus-and-so conditioned", play the role of a material demonstrative, picking out (in a particular house, or man) a particular generic matter underlying the final form of the species in question; and the contrast is very explicit between "this" as referring to such an underlying subject of final differentiation, and the "this" that would refer to the individual man or house as a whole.[7]

Let our canonical idiom for this employ "I_m" for material demonstrative, parallel to the use of "V_m" for material quantifier; then the philosophical grammar for "this is a S" according to the indications of Zeta 17 and Eta 2 would be:

$$(5) \qquad \text{this is a } S \leftrightarrow (I_m \, g_1) \overbrace{}^{D_n}_{g_1} \, ,$$

– the convention of course being that the reference of the material demonstrative on the right is the proximate generic matter of the *same* individual as is the reference of the ordinary, objectual demonstrative on the left.

(iii) *The relationship reconsidered between SOCRATES and MAN: in one sense trivial, in another, significant*

The last-developed idiom allows us to fix upon a particular one of the individuals coming down through time in the manner suggested by the "total world-view"; and with the obvious device of attaching temporal subscripts to our new variable-binding operator as to the previous, it becomes possible to see the connection of an individual, as presently so fixed upon, with itself at earlier phases of its career. For example, imagine us to be sitting amongst a group of conversants in the prison courtyard, on the day of the ship's return to Athens from Delos in year 399: we now are

---

7 This contrast is precisely the chief moral of Zeta 17, *dioristeon hoti tade tode,* "it's got to be separated out, that *these* are *this*', cf. 1041ᵇ2.

in a position to understand that *this man here now is one and the same man as a man somewhere then, in 470,* the earliest of the three S_bs depicted in our trial world-diagram (p. 272):

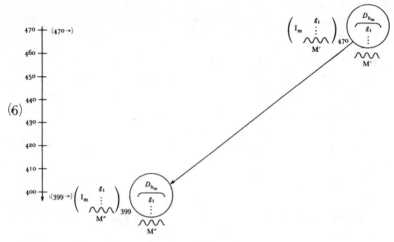

(6)

This man here now (ostending if necessary) is of course none other than Socrates, picked up at a moment very late in his career, which can be seen extending upward (or better, receding away before us into the temporal distance) through its earlier phases toward its beginning. He being thus conveniently before us, we may inquire more closely, in the light of the foregoing developments, into what the philosophical grammar is of *him*: him, and the man he is.

Looked at in one way, the circumstance that *Socrates is a man* can be seen as a kind of "trifling proposition" or truth by definition, stemming from the capital point of principle in this theory, the identity of being any individual and being a specimen of the specific form it is a specimen of;[8] in a metaphysically perspicuous language that would transparently show forth such relationships (the type of language in which the Cosmic Registry is surely composed), this linkage of individual to species would be mirrored in a typographic connection of proper name to species-name (like the *Cats.* cognomen "the individual man", and unlike the proper name "Socrates", which in ordinary Greek or English *could* be a name of anything at all – horse, house, substance, nonsubstance, anything). For example, if the various substantial species are marked by subscripts: S_a, S_b, . . . (where S_a = Lion, S_b = Man, etc.), then the substantial individ-

---

8 The relationship that started as the substantial case of "being synonymously called after" in the *Categories* (§4), and has since evolved into exemplifying (§20(iii)), the having$_{(3-2)}$ of an essence (§23(iii)), etc.

uals "synonymously called after" their species should be explicitly so baptized with names identically subscripted. Then, they need also be indexed with superscripts to distinguish co-specific specimens from one another, so that the individuals of species S_a are $s_a^1, s_a^2, \ldots$; of species S_b, $s_b^1, s_b^2, \ldots$ (let $s_b^7 =$ Socrates, s_b^{31} Callias; and generally let the indexical order be chronological order of formation; in case of ties, then first more westerly longitude of place of formation, and second more northerly latitude). Thus in the language of *is form of* that relates form to individual (§20(iii)), the circumstances that *Socrates is a man* would be rendered:

(7) $\qquad\qquad S_b$ is form of s_b^7,

which now can be seen to be aptly crafted to represent the aspect that according to substance theory is "trivial".[9]

On the other hand, the circumstances that *this man here now is Socrates* is no triviality but a significant and possibly even momentous affair: to assert that it obtains is to state that a certain individual (canonically, in whose presence the statement is made – thus bracketing tour guides lecturing before historical paintings, etc.), in the prison courtyard here and now in year 399, is *one and the same man* as the man who (selecting arbitrarily, and stipulating the history) e.g. made the memorable, defiant Apology in the court of justice, who earlier elenched concerning Virtue with all comers everywhere about town, who earlier still saved and was saved by Alcibiades during Athenian military operations in the (now-disastrously-concluded) Peloponnesean War, and who, seventy eventful years back, was born in Athens to Sophroniscus and Phaenarete (and, it so happens, was named by them "Socrates", though of that more shortly).

Part of this circumstance has already been captured in the analytical framework being built on the foundations of *Meta* Eta 2, namely in (6) (p. 280); what is needed to complete the picture is to see how to depict the fact that that temporally extended entity is not an arbitrary S_b stretching between those particular temporal termini but *Socrates*, i.e., s_b^7. To this end, let us ask: can an analysis in the spirit of Eta 2 be given of (7), that contextually redistributes Socrates into a final differentia and a generic-plus-sensible matter, in the manner of the analys*antia* of (1) and (4) (symbolically, those of (2) and (5)) with respect to their respective analys*anda*? In other words, can (7), which is stated in terms of "is form of ", be reformulated in terms of "informs"?

9 Although overlying problems of great depth: see Furth (1986), on *Meta*. Gamma 4.

The answer is: when a couple of complications are dealt with, Yes. There are two factors in this case that were not involved in $(1)/(2)$ and $(4)/(5)$: first, the presence of the superscript numeral "7" which renders the name a name of *Socrates*, and second, the need to accommodate the in-principle possibility of continuous and even total exchange of sensible matter (not directly capturable in the synchronic terms of $(1)/(2)$ and $(4)/(5)$).

To begin, at any given moment t_i, Socrates is contextually re-distributable into the final differentia of S_b and the full column of vertical differentiation underlying it, differentiating the sensible matter of which he is composed at t_i; i.e., we have something of the general form:

As yet, however, the most that this depicts is *there is a S_b at t_i*; the first question is, where in the analysans should be placed the required index that will singularize it to *Socrates* at t_i? Not, I think, as an index on the D_b, for that would suggest that the final differentia was *peculiar* to Socrates and foreclose the preferable view that it, like the rest of the form, is shared by all specimens of the species – it has indeed been argued above that advent and retention of final differentia equals coming-to-be and continuing-to-be of full-fledged individual (§15(i), §17(iii), ff.), but this is true, individual by individual, species-wide, not for Socrates alone. Nor, it seems, should the Socratic index attach to the material subject,

for that includes much that only fleetingly composes him, as well as (on the "strange hypothesis" of §15(i)) not of itself adding up to a full individual in any case. It appears that the superscript index must be affixed to the entire vertical context

$$\overbrace{\begin{array}{c} D_b \\ g_1 \\ \vdots \\ \wedge\!\wedge\!\wedge \\ M \end{array}} \quad ,$$

in the spirit that only this can represent the intersection at t_i of both the momentarily constituting matter and the temporally continuing form, which *is* what we want: the "knot" that is Socrates, caught at t_i. Thus, returning now to the prison courtyard, the existence of *the man Socrates* here at 399 is:

$$\left(V_m \overset{\overset{g_1}{\vdots}}{\underset{M}{\sim\!\sim\!\sim}}\right)_{399}\left\{\overset{\overbrace{\overset{D_{b_m}}{\underset{\overset{g_1}{\vdots}}{}}}}{\underset{M}{\sim\!\sim\!\sim}}\right\}^7,$$

and the circumstance that *this man here now is Socrates* assumes the form:

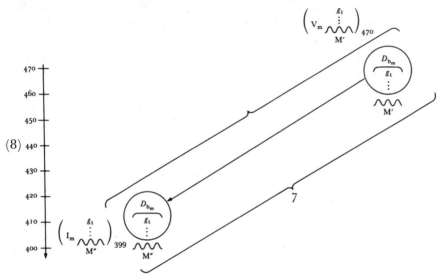

(An alternative ordinary-language rendering of (8) might be: "this man here now is Socrates and always has been".) Here as previously, the portion

represents the continuity of the form – the entire column of vertical differentiation, down to the level of exchangeable matter, whatever that may be. Also as before, the variable-binding operators

$$\text{``}\left(V_m \overset{\overset{g_1}{\vdots}}{\underset{M}{\sim\!\sim\!\sim}}\right)\text{''} \text{ and } \text{``}\left(I_m \overset{\overset{g_1}{\vdots}}{\underset{M}{\sim\!\sim\!\sim}}\right)\text{''}$$

quantify into the entire substantial contex to pick out the sensible-and-generic matter of which the substance is composed at those points of its existence.

What is new here is the index "7", assigned, among S_bs, to Socrates, drawn so as to bracket the entire four-dimensional extent of this particular "knot", including the sensible matter that composes it at each moment. The "7" as it functions here (unlike its function in "s^7_b") is not really a name or a part of a name, but should be understood more in this way: taking the "then" and the "now", 470 and 399, as the first and last moments of Socrates' existence, the first moment (some months before his birth, remember) marked the advent, upon the final differentiation of the as-yet-only-generically-defined *kuema*, of *that particular individual*, identifiable with his own entry in the Cosmic Registry as: S_b Number Seven. (Of course, the historical circumstance that his parents named him "Socrates" – or "s^7_b", or whatever it was – is a different fact, of importance only to a few of us other S_bs, who may wish to *talk* about him, or to call to him when he is beyond seizing range and, unlike Polemarchus, have no servant to bid run and seize him – i.e., as Polemarchus said to the servant: "him!".)

BIBLIOGRAPHY

A guide to some pertinent literature, not all of which is specifically referenced in the text or notes. (A very few items are so referenced in especially remote allusions and are not included here.)

Ackrill, J. L. (1963), notes to *Aristotle's Categories and de Interpretation* (Oxford, 1963), 71–155

   (1972–3), "Aristotle's definitions of *psuche*", *PAS* 73 (1972–3), 119–33. Reprinted in Barnes-Schofield-Sorabji (1975), 65–75

   (1981), *Aristotle the philosopher* (Oxford, 1981)

Albritton, R. (1957), "Substance and form in Aristotle", *Journ. Philos.* 54 (1957), 699–708

Alexander of Aphrodisias (c. 200), *In Aristotelis Metaphysica commentaria*, ed. M. Hayduck (Berlin, 1891)

Allen, R. E. (1969), "Individual Properties", *Phron.* 14 (1969), 31–9

Annas, J. (1974), "Individuals in Aristotle's *Categories*: two queries", *Phron.* 19 (1974), 146–152

Anscombe, G. E. M. (1953), "The principle of individuation", *PAS* s.v. 27 (1953), 83–93

   (1956), "Aristotle and the Sea-Battle", *Mind* 65 (1956), 1–15

   (1961), "Aristotle", in Anscombe, G. E. M. and Geach, P. T., *Three Philosophers* (Oxford, 1961), 5–63

Anton, J. P. (1968), "The Meaning of *ho logos tēs ousias* in Aristotle's *Categories* 1a", *Monist* 52 (1968), 252–67

Apelt, O. (1891), "Die Kategorienlehre des Aristoteles", in *Beiträge zur Geschichte der griechischen Philosophie* (Leipzig, 1891), 101–216

Arpe, C. (1937), *Das TI HN EINAI bei Aristoteles*, dissertation (Hamburg, 1937)

Aubenque, P. (1962), *Le problème de l'être chez Aristote* (Paris, 1962)

Balme, D. M. (1960), "Aristotle's use of differentiae in biology", in *Studia Aristotelica* 2, 195–212, repr. revised in Barnes-Schofield-Sorabji (1975), vol. 1, 183–93

   (1962), "*genos* and *eidos* in Aristotle's biology", *Class. Quart.* 12 (1962), 81–98

   (1965), "Aristotle's use of the teleological explanation", inaugural lecture, Queen Mary College, London, 1965

   (1970a), "Aristotle: natural history and zoology", in Gillispie (1970), vol. 1, pp. 258–66

   (1970b), "Aristotle and the beginnings of zoology", *Journal of the Society for the Bibliography of Natural History* 5 (1970), 272–85

   (1972), *Aristotle's de Partibus Animalium I and de Generatione Animalium I* (Oxford, 1972) (cited as "*PAGA I*")

   (1980), "Aristotle's biology was not essentialist", *Arch. Gesch. Philos.* 62 (1980), 1–12

Barnes, J. (1975), notes to *Aristotle's Posterior Analytics* (Oxford, 1975), pp. 83–277

Barnes, J., Schofield, M. and Sorabji, R. (1975), *Articles on Aristotle* (4 vols.) (London, 1975)

Blersch, K. (1937), *Wesen und Entstehung des Sexus im Denken der Antike* (Stuttgart–Berlin 1937), *Tübinger Beiträge zur Altertumswissenschaft*, vol. 29

Bogen, J., and McGuire, J. E. (eds.) (1985), *How things are: studies in predication and the history of philosophy and science* (Dordrecht, 1985)

Bolton, R. (1976), "Essentialism and semantic theory in Aristotle", *Philos. Rev.* 85 (1976), 514–44

Bonitz, H. (1849), *Aristotelis Metaphysica* (Berlin, 1949)

    (1853), "Über die Kategorien des Aristoteles", *Sitzungsberichte der kaiserlichen Akademie der Wissenschaften, Phil.-Hist. Klasse* x (1853) (Vienna, 1853), 591–645 (repr. Darmstadt, 1967)

    (1870), *Index Aristotelicus* (Berlin, 1870, repr. Graz, 1955)

Bourgey, L. (1955), *Observation et Expérience ches Aristote* (Paris, 1955)

Boylan, M. (1983), *Method and practice in Aristotle's biology* (Lanham, Md., University Press of America, 1983)

Brentano, F. (1975), *On the several senses of being in Aristotle* (Berkeley, 1975) (tr. by R. George of *Von der mannigfachen Bedeutung des Seienden nach Aristoteles* (Freiburg im Breisgau, 1862))

Burnyeat, M. F. (1981), "Aristotle on understanding knowledge", in *Studia Aristotelica* (*q.v.s.v.*), 8

Case, T. (1911), "Aristotle", *Encyclopaedia Britannica*, 11th ed.

Charlton, W. (1970), notes to *Aristotle's Physics, Books I and II* (Oxford, 1970), 51–145

Chen, Chung-hwan (1957a), "Aristotle's concept of primary substance in books Z and H of the *Metaphysics*", *Phron.* 2 (1957), 46–59

    (1957b), "Aristotle's two expressions *kath' hupokeimenou legesthai* and *en hupokeimenôi einai*", *Phron.* 2 (1957), 148–59

    (1958), "The relation between the terms *energeia* and *entelecheia* in the philosophy of Aristotle", *Class. Quart.* NS 8 (1958), 12–17

    (1964), "Universal concrete", *Phron.* 9 (1964), 48–57

Cherniss, H. (1944), *Aristotle's criticism of Plato and the Academy*, 1 (Baltimore, 1944)

Clark, S. R. L. (1975), *Aristotle's Man* (Oxford, 1975)

Code, A. (1976), "The Persistence of Aristotelian Matter", *Philos. Studies.* 29 (1976), 357–67

    (1978a), "No universal is a substance: an interpretation of *Metaphysics* Z 13 1038b8–15", *Paideia* 7 (1978), 65–74

    (1978b), "What is it to be an individual?" (abstract), *Journ. Philos.* 75 (1978), 647–8

    (1984), "The aporematic approach to primary being in *Metaphysics* Z", *Can. Journ. Philos.*, s.v. 10 (1984), 1–20

    (1985a), "Aristotle: Essence and accident", in *Philosophical Grounds of Rationality*, ed. R. Grandy and R. Warner (Oxford, 1985), 409–37

    (1985b), "On the origin of some Aristotelian theses about predication", in Bogen and McGuire (1985), 101–31; "Appendix on the Third Man argument", 323–6

    (1986), "Aristotle's treatment of a basic logical principle I", *Can. Journ. Philos.* 16 (1986), 341–357

Cohen, S. M. (1978) "Individual and essence in Aristotle's *Metaphysics*", *Paideia* 7 (1978), 75–85

(1984), "Aristotle and individuation", *Can. Journ. Philos.*, s.v. 10 (1984), 41–65

Cole, F.J. (1930), *Early theories of sexual generation*, Oxford 1930.

Cooper, J.M. (1982), "Aristotle on natural teleology', in Nussbaum & Schofield (1982)

Crick, F.H.C. (1966), *Of Molecules and Men* (Seattle, 1966)

Dancy, R.M. (1975a), *Sense and contradiction: a study in Aristotle* (Dordrecht, 1975)

    (1975b), "On some of Aristotle's first thoughts about substances", *Philos. Rev.* 84 (1975), 338–73

    (1978), "On some of Aristotle's second thoughts about substances: matter", *Philos. Rev.* 87 (1978), 372–413

Darwin, C. (1868), *Variation of Animals and Plants under Domestication* (New York, 1868)

Davis, W. (1986), *The serpent and the rainbow* (New York, 1986)

Delbrück, M. (1971), "Aristotle-totle-totle", in Monod, J. and Borek, E., eds., *Of microbes and life* (New York, 1971).

Diels, H. and Kranz, W. (1966), *Die Fragmente der Vorsokratiker*, 6th ed. (Dublin/Zurich, 1966)

Driscoll, John A. (1981), "*Eidē* in Aristotle's earlier and later theories of substance", in O'Meara (1981), 129–59

Düring, I. (1943), *Aristotle's De Partibus Animalium: Critical and literary commentaries* (Göteborg, 1943)

    (1960), "Aristotle's method in biology", in *Studia Aristotelica* 2, 213–21

    (1966), *Aristoteles: Darstellung und Interpretation seines Denkens* (Heidelberg, 1966)

Frede, M. (1978), "Individuen bei Aristoteles", *Antike und Abendland* 24 (1978), 16–39

    (1981), "Categories in Aristotle", in O'Meara (1981), 1–24

Furth, M. (1967), "Elements of Eleatic Ontology", *Journ. Hist. Philos.* 6 (1967), 111–32. Repr. in A.P.D. Mourelatos, ed., *The Pre-Socratics: a collection of critical essays*, Garden City, 1974, 241–70

    (1978), "Transtemporal Stability in Aristotelian Substances", *Journ. Philos.* 75 (1978), 624–646. Repr. in *The Philosopher's Annual*, vol. 2, ed. D.L. Boyer, P. Grim and J.T. Sanders (Totowa, N.J. 1979), 88–110

    (1985), notes to *Metaphysics, Books Zeta, Eta, Theta and Iota* (Indianapolis, 1985), 103–40

    (1986), "A note on Aristotle's Principle of Non-Contradiction", *Can. Journ. Philos.* 16 (1986), 371–81

Geach, P.T. (1962), *Reference and Generality*, (Ithaca, N.Y., 1962)

Georgiadis, Constantine (1973), "Two conceptions of substance in Aristotle", *The New Scholasticism* 47 (1973), 22–37, repr. O'Hara (1982), 172–87

Gigon, O. (1946), "Die naturphilosophischen Voraussetzungen der antiken Biologie", *Gesnerus* 3 (1946), 35–58

Gill, M.L. (forthcoming) "Laying the ghost of prime matter"

Gillispie, C.C. (1970), *Dictionary of Scientific Biography* (New York, 1970)

Gomez-Pin, Victor (1976), *Ordre et Substance: L'Enjeu de la Quête Aristotélicienne*, (Paris, Éditions Anthropos, 1976)

Gotthelf, A.S. (1976), "Aristotle's conception of final causality", *Rev. Metaph.* 30 (1976–7), 226–54

Gotthelf, A.S. and Lennox, J.G. (1987), *Philosophical issues in Aristotle's biology* (Cambridge, 1987)

Gould, S.J. (1976), "D'Arcy Thompson and the science of form", in Grene and Mendelsohn (1976)

Grene, M. (1963), *A portrait of Aristotle* (Chicago, 1963)

(1972), "Aristotle and modern biology", *Journ. Hist. Ideas* 33 (1972), 395–424, repr. in Grene and Mendelsohn (1976)

Grene, M., and Mendelsohn, E., eds. (1976), *Topics in the Philosophy of Biology* (Dordrecht/Boston 1976: BSPS, vol. 27.)

Hantz, H.D. (1939), *The biological motivation in Aristotle* (New York, 1939)

Happ, H. (1971), *Hyle: Studien zum aristotelischen Materia-Begriff* (Berlin/New York, 1971)

Hardie, W.F.R. (1964), "Aristotle's treatment of the relation between soul and body", *Philos. Quart.* 14 (1964), 53–72

Haring, E.S. (1957), "Substantial form in Aristotle's *Metaphysics* Zeta", *Rev. Metaph.* 10 (1956–7), 308–32, 482–501, 698–713

Harter, E.D. (1975), "Aristotle on Primary Ousia", *Arch. Gesch. Philos.* 57 (1975), 1–20

Hartman, E. (1976), "Aristotle on the identity of substance and essence", *Philos. Rev.* 85 (1976), 545–61. Repr. revised in Hartman (1977)

(1977), *Substance, Body and Soul* (Princeton, 1977)

Harvey, W. (1653), *Disputations touching the Generation of Animals* (tr. by G. Whitteridge of *Exercitationes de generatione animalium*) (Oxford, Blackwell Scientific Publications, 1981)

Heinaman, R. (1981), "Non-substantial individuals in the *Categories*", *Phron.* 26 (1981), 295–307

Hertz, R. (1960), *Death and the right hand* (tr. by R. and C. Needham) (New York, 1960)

Hintikka, J. (1957), "Necessity, universality and time in Aristotle", *Ajatus* 20 (1957), 65–91. Revised and repr. in Hintikka (1973), ch. 5

(1973), *Time and necessity: studies in Aristotle's theory of modality* (Oxford, 1973)

Horowitz, M.C. (1976), "Aristotle and woman", *Journ. Hist. Biol.* 9 (1976), 183–213

Jacob, F. (1973), *The Logic of Life: A History of Heredity* (New York, 1973). Orig. *La Loqique du Vivant: une histoire de l'hérédité* (Paris, 1970)

Jaeger, W. (1934), *Aristotle: fundamentals of the history of his development*, tr. R. Robinson (Oxford, 1934)

Joachim, H.H. (1922), *Aristotle on coming-to-be and passing-away* (Oxford, 1922) (repr. Hildesheim/New York, 1970)

Jones, B. (1972), "Individuals in Aristotle's *Categories*", *Phron.* 17 (1972), 107–23

(1974), "Aristotle's introduction of matter", *Philos. Rev.* 83 (1974), 474–500

King, H.R. (1956), "Aristotle without *materia prima*", *Journ. Hist. Ideas* 17 (1956), 370–89

Kirk, G.R. and Raven, J.E. (1960), *The presocratic philosophers* (Cambridge, 1960)

Kirwan, C. (1971), notes to *Metaphysics, Books Gamma, Delta and Epsilon* (Oxford, 1971), 75–200

Kosman, L.A. (1984), "Substance, being and energeia", *Ox. Stud. in Anc. Philos.* 2 (1984), 121–49

Kullmann, W. (1974), *Wissenschaft und Methode, Interpretationen zur aristotelischen Theorie der Naturwissenschaft* (Berlin/New York, 1974)

(1979), *Die Teleologie in der aristotelischen Biologie: Aristoteles als Zoologe, Embryologe und Genetiker*. Sitzungsberichte der Heidelberger Akademie der Wissenschaften, Phil.-hist. Klasse (Heidelberg, 1979)

Lear, J. (1980), *Aristotle and logical theory* (Cambridge, 1980)

Le Blond, J.–M. (1938), *Eulogos et l'argument de convenance chez Aristote* (Paris, 1938)

(1939), *Logique et méthode chez Aristote* (Paris, 1939)

(1945), *Aristote: philosophe de la vie. Le livre premier du traité sur les parties des animaux* (Paris, 1945)

Lee, H. D. P. (1948), "Place-names and the date of Aristotle's biological works", *Class. Quart.* 42 (1948), 61–7

Lennox, J. G. (1980), "Aristotle on genera, species, and 'the more and the less'", *Journ. Hist. Biol.* 13 (1980), 321–46

(1984), "Recent philosophical studies of Aristotle's biology", *Anc. Philos.* 4 (1984), 73–82. (Review of Pellegrin (1982), Morsink (1982), Boylan (1983))

Lesher, J. (1971), "Aristotle on form, substance and universals: a dilemma", *Phron.* 16 (1971), 169–78

Lesky, E. (1950), *Die Zeugungs- und Vererbungslehren der Antike and ihr Nachwirken* (Wiesbaden, 1950). Akademie der Wissenschaften und der Literatur [Mainz], Abhandlungen der Geistes- and Sozialwissenschaftlichen Klasse, Jahrgang 1950, no. 19

(1957), "Harvey und Aristoteles", *Sudhoffs Archiv* 41 (1957), 289–316, 349–78

Lewis, F. A. (1982), "Accidental sameness in Aristotle", *Phil. Studies* 42 (1982), 1–36

(1984). "What is Aristotle's theory of essence?", *Can. Journ. Philos.* s.v. 10 (1984), 89–131

(1985), "Form and predication in Aristotle's *Metaphysics*", in Bogen & McGuire (1985), 59–83

Lloyd, A. C. (1962), "Genus, species, and ordered series in Aristotle", *Phron.* 7 (1962), 67–90

(1970), "Aristotle's principle of individuation", *Mind* 79 (1970), 519–29

(1981), *Form and universal in Aristotle* (Liverpool, 1981)

Lloyd, G. E. R. (1961), "The development of Aristotle's theory of the classification of animals", *Phron.* 6 (1961), 59–81

(1962), "Right and left in Greek philosophy", *Journ. Hell. Stud.* 82 (1962), 56–66

(1968), *Aristotle: the growth and structure of his thought* (Cambridge, 1968)

(1975), "The empirical basis of the physiology of the *Parva Naturalia*", in *Studia Aristotelica* 7, 215–39

(1979), *Magic, Reason and Experience* (Cambridge, 1979)

Louis, P. (1975), "Monstres et monstruosites dans la biologie d'Aristote", *Monde Grec* (1975), 277–84

Loux, M. J. (1979), "Form, species and predication in *Metaphysics Z, H* and *Θ* ", *Mind* 88 (1979), 1–23

Mansion, S. (1973), "Deux définitions différentes de la vie chez Aristote?", *Revue Philos. de Louvain* 71 (1973), 425–50

(1975), "Soul and life in the *de Anima*", in *Studia Aristotelica* 7, 1–20

Matthen, M. (1984), "Aristotle's semantics and a puzzle concerning change", *Can. Journ, Philos.*, s.v. 10 (1984), 21–40

Matthews, G.B. and Cohen, S.M. (1968), "The one and the many", *Rev. Metaph.* 21 (1967–8), 630–55

McMullin, E. (1965), *The concept of matter in Greek and medieval philosophy* (Notre Dame, 1965)

Meyer, A.W. (1936), *An analysis of the de Generatione Animalium of William Harvey* (Stanford, 1936)

(1939), *The rise of embryology* (Stanford, 1939)

Meyer, H. (1919), "Das Vererbungsproblem bei Aristoteles", *Philologus* 75 (1918), 323–363

Meyer, J.B. (1855), *Aristoteles Thierkunde, ein Beitrag zur Geschichte der Zoologie, Physiologie und alten Philosophie* (Berlin, 1855)

Miller, H. (1952), "*Dynamis* and *physis* in *On Ancient Medicine*", *Trans. and Proc. of Amer. Philol. Assoc.* 83 (1952), 184–97

Minio-Paluello, L. (1970), "Aristotle: tradition and influence", in Gillispie (1970), vol. 1, pp. 267–81

Modrak, D.K. (1979), "Forms, types and tokens in Aristotle's *Metaphysics*", *Journ. Hist. Philos.* 17 (1979), 371–81

(1985), "Forms and compounds", in Bogen & McGuire (1985), 85–99

Moravcsik, J.M.E. (1967), ed.: *Aristotle: a collection of critical essays* (Garden City, N.Y., 1967)

Morsink, J. (1979), "Was Aristotle's biology sexist?", *Journ. Hist. Biol.* 12 (1979), 83–112

(1982), *Aristotle on the generation of animals: a philosophical study* (Lanham, Md., University Press of America, n.d. [1982])

Needham, J. (1955), *A history of embryology*, rev. ed. (New York, 1955)

Nussbaum, M.C. (1978), *Aristotle's de motu animalium* (Princeton, 1978)

Nussbaum, M.C. and Schofield, M. (1982), *Language and Logos: studies in ancient Greek philosophy* (Cambridge, 1982)

O'Hara, M.L. (1981), ed., *Substances and things: Aristotle's doctrine of physical substance in recent essays* (Washington, University Press of America, 1981)

O'Meara, D.J. (1981), ed., *Studies in Aristotle* (Washington, D.C., 1981)

Owen, G.E.L. (1957) "Logic and metaphysics in some earlier works of Aristotle", in *Studia Aristotelica* 1, 163–90

(1960), "Tithenai ta phainomena", in *Studia Aristotelica* 2, 83–103, repr. in Barnes–Schofield–Sorabji (1975), vol. 1, 113–26

(1965a), "The Platonism of Aristotle", *Proc. Brit. Acad.* 51 (1965), 125–50

(1965b), "Inherence", *Phron.* 10 (1965), 97–105

(1965c), "Aristotle on the snares of ontology", in R. Bambrough (ed.), *New essays on Plato and Aristotle* (London, 1965)

(1970), "Aristotle: Method, physics and cosmology", in Gillespie (1970), vol. 1, pp. 250–8

(1978), "Particular and general", *PAS* 79 (1978–9), 1–21

Owens, J. (1960), "Aristotle on Categories", *Rev. Metaph.* 14 (1960–1), 73–90

(1951), *The doctrine of being in the Aristotelian Metaphysics* (Toronto, 1951); 2nd ed. 1963; 3rd ed. 1978; cited as (*DOB*) with ed. superscript

(1966), "The Aristotelian argument for the material principle of bodies", in *Studia Aristotelica* 4, 193–209 [?]

(1981), *Aristotle: The collected papers of Joseph Owens*, ed. J.R. Catan (Albany, SUNY, 1981)

Peck, A.L. (1931), "Anaxagoras: predication as a problem in physics", *Class. Quart.* 25 (1931), 27–37, 112–20

(1953), "The connate pneuma: an essential factor in Aristotle's solution to the problems of reproduction and sensation", in: E.A. Underwood, ed., *Science, medicine and history, essays in honour of Charles Singer* (London, 1953), vol. 1, 111–21

(1961), "Foreword" to translation of *Parts of Animals* in Loeb Classical Library, rev. ed. (London, 1961), 3–50

(1963), "Preface" to translation of *Generation of Animals* in Loeb Classical Library, rev. ed. (London, 1963), v–lxxviii

(1965), "Introduction" to translation of *Historia Animalium* in Loeb Classical Library, rev. ed. (London, 1965), v–xcvii

Pellegrin, P. (1982), *La classification des animaux chez Aristote: statut de la biologie et unité de l'Aristotélisme* (Paris, 1982) Tr. by A. Preus as *Aristotle's classification of animals: biology and the conceptual unity of the Aristotelian corpus* (Berkeley, 1987)

Platnauer, M. (1921), "Greek colour-perception", *Class. Quart.* 15 (1921), 153–62

Preiswerk, A. (1939), "Das Einzelne bei Platon und Aristoteles", *Philologus*, Supplementband 32, Heft 1 (Leipzig, 1939), 1–196

Preus, A. (1970), "Science and philosophy in Aristotle's Generation of Animals", *Journ. Hist. Biol.* 3 (1970), 1–52. Repr. in Preus (1975)

(1975), *Science and philosophy in Aristotle's biological works* (Hildesheim, 1975)

(1977), "Galen's criticism of Aristotle's conception theory", *Journ. Hist. Biol.* 10 (1977), 65–85

Reale, Giovanni, *The concept of first philosophy and the unity of the Metaphysics of Aristotle* (ed. and tr. J.R. Catan) (Albany, SUNY, 1980)

Regis, E., Jr. (1976), "Aristotle's principle of individuation", *Phron.* 21 (1976), 157–66

Robinson, H.M. (1974), "Prime matter in Aristotle", *Phron.* 19 (1974), 168–88

de Rijk, L.M. (1952), *The place of the categories of being in Aristotle's philosophy* (Assen, 1952)

Rorty, R.M. (1973), "Genus as matter: a reading of *Metaphysics* Z–H", in: *Exegesis and argument: studies in Greek philosophy presented to Gregory Vlastos*, ed. E.N. Lee, A.P.D. Mourelatos and R.M. Rorty (*Phron.* s.v. 1, 1973), 393–420

Ross, W.D., *Aristotle's Metaphysics* (Oxford, 1953) (cited as AM)

Aristotle's Prior and Posterior Analytics (Oxford, 1965) (cited as APPA)

Sellars, W. (1957), "Substances and form in Aristotle", *Journ. Philos.* 54 (1957), 688–99

(1959), "Aristotle's Metaphysics: An interpretation", in *Philosophical Perspectives* (Springfield, Ill.: Thomas Publishers, 1959, 73–124

Shartin, D.C. (1984), *Aristotle's theory of substance and essence in the Categories and Book Zeta of the Metaphysics*, doctoral dissertation, UCLA, 1984

Shaw, J.R. (1972), "Models for cardiac structure and function in Aristotle", *Journ. Hist. Biol.* 5 (1972), 355–88

Singer, C. (1922), *Greek biology and Greek medicine* (Oxford, 1922), repr. New York, AMS Press, 1979

Smith, J.A. (1921), "*Tode ti* in Aristotle", *Class. Rev.* 35 (1921), 19

Sokolowski, R. (1970), "Matter, elements and substance in Aristotle", *Journ. Hist. Philos.* 8 (1970), 263-88, repr. in O'Hara (1982), 91-116

Solmsen, F. (1950), "Tissues and the soul", *Philos. Rev.* 59 (1950), 435-68

(1958), "Aristotle and prime matter: a reply to H.R. King", *Journ. Hist. Ideas* 19 (1958), 243-52

(1960), *Aristotle's system of the physical world: a comparison with his predecessors* (Ithaca, 1960)

Sorabji, R. (1974), "Body and soul in Aristotle", *Philos.* 49 (1974), 63-89

Stahl, D.E. (1981), "Stripped away: some contemporary obscurities surrounding Metaphysics Z 3 (1029a10-26)", *Phron.* 26 (1981), 177-80

Studia Aristotelica (references to these are dated by year of symposium, rather than year of publication of volume):

(1. 1957) Düring & Owen, eds., *Aristotle and Plato in the mid-fourth century* (Göteborg, 1960)

(2. 1960) Mansion, S., ed., *Aristote et les problèmes de méthode* (Louvain, 1961)

(3. 1963) Owen, G.E.L., ed., *Aristotle on Dialectic* (Oxford, 1968)

(4. 1966) Düring, I., ed., *Naturphilosophie bei Aristoteles und Theophrast* (Heidelberg, 1969)

(5. 1969) Moraux, P., ed., *Untersuchungen zur eudemische Ethik* (Berlin, 1971)

(6. 1972) Aubenque, P., *Études sur la métaphysique d'Aristote* (Paris, 1979)

(7. 1975) Lloyd, G.E.R. and Owen, G.E.L., eds., *Aristotle on mind and the senses* (Cambridge, 1978)

(8. 1978) E. Berti, ed., *Aristotle on science: the 'Posterior Analytics'* (Padua, 1981)

(9. 1981) Moraux, P., and Wiesner, J., eds., *Zweifelhaftes im corpus Aristotelicum* (*Peripatoi*, v. 14) (Berlin, 1983)

Thompson, D.W. (1910), translation of *Historia Animalium* (Oxford, 1910)

(1913), *On Aristotle as a biologist* (Oxford, 1913)

(1917), *On growth and form* (Cambridge, 1917; 2nd ed., 1942)

Trendelenburg, A. (1833), *de Aristotelis categoriis prolusio academica* (Berlin, 1833)

(1846), *Geschichte der Kategorienlehre* (Berlin, 1846)

Tugendhat, E. (1958), *Ti kata tinos* (Freiburg, 1958)

Waterlow, S. (1982), *Nature, change and agency* (Oxford, 1982)

Wedin, M.V. (1979), "'Said of' and 'predicated of' in the *Categories*", *Philos. Res. Archives*, Vol. 5, no. 1301, 1-13

(1982), "Aristotle on the range of the principle of non-contradiction", *Logique et Analyse* 25 (1982), 87-92

(1984), "Singular statements and essentialism in Aristotle", *Can. Journ. Philos.*, s.v. 10 (1984), 67-88

White, N.P. (1971) "Aristotle on sameness and oneness", *Phil Rev* 80 (1971), 177-97

(1972) "Origins of Aristotle's essentialism", *Rev Metaph* 26 (1972-3), 57-85

Whiting, J.E. (1984) *Individual forms in Aristotle*, doctoral dissertation, Cornell University, 1984

Wieland, W. (1962), *Die aristotelische Physik* (Göttingen, 1962). Portions transl. and repr. in Barnes-Schofield-Sorabji (1975), vol. 1

Wiggins, D. (1980), *Sameness and substance* (Cambridge (USA), 1980)

Wilson, L.G. (1970), "Aristotle: anatomy and physiology", in Gillispie (1970), vol. 1, pp. 266-7

Witt, Charlotte (1985), "Form, reproduction and inherited characteristics in Aristotle's *Generation of Animals*", *Phron.* 30 (1985), 46–57

Woods, M.J. (1967), "Problems in Metaphysics Z, Chapter 13", in Moravcsik (1967) (1975), "Substance and essence in Aristotle", *Proc Soc* 75 (1974–5), 167–180

Wright, M.R. (1981), *Empedocles: the extant fragments* (New Haven/London, 1981)

INDEX OF TOPICS

INDEX OF NAMES

THE LIBRARY
ST. MARY'S COLLEGE OF MARYLAND
ST. MARY'S CITY, MARYLAND 20686